# The Countryside in the Age
# of Capitalist Transformation

# The Countryside in the Age of Capitalist Transformation

ESSAYS IN THE SOCIAL HISTORY

OF RURAL AMERICA

EDITED BY STEVEN HAHN AND

JONATHAN PRUDE

THE UNIVERSITY OF NORTH CAROLINA PRESS

CHAPEL HILL AND LONDON

© 1985 The University of North Carolina Press
All Rights Reserved
Manufactured in the United States of America

Library of Congress Cataloging in Publication Data
Main entry under title:

The Countryside in the age of capitalist
   transformation.

   Includes index.
   1. United States—Rural conditions—Addresses,
essays, lectures.   2. United States—Social
conditions—To 1865—Addresses, essays, lectures.
3. Sociology, Rural—United States—History—
Addresses, essays, lectures.   I. Hahn, Steven,
1951–     .   II. Prude, Jonathan.
HN57.C68   1985      307.7'2'0973      85-2847
ISBN 0-8078-1666-3
ISBN 0-8078-4139-0 pbk.

# Contents

# Maps and Figures

# Tables

# Acknowledgments

Collections of essays, even of previously unpublished essays, rarely benefit from the rounds of advice and criticism that customarily attend the completion of scholarly studies. Ours is no exception. We are, of course, grateful for the excellent editorial assistance of Iris Tillman Hill and Gwen Duffey, and for the early interest of Lewis Bateman—all of the University of North Carolina Press. Individual contributors have made separate acknowledgments where appropriate, and some of them have aided us in determining the format and thematic direction of the volume. Still, we would like to add a special word of thanks.

At a very crucial stage, the late Herbert G. Gutman lent important encouragement and helped us bring this undertaking to fruition. We shared his long-standing insistence that the history of labor form part of the larger history of capitalism in the United States, and that the history of capitalism embrace the country as well as the town and city. Our own understanding of rural America in the "age of capitalist transformation" has been influenced by Professor Gutman's work, and the same can be said for many of the contributors to this volume and for many other scholars now studying the American countryside in the eighteenth and nineteenth centuries. We are all diminished by his loss. But his presence will always be felt.

# The Countryside in the Age
# of Capitalist Transformation

STEVEN HAHN & JONATHAN PRUDE

# Introduction

I

American history was launched from the countryside. We can see this, first and most obviously, in the persistent rural character of American society. Indeed, even before European settlement commenced, the cultures fashioned by North American Indians—though stunningly diverse and occasionally marked by concentrated residential patterns—were virtually never rooted in cities and were typically organized around hunting and agriculture.[1] And so the pattern continued. As late as 1750, well over a century after a permanent European presence took root on the Atlantic coast, forests remained so thick that sailors approaching the New World from the east could smell the pine trees before they saw land.[2] In 1800, only 3 percent of inhabitants in the new United States lived in cities, and the same statistics that textbooks assemble to demonstrate increasing urbanization during the nineteenth century may with equal logic be marshaled to document an abiding commitment to rural life. The proportion of Americans living outside cities was five out of six in 1860 and two out of three in 1900. Only in the 1880s, according to a classic text in the field, did urbanization become a "controlling factor in national life," and a widely accepted reckoning holds that not until 1920 did a majority of Americans begin living in "urban" areas.[3]

But the rural propulsion of American history is equally evident when we consider "history" as the product of historians: as the literature produced by self-conscious students of the past. A sensitivity to the hinterland proved critical in shaping the way American history came to be conceptualized and written down.

The first white historians of the British colonies were committed to chronicling the settlement of an unknown New World, and the countryside was consequently often experienced and described as the wilderness—the unchartered, vast rural hinterland—that Europeans saw before them. It was the forest William Bradford felt as so enormous and pressing so close to seventeeth-century Plymouth: the "woods" that were home to Indians and where "John Billington lost him selfe . . . and wandered up and downe some 5 days, living on beries and what he could find."[4] In less threatening form, it was the pastoral vista Robert Beverley evoked toward the end of his

3

early eighteenth-century *History and Present State of Virginia*. "Here all their Senses are entertain'd with an endless Sucession of Native Pleasures. Their Eyes are ravished with the Beauties of naked Nature. Their Ears are Serenaded with the perpetual murmur of Brooks, and the thorow-base which the Wind plays, when it wantons through the Trees."[5]

The great narrative historians of the nineteenth century also gave attention to the countryside. Again it was the rural wilderness—and the dramatic saga of European entry upon that wilderness—that drew their attention. Thus Francis Parkman and W. H. Prescott devoted their energies specifically to the stories of New World empire building by the British, French, and Spanish. And even George Bancroft (as Richard Hofstadter later pointed out) glimpsed "the importance of the West in American character."[6]

This brief scattering of examples scarcely hints at the myriad and complex ways in which early historians acknowledged the nonurban dimension of American history. But the sampling is perhaps sufficient to document that this dimension was acknowledged. And it provides background to Frederick Jackson Turner, whose contribution it was to place rural America at the heart of an extraordinarily powerful and evocative historical "thesis."

The "rural" with which Turner concerned himself was once more, of course, the unsettled hinterland—more precisely, the frontier. In articles, papers, and books extending from the 1890s through the 1920s, he advanced the central argument that America's sequential frontiers—"the existence of an area of free land, its continuous recession, and the advance of American settlement westward"—could "explain American development." He maintained that life along America's moving frontier promoted democracy, dissolved ethnic particularities into a buoyant nationalism, and encouraged individualism and self-sufficiency; at the same time, access to the frontier served as a "safety-valve" for the pressures and human casualties spawned amid Eastern commercialization and industrialization. In sum, "the advance of the frontier has meant a steady movement away from Europe, a steady growth of independence on American lines. And to study this advance, the men who grew up under the conditions, and the political, economic, and social results of it, is to study the really American part of our history." It naturally followed that the closing of the frontier in the late nineteenth century marked the end of "the first period of American history."[7]

First articulated in 1893, the "frontier thesis"—and the radical preoccupation with rural Americana it embraced—came in time to rank among the most widely applauded synthetic visions in all of American historiography.[8] Its popularity was perhaps partly due to the rural Western brio with which Turner (a native of Wisconsin) pressed his case. Though a product of the Johns Hopkins doctoral program, he was reacting strongly against the tendency among Eastern scholars of his day to dwell on the European (and especially Teutonic) origins of American institutions. Indeed, in an important sense Turner spoke for all Americans living west of the Appalachians— by 1900 a majority of the nation's population—who were weary of Eastern cultural hegemony and proud to have the master switch of American history placed amidst their plains and mountains.[9]

From another perspective, however, Turner's formulation may have captured the blend of nostalgia and bitter anxiety gripping rural areas in both the West and the East during the late nineteenth century. For did not the end of the frontier (the end of "the first period of American history") come at a time when cities were finally beginning to assert "controlling" influence over national life; when the countryside, though still supporting most American residents, was increasingly judged by pundits to be stultifying, a benighted second best to the growing metropolises; when the policies of powerful—and often urban-based—businessmen could affect the prosperity of even the most isolated yeomen? The sense of closure, of a culture growing old, that winds through the frontier thesis, may thus have neatly mirrored the sensibility of country folk who felt left behind, or exploited, or devalued, by the sweeping changes of fin de siècle America.[10]

But for our purposes, Turner's most important resonance was among other historians. It is by now clear that throughout the first half of the twentieth century his impact on scholarship was considerable. And although certain writers may have followed Turner out of one or another brand of visceral commitment to rural life, a good number were attracted simply by the rich insights and implications embroidered into Turner's propositions. The frontier thesis ramified into many offshoots of American history, but it played a particularly significant role in shaping a whole new branch of rural studies. Perhaps not surprisingly, many such post-Turnerian investigations of the countryside focused on the Far West. Others, reflecting Turner's general emphasis on ecological factors, produced environmentally sensitive works covering both the frontier and postfrontier eras of the Great Plains, the southern grasslands, and the component segments of eastern agriculture.[11] Then too, on a more general level, rural historians after Turner reflected the master's influence in the variety of materials they drew upon and in their intense interest in the daily lives of unexceptional people. For it was also Turner's contribution—offered just at the moment professional scholarship was emerging—to demonstrate that historians might properly deal with almost every aspect of human life, and with common folk as well as leaders.[12]

We have lingered over Turner because of his demonstrably long shadow. But there was never a Turner hegemony. Almost from the outset (and especially during the 1930s and 1940s), there were telling criticisms, ranging from attacks on loose definitions of key concepts (including "frontier") to questions about precisely how frontiers (whatever they were) "explain"

America. Indeed, it turns out that many rural historians who followed Turner with regard to subject matter and methodology were actually *testing* his arguments—and finding them wanting. Since the 1950s students pausing to consider Turner's outlook have, it is true, adopted a somewhat more accepting attitude.[13] Ironically, however, this latter-day tolerance has come at a time when the validity of the frontier thesis no longer seems to matter as much as it once did. Although still often serving as a point of departure,[14] Turner's angle of vision has been largely shunted aside over the last ten to twenty years in favor of research with little time for the West, the frontier, or indeed rural history of any kind.

The shift is especially evident in social history. Perhaps reflecting the post–World War II growth of major metropolitan regions, the current generation of social historians has tended to pursue topics in urban rather than rural contexts. Studies of social structure and social mobility, analyses of family and women's history, probings into labor history, and (what is often the underlying concern of these projects) investigations "from the bottom up" into commercialization and industrialization: in sum, the whole swath of varied and methodologically innovative enquiries whose appearance marked the authentic coming of age of "the new social history"—such enquiries commonly have found urban settings most congenial.[15] Indeed, "urban history" itself has emerged in this period as a self-consciously discrete field of teaching and research.[16]

Now it is true that in certain ways (for example, in their hypothesis that upward social mobility was the real American "safety-valve") some new social historians have effectively continued the debate over Turner's ideas.[17] And it is also true that because of their intrinsically rural subject matter, some investigations in social history published during the last few decades have confronted the countryside head on—and sometimes have linked this focus with further invocations of Turner's categories and arguments. The New England colonial community studies that began appearing in the late 1960s come to mind here, as do certain studies of the South in both colonial and antebellum periods.[18] Yet, the central point remains. Many of the most sophisticated, intelligent, and energetic forays into American social history during recent decades have tended to bypass the countryside.

There are signs, however, that this situation is starting to change. A resurgent interest in rural history has begun to find expression. It is an interest that has the potential to extend through all periods of the American story; an interest covering all regions, and embracing settled areas as well as frontiers; an interest that has by now achieved sufficient momentum to require recognition in present-day historiography.[19] Inevitably, this "new rural history" has been shaped by—and can only be understood in light of—its intellectual traditions, the frontier thesis especially. But rural history in its latest guise does not seek to resuscitate Turner (or any other scholar) so much as to meld what is useful in earlier writings with techniques and themes found in various branches of contemporary social history. It follows that this new rural history aims to supplement, not supplant, interpretations provided by, say, family and labor historians. It follows, too, that this rural history views the countryside, not as a central explanation for all "American development," but more modestly as a factor that needs to be threaded back into American history in a careful and balanced manner.

All of which, of course, is by way of identifying the orientation of this book. The essays occasionally start with, but are not confined by, discussions of Turnerian hypotheses; they range in subject matter from treatments of mill dams in the colonial and post-Revolutionary eras to rural ethnic and labor patterns in the twentieth century; they extend geographically from New England and Georgia in the East to Minnesota and California in the West. This collection is intended to illuminate the breadth and possibilities of the new rural history. In short, we mean to show what can be learned by centering new kinds of attention on the milieu in which most Americans have lived during most of American history.

## II

At this point we should specify more fully the nature of this new rural history. How do students of the countryside (including contributors to this book) currently conceptualize their subject—or how might they usefully consider conceptualizing it?

First, a negative specification: Today's rural historians do *not* typically feel constrained to demonstrate the transcendent worth of country life. These scholars often catalog the conflicts and hardships generated when rural norms were disrupted; at times these same scholars may evince sympathy for the institutions and attitudes thus undermined. Yet there is little effort to argue that what might be judged admirable in rural society—patterns of cooperation, for example, or notions of independent "virtue"— were known *only* in the hinterland. Rural history today neither expresses nor taps any broad nostalgia for country existence. What it does do (to appropriate the agenda suggested by one practitioner) is provide "systematic study of human behavior over time in rural environments."[20] But this, of course, merely raises the knotty problem of deciding what we mean by "rural environment."

The point of departure for definitions of "rural" usually has been demographic density: The countryside is reckoned to have fewer people within a given geographic area of analysis than nonrural locales. The difficulty is that the threshold figure above which "rural" becomes "urban" is notoriously vague. A glance at the monographic literature reveals that the cutting edge can vary from 2,500 to 4,000 to 10,000 people; the *International Encyclopedia of the Social Sciences* can do no better than inform us that "in most countries the dividing line between rural and urban is set at population aggregates of somewhere between 1,000 and 5,000 inhabitants."[21] In an important sense such uncertainty is inevitable. The comparative element (the continuing contrast with urban concentrations), which is intrinsic to the concept of "rural" population aggregates, would appear to encourage demographic definitions that shift through time. It is scarcely reasonable, for example, that the same population standard separating rural from urban settings in 1860 (when the republic's five largest cities all held more than 100,000 souls) should be applied in 1760 (when the fifth largest settlement in British North America held only 7,500).[22] Then, too, we must bear in mind that even coexistent rural areas could demonstrate significant economic, social, and cultural variation. An 1860 demographic indicator of, say, 2,500 might well be suitable for some areas, but it might also end up defining as "urban" various small northeastern townships that bore little resemblance to the major metropolises thriving in the same region by mid-century.

Plainly then, we should be wary of static and overly uniform demographic specifications. On the other hand, the basic correlation of rural with (relatively) low population levels is surely valid. If we are careful to avoid relying too heavily on a single figure, a population benchmark is useful as a *rough* indicator of our subject. In the context of this collection—dealing as it does mainly with the nineteenth and early twentieth centuries, and exploring as it does both frontier and long-inhabited zones of the countryside—we propose a cutoff figure of approximately 5,000. This does not mean all the areas and communities explored in the following pages contained anywhere near this many people. But it does suggest that we view "rural" as encompassing a range of settlement patterns, including villages and small towns.

Of course criteria other than population levels may be used to mark off rural terrains. A widely accepted occupational sine qua non of country life, for example, is a commitment to agriculture (or more broadly "the collection and cultivation of plants and animals").[23] Again there is surely a measure of truth here, but again we must be careful. One of the strengths of the new rural history lies in its effort to unravel the complex transformations of rural economies—and so move beyond merely documenting an allegiance to husbandry. Many contemporary students of the American countryside (including several contributors here) focus on the ways in which farmers became (or actively resisted becoming) more involved in the market. Or they explore the ways in which mercantile, handicraft, and even large-scale industrial enterprises entered rural settings. From this perspective, neither a shift in the nature of farming nor the emergence of nonfarming activities signaled the end of "ruralness."[24] Small communities with an agricultural past could still be tallied as country towns when they acquired stores, smithies, and factories.

A final element commonly attached to definitions of "rural environments" involves the proposition that "ruralness" connotes "more than location or an occupation; it is a way of life,"[25] a discrete social structure, a unique weltanschauung. Obviously, this notion finds strong resonance in Turner, who saw the hinterland as especially supportive—indeed, as the American breeding ground—of key attitudes and patterns in national life. Arthur Schlesinger presented his own version of this idea when, in his 1933 study of *The Rise of the City*, he contrasted two "cultures": "one static, individualistic, agricultural, the other dynamic, collective, urban." More recent writers offer still other versions, again usually organized around comparisons with urban situations. The countryside is said to exhibit "close personal, primary group relations," or "extended family networks . . . and an attitude of complacency in the face of nature's forces," or relatively low rates of transiency, or (reversing Turner's belief in rural individualism) an overall communal solidarity (with or without nucleated settlements), and a sense of mutuality.[26]

The problem here is not simply the scholarly disagreements over what constituted the distinctly rural "way of life." Nor is it only that variations in rural America make it unlikely there was ever anything approaching a single rural ethos or social structure (just as variations among cities make it unlikely there was ever a single urban modus vivendi). The chief problem is that many of the norms and structures once thought of as exclusive characteristics of the countryside are equally characteristic of urban settings. Anthropologist Robert Redfield acknowledged this almost thirty years ago when he concluded that "folk and urban ways" can coexist in the same locale. Building on the famous categories of the German social theorist Ferdinand Tonnies, historian Thomas Bender recently offered essentially the same view. Gemeinschaft and gesellschaft, he writes, should be thought of as "permanent aspects of all social life."[27]

The point here, we should stress, is not to deny that rural life has possessed distinctive elements. The point is to determine how to illuminate such elements fully but without exaggeration. And the answer is perhaps to turn the whole issue around. Instead of stressing the separateness of the countryside, it might well prove more fruitful to explore rural regions by placing them in context: by understanding their history as one dimension of broad social and economic transformations that, in different forms and degrees, affected *all* of American society, and by seeing rural and urban history as distinct but linked aspects of, for example, the spread of market relations or the variegated process of industrialization.[28] Conceived in this way, our enquiries are not, from the outset, obliged to prove the existence of this or that putatively unique rural characteristic. Instead, the special rhythms and textures of rural history can emerge after the fact; they are what we *may* deduce from exploring the various ways fundamental social, economic, and cultural developments penetrated the American countryside. In the meantime we have before us the rural chapter of these developments.

## III

Yet we may also have more. We may have a new way of thinking about how the countryside helped precipitate and shape those changes. For if the story of rural America—as told by Turner, his disciples, and his critics—tended to take on a rearguard or merely reflective character in relation to the forces of modernization and modernity, it now appears to be assuming a more innovative and dynamic character. We are coming to recognize that the countryside not only launched American history, but launched the modern world as well.

That recognition owes a great deal to the increasingly internationalist orientation of much recent scholarship, although the connection has been neither immediate nor direct. The initial appeal of research being completed by students of other rural societies—in Europe, particularly—had, in fact, more to do with methodological than with comparative concerns: Historians of America became very interested in the material culture, social relations, and *mentalité* of common people, and historians of Europe and of parts of the Third World had already conducted pioneering, and often brilliant forays into those areas. The works of the English demographers and social historians and of the French *Annalistes*—with their path-breaking studies of population and the life cycle, family reconstitution and inheritance, popular rituals and customs, and the links between geography and technology—have been of special importance.[29] To this, Turner could scarcely have objected, given his own contribution to legitimizing the integrity of ordinary Americans and his own structuralist and environmentalist inclinations. But the questions, issues, and methods elaborated by the students of other nations have enabled the newer rural historians to fashion an environmentalism far more sophisticated than anything Turner offered. Rather than imposing inflated causal responsibilities upon physical settings (as Turner did), and rather than treating those settings as incidental backdrops to historical processes (as do some contemporary historians reacting against Turner), a good deal of recent rural history seeks to present human behavior as the product of complex interactions between specific environments, on the one hand, and social, economic, and cultural pressures, on the other.[30]

But the internationalist leanings of the new rural history soon passed beyond the methodological and, in so doing, have managed to confront

Turner's legacy more explicitly. Gradually but steadily, rural historians, like social historians generally, have burst the idea advanced by Turner which may well be even more powerful than his frontier thesis: the idea of American exceptionalism, of a peculiarly distinct national experience beholden to few if any theories and generalizations relevant to other areas of the globe (save, perhaps, as negative reference points). This has happened largely because the effort to reconstruct the lives of the "inarticulate" tended to spur (or in some cases to follow) an interest in the general economic evolution of American society. Here again, the most significant and challenging results were emerging from the fields of European, Latin American, Asian, and comparative history, at times from the same scholars responsible for the methodological breakthroughs. And as Americanists began attempting to link the "structures of everyday life" with broader conceptions of socioeconomic development, it became apparent that the United States shared in a worldwide unfolding of events.

Historians of the South were among the first to glimpse these vistas. Attempting to locate slavery and the plantation system within the sweep of regional and national political economies, they were struck by the way the South appeared at once out of step with the rest of the nation yet in step with many other parts of the world. A number of important features of Southern life seemed to call for a comparative vision and to encourage serious consideration of America's place in the rise of world capitalism: forced labor, large estates, staple agriculture, social hierarchy, landed and merchant capital, race and class, and a developing colonialism. Scholars turned initially, and logically, to Latin America, where black slavery first established a foothold in the Western Hemisphere and where the attendant problems of exploitation, racial conflict, and economic backwardness left an indelible imprint.[31] Often with a contemporary political agenda, historians of Latin America had begun to analyze, in an explicitly theoretical fashion, the changing sociopolitical character of their overwhelmingly rural societies, the rise and interaction of various productive systems, and the relationships between colony and metropolis. Few doubted that the colonization of Latin America had its roots in the commercial expansion of Western Europe, or that metropolitan regimes received the vast share of economic rewards. Far less certain was the nature of the Latin American societies that European expansion had thus created.

Some authorities argued that Latin America took on aspects of feudalism, characterized as it was by patrimonial land grants, *latifundia*, a rigidly hierarchical social structure, a dependent laborforce (whether African or Indian), an aristocratic ruling class, and a small and weak bourgeoisie.[32] Some argued that Latin America witnessed the appearance of "dual economies": a market-oriented sector associated with the ports, plantations, and mines, and a traditional sector in the hinterlands given over to subsistence agriculture.[33] Some argued that Latin America was quickly integrated into a world capitalist economy, though within the context of "dependency" relations (reaching out from European metropolises to colonial towns, landed estates, and the backlands) through which European powers tapped labor and material resources.[34] And finally, some argued that although Latin America participated in—indeed helped propel—the rise of a world capitalist system based in Europe, it remained dominated by a variety of precapitalist social relations.[35] These disagreements, it should be noted, stem chiefly from differences in definition (and political orientation). Those who define capitalism in terms of commodity exchange confront those who define it in terms of how surpluses are extracted from direct producers. Nonetheless, the debate over the nature of Latin American society has illuminated a paradox that historians of the South have been pondering for some time now: Forced rural labor proved necessary to early capitalist development and yet ultimately had to be swept away to permit further advances.[36]

Rural social relations have figured centrally—and for American historians most instructively—in the even more long-standing debate over the European transition from feudalism to capitalism. For Europeanists have come to argue that the rise of commercial and industrial capitalism depended upon a transformation of the countryside. Earlier interpretations had assigned the dynamic role to cities and towns where (it was suggested) the market economy took shape, forged short- and long-distance trading networks by land and sea, and ultimately broke down the insular, self-sufficient feudal order in the hinterlands.[37] But with the work of Marc Bloch and, later, of Maurice Dobb, Rodney Hilton, Eric Hobsbawm, Georges Duby, Immanuel Wallerstein, Emmanuel Le Roy Ladurie, and Robert Brenner, among others, attention shifted and exciting new questions were raised.[38] On the one hand, the feudal economy began to be seen as more dynamic than previously assumed, and subject to its own logic of expansion and crisis. On the other hand, the towns came to be judged as less transformative. Indeed, it became clear that the full progress of capitalism, customarily associated so closely with the urban world, rested chiefly on what transpired in the rural world.

It became clear because of some perplexing problems presented by the European story. In the first place, a long period of time separated the initial erosion of feudal relations (notably serfdom) and the onset of industrialization—perhaps four centuries. Furthermore, the areas that at first appeared most advanced in commerce and manufacturing—the Italian city-states, the Baltic states, the Netherlands, the Iberian peninsula—failed to make the vital breakthrough and eventually lapsed into decline. Wherever scholars chose to find the precise causal connections, they could not help but focus on the slow and incomplete, if not obstructed, process of revolutionizing the countryside. Capitalist development, after all, requires both a mobile laborforce and a large domestic market for manufactured goods; it requires, in other words, that rural producers be not only liberated from compulsory dues and obligations, but also severed from proprietary claims to productive resources, and so rendered incapable of subsisting without recourse to the market. In England, which emerged in the forefront of industrialization, the most dramatic strides were taken by means of enclosures, the consolidation of holdings, and the advent of large-scale farming based on tenantry and wage labor.[39] On the continent, where industrialization was later in coming, traditional rural relations proved far more resilient.

Indeed, the continuing strength of the rural sector in much of continental Europe is particularly striking. There was, to be sure, considerable variety in the forms of economic and political organization: In some regions the seigneurial order persisted into the eighteenth and early nineteenth centuries, in others quasi-independent peasant farming secured relatively stable footing. Although it is possible to make broad distinctions between patterns in Eastern and Western Europe, a wide array of relations and arrangements could be found even within the same national boundaries. In any case, there were substantial barriers to primitive accumulation, increased productivity, agricultural innovation, and the domination of the marketplace.[40]

What has this awareness of European economic development meant for historians of rural America? In a general sense it has already promoted a more subtle and textured understanding of social change in the countryside, as well as richer and more satisfying explanations of how such changes contributed—were in fact intrinsic—to the emerging political economy of the contemporary world. But it also has implications for what rural historiography *should* do, for the directions future ventures in American rural history might pursue.

Perhaps the key point here is, ironically, the need to avoid a careless equation of the American situation with *all* of Europe. Despite America's pronouncedly British heritage, for example, scholars should realize that developments in America and Great Britain were often quite different. This is partly because the byways of British rural history in the "modern" period were both varied among themselves and generically unique: They were distinct both from developments in the New World and from patterns unfolding in continental Europe.[41] It is also the case that America evinced its own measure of uniqueness. Thus it bears notice that, save for the range cattle industry and the very brief appearance of "bonanza" farms on the Northern Plains, the "classic" three-tiered format of English capitalist agriculture (resting heavily on wage laborers) was not widespread in either the American colonies or the United States. Instead, either family or unfree labor prevailed.[42] Nor should it be overlooked that the transition from agriculture to handicrafts and factories in New England—the region in which rural industrialization has been investigated most extensively—displayed distinct characteristics. For in the post-Revolutionary northeastern country-side we find an agricultural economy that was declining but remained inno-cent of enclosures; that embraced the market only slowly and grudgingly yet generated capital for nonfarming investments; that encouraged widespread exodus from family farms, but until the post-1840 wave of foreign immi-grants (itself a unique American development) never spawned a consistent labor surplus for the region's rural manufactories.[43]

All of this, of course, simply underscores the need, not to avoid foreign comparisons, but to construct them carefully. There is no reason historians of the American South would not profit from looking at Eastern Europe—especially Prussia—where a "second serfdom" took hold at roughly the same time slavery was established in the Western Hemisphere. For their part, historians of New England, the Middle Atlantic, and the Midwest might usefully focus on Western Europe—particularly western Germany and France—where seigneurial exactions were limited or light and where household production based upon reasonably secure tenures predominated. And so long as they avoid rigidly linear notions of "modernization," these same scholars might also ponder what historians of Europe have termed "proto-industrialization": a process in which the integrity of the family unit was maintained even as it was drawn into the sphere of commodity produc-tion under the auspices of merchant capital.[44] It was a process that may hold some clues for understanding the gradual commercialization of family farming.

Comparisons such as these might also shed new light on the nature and meaning of political conflict in the United States during the eighteenth and nineteenth centuries. Pioneering work of this sort is already under way among scholars examining the transition from slavery to freedom in the South, with important insights culled from both European and Latin American examples.[45] But the legal emancipation of slaves and peasants was only part of the story of political contention and popular unrest accom-panying the modernization of rural societies throughout much of the world. Without pushing comparisons too far, there is much to be learned from rural resistance to the incursions of the market and the state, from popular hostility to enclosures and related agricultural "reforms," and from those moments when local peasant unrest grew into larger rebellions. Certainly our perspective on the bitter skirmishes in America over grazing and water rights, eminent domain, and rural cooperatives, not to mention over the more imposing national issues of land, money, and banking, might be sharpened considerably.

We need, finally, to place the American rural experience in a truly inter-national rather than simply comparative context. After all, the great transat-lantic migrations of the nineteenth century at once denoted the transformation of rural Europe and helped shape the transformation of rural America. It is becoming increasingly clear (and this collection helps to confirm) that immigration contributed to rural as well as urban ethnic diversity. Moreover, immigration may help explain how the United States managed to industrialize rapidly while geographical expansion, liberal land policies, and family farming persisted in the North and West, and while staple agriculture continued to hold sway in the South—rural conditions that elsewhere slowed economic development considerably. What was exceptional about the American road to industrial capitalism may thus, in a significant sense, have depended on a worldwide process of which America was only a small part.

## IV

The essays gathered here reflect and advance many of the conceptual and methodological insights we have been discussing. The result, it must be admitted, is not a comprehensive collection. The articles are concerned with milieus that are linked frequently, but not exclusively, to agriculture and that range from sparsely settled wilderness to villages and towns. Although different geographical areas are considered, there is no effort to examine every separate kind of rural setting, and the three broad regions these essays traverse—the Northeast, South, and West—are explored in both different and overlapping periods. Similarly, although these essays cover a variety of subjects, they cannot pretend to illuminate every important historical and historiographical issue relating to America's rural past. For example, the collection touches only obliquely on the question of how America's attitude toward, and image of, the countryside changed over time.[46]

The essays were selected, first, because we regard them as representative examples of new work in American rural history. But they were also chosen because in fact, taken together, they do display thematic coherence. Despite their varying approaches, arguments, and topics, our contributors focus, in one degree or another, on the complex and often conflicted development of commercial and industrial capitalism in the countryside. From different vantage points, and with differing emphases, the authors attempt to place rural areas and communities within the larger context of America's "Great Transformation."

We begin in the Northeast, where the pressures of commercialization extended early into the hinterland and where industrial capitalism first made itself felt in the countryside before migrating to the cities and towns. Gary Kulik explores an initial bitter conflict between farmers and mill owners over riparian rights, highlighting the legal, cultural, and economic divisions that ruptured rural New England from the mid-eighteenth through the early nineteenth centuries. Thomas Dublin examines the proliferation of outwork—specifically the making of palm-leaf hats—that drew New England farm households into an emerging national economy and rural labor into the service of industrialism. Jonathan Prude considers the growing frictions between the mill villages that came to dot southern New England and the agricultural communities surrounding them, suggesting the perceptions and associations that went into the definition of deep and lasting tension. David Jaffee uncovers the world of the little-known portrait makers, often self-taught itinerants, who wended through rural settlements and villages, at once tapping and helping to create a market for mass-produced art and the bourgeois tastes that sustained it.

Although the Great Transformation is most commonly associated with industrialization, the experience of middle to late nineteenth-century Southerners demonstrates that the two are not synonymous. The South would remain overwhelmingly agricultural well into the twentieth century, and yet the period following the Civil War witnessed the rapid extension of market relations along with mounting incidents of rural unrest. On the one hand, there was the abolition of black slavery; on the other hand, white farm families were soon absorbed into the cotton economy. John Scott Strickland opens this story by describing the transition from slavery to freedom in the South Carolina Low Country, where a unique system of labor organization gave shape to the dramatic struggle over social relations in the postwar era. Steven Hahn shifts our focus to the Georgia Upcountry, a nonplantation region during the antebellum period, where communities of white yeomen farmers moved from semisubsistence to commercial agriculture. Robert C. McMath, Jr. takes us to another locale, the sandy lands of east Texas, and analyzes the social and cultural foundations of agrarian radicalism—specifically, the early organization of the Texas Farmers' Alliance. Given the very different settings, circumstances, and conditions that they explore, these three case studies also help us identify historical threads running through the entire region.

The West is customarily viewed as unique and yet also archetypically American: rugged, democratic, individualistic, commercial, and competitive. But as the contributors to this section of the volume make plain, the West displayed considerable diversity even as it embraced the central experiences of the South and the East. John Mack Faragher, in his study of pre–Civil War settlement in Sugar Creek, Illinois, and Kathleen Neils Conzen, in her investigation of nineteenth- and early twentieth-century immigrant inheritance patterns in rural Minnesota, both suggest that the social relations and sensibilities found in precapitalist communities of Europe and seaboard America were reproduced as settlers moved westward. In his sweeping essay, Howard Lamar draws conclusions about the social impact of the frontier very different from those of Frederick Jackson Turner. Lamar argues that the conditions of frontier life very often encouraged the development of forced labor systems and a protracted transition from legal bondage to coercive contract. Thus it was that the Midwest, Plains, and Far West also felt the currents of the larger transformation.

What happened in rural communities after the transformation occurred? Stagnation and decline, occasioned by the increasing hegemony of cities and industry, have normally been the answer. In the volume's concluding essay, however, Hal S. Barron offers a different assessment. Looking particularly at the story of Chelsea, Vermont, but with implications reaching well beyond, Barron suggests an economic and demographic stabilization made possible by creative strategies designed to transmit and preserve viable farmsteads and a mixed agriculture capable of circumscribing the full impact of market fluctuations.

The rural history represented by these eleven essays remains in its formative stages. Questions, issues, and perspectives are still being defined and refined. A new synthesis is yet to be written. We hope that this volume will serve as a valuable introduction to students and a guidepost for those interested in pursuing research in the field. Above all we hope it will suggest the complex and powerful ways in which the countryside shaped American history.

NOTES

1. Gary B. Nash, *Red, White and Black: The Peoples of Early America* (Englewood Cliffs, N.J., 1982), 8–16.

2. Richard Hofstadter, *America at 1750: A Social Portrait* (New York, 1971), xi.

3. Arthur Schlesinger, *The Rise of the City, 1878–1898* (New York, 1933), 79. T. Harry Williams, Richard N. Current, and Frank Freidel, *A History of the United States*, 2d ed., 2 vols. (New York, 1966), 1:253; Richard N. Current, T. Harry Williams, Frank Freidel, and Alan Brinkley, *American History: A Survey*, 6th ed., 2 vols. (New York, 1983), 2:545.

4. William Bradford, *History of Plymouth Plantation, 1620–1647*, 2 vols. (New York, 1912), 1:222.

5. Robert Beverley, *The History and Present State of Virginia*, ed. with intro. by Louis B. Wright (Chapel Hill, N.C., 1947), 298.

6. Richard Hofstadter, *The Progressive Historians: Turner, Beard, Parrington* (New York, 1968), 12, 17.

7. Frederick Jackson Turner, "The Significance of the Frontier in American History," quoted in Ray Allen Billington, ed., *The Frontier Thesis: Valid Interpretation of American History?* (New York, 1966), 9, 11.

8. In Charles Beard's opinion, Turner's paper had "a more profound influence on thought about American history than any other essay or volume ever written on the subject." See Hofstadter, *The Progressive Historians*, 47–48.

9. Ibid., 50, 54, 65–66.

10. Schlesinger, *The Rise of the City*, 58–61. Hofstadter, *The Progressive Historians*, 61.

11. Walter Prescott Webb, *The Great Plains* (Boston, 1931); James C. Malin, *The Grassland of North America: Prolegomena to its History* (Lawrence, Kans., 1947); Percy W. Bidwell and John I. Falconer, *History of Agriculture in the Northern United States, 1620–1860* (Washington, D.C., 1925); Lewis C. Gray, *History of Agriculture in the Southern United States to 1860*, 2 vols. (Washington, D.C., 1933); Fred A. Shannon, *The Farmer's Last Frontier: Agriculture, 1860–1897* (New York, 1945).

12. Hofstadter, *The Progressive Historians*, 72.

13. Billington, ed., *The Frontier Thesis*, 3–7.

14. See, for example, the treatment of Turner in Alan Dawley, *Class and Community: The Industrial Revolution in Lynn* (Cambridge, Mass., 1976), 54.

15. For example: Stephan Thernstrom, *Poverty and Progress: Social Mobility in a Nineteenth Century City* (Cambridge, Mass., 1964); Peter Knights, *The Plain People of Boston, 1830–1860: A Study in City Growth* (New York, 1971); Thomas Dublin, *Women at Work: The Transformation of Work and Community in Lowell, Massachusetts, 1826–1860* (New York, 1979); Bernard Farber, *Guardians of Virtue: Salem Families in 1800* (New York, 1972); Bruce Laurie, *Working People of Philadelphia, 1800–1850* (Philadelphia, 1980); Gary B. Nash, *The Urban Crucible: Social Change, Political Consciousness, and the Origins of the American Revolution* (Cambridge, Mass., 1979).

16. The "new" urban history usually marks its emergence with the publication of Stephan Thernstrom and Richard Sennett, eds., *Nineteenth-Century Cities: Essays in the New Urban History* (New Haven, Conn., 1969). But see also Oscar Handlin and John Burchard, eds., *The Historian and the City* (Cambridge, Mass., 1963).

17. Thernstrom, *Poverty and Progress*.

18. For example: Charles S. Grant, *Democracy in the Connecticut Frontier Town of Kent* (New York, 1961); Richard Bushman, *From Puritan to Yankee: Character and the Social Order in Connecticut, 1690–1765* (Cambridge, Mass., 1967); Kenneth A. Lockridge, *A New England Town: The First Hundred Years, Dedham, Massachusetts, 1636–1736* (New York, 1970); Philip G. Greven, *Four Generations: Population, Land, and Family in Colonial Andover, Massachusetts* (Ithaca, N.Y., 1970); Robert A. Gross, *The Minutemen and Their World* (New York, 1976).

19. Several essays have drawn particular attention: James A. Henretta, "Families and Farms: *Mentalité* in Pre-Industrial America," *William and Mary Quarterly* 3d ser. 35 (1978): 3–32; Christopher Clark, "The Household Economy, Market Exchange and the Rise of Capitalism in the Connecticut Valley, 1800–1860," *Journal of Social History* 13 (1979): 169–89; Michael Merrill, "Cash Is Good to Eat: Self-Sufficiency and Exchange in the Rural Economy of the United States," *Radical History Review* 3 (1977): 42–71.

20. Robert P. Swierenga, "Theoretical Perspectives on the New Rural History: From Environmentalism to Modernization," *Agricultural History* 56 (1982): 495.

21. Such estimates are drawn from Thomas Bender, *Community and Social Change in America* (New Brunswick, N.J., 1978), 12; Thomas Bender, *Toward an Urban Vision: Ideas and Institutions in Nineteenth Century America* (Lexington, Ky., 1975), 29; Schlesinger, *The Rise of the City*, 67; David L. Sills, ed., *International Encyclopedia of*

*the Social Sciences*, 16 vols. (New York, 1968), 13:582. (Statistics cited in n. 3, above, use a standard of 8,000.) See also Michael Frisch, *Town Into City: Springfield, Massachusetts and the Meaning of Community, 1840–1880* (Cambridge, Mass., 1972), 1–6.

22. Williams, Current, and Freidel, *A History of the United States*, 1:59, 460.

23. Sills, ed., *International Encyclopedia of the Social Sciences*, 13:582. Swierenga, "Theoretical Perspectives on the New Rural History," 496.

24. Thomas Bender has pointed out that early nineteenth-century Americans assumed rural areas could embrace commercialization and industrialization. See Bender, *Toward an Urban Vision*, ch. 2.

25. Swierenga, "Theoretical Perspectives on the New Rural History," 496.

26. Schlesinger, *The Rise of the City*, 53; Sills, ed., *International Encyclopedia of the Social Sciences*, 13:582; Swierenga, "Theoretical Perspectives on the New Rural History," 496; Michael B. Katz, Michael J. Doucet, and Mark J. Stein, "Migration and the Social Order in Erie County, New York: 1855," *Journal of Interdisciplinary History* 8 (1978): 669–701; Bender, *Community and Social Change*, ch. 2.

27. Sills, ed., *International Encyclopedia of the Social Sciences*, 13:581–82; Bender, *Community and Social Change*, 33, 42.

28. Several of the essays in this book (for example those by Barron and Prude) stress the particularity of rural economic transformations. But this hardly contradicts the view that, in a general sense, rural and nonrural areas underwent—and contributed to—the overall commercialization and industrialization of American life. Sensitivity to rural experiences discloses both the connections and heterogeneity within economic development. In this regard it is useful to consider recent formulations of Turner's notion of the frontier-as-safety-valve that underscore the melding of rural and urban contributions to national economic growth. See Ellen Von Nardoff, "A Resources and Sociopsychological Safety Valve" in Billington, ed., *The Frontier Thesis*, 51–62. See also Diane Lindstrom, *Economic Development in the Philadelphia Region, 1810–1850* (New York, 1978). A comparable perspective, albeit from a very different vantage point, is found in Raymond Williams, *The Country and the City* (New York, 1973).

29. See, for example, E. A. Wrigley, *An Introduction to English Historical Demography from the Sixteenth to the Nineteenth Century* (London, 1966); Peter Laslett, *The World We Have Lost* (London, 1965); Lawrence Stone, *The Family, Sex, and Marriage in England, 1500–1800* (New York, 1977); E. P. Thompson, "The Moral Economy of the English Crowd in the Eighteenth Century," *Past and Present* 50 (1971): 76–136; Jack Goody, Joan Thirsk, and E. P. Thompson, eds., *Family and Inheritance: Rural Society in Western Europe, 1200–1800* (Cambridge, Eng., 1976); Fernand Braudel, *The Mediterranean and the Mediterranean World in the Age of Philip II*, 2 vols. (New York, 1972); Emmanuel Le Roy Ladurie, *Les Paysans de Languedoc*, 2 vols. (Paris, 1966); Emmanuel Le Roy Ladurie, *Montaillou: The Promised Land of Error* (Paris, 1975).

30. Eric Lampard, "American Historians and the Study of Urbanization," *American Historical Review* 67 (1961): 49–61. For a general critique of contemporary urban historiography see Theodore Hershberg, "The New Urban History: Toward an Interdisciplinary History of the City," in Theodore Hershberg, ed., *Philadelphia: Work, Space, Family, and Group Experience in the Nineteenth Century—Essays Toward an*

*Interdisciplinary History of the City* (New York, 1981), 3–35. For a recent contribution that treats the rural milieu simply as a backdrop see Anthony F. C. Wallace, *Rockdale: The Growth of an American Village in the Early Industrial Revolution* (New York, 1978).

31. Frank Tannenbaum, *Slave and Citizen* (New York, 1946); Stanley M. Elkins, *Slavery: A Problem in American Intellectual and Institutional Life* (Chicago, 1959); Eugene D. Genovese, *The World the Slaveholders Made: Two Essays in Interpretation* (New York, 1969); Eugene D. Genovese, *In Red and Black: Marxian Explorations in Southern and Afro-American History* (New York, 1971); David Brion Davis, *The Problem of Slavery in Western Culture* (Ithaca, N.Y., 1967).

32. Gilberto Freyre, *The Masters and the Slaves: A Study in the Development of Brazilian Civilization*, trans. by Samuel Putnam (New York, 1946); Frank Tannenbaum, *Ten Keys to Latin America* (New York, 1962).

33. Cyril S. Belshaw, *Traditional Exchange and Modern Markets* (New York, 1965). For a classic literary representation see Euclides da Cunha, *Rebellion in the Backlands*, trans. by Samuel Putnam (Chicago, 1944).

34. This has been argued most forcefully by Andre Gunder Frank, *Capitalism and Underdevelopment in Latin America* (New York, 1967).

35. See, in particular, Ernesto Laclau, "Feudalism and Capitalism in Latin America," *New Left Review* 67 (1971): 19–38.

36. A number of economic historians and econometricians have argued that slavery presented no real impediment to economic growth and industrialization. Still, they have yet to provide an example of a slave society that moved along that route. See Robert W. Fogel and Stanley L. Engerman, *Time on the Cross: The Economics of American Negro Slavery* (Boston, 1974).

37. See Henri Pirenne, *Economic and Social History of Medieval Europe* (New York, 1937).

38. Marc Bloch, *French Rural History: An Essay on its Basic Characteristics* (Berkeley, Calif., 1966); Maurice Dobb, *Studies in the Development of Capitalism* (London, 1946); Georges Duby, *The Early Growth of the European Economy: Warriors and Peasants* (London, 1974); Rodney Hilton, *The Decline of Serfdom in Medieval England* (New York, 1969); Immanuel Wallerstein, *The Modern World-System: Capitalist Agriculture and the Origins of the European World-Economy in the Sixteenth Century* (New York, 1974); Le Roy Ladurie, *Paysans de Languedoc*; E. J. Hobsbawm, "The General Crisis of the European Economy in the Seventeenth Century," *Past and Present* 5 (1954): 33–53, 6 (1954):44–65; Robert Brenner, "Agrarian Class Structure and Economic Development in Preindustrial England," *Past and Present* 70 (1976):30–75. Brenner's article stirred an important debate in the pages of *Past and Present*, most of which will be reprinted in T. H. Aston and C. H. E. Philpin, eds., *The Brenner Debate* (Cambridge, Eng., forthcoming).

39. The ways in which shifting patterns of agriculture facilitated English industrialization are noted even in analyses that play down the social cost of enclosure. Such treatments cite the increasing productivity of eighteenth-century agriculture as the cause of lower food prices (despite a rising population) and hence as the source of potentially rising domestic demand for manufactured products. Heightened agricultural efficiency is in turn attributed partly to the gradual extension of farming techniques introduced even before 1700, and partly to the more "rational" (and more thoroughly wage-dependent) labor systems introduced through enclosures and the

three-tiered structure of farming. See Roderick Floud and Donald McCloskey, eds., *The Economic History of Britain Since 1700, Vol. 1* (Cambridge, Eng., 1981), esp. ch. 1, 3, 4.

40. Jerome Blum, *The End of the Old Order in Rural Europe* (Princeton, N.J., 1978).

41. See Maxine Berg, Pat Hudson, and Michael Sonenscher, eds., *Manufacture in Town and Country Before the Factory* (Cambridge, Eng., 1983); Gareth Stedman Jones, *Languages of Class: Studies in English Working Class History* (Cambridge, Eng., 1983), 3–7.

42. The postemancipation system of tenantry and sharecropping in the South took on some of the legal and organizational aspects of wage labor, although they developed gradually and incompletely.

43. See Clarence H. Danhof, *Change in Agriculture: the Northern United States, 1820–1870* (Cambridge, Mass., 1969); Thomas Dublin, *Farm to Factory: Women's Letters, 1830–1860* (New York, 1981); Clark, "The Household Economy, Market Exchange and the Rise of Capitalism in the Connecticut Valley, 1800–1860"; Jonathan Prude, "The Social System of Early New England Textile Factories: A Case Study, 1812–1840," in Michael H. Frisch and Daniel J. Walkowitz, eds., *Working-Class America: Essays on Labor, Community, and American Society* (Urbana, Ill., 1983), 1–36.

44. See Hans Medick, "The Proto-industrial Family Economy: The Structural Function of Household and Family During the Transition from Peasant Society to Industrial Capitalism," *Social History* 3 (1976): 291–315. Cautionary criticisms of proto-industrialization are found in Berg, Hudson, and Sonenscher, eds., *Manufacture in Town and Country Before the Factory*, ch. 1.

45. Eric Foner, *Nothing But Freedom: Emancipation and Its Legacy* (Baton Rouge, La., 1983); Eugene D. Genovese, *From Rebellion to Revolution: Afro-American Slave Revolts in the Making of the Modern World* (Baton Rouge, La., 1979); Jonathan M. Wiener, *Social Origins of the New South: Alabama, 1860–1885* (Baton Rouge, La., 1978); Dwight Billings, *Planters and the Making of a 'New South': Class, Politics, and Development in North Carolina, 1865–1900* (Chapel Hill, N.C., 1979); C. Vann Woodward, "The Price of Freedom," in David Sansing, ed., *What Was Freedom's Price?* (Jackson, Miss., 1978), 93–113; Thomas C. Holt, "'An Empire Over the Mind': Emancipation, Race, and Ideology in the British West Indies and the American South," in J. Morgan Kousser and James M. McPherson, eds., *Region, Race, and Reconstruction: Essays in Honor of C. Vann Woodward* (New York, 1982), 283–313.

46. See, for example, Williams, *The Country and the City*, and Leo Marx, *The Machine in the Garden: Technology and the Pastoral Ideal in America* (New York, 1964).

# PART I

# The Northeast

GARY KULIK

# 1. Dams, Fish, and Farmers

DEFENSE OF PUBLIC RIGHTS IN

EIGHTEENTH-CENTURY RHODE ISLAND

I

In the late summer of 1839, Henry David Thoreau committed to his note-book a half-dozen lyrical pages on the coming of factories to the New England countryside. It was for him, as for his contemporaries, a familiar subject. Yet he chose to address it in an unconventional way. The occasion was his celebrated journey on the Concord River. He had come upon the Billerica dam, and he began to reflect upon the connections between factory dams and fish. "Salmon, shad and alewives were formerly abundant here," he wrote, "until the dam . . . and the factories at Lowell put an end to their migration hitherward."[1] Dams thwarted the instincts of anadromous fish—salt-water fish that annually spawned in the shallow headwaters of the re-gion's rivers. Moved by their plight, Thoreau imagined a time "a thousand years hence" when "nature will have leveled the Billerica dam, and the factories at Lowell, and the Grass-ground river run clear again."[2] As he further reflected on the ways in which human agency had so fundamentally altered the rhythms of nature, he could imagine a solution independent of nature. "Who knows," he asked, "what may avail a crow-bar against that . . . dam."[3]

Dams troubled not only fish, but farmers too. New England farmers had long valued fish as an important source of protein, and river fish were free for the taking. Seventeenth-century writers had marveled at the numbers of fish that filled New England's rivers in the spring. Yet the numbers of migratory fish were declining, and the decline was noticeable as early as the 1770s. Dams were the cause. In addition, all dams raised water levels, and some flooded good farm land. All this provoked increasing resentment, and Thoreau gave voice to it when he wrote: "At length it would seem that the interests, not of the fishes only, but of the men of Wayland, of Sudbury, of Concord, demand the leveling of that dam."[4]

It was Thoreau's genius to evoke the passing of an eighteenth-century social order whose values were no longer resonant in his time in a language

25

that seems to ring clearly in twentieth-century ears. More than most, Thoreau understood the costs of technical and economic progress, and the threat a commercial and industrial order posed to the rural economy of antebellum New England. Yet his reflections on the unequal contest between dams and fish, between factory owners and farmers, had the quality of a personal lament. There is no indication that Thoreau recognized the issue which so vexed him in 1839 had deep historical roots and had once vexed whole communities.

By the time Thoreau wrote, the issue had been essentially decided. The Atlantic salmon would soon disappear from the upper reaches of New England's rivers, not to reappear again until the 1980s, and then only in miniscule numbers. As early as the 1830s, cotton-mill owners, the largest users of New England's waterpower, had effectively imposed their claims to water against all competing users. Morton Horwitz and William Nelson have analyzed the legal context. Changes in the law of water rights, Horwitz has argued, were at the center of a fundamental reinterpretation of eighteenth-century property law. Traditional definitions of ancient use and permissible injury came to be subordinated to a utilitarian legal calculus whose principal beneficiaries were the cotton-mill owners of the early nineteenth century. Both Horwitz and Nelson based their arguments on court cases in which mill owners interfered with the individual rights of other riparian proprietors. Both historians neglected conflict over fishing rights, a conflict that expressed itself, not as a defense of individual property rights, but as a defense of public rights, and whose arena was typically the legislature rather than the law courts. Nevertheless, contests over fishing rights unfolded in ways that confirm Horwitz's and Nelson's interpretations. The claims of unhindered economic development came to outweigh both the customary precepts of property law discussed by Horwitz and Nelson, and the claims of public rights. The new legal dispensation made it increasingly permissible for large textile-mill owners to flood upstream farm land, to disrupt and even injure the operation of smaller mills (sawmills, gristmills, and the like), and to obstruct migratory fish. Mill owners had not always had such license.[5]

For more than a century, New England farmers defended their entitlement to fish—through statute law, through petitions, through lawsuits, and, at least twice in Massachusetts, through the direct removal of offending dams. For the better part of the eighteenth century they were successful. The owners of blast furnaces, the first capitalists in the countryside, were also the first to challenge the rights of farmers. They did so most visibly in Rhode Island, beginning in the late 1740s. Cotton-mill owners later continued the challenge, even more effectively and with more far-reaching consequences. Farmers, however, were far from passive. They believed that both law and custom were on their side. Fish were important to their economy, not principally as commodities to be bought and sold, but as food for their own consumption. Yet they were defending more than narrow economic interest. They were defending a deeply felt definition of the public good and a sense of the proper balance between public and private rights. They saw their rights to fish as emblems of a rural order delicately poised between economic individualism and public virtue.[6]

The growth of economic individualism and the decline of a corporate social order has been a significant theme of New England's colonial history since the work of Perry Miller. Over the last fifteen years, a new generation of colonial historians has redefined this declension, largely in the language of modernization theory, extending Miller's argument to cover not only religious thought but demography, material culture, political ideology, and the law. The work of Kenneth Lockridge, Daniel Scott Smith, James Deetz, and many others, has made it more difficult to claim, as Louis Hartz once did, that America was liberal, capitalist, and individualist from its inception. Studies of the pace and extent of social change in early America have thus proliferated. But they constitute, as Michael Zuckerman has wryly argued, an "advancing embarrassment." There is no agreement on the scope, the timing, even the basic units of change. Did a "modern" America emerge in the 1660s, the 1690s, the 1720s, or in the era of the Revolution? Or did important traditional forms persist even later? Are the keys to modernity to be found in the expansion of markets, in the Great Awakening, in the birth rate, in political ideology, in Georgian house forms, in gravestone markings, or in some combination of these, in a synthesis yet unwritten?[7]

In recent years, a series of essays on the character of the early American rural economy has given a different form to these questions. At issue is the extent of commercial farming in the eighteenth and early nineteenth centuries, and the relationship between the economy of rural America and the consciousness of its farmers. At a deeper level, the argument is over the rise of capitalism: how it should be defined and when it happened.

There are three general arguments. The first argument is that commercial farming was widespread in early America and that farmers were economic individualists intent on maximizing profit. This is the inheritance of Louis Hartz, given more recent support by Charles Grant and James Lemon. The second argument is that commercial farming opportunities were limited and subsistence farming was the norm, but that the entrepreneurial instincts of American farmers were only temporarily repressed. This is the position taken a generation ago by Percy Bidwell and John Falconer. The third argument is that the farm economy was based neither on commercial markets nor on household subsistence, but on a combination of subsistence, local barter, communal labor (i.e., house raising and husking bees), and limited market agriculture. In such an economy, economic individualism was hedged by considerations of kin, community, and reciprocity.

Variants of this argument, inspired by both recent anthropology and British Marxist history, have been advanced by Michael Merrill, James Henretta, and Christopher Clark, among others. Intent on revealing the contours of a precapitalist America, they have reopened a debate important to the understanding of social change in early America. They have not made their case in sufficient detail, however, or with sufficient attention to time and space, to compel belief.[8]

This essay, based upon Rhode Island sources, brings new evidence to bear on the eighteenth-century rural economy, the consciousness of farmers, and the rise of capitalism. Definitions are in order. I understand capitalism to mean a system of production based upon wage labor, and as such distinct from that general constellation of economic forces—the growth of commerce, finance, and a market economy—conventionally subsumed under the rubric of commercial revolution. The interior communities of northern and western Rhode Island, where conflict over fishing rights was most pronounced, had economies that were neither capitalist nor strongly commercial. Backcountry farmers were not opposed to the introduction of blast furnaces, though more had reservations about cotton mills, but they were insistent that capitalist manufacturers respect their rights. It was not simply that farmers had different economic interests, though they did. They were concerned with defending an economy, a polity, and a way of life at odds with the emergence of an industrial and capitalist America. To this extent, the evidence of my essay lends support to the perspectives of Merrill, Clark, and company, though it does so by pointing in unexplored directions—to the impact of the American Revolution and of the anticapitalist strands of "Country thought" on the consciousness of backcountry farmers defending their rights to fish.[9]

II

All contests over water rights in Britain and America turned on questions of law. The social history of water-rights law in Britain remains to be written, but its general outlines are clear. No British subject had the right to obstruct the passage of migratory fish. The principle derived from the common law and had been expressed in Magna Carta. Parliament reaffirmed it in 1285, again in 1384, three times during the fifteenth century, and once more, emphatically, in 1714 when it prohibited the construction of dams or weirs hindering the passage of salmon on seventeen British rivers. The principle was unambiguous. The public had the right to expect that Britain's stock of salmon, shad, and other anadromous fish would be perpetually replenished by the great spring fish runs. And in a largely agricultural economy, that right took precedence over the rights of mill owners to exploit fully Britain's potential waterpower.[10]

The legal remedy available to those whose rights were abridged was equally unambiguous. Under the common law, all river obstructions could be defined as public nuisances. All public nuisances were subject to the summary remedies of the common law and could be removed at will. Appeals to local courts then followed; they did not precede removal. Thus an aggrieved individual had the common-law right to "enter the close of his neighbor, for the purpose of abating or removing the cause of injury."[11] Carefully phrased in the bloodless language of legal prose, the abatement of a public nuisance involved nothing less than the physical destruction of another's property. Those who destroyed their neighbor's dam might well be acting with the law of England on their side.[12]

Yet mill dams were rarely destroyed. England's medieval watermills, most of which ground grain, were too important. As processors of the preindustrial harvest, many could trace their rights and privileges to Domesday Book; others were owned by powerful nobles or religious orders. They were important, however, less as distinct "industrial" enterprises such as those common to the nineteenth century, than as integral elements of England's agricultural economy. The common law, itself the product of an overwhelmingly agrarian society, may have subordinated the rights of mill owners to the larger needs of agriculture, but it did not seriously disadvantage the owners of established mills. It did, however, effectively restrain the construction of new mills and the enlargement or intensified use of old mill sites. As long as the characteristic constraints of preindustrial economies operated to limit mill owners' abilities to expand, the needs of mill owners and the common law remained in harmony. But as opportunities for industrial development increased in the eighteenth century, mill owners and their supporters attempted to modify the common law.[13]

The most direct way to do so was by statute. During the first half of the eighteenth century, Parliament passed laws (8 Anne c. 3 and 15 George II c. 6) that enhanced the legal security of mill owners. Henceforth, it would be an offense, not to build a dam that obstructed fish, but only to fail to provide fish passageways. Moreover, the remedy would no longer be abatement, but a suit at law or a formal complaint to the appropriate political authority. As waterpower became more important, courts and legislatures found it necessary to accommodate the claims of mill owners. Yet they tried to do so in ways that acknowledged the public's interest in both watermills and fish.[14]

It was in this context that New Englanders first addressed the issue of competing claims to river use. New England's economy in the early eighteenth century was far less complex than its British counterpart, but the problem of balancing rights to waterpower with rights to fish was even more urgent—for New England needed mills. The work of grain millers, sawyers, and others who employed waterpower was critical to the region's farm economy. Some towns encouraged the construction of new mills through the use of bounties and land grants, while others treated mill dams as they did roads and considered their repair a public duty. These same towns also sought to protect the public's right to fish. As the population of rural New England grew substantially during the first third of the eighteenth century, colonial legislatures found it necessary both to encourage and to regulate the construction of mill dams. They did so by enacting two distinct sets of statutes, the Mill Acts and the Fish Acts.[15]

Rhode Island passed its Mill Act in 1734, modeling it on the first such law in the colonies, the Massachusetts Act of 1713. The Rhode Island Act gave watermill owners the right to build dams and to flood upstream farm land "without any Molestation," subject only to the payment of court-assessed damages in the form of an annual rent to those whose lands were flooded.[16] In effect, the act was a form of eminent domain, sanctioning the enforced loan of privately held land. The Rhode Island Act was an exclusive remedy, prohibiting any common-law actions, whether for trespass or nuisance. A century later, New England cotton-mill owners would interpret the Mill Acts to justify their intensive, private use of the region's waterpower. Yet the acts were principally intended neither to free entrepreneurial energy nor to promote extensive economic development, but to draw a proper balance between public and private rights.[17]

The essential rights at stake were the rights of New England towns to attract and support the water-powered mills necessary to their agricultural economies. To this end, towns were willing to sacrifice small tracts of upstream land. In most cases, the loss was inconsequential, for the dams of grain millers and sawyers did not raise water levels substantially. Land was still plentiful, much of it was poor, and New England farmers did not practice a land-intensive agriculture. In cases in which valuable land was threatened, however, the calculus of public interest could be quite different. When John Sawin's sawmill in Natick, Massachusetts, flooded good meadow land in 1720, neighboring townsmen ordered it moved to another site. Watermills were important, but they were expected to serve the needs of agriculture. New England towns did not conceive of their mills as independent commercial ventures, but as extensions of their farm economies, and they generally supported only as many as they actually needed. The Mill Acts clearly encouraged the growth of mills, but they provided no license for unhindered economic development.[18]

The encouragement the Mill Acts provided was further balanced by the restrictive character of New England's Fish Acts. Fish were an important source of protein for the region's farmers, and the great spring fish runs came just at a time when stocks of food were running low after the long New England winters. More frequently invoked than the Mill Acts, the Fish Acts protected the rights of the public by regulating the building and operation of mill dams. In the interest of the rural economy, eighteenth-century mills might be allowed to flood upstream land, but they would not be permitted to obstruct the passage of migratory fish.[19]

Consider the laws Rhode Island legislators passed during the first half of the eighteenth century. In 1719, just five years after Britain's comprehensive effort to protect its salmon, the Rhode Island General Assembly approved an act "to preserve and improve the fishing of the [colony's] several rivers . . . and to prevent obstructions from being made to hinder the same."[20] More than one town had complained of dams obstructing the passage of fish—obstructions, in the language of the act, "prejudicial to the Inhabitants of Such Towns and Especially to the poor of the Neighborhood."[21] In response, the General Assembly gave each town the power to remove dams and stipulated that no dams restricting fish could be built without the permission of the respective town. In 1735, the Assembly went much further and detailed the specific responsibilities of dam owners. It did so within months of its passage of the Mill Act, attempting to balance encouragement with strict regulation. Under the new act, any mill owner erecting a dam across water where migratory fish normally passed had to provide a fishway during the spring runs, specifically from 10 April to 20 May, "annually, forever."[22] Complaints were to be heard by local justices of the peace. Two deputies from Scituate, a rural township in west-central Rhode Island, introduced the act in order to protect large numbers of herring that customarily found their way into "Moswansicut and other ponds in the western part of the Colony."[23] Drawing on the act, further regulations were formulated for some of the more populous parts of southern Rhode Island—for Point Judith Pond and the "Petaquamscut" River in 1736, for all of South Kingstown in 1739, and for the Pawcatuck River in the southwest corner of the colony in 1742.[24] (See Map 1.1.)

The Fish Acts, and the petitions that led to their passage, expressed the belief of Rhode Island farmers that unregulated mill dams threatened their right to fish. For mill owners, the colony's streams were chiefly a source of power; for most farmers, they were a source of sustenance. Such differences were bound to produce friction. Yet evidence of overt conflict between farmers and mill owners during the first third of the eighteenth century is rare. Grain millers or sawyers may have resented the Fish Acts and the restrictions they imposed, but they seem to have accepted them without public opposition.

In at least one instance, a family of mill owners willingly accommodated the needs of farmers. In 1714, the Jenckes family of Pawtucket Falls, proprietors of a forge and sawmill, granted William Arnold and four others,

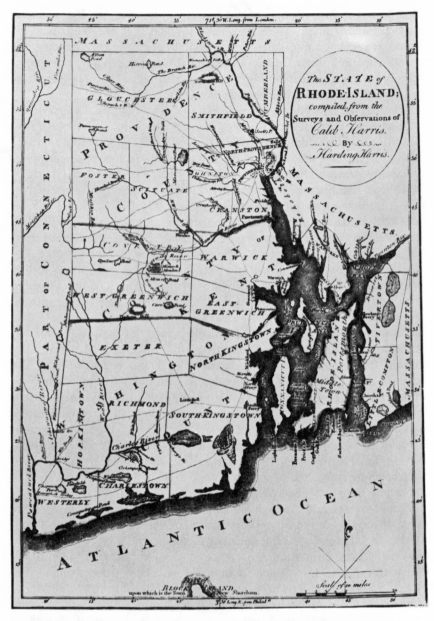

1.1. *The State of Rhode Island by Caleb Harris, Philadelphia, 1814 (courtesy The Rhode Island Historical Society)*

along with "each and every" inhabitant of Rhode Island and Massachusetts, permission to dig a channel on the west side of the falls to serve as a fish passage. Pawtucket Falls, the colony's largest waterpower site, was approximately 14 feet high. Local residents recalled the sight of salmon struggling over the waterfall in a series of fitful leaps. But smaller fish had no chance. Before 1714, according to the first historian of Pawtucket Falls, farmers had taken pains to smooth the falls' jagged rocks "by battering down the projecting points, that the fish, in the time of their running, might more easily ascend."[25] A permanent fishway, however, seemed to offer a better solution. The construction of Sargeant's Trench, as it came to be known, was a measure of the importance farmers attached to fish. (See Map 1.2.) Within a generation, the trench would become a source of discord between farmers and mill owners, and would remain so for almost a century. Still, the trench had its origins not in conflict, but in cooperation.[26]

Conflict between farmers and mill owners in the early eighteenth century was rare for several reasons. Mill owners were not a separate "industrial" interest, for much of what constituted industrial production in the eighteenth century—the grinding of grain, the sawing of wood, the fulling of woolen cloth—was closely tied to agriculture. Farmers and mill owners were thus integral parts of a single and largely undifferentiated economy, and most mill owners did at least some farming. Moreover, the work of mill owners was either seasonal or episodic. For grain millers who worked largely in the fall, or for the proprietors of small sawmills who worked only when work was available, it was no particular hardship to construct a fishway or to open a portion of their dam during the annual fish runs. They might resent having to do so, but it did not threaten their livelihood.[27]

The farmers, grain millers, and sawyers of the Rhode Island interior sought their livelihoods in an economy only tenuously tied to market production. Unlike the fertile coastal lands of southern Rhode Island, home of the pastoral economy of the Narragansett planters, the colony's northern and western lands were poor and unproductive. Backcountry farmers tended small herds of livestock and cultivated few market crops. Most of what they grew they consumed themselves. A few northern Rhode Island farmers raised small amounts of tobacco and flaxseed oil for international markets, yet the area produced so few provisions for the European or West Indian trade that Providence merchants had to send their agents into central Massachusetts to fill their ships. Local markets were also thin. Providence, the only city of northern Rhode Island, had no market house until 1774; like Boston, it was a net importer of food. In such an economy, the availability of free fish in the countryside was important. And river fish were generally consumed by those who caught them. Such fish were rarely marketed, for backcountry farmers could not compete, even if they wished, with the ocean fisheries of the Atlantic coast. The relative absence of a market

1.2. *Sargeant's Trench (courtesy The Rhode Island Historical Society)*

economy muted tensions over water rights. As long as the economic stakes
were low, conflict could be accommodated. But the stakes would not remain
low.[28]

## III

Conflict over water rights increased in Rhode Island with the introduction
of blast furnaces at mid-century. Unlike gristmills and sawmills, furnaces
depended on wage labor, were fully committed to market production, and
required continuous amounts of waterpower. No other enterprises placed
comparable demands on the colony's rivers and streams, because furnaces
operated around the clock, for months at a time. No other users of waterpower were as concerned with both technical efficiency and profit.[29]

   The Furnace Unity provoked the colony's first serious conflict. Owned by
two Boston merchants and located on the Blackstone River about 9 miles
above Pawtucket Falls, the Unity cast hollowware for both local and regional
markets as well as cannon and shot used in King George's War. (See Map

1.1.) On 27 April 1748 upstream residents claimed before the local justice of the peace that the furnace's dam hindered the passage of fish. The judge agreed, and ordered that "the said Dam should be broken and a way made through the same," by April of the following year.[30] The two owners, referring to the plaintiffs as "certain malicious persons," petitioned the General Assembly in October 1748 to void the court's directive. The owners claimed that salt-water fish were not hindered, that breaking the dam would not promote the passage of fish, and moreover, would spoil a "useful grist mill now standing in such dam." The owners, however, made no claim for the local utility of the furnace. Their petition was signed by thirty-seven freemen. Even if some of them were furnace workers, it is apparent that local opinion was divided. The General Assembly agreed with the furnace owners and their supporters, its reasoning unknown, and preserved the dam.[31]

Any other solution might have threatened the very existence of the furnace. Not only did blast furnaces have to be run continuously, they were customarily put in blast in the spring, in the midst of the annual fish runs. New England winters were too severe for prolonged outdoor work, and winter frosts adversely affected furnace operation. In the fall, water was likely to be scarce. And the summer, in the words of one ironmaster, was "too hot for the constitution of the workmen to endure it."[32] Only the spring offered ideal weather and plentiful water. Knowing this, the owners of Furnace Unity had taken no chances. They drafted a carefully worded petition, and cogently argued their case before the Assembly. The stakes were high. Though local opinion was divided, the decision of the local justice of the peace had given notice of a culture that placed a higher value on public and customary rights than on economic development in the hands of absentee ironmasters. Moreover, such values had been legitimated by local authority. The furnace owners had prevailed only by appealing over of the heads of that authority, to colonywide interests apparently more amenable to their influence. Ironmasters would not always be so successful.

Public conflict over fish intensified sharply in the years after 1765, as ironmasters sought exemption from the colony's Fish Acts. Farmers, in response, came to defend their rights with a new sense of urgency—an urgency shaped by the Revolutionary crisis. The rising conflict over fish was clearly the product of that extraordinary convergence of economic and ideological change which marked the years from 1765 to 1776.

By the 1760s, population growth was pressing against the limits of available economic resources. In the settled portions of New England, land had grown scarce, and so apparently had the numbers of river fish. The Swedish naturalist Peter Kalm, in his travels through New England, reported the claims of Boston-area farmers that fish were in short supply and that mill dams were the cause. Some ironmasters thus appeared to be profiting from their control of an increasingly scarce public resource. The objections of farmers, which at some other time might simply have festered beneath the surface of public life, achieved both voice and legitimacy in the context of the American Revolution.[33]

The growth of a contentious and popularly based politics in the years after 1765 encouraged backcountry farmers to seek redress for their grievances, and their grievances struck a louder and more responsive chord than they had a decade earlier. The issues they raised about dams, fish, and water rights had no direct connection to the momentous issues of the Revolution, but they drew upon a common sensibility—distrust of corrupt and arbitrary power. Farmers saw their rights to fish threatened by powerful ironmasters closely tied to the colony's political leadership and intent, so they believed, on turning manifestly public resources to private advantage. In responding to these threats, farmers sought to defend both their specific economic interests and their sense of public virtue, for the public good, as they understood it, demanded that individual economic rights be subordinated to the general will.[34]

Concerns such as these derived their resonance from Anglo-American "Country thought," a cluster of ideas about power and liberty, virtue and corruption, private interests and public good, associated with the English Commonwealthmen and widely accessible to colonists during the final third of the eighteenth century. Country thought provided the language of patriot resistance at its most articulate levels. It was a language of moral regeneration, inspired by classical antiquity, implicitly anticapitalist, suspicious of wealth, power, and the influence of commerce. Historians are divided about the extent to which the Commonwealth tradition impelled the less articulate farmers, mechanics, and laborers of the colonial seaboard. The evidence from Rhode Island is sketchy but suggestive. The petitions of the colony's backcountry farmers were the product of their immediate experience, not an explicit expression of the Commonwealth tradition. But Country sensibilities lent shape to that experience, structured its meaning, and legitimated its expression. It was no accident that conflict over fish and conflict over empire overlapped in time and elicited similar fears—the fear of arbitrary power and corrupting influence, and the fear that rapacious private interests might overwhelm a fragile, and traditionally defined, public good.[35]

Consider the pattern of conflict. In August 1765, Stephan Hopkins, Israel Wilkinson, and Nicholas Brown and his partners petitioned the Rhode Island General Assembly for an exemption to the Fish Act of 1735. They sought to build an iron furnace on the north branch of the Pawtuxet River. (See Map 1.1.) This was the Hope Furnace, the colony's largest and best known. Its supporters were men of prominence. Stephan Hopkins would later serve as colonial governor. Nicholas Brown's partners were his broth-

ers John, Joseph, and Moses—the "Browns of Providence Plantations"—
one of the colony's wealthiest families. In addition, Moses Brown, who
would later play a critical role in the beginnings of the American textile
industry, was a member of the Assembly's lower house. That body quickly
granted the company's petition. The upper house, however, initially sought
to defer the issue until meetings of local residents could be held. No record
of such meetings survives, and the upper house eventually concurred. But it
did so only after stipulating that the furnace owners construct a fishway
whose effectiveness would be judged by three knowledgeable freemen. If
these freemen decided that the fishway was unsuccessful, then the Act of
1735 would apply. Despite the furnace owners' formidable influence, they
had not been wholly successful. The full efficiency of the Hope Furnace
had been sacrificed to preserve a customary entitlement to fish. A century
later, the first historian of Providence County claimed that this decision,
along with other similar water-rights decisions, "tended greatly to retard the
progress of manufacture."[36] In this case, however, the retardation was only
temporary. Four years later, the owners submitted another petition request-
ing full exemption from the Act of 1735. This time, with Stephan Hopkins
himself in the governor's chair, it was granted.[37]

The colony's major furnace owners had succeeded, though not easily and
not without opposition. Smaller mill owners were not as fortunate. Farmers
were becoming increasingly prickly about their rights to fish, and suspicious, not only of ironmasters, but of all mill owners. In May 1766, sixty
upcountry famers in the Pawtuxet Valley presented a petition to the Assembly opposing the effort of Samuel Greene to build a corn mill near Gorton's
Pond. The farmers claimed that Greene's proposed mill would block the
passage of fish, and, in addition, was unnecessary to the local economy.
Their community already had a corn mill. In June, Greene formally applied
for an exemption to the colony's Fish Act. The Assembly deferred its decision while demanding that Greene, in the interim, comply with the law. It
never again acted on the question, effectively denying Greene his exemption. Samuel Greene had less influence than the colony's ironmasters, and
popular pressure was mounting.[38]

During the same year, three other petitions arrived in the Assembly raising new issues and introducing new protagonists. Mill owners and ironmasters were not the only ones to threaten the rights of farmers; so too did
commercial fishermen. In February 1766, thirty-three farmers living near
the Pawcatuck River asked the Assembly to regulate the use of fishing nets.
(See Map 1.1.) Some farmers used small nets during the spring runs to
catch as many fish as they could, curing them to eat throughout the year.
But it was commercial fishermen, whose presence first became an issue
in this period, who made extensive use of large nets and whose actions
fundamentally threatened supplies of fish. Deploying their nets directly

downstream of mill dams, they used the dams as barriers to trap migratory fish. Carefully maneuvering their boats, they drove the great spring schools toward their nets. The petitioners, invoking a "moral economy" of a kind revealed in E. P. Thompson's studies of eighteenth-century England, claimed that these commercial fishermen then charged an "extravagant price," depriving poor families of fish "that Divine Providence had bestowed upon them."[39] They requested that the Assembly outlaw the use of nets annually from 1 March to 1 June, and that it impose a fine of 50 pounds on those who failed to open their dams during the spring runs. In May, over seventy residents of Cranston forwarded a petition to the legislature protesting the "great neglect of timely opening of mill dams,"[40] and demanding stiff penalties for those using nets at Pawtuxet Falls. And in August, residents of Westerly and Hopkinton submitted a third petition asserting that the current laws protecting fish were ineffective and had thus done "great damage [to] the poor."[41] They too wanted stiffer laws mandating the opening of dams and restricting the use of nets. The General Assembly listened, and in February 1767 passed an act prohibiting the use of nets, or seines, from 25 March to 1 June on the entire Pawcatuck River and on a specified area below Pawtuxet Falls.[42]

The popular pressure of these years was also evident at Pawtucket Falls on the Blackstone River. By the 1760s, the Jenckes family had dammed Sargeant's Trench and built two anchor shops upon it, converting what had originally been a fishway into a power canal. (See Map 1.2.) The rise of shipbuilding in Providence provided the incentive. Upcountry farmers did not immediately protest this abridgment of their rights, but in October 1761, John Dexter of Cumberland, along with seventeen others, requested that the General Assembly authorize a lottery to pay for improvements at the falls. Dexter and his fellow petitioners claimed that a great many fish of "several sorts" entered the river below the falls, but could not pass easily upstream. For 1,000 pounds, Dexter argued, a new fish passage could be constructed to allow fish "that choose fresh water to pass with ease." The Assembly granted the request.[43]

Dexter's petition was signed by all of the mill owners then working at Pawtucket Falls—David and Hugh Kennedy, James and Nehemiah Bucklin, and seven members of the Jenckes family. They no doubt believed that supporting a new fishway was far preferable to giving up their rights in Sargeant's Trench, on which upcountry farmers might well have insisted. Farmers and mill owners at Pawtucket Falls were not yet in conflict, though their interests were clearly beginning to diverge. The new fishway worked, at least for a time. The General Assembly later claimed that the lottery had demonstrated its "public utility," benefiting farmers above the falls—"especially the poorer Sort of People."[44]

By 1773, however, backcountry farmers had come to believe that the fishway was ineffective; now they convinced the Assembly to push the issue one critical step further. In August of that year the Assembly passed legislation with the ominous title, "An act making it lawful to break down and blow up Rocks at Pawtucket Falls to let fish pass up."[45] The traditional common-law remedy for river obstructions had been affirmed by statute. It was now legal "for any person or persons whatsoever, at their own proper expense, to blow up or break down any rock or rocks in the falls . . . that obstruct the passage of fish up the said river, the said river being hereby declared a public river."[46] The act was a major victory for northern Rhode Island farmers, clearly and unambiguously affirming the importance attached both to fish and to public rights.

The act was also more than the mill owners at the falls were willing to tolerate. The Jenckeses, the Bucklins, and one Richard Fenner, a miller on the west bank, responded to the Assembly at its next session. Asserting that they had been "peaceably and quietly possessed" of their mill privileges for decades, and that they had gone to great expense to maintain watermills frequently subject to floods, they did not now want to face the hazards of new law which would empower anyone "to judge of the propriety of destroying the dams at the Falls."[47] Any person, they claimed, able to "procure a pound of gunpowder, actuated by the worst motives, may at any time in the space of a few hours, blow our interest to the amount of several thousands of dollars to irretrievable destruction."[48] They requested that the law be repealed, and ninety-three freemen who signed their petition agreed with them—their numbers testimony to a growing divisiveness based on diverging economic interests.

Although it did not repeal the law, the Assembly in June 1774 claimed that it had been "misunderstood," and that "many Disadvantages have happened."[49] The "Disadvantages" were not specified, but the Assembly formed a committee consisting of Stephan Hopkins, Darius Sessions, and Moses Brown—two of whom, as owners of the Hope Furnace, had a direct stake in amending the Fish Acts—to see that the new act was "truely executed." No rocks could be removed unless under their direction.[50]

Yet removal proceeded. Moses Brown later testified that "he directed the blowers where not to blow," as fishways were created on both sides of the falls.[51] These fishways, once again, seemed to work. A later petition asserted that "country" interests had been secured and that fishing continued to prove valuable, "particularly to the poorer inhabitants."[52] The same petition also claimed that the mill privileges had not been damaged, although on this there is contrary evidence. Testifying in a later unrelated case, one Israel Arnold asserted that the mills lay idle, and the dam unrepaired, for three to four years after the blastings at Pawtucket Falls.[53]

This victory for the farmers of northern Rhode Island came at the expense not of the colony's ironmasters—whose efforts to exempt themselves from the Fish Acts had initially provoked conflict—but at the expense of a less powerful group of grain millers, blacksmiths, and fullers. This was the first time in Rhode Island's history that farmers and the owners of small mills had seriously contested each other. In doing so, they revealed the distance that had come to separate their interests.

Now firmly tied to a market economy based upon shipbuilding and commerce, the mill owners of Pawtucket Falls were far less willing to accommodate the needs of farmers than their ancestors had been fifty years earlier. The rise of Providence port had made the difference. What had once been a fishway, mutually constructed by farmers and mill owners, was now a power canal. The colony's waterpower increasingly served the needs of an international economy. The economic stakes were higher and some men had come to believe that the public good now required that customary rights to fish be subordinated to the needs of commerce and manufacturing.[54]

The farmers of the northern Rhode Island backcountry disagreed. Unlike some of their mill-owning neighbors, they had not grown more closely tied to a market economy. And they remained intent on protecting their rights to fish, even if that meant discouraging the full commercial use of the colony's rivers. The ferment of the Revolutionary years had given them the voice and the opportunity to reclaim rights once unambiguously theirs. They would continue their efforts to uphold those rights into the nineteenth century. But their power to do so would diminish.[55]

IV

During the 1780s and 1790s, growing support for home manufactures increased the importance of waterpower and helped to redefine the nature of public benefit. Rhode Island's General Assembly became less willing to restrict the prerogatives of mill owners, and the rights of farmers to fish gradually counted for less. Yet conflict over water rights continued, and in one area of the state, backcountry farmers did manage to defend their rights to fish.

The Pawcatuck River valley, located in the southwest on the Connecticut border, had been the locus of sporadic conflict over water rights since the 1760s. Because the river had never been important to the colony's ironmasters, the protagonists did not include the owners of furnaces or forges. They did include farmers, commercial fishermen, and small-scale mill owners. During the 1780s conflict flared. The Assembly referred to "great Disturbances" and "Disorders and Breaches of the Peace," and in response, passed strong legislation in 1785.[56] The new law sharply limited the rights of mill owners, forbidding the operation of any sawmills during the spring runs, from 20 March to 1 June, and requiring that the dam nearest the mouth of the Pawcatuck be opened a full 15 feet during the same period. Acting alone, without the support of powerful local ironmasters, the river's grain millers and sawyers proved no match for the area's farmers. Commercial fishermen fared better. Previously banned from using nets during the spring runs, they gained the right to use nets two days a week, though only for an hour at a time. Despite growing opposition to the Act of 1785, and despite the later emergence on the Pawcatuck of cotton-mill owners wealthier and more powerful than their predecessors, the act remained in force on the river into the 1830s.[57]

Elsewhere in the state, farmers were not as successful. While opposition to dams that restricted fish passage continued, its political effectiveness diminished. On 4 June 1785, sixty-six farmers from Cranston and Warwick petitioned the Assembly to claim that dams and nets at Pawtuxet Falls prevented alewives from reaching their spawning grounds. "Before said obstructions," the petitioners asserted, "said fish were taken in great plenty and were of infinite advantage to the Poor and middling sort of people."[58] The farmers defined their fishing privilege in the new language of the Declaration of Independence—as an "unalienable right."[59] In August, the Assembly formed a committee to inspect the falls. Claiming that fish could pass, that nets posed no problem, and that the Act of 1735 remained effective, the committee denied the farmers' petition. Less than a year later, the Assembly amended the law of 1767, which prohibited the use of nets below the falls during the spring runs, to allow fishermen to use nets four days of the week.[60]

Farmers from Smithfield and Cumberland also found the Assembly less amenable to their influence. In June 1786, 168 of them, more than had ever previously signed a water-rights petition in Rhode Island, sought the Assembly's approval to organize a lottery for excavating a new trench around Pawtucket Falls. (See Map 1.2.) The fishway of 1774 had evidently failed. The owners of mill sites on the old trench were willing to allow the new fishway so long as their works were not injured. Yet the Assembly did not approve the lottery. The area's farmers, acting on their own and with the apparent consent of the mill owners, did make some improvements to the trench and, in May 1787, managed to convince the Assembly to restrict the use of nets and lines in and near its mouth. It was a minor victory, a pale reflection of what farmers had won fourteen years earlier on the same river.[61]

Conflict over dams, fish, and water rights in Rhode Island took a decisive turn in the 1790s. A dam was destroyed for the first time, new issues emerged, and conflict among mill owners dramatically increased. The new protagonists were the owners of cotton mills. Like blast furnaces, cotton mills were capitalist enterprises and required waterpower that was consistently available. Between 1790 and 1820, cotton mills would multiply in number, grow in size, and make unprecedented demands on the rivers and streams of Rhode Island. At one level, cotton-mill owners simply took up where the state's economically declining ironmasters left off—demanding that the Fish Acts be amended or ignored, to suit their interests. At another level, however, they fundamentally redefined the rules of the game.[62]

Again, Pawtucket Falls was at the center of the story. The precipitating incident, however, had nothing to do with the fishing rights of farmers, though the ensuing conflict would have a damaging impact on those rights. The story begins with an Englishman, Samuel Slater, who established the first water-powered cotton mill in North America at the falls in 1790. Two years later, he and his partners, financed by Moses Brown, sought to build a new mill. They chose a site 200 yards above the falls, and began work on a new dam in the summer of 1792. Some 6 to 7 feet high and approximately 200 feet long, the new dam was arguably the largest yet built in America. On 31 August, the owners of watermill privileges at Pawtucket Falls, Stephan and Eleazar Jenks, blacksmiths, and John Bucklin, grain miller, entered Brown's property and, in the language of the subsequent charges, "did . . . utterly subvert, pull down & destroy" the partially finished dam.[63]

At their trial, Bucklin and the two Jenkses claimed that the new dam was a nuisance, that it diverted "the natural stream" of the river and "prevented the Water . . . from running to and carrying [their] Mills in such a manner as it had before run . . . from time immemorial."[64] The issue for them was not rights to fish, but rights to the river's flow. Invoking the customary remedy of the common law, they freely admitted destroying the dam, "as Lawfully they might."[65]

Rhode Island's eighteenth-century mill owners had, on occasion, quarreled with each other over water rights, but never to this extent. The conflict at Pawtucket Falls involved more than competing economic interests. In truth, the obstruction created by the new dam was only temporary, a product of the building of the dam rather than of the dam itself. The flow of the river remained the same, and the same amount of water would soon have been available to the mill owners at the falls. Why then had a merely temporary obstruction elicited such conflict? The Jenkses and the Bucklins had long occupied mill sites at the falls; the former since the 1670s, the latter since the middle of the eighteenth century. Their trades had been disrupted, however temporarily, by a new business larger in scale and more demanding of waterpower than any previous business in the village's history. The new company was controlled by outsiders—Providence merchants—its most visible representative was an English immigrant, and it carried the taint of English industrialism. There was prejudice against Slater, according to the village's first historian and a contemporary of Slater's, because he was

English—"prejudice which lasted some time and attached to everything pertaining to cotton manufacture."[66] Not everyone opposed the new mill but for many, cotton mills evoked special fears, namely, of mill owners corrupted by power and of landless and dependent mill workers powerless to exercise their republican liberties.[67]

After a complex series of trials, Bucklin and the Jenkses won their case. The decision turned not on whether the new dam had a right to stand, but on whether the construction of the dam temporarily impeded the flow of water to the mills below. The court ruled that it did. The cotton-mill owners, however, had rebuilt the dam even before the case went to court, and rebuilt twice more, it still stands.[68]

The mill owners at Pawtucket Falls did not acquiesce gracefully in the rebuilding of the dam. Bucklin and the two Jenkses raised *their* dam by 2 feet. They did so, according to Moses Brown, "with a view . . . to cause backwater to flow upon the wheels above," directly threatening the operation of Slater's mill.[69] But their act also threatened others. By the 1790s, Pawtucket village was a warren of small-scale water-powered industry. Two anchor forges, three snuff mills, three fulling mills, a clothier's shop, a linseed-oil mill, a slitting mill, two machines for cutting nails and one for cutting screws clustered about the falls and along Sargeant's Trench. Several mills and shops on the trench were located above the falls, and their owners were no more willing than Brown and Slater to risk injury. They would join with the cotton-mill owners to oppose the 2-foot addition at Pawtucket Falls.[70]

There were others opposed as well, and for familiar reasons. Backcountry farmers saw both dams as threats to their fishing rights, and in November 1792 they petitioned the General Assembly. The addition to the old dam, they claimed, would make it impossible for fish to pass up river and the new dam had no fishways at all. The farmers suggested that a committee be appointed with power to remove all obstructions. The Assembly complied.[71]

But in February 1793, the Assembly reversed itself on one critical point. It redefined the committee's charge and placed the cotton-mill dam outside the committee's jurisdiction. Moses Brown's long experience in dealing with the Assembly over questions of water rights had proven invaluable. It was an important moment. For the first time in Rhode Island's history, a major water-rights issue had been removed from the political process, insulated from popular pressure. In the strict sense, this did not serve as a precedent, for other cotton-mill owners were not as politically adept as Moses Brown. Nevertheless, the decision left no doubt where power lay, and confirmed the worst fears of those ardently opposed to cotton mills. Brown and Slater had violated the state's Fish Act, but they would never be called to account. No fishways were ever built on the Slater mill dam.[72]

The committee completed its work in March 1793 by demanding that the 2-foot addition at the falls be removed. A month earlier, the mill and shop owners along the trench had drafted their own petition urging the Assembly to so decide. The addition, they believed, increased the risk of flood. With its removal, the threat to the Slater mill and to the works on the trench was eased. The mill owners at the falls had succeeded only in dividing the village. They were the immediate losers, while the cotton-mill owners, along with their allies, had triumphed.[73]

The contest they won was different from previous struggles over water rights in Rhode Island. It was both more complex and more intense, and the economic stakes were higher. The Assembly's decision not only placed the Slater mill dam above the law, but effectively excluded the interests of backcountry farmers. The conflict at Pawtucket Falls had begun and ended as a conflict among mill owners—riparian proprietors, individual property owners with specific and direct economic interests. Backcountry farmers, defenders not of individual property rights but of larger notions of public right and public virtue, were the real losers. Contests over water rights would continue at Pawtucket Falls for another thirty years, as mill owners quarreled over issues of fair apportionment. Now, however, the contest was one in which they were the only players—a contest in which the most powerful among them, the cotton-mill owners, would soon emerge victorious.[74]

The state's Fish Act, as it applied to the Blackstone River, would remain on the books until 1829, though northern Rhode Island farmers would never enforce it again. Their powerlessness to do so had other consequences. With the passage of migratory fish now almost completely obstructed, it was only a matter of time before commercial fishermen seized their opportunity. In 1804, they and their supporters petitioned the General Assembly to repeal the Act of 1787, which restricted the use of nets below the Falls. In 1805, the Assembly agreed. The commercial fishermen justified their request as beneficial to the public, claiming that they would furnish fish to "indigent people" more cheaply and more regularly than previously while insuring that large numbers of fish were not lost to the community. As there would now be far fewer fish reaching the upper Blackstone, they may have been correct. But in associating the public good with the commercial use of fishing nets, their argument reversed long-standing assumptions about what constituted the public good.[75]

Cotton-mill owners made the same kind of argument. During the first half of the nineteenth century, they effectively hid their economic interests in the cloak of public benefit, successfully arguing that their need for waterpower should take precedence, as one of their number sarcastically put it, over "a trifling shad and alewife fishery that does not pay for the grog expended in taking the fish."[76] The rights of individual property owners had come to dwarf older notions of public right. In 1828, the U.S. Circuit Court echoed the trend when it decided that Rhode Islanders could not cross the property of others in order to fish. It was irrelevant that people had been doing so for years. An appeal to customary rights could not justify trespass on private property.[77]

Conflict between farmers and mill owners over fishing rights continued into the nineteenth century—in Rhode Island's Pawcatuck Valley; in Newton, Pembroke, and Weymouth, Massachusetts; and in Shelton, Connecticut. In some places, farmers were able to insist upon the maintenance of fishways, but their efforts had little impact. Dams multiplied and grew larger, while fishways proved ineffective. By the middle of the nineteenth century, the number of anadromous fish in the rivers of New England had been reduced dramatically, and the Atlantic salmon could no longer be found in its customary spawning grounds.[78]

Yet Thoreau's vision—of clear rivers, of leveled factories, and of the salmon's return—was not wholly a dream. New England's textile mills have been dormant for the last fifty years, the victims not of nature, as Thoreau imagined, but of the international economy. New England's mill dams, with few exceptions, are no longer generating power and New England's rivers are slowly being converted to recreational uses. In the last few years, Atlantic salmon have found their way, assisted by fishery experts, to the upper reaches of the Connecticut River.[79]

## V

Conflict over dams and fishing rights in eighteenth-century Rhode Island was, at heart, a conflict over the coming of industrial capitalism. The annual spring migration of salmon, shad, and alewives furnished the noncommercial farmers of the Rhode Island backcountry with an important source of food. Their rights to fish were protected by both law and custom. Sawyers, grain millers, and other owners of small rural mills closely linked to local farm economies, easily accommodated those rights. The owners of blast furnaces, the first capitalists in the countryside, could not. Their technology and their capital investment required the intensive use of waterpower. As they sought to alter older patterns of river use, they also tried to alter the laws that protected the fishing rights of farmers. The conflict that furnace owners provoked paralleled the years of crisis leading to the American Revolution.

Farmers defended not just their economy, but their sense of public right and public virtue. They feared, not only the loss of fish, but the unrestrained pursuit of private advantage by mill owners. They were disturbed by the power of mill owners to impress their will on courts and legislatures.

And as events would demonstrate, they had reason. Their apprehension had no direct connection to the issues of the Revolution, but drew upon a common sensibility—a sensibility expressed in Anglo-American Country thought. Country sensibilities lent shape to the experience of farmers and legitimated their concerns. Rhode Island farmers defended their fishing rights most effectively during the years from 1765 to 1772. After the Revolution, they continued to defend those rights, upholding an ideal of public virtue anticapitalist in its implications. Then their power declined. The growing commercial uses of waterpower, in particular the rise of cotton mills, fundamentally eroded the fishing rights of farmers. The pattern of conflict over dams and fish in eighteenth-century Rhode Island reveals the complex and contested nature of the American transition to industrial capitalism.

NOTES

1. Henry David Thoreau, *A Week on the Concord and Merrimack* (Cambridge, Mass., 1894), 39.

2. Ibid., 39–40.

3. Ibid., 44.

4. Ibid., 45; William Wood, *New England's Prospect* (1634), ed. by Alden Vaughan (Amherst, Mass., 1977), 56; Thomas Morton, *New England Canaan* (1632), in Charles Francis Adams, Jr., ed., *Pubs. of the Prince Society*, 29 vols. (Boston, 1883), 14:222; William Root Bliss, *Colonial Times on Buzzard's Bay* (New York, 1888), 196–99; Peter Kalm, *Travels in North America*, 2d. ed. (1772), in John Pinkerton, ed., *A General Collection of the Best and Most Interesting Voyages and Travels in all Parts of the World*, 17 vols. (London, 1812), 13:470–71; Richard Bayles, *History of Providence County, Rhode Island*, 2 vols. (New York, 1891), 2:235; Howard S. Russell, *A Long, Deep Furrow: Three Centuries of Farming in New England* (Hanover, N.H., 1976), 79, 319; David Starr Jordan and Barton Warren Evermann, *American Food and Game Fishes* (New York, 1904), 105–8; Charles A. Atwood, *Reminiscences of Taunton* (Taunton, Mass., 1880), 5–6.

5. Zadock Thompson, *History of Vermont* (Burlington, Vt., 1842), 128, 140; Morton J. Horwitz, *The Transformation of American Law, 1780–1860* (Cambridge, Mass., 1977), 29–53; Morton J. Horwitz, "The Transformation in the Conception of Property in American Law, 1780–1860," *University of Chicago Law Review* 40 (1973): 248–90; William E. Nelson, *The Americanization of the Common Law: The Impact of Legal Change in Massachusetts Society, 1760–1870* (Cambridge, Mass., 1975), 159–65; J. R. Pole, *Paths to the American Past* (New York, 1979), 75–108.

6. On dam breaking in Massachusetts, see Alonzo Lewis, *The History of Lynn* (Boston, 1844), 154; William S. Pattee, *A History of Old Braintree and Quincy* (Quincy, Mass., 1878), 462–64; Charles Francis Adams, Jr., *Three Episodes of Massachusetts History*, 2 vols. (Boston, 1892), 2:831–34; Edward N. Hartley, *Ironworks on the Saugus* (Norman, Okla., 1957), 262–65.

7. See especially Michael Zuckerman, "The Fabrication of Identity in Colonial

America," *William and Mary Quarterly* 3d ser. 34 (1977): 183–214; Kenneth A. Lockridge, "Social Change and the Meaning of the American Revolution," *Journal of Social History* 6 (1973): 403–39; Kenneth A. Lockridge, *A New England Town: The First Hundred Years, Dedham, Massachusetts, 1636–1736* (New York, 1970); James Deetz, *In Small Things Forgotten* (New York, 1977); Daniel Scott Smith, "Population, Family, and Society in Hingham, Massachusetts, 1635–1880," Diss., University of California, Berkeley, 1973. The classic statements are Perry Miller, *The New England Mind: The Seventeenth Century* (New York, 1939); Perry Miller, *The New England Mind: From Colony to Province* (Cambridge, Mass., 1953); and Louis Hartz, *The Liberal Tradition in America* (New York, 1955). A recent intervention in this old debate is Stephan Innes, *Labor in a New Land: Economy and Society in Seventeenth-Century Springfield* (Princeton, N.J., 1983).

8. Charles S. Grant, *Democracy in the Connecticut Frontier Town of Kent* (New York, 1961); James T. Lemon, *The Best Poor Man's Country: A Geographical Study of Early Southeastern Pennsylvania* (Baltimore, 1972); Percy W. Bidwell and John I. Falconer, *History of Agriculture in the Northern United States, 1620–1860* (Washington, D.C., 1925); Michael Merrill, "Cash Is Good to Eat: Self-Sufficiency and Exchange in the Rural Economy of the United States," *Radical History Review* 3 (1977): 42–71; James A. Henretta, "Families and Farms: *Mentalité* in Pre-Industrial America," *William and Mary Quarterly* 3d ser. 35 (1978): 3–32; Christopher Clark, "The Household Economy, Market Exchange and the Rise of Capitalism in the Connecticut Valley, 1800–1860," *Journal of Social History* 13 (1979): 169–89; Robert E. Mutch, "The Cutting Edge: Colonial America and the Debate about the Transition to Capitalism," *Theory and Society* 9 (1980): 847–63. Winifred B. Rothenberg, "The Market and Massachusetts Farmers, 1750–1855," *Journal of Economic History* 41 (1981): 283–314; Carole Shammas, "How Self-Sufficient Was Early America?" *Journal of Interdisciplinary History* 13 (1982): 247–72; Bettye Hobbs Pruitt, "Self-Sufficiency and the Agricultural Economy of Eighteenth-Century Massachusetts," *William and Mary Quarterly*, 3d ser. 41 (1984): 333–64.

9. On "Country thought," see Bernard Bailyn, *The Ideological Origins of the American Revolution* (Cambridge, Mass., 1967); Gordon Wood, *The Creation of the American Republic, 1776–1787* (Chapel Hill, N.C., 1969); J. G. A. Pocock, *The Machiavellian Moment: Florentine Political Thought and the Atlantic Republican Tradition* (Princeton, N.J., 1975); and discussion later in this essay.

10. Humphrey W. Woolrych, *A Treatise of the Law of Waters*, 2d. ed. (London, 1851), 195; *Halsbury's Laws of England*, 3d. ed., 34 vols. (London, 1956), 17:317–18, 343–49; Anthony Netboy, *The Atlantic Salmon: A Vanishing Species?* (London, 1968), 165–85.

11. Joseph K. Angell, *A Treatise on the Common Law in Relation to Water-Courses* (Boston, 1824), 74–75.

12. *The King* v. *Wharton*, 12 Mod. 510, 86 Eng. Rep. 1056 (K. B., 1701), cited in T. E. Lauer, "The Common Law Background of the Riparian Doctrine," *Missouri Law Review* 28 (1963): 60–107.

13. Woolrych, *Treatise of the Law of Waters*, 85–86, 169; Lauer, "The Common Law Background of the Riparian Doctrine"; Netboy, *The Atlantic Salmon*, 165–85.

14. Woolrych, *Treatise of the Law of Waters*, 85–86, 169, 195; Netboy, *The Atlantic Salmon*, 178–85; Fred S. Thacker, *The Thames Highway*, 2 vols. (London, 1914),

1:3–4. For general conflict over water rights in Britain see T. S. Willen, *River Navigation in England, 1600–1750* (London, 1936), 16–51; L. T. C. Rolt, *The Inland Waterways of England* (London, 1950), 15–36; Leslie Syson, *British Water-Mills* (London, 1965), 42–45; John Rodgers, *English Rivers* (London, 1947), 11–17; Christopher Hill, *Reformation to Industrial Revolution* (London, 1967), 167; John Sutcliffe, *A Treatise on Canals and Reservoirs* (Rochdale, Eng., 1816), 246.

15. Horwitz, *Transformation of American Law*, 47–48; Angell, *Treatise on the Common Law*, 124, 507–14; "The Law of Water Privileges," *The American Jurist and Law Magazine* 2 (1829): 25–38; *Report of Committee on the Mill*, 6 October 1821, City Hall Archives, Providence, R.I.; J. Leander Bishop, *A History of American Manufactures*, 3 vols. (Philadelphia, 1861), 1:122–32; B. Cowell, *Ancient Documents Relative to the Old Grist Mill* (Providence, 1829).

16. R.I. Colony Records (1729–45), vol. 5, 185–86, R.I. State Archives, Providence.

17. Horwitz, *Transformation of American Law*, 47–53.

18. William Biglow, *History of the Town of Natick* (Boston, 1830), 8–9.

19. Bayles, *History of Providence County*, 2:235; Russell, *A Long, Deep Furrow*, 79, 319.

20. R.I. Colony Records, vol. 4, 221.

21. Ibid.

22. Public Laws of Rhode Island, 1744, 185–87, R.I. State Archives, Providence.

23. Cyrus Walker, "A History of Scituate," manuscript, n.d., 187, Town Clerk's Office, N. Scituate, R.I.

24. R.I. Petitions, vol. 4, 3, R.I. State Archives, Providence; Public Laws of Rhode Island, 1744, 190–91, 254–55, 258.

25. David Benedict, "Reminiscences No. 19," *Pawtucket Gazette & Chronicle*, 29 July 1853; Robert Grieve, *An Illustrated History of Pawtucket, Central Falls, and Vicinity* (Pawtucket, R.I., 1897), 32–44, 104–15.

26. Introductory Deposition, Equity Register, *Tyler et al.* v. *Wilkinson et al.*, 24 Fed. Case 472, 474 (no. 14,312) C. C. D. R. I., 1827, Federal Record Center, Waltham, Mass.

27. Carl Bridenbaugh, *The Colonial Craftsmen* (New York, 1950), 33–64; Louis C. Hunter, *A History of Industrial Power in the United States, 1780–1930, Vol. 1: Waterpower in the Century of the Steam Engine* (Charlottesville, Va., 1979), 1–50, n. 386.

28. Carl Bridenbaugh, *Fat Mutton and Liberty of Conscience, Society in Rhode Island, 1636–1690* (Providence, 1974); James Hedges, *The Browns of Providence Plantations, the Colonial Years* (Cambridge, Mass., 1952); Lynne Withey, *Urban Growth in Colonial Rhode Island: Newport and Providence in the Eighteenth Century* (Albany, N.Y., 1984).

29. Hunter, *History of Industrial Power*, 1, 6, n. 386; Arthur Cecil Bining, *Pennsylvania Iron Manufacture in the Eighteenth Century* (Harrisburg, Pa., 1938), 55–81.

30. R.I. Petitions, vol. 4, 70.

31. Ibid., vol. 7, 2; Israel Wilkinson, *A Memoir of the Wilkinson Family in America* (Jacksonville, Ill., 1869), 101–2, 403; Bishop, *A History of American Manufactures*, 1:503.

32. R.I. Petitions, vol. 13, 132.

33. Kalm, *Travels in North America*, 470–71.

34. On the general issues, see Kenneth A. Lockridge, "Social Change and the Meaning of the American Revolution"; J. G. A. Pocock, "Virtue and Commerce in the Eighteenth Century," *Journal of Interdisciplinary History* 3 (1973): 120–34; Edmund S. Morgan, "The Puritan Ethic and the American Revolution," *William and Mary Quarterly* 24 (1967): 3–43.

35. See Bailyn, *The Ideological Origins of the American Revolution*; Wood, *The Creation of the American Republic*; Pocock, *The Machiavellian Moment*; and Gary B. Nash, *The Urban Crucible: Social Change, Political Consciousness, and the Origins of the American Revolution* (Cambridge, Mass., 1979); John Murrin, "The Great Inversion, or Court versus Country: A Comparison of the Revolution Settlements in England (1688–1721) and America (1776–1816)," in J. G. A. Pocock, ed., *Three British Revolutions, 1641, 1688, 1776* (Princeton, N.J., 1980), 368–453.

36. R.I. Petitions, vol. 11, 206; Hedges, *The Browns of Providence, Colonial Years*, 123–54; Mack Thompson, *Moses Brown, Reluctant Reformer* (Chapel Hill, N.C., 1962).

37. R.I. Petitions, vol. 13, 77.

38. Ibid., vol. 13, part 2, 11, 15, 17.

39. Ibid., vol. 13, part 2, 10; E. P. Thompson, "The Moral Economy of the English Crowd in the Eighteenth Century," *Past and Present* 50 (1971): 76–136.

40. R.I. Petitions, vol. 13, part 2, 20.

41. Ibid., vol. 13, part 2, 41.

42. Acts and Resolutions of the R.I. General Assembly, vol. 11, 52, R.I. State Archives, Providence.

43. Introductory Deposition, *Tyler* v. *Wilkinson*; R.I. Petitions, vol. 10, 176.

44. R.I. Colony Records, vol. 7, 413–14; vol. 9, 61.

45. Ibid., vol. 9, 61.

46. Ibid.

47. R.I. Petitions, vol. 15, 105.

48. Ibid.

49. R.I. Colony Records, vol. 9, 118.

50. Deposition of Moses Brown, 27 January 1824, *Tyler* v. *Wilkinson*.

51. Ibid.

52. R.I. Petitions, vol. 27, 83.

53. Deposition of Israel Arnold, *Tyler* v. *Wilkinson*.

54. See Peter Coleman, *The Transformation of Rhode Island, 1790–1860* (Providence, 1969), 3–25; Sydney V. James, *Colonial Rhode Island* (New York, 1975), 262–66.

55. Evidence on the eighteenth-century economy of northern Rhode Island is drawn from my unpublished study of probate records, now being reworked into a larger manuscript. Evidence available from author.

56. J. R. Bartlett, ed., *Records of the State of Rhode Island*, 10 vols. (Providence, 1865), 10:113–14, 135–39; Frederic Denison, *Westerly and its Witnesses, 1626–1876* (Providence, 1878), 223–25.

57. Denison, *Westerly*, 225.

58. R.I. Petitions, vol. 22, 90.

59. Ibid.

60. R.I. Colony Records, vol. 13, 476–78.

61. R.I. Petitions, vol. 27, 83; vol. 36, 22; Introductory Deposition, *Tyler* v. *Wilkinson*; Grieve, *An Illustrated History*, 106.

62. Coleman, *Transformation of Rhode Island*, 71–107.

63. *Kennedy et al.* v. *Bucklin et al.*, Court of Common Pleas, Bristol County, vol. 12, 214–15, 289–91; *Bucklin et al.* v. *Arnold et al.*, vol. 12, 257; *Jenks* v. *Kennedy*, vol. 12, 236–37, Bristol County Superior Court, Taunton, Mass. By the late eighteenth century, most members of the Jenckes family had simplified the spelling of their name to Jenks.

64. *Kennedy* v. *Bucklin*.

65. Ibid.

66. David Benedict, *Report of the Centennial Celebration of the 24th of June, 1865, at Pawtucket, of the Incorporation of the Town of North Providence* (Providence, 1865), 87–88.

67. See Drew McCoy, *The Elusive Republic: Political Economy in Jeffersonian America* (Chapel Hill, N.C., 1980), 105–19.

68. Deposition of Moses Brown, *Tyler* v. *Wilkinson*.

69. Ibid.

70. Timothy Dwight, *Travels in New England and New York*, 4 vols. (New Haven, Conn., 1821), 2:27.

71. R.I. Petitions, vol. 27, 83.

72. R.I. Colony Records, vol. 14, 274–75.

73. Bartlett, ed., *Records of the State of Rhode Island*, 10:508; R.I. Petitions, vol. 27, 83, 116.

74. See *Tyler* v. *Wilkinson*.

75. R.I. Petitions, vol. 36, 22.

76. *Pawtucket Chronicle*, 24 January 1829.

77. *Smith* v. *Miller*, 5 Mason's Rep., 191. See also *Kenyon* v. *Nichols*, R.I. Rep., vol. 1, 106.

78. See Denison, *Westerly*, 175; *Towns of Stoughton, Sharon, and Canton* v. *Baker and Vose*, 4 Mass. Rep., 552–532 (1808); *Commonwealth* v. *Chapin*, 5 Pick., 199 (1826); Francis Jackson, *History of the Early Settlement of Newton* (Boston, 1854), 107–8; Orra L. Stone, *History of Massachusetts Industries*, 4 vols. (Boston, 1930), 2:1134, 1214–15; Matthew Roth, *Connecticut: An Inventory of Historic Engineering and Industrial Sites* (Washington, D.C., 1981), 33–34.

79. Nelson Bryant, "History Made on Connecticut," *New York Times*, 14 June 1981, 10S.

THOMAS DUBLIN

# 2. Women and Outwork in a Nineteenth-Century New England Town

## FITZWILLIAM, NEW HAMPSHIRE,

## 1830–1850

I

The transformation of New England agriculture with the growth of industrial capitalism in the antebellum decades has been a staple theme of American social and economic history since Percy Bidwell explored the issue in the 1920s.* The basic outlines of the process are clear and uncontroversial. With the growth of factory textile production there was a dramatic decline in the household manufacture of yarn and cloth. As spinning, and later weaving, moved from home to factory, increasing numbers of farmers' daughters left their homes and entered the mills that dotted New England's riverbanks. Simultaneously, growing urban markets and improved transportation led to the growth of market-oriented production that spelled the demise of an earlier agricultural regime. Farming families who had been relatively self-sufficient or whose exchanges were primarily local in character became enmeshed in wider economic transactions and were increasingly integrated into a New England-wide economy. The broad contours of the changes between 1800 and 1860 are known, but little has been written about how this transformation occurred. One aspect of this larger process

*Research for this article was supported by grants from the Committee on Research, University of California, San Diego; the Charles Warren Center for Studies in American History, Harvard University; the Henry A. Murray Center of Radcliffe College; and the National Endowment for the Humanities. I would like to express my thanks to Deborah Bruns and Seth Kreisberg for able research assistance and to Caroline Sloat and Jane Nylander of Old Sturbridge Village for sharing their expertise. I presented earlier versions of the article at meetings of the American Historical Association and the Deutsche Gesellschaft für Amerikastudien. I thank James Allen, David Jaffee, Michael Merrill, Joan Scott, and Caroline Ware for their critical comments on that work.

has been particularly neglected: the role of industrial outwork in the changing rural economy.[1]

We would do well to avoid thinking in terms of a strict opposition between urban industry and rural agriculture in this period. For young men and women in the countryside, migrating to the city or remaining at work on the farm were not the only alternatives. Although many young people migrated cityward, urban merchants and manufacturers sent large quantities of raw materials and semifinished goods out to the countryside to take advantage of an underemployed farm laborforce. In other words, industry spread into the countryside. The resulting outwork networks extended from Connecticut to Maine.

Industrial outwork—the distribution of raw materials to farming families for fabrication and subsequent sale beyond the local market—played an important role in the penetration of capitalist market practices and values into the countryside. Between 1810 and 1880, members of farming families produced a succession of consumer goods for mass urban and Southern markets. Handloom weaving, shoe binding, the braiding of straw and palm-leaf hats, and sewing occupied several generations of farmers' daughters and wives and provided considerable supplementary income for rural families. Through these means urban markets and capitalist institutions had an influence that extended far beyond city limits.

It may be useful to consider one such putting-out industry in some detail to appreciate the character and magnitude of outwork. Brief descriptions in numerous local histories of New Hampshire and Massachusetts towns attest to the importance in the 1830s and 1840s of palm-leaf hat manufacturing, an industry conducted entirely through the putting-out system.[2] Boston wholesalers purchased palm leaf, usually imported from Cuba or the Virgin Islands, which they in turn supplied to country storekeepers in central Massachusetts or southern New Hampshire. Storekeepers split the leaf and sold it to customers, who would weave or braid inexpensive men's or children's hats. Women and children, working in their own homes, fashioned the crude hats during periods of slack demand for labor on their farms. A teenager could make a hat in about three-fourths of a day, for which the pay would be 20 cents. Storekeepers bought back the finished hats, paying for them with credit toward store purchases. After bleaching and pressing, the hats were forwarded to wholesale merchants in Boston, New York, Philadelphia, and Baltimore to be sold primarily as farm laborers' or slaves' hats in the West or South.[3]

Although we know very little about this industry, our ignorance is no measure of its importance in the antebellum decades. Residents of Worcester County, Massachusetts, the center of the industry, made 1.5 million palm-leaf hats in 1832 and more than 2 million in 1837. Had everyone making the hats been working full time, it would have taken about 5,000 workers to produce this quantity. This laborforce is not insubstantial, especially when compared to the 5,700 women employed in Lowell's more famous cotton textile mills at this date.[4] As very few of the women and children worked full time, however, the actual number making hats at some point in the year in Worcester County was probably closer to 20,000. For the state as a whole, there were about 33,000 palm-leaf hatmakers, a figure exceeding the 20,000 cotton textile workers statewide.[5]

These numbers demonstrate that palm-leaf outwork was a widespread activity in Massachusetts in the 1830s. I would not argue, however, that it was of greater importance than cotton textiles or shoemaking. Hatmaking was entirely a handicraft operation and consequently the value of hats and the earnings of hatmakers remained small. The value of the 3.3 million hats made in Massachusetts in 1837 was only about $700,000, or just over $20 per worker. By contrast, cotton textiles manufactured in the state that year sold at wholesale for $13.1 million, a figure almost nineteen times that for palm-leaf hats.[6] Still, although the market value of the hats is not impressive, palm-leaf hatmakers in Massachusetts put in about 2.5 million persondays of labor annually in the 1830s, making this activity an important element in the lives of farming families.

European historians have been more interested in the growth of the putting-out system than have their American counterparts. Recent research on the putting-out system in Europe has included theoretical discussion and detailed case studies. Using the term "proto-industrialization," Franklin Mendels has argued that the growth of market-oriented, but traditionally organized, rural industry played a crucial role in the development of industrial capitalism in early modern Europe. Hans Medick's work has explored the ways in which proto-industrialization bridged two worlds, arguing that rural families engaged in new productive activities for traditional reasons, but in this process became involved in newly emerging market relations. He points to the contradictions between the needs of individual families and of the broader economy, which are evident most strikingly in the plight of the handloom weavers in Great Britain in the first half of the nineteenth century. David Levine and Rudolph Braun have focused their studies on the demographic implications of this rural industry in local English and Swiss settings. All in all, there is a lively discussion of the putting-out system and its consequences among European historians that Americanists would do well to follow.[7]

Putting-out industries in New England differed from their European counterparts in several important respects, and I hesitate to appropriate the European term, "proto-industrialization," to describe the American phenomenon. European proto-industrialization was a long, drawn-out phenomenon with a significant impact on the rural political economy over several centuries; in contrast, putting-out work in New England had a much later start and played a major role for only about two generations. European outwork largely anticipated factory production; in New England it complemented factory textile production. Whereas the rise and decline of putting-out work in European countries extended over several hundred years, similar processes in the United States had a much more compressed history. One cannot expect demographic changes in the United States to be so striking as those in European countries. The putting-out system in the United States simply did not have such a long time period in which to influence rural patterns of marriage and fertility and, because it was contemporaneous with factory production, its effects were mixed with those due primarily to the factory influence. Given these differences between the American and the European contexts, it is important to examine outwork in the American context rather than simply infer its character from European studies to date.

II

A word about the setting for this study will be helpful. I focus on a palm-leaf hatmaking network centered around the country store of Dexter Whittemore of Fitzwilliam, New Hampshire, a rocky, hill-country town in the southwestern corner of the state.[8] Like most New Hampshire towns, Fitzwilliam was a farming community with a large majority of residents engaged in agricultural pursuits. The town differed in several important respects, however, from other rural towns in the state. First, it had a much larger proportion of nonagricultural workers than did surrounding towns. More than 32 percent of Fitzwilliam men in 1840 pursued occupations outside of farming, compared with fewer than 23 percent for the county as a whole. Furthermore, while other towns lost residents in the decades between 1820 and 1850, Fitzwilliam's population rose from 1,167 to 1,482, or by about 27 percent. The growth of palm-leaf hatmaking contributed to the prosperity of the town, but the expansion of the manufacture of wooden bowls and pails and the opening up of granite quarries played roles as well. Fitzwilliam developed a relatively diverse economy for a rural community in the antebellum years.[9]

While Fitzwilliam grew moderately in these decades, Dexter Whittemore's business boomed. Whittemore sold his first split palm-leaf supplies in the spring of 1828 and by the early 1830s was marketing about 23,000 hats annually. This figure climbed steadily to about 80,000 a year in the 1850s. As the quantity of hats increased, so did the number of hatmakers; from about 250 in the 1829–1831 ledger, the number grew to more than 800 twenty years later.[10] The network also expanded in geographical terms as Whittemore drew in increasing numbers of residents from neighboring towns. In 1830 only 21 percent of customers (who were also outworkers) came from outside of Fitzwilliam; by 1850, nonresidents accounted for 52 percent of those trading with Whittemore. The hat network grew steadily until the winter of 1856–57 when Whittemore closed up the store and left town. The store remained closed for over a year, reopening in April 1858 under the direction of Dexter Whittemore's son Joel. When the store reopened, however, palm-leaf hats were no longer a significant aspect of the business.[11]

The Whittemore ledgers offer insights into the operation of one country store deeply embedded in a system of rural outwork, but they are also a rich source for understanding the range of economic activities in the town. Whittemore's country store served as the nexus joining the farms of Fitzwilliam with the broader New England economy. Local residents purchased from Whittemore a wide variety of food supplies, yarn and cloth, clothing, household furnishings, and farm implements. To finance these purchases they sold Whittemore butter, eggs, cheese, and other farm products. And most important for this study, a great many families took split palm leaf from the store, braided hats, and brought them back to Whittemore. For the goods they sold to the store or the labor services they provided making hats, local residents received credits on store ledgers. Periodically Whittemore would total the debits and the credits in each account and strike a balance. At such times he would either carry the balance forward into another ledger or ask his customer to settle the account. Accounts could be settled by the sale of products, a cash payment—an unusual event—or by a note payable by some future date. Rarely was interest recorded on either side of the ledgers, though occasionally a long-standing IOU led Whittemore to charge interest.

The ledger accounts offer the historian an unusual view of economic activity in a farming community recently integrated into the broader New England economy. By analyzing the kinds of credits recorded in ledger accounts we can illuminate the nature of economic exchanges within the town. The most common credits were hat credits, found in over 83 percent of all accounts in both 1830 and 1850 (Table 2.1). Hat credits remained a fairly steady item in ledger accounts over the two decades, accounting for about 48 percent of total credits in 1830 and 45 percent in 1850 (Table 2.2). Other sorts of credits, however, showed more dramatic shifts over the period. For instance, the relative frequency of credits for agricultural products declined. In 1830 fully 49 percent of accounts had some agricultural credits; by 1850 only about 30 percent had any credits of this sort. The proportion of accounts with any textile or miscellaneous credits declined as well. Finally, third-party payments recorded in accounts also dwindled.[12]

This last trend deserves some elaboration. In 1830, except for hats the most frequent credits in Whittemore's accounts were third-party pay-

2.1. *Proportions of Whittemore Accounts with Credits in Various Categories,*
*1830 and 1850*

| Type of Credit | 1830 (%) | 1850 (%) |
|---|---|---|
| Hat credits | 84.6 | 83.1 |
| Agricultural goods | 49.0 | 30.5 |
| Third-party payments | 50.0 | 26.6 |
| Miscellaneous credits | 47.7 | 19.9 |
| Cash payments | 43.3 | 62.5 |
| Notes (IOUs) | 24.8 | 35.7 |
| Textiles, clothing | 21.5 | 14.1 |
| Total cases | 298 | 971 |

ments. Third-party payments were essentially "banking" transactions in
which Whittemore simultaneously debited one account and credited another; in this manner he permitted customers to settle their mutual obligations through the credit system maintained in the store's books. The frequency of this sort of payment is indicative of a wide network of debts that
extended beyond Whittemore's store. These payments show that individuals
who owed money to Whittemore often stood as creditors to others who
would pay off these debts through credit transactions in Whittemore's account books. Whereas half of Whittemore's accounts had credits of this sort
in 1830, by 1850 the proportion had declined to slightly more than one-
fourth. Over time the network of debt and exchange shrank. In place of the
complicated creditor–debtor relations among members of the community
that prevailed in 1830, we see the emergence of a more neatly structured
network in which Whittemore's customers stood in parallel relationships
with him, distinct from their relationships with one another.[13]

As individuals came to rely less on settling accounts with farm products
other than hats and as third-party payments declined, account holders had
to find some way to pay for the supplies they continued to buy from Whittemore. Increasingly they used cash and notes to cover their purchases. The
proportion of accounts settled with cash payments increased from 43.3 percent in 1830 to 62.5 percent in 1850 (see Table 2.1). The average amount
of cash in each account increased from $2.83 to $12.06, and the proportion
of all credits accounted for by cash payments grew from 6.6 percent to 26.1
percent (see Table 2.2). In addition, a rising proportion of account holders
signed IOUs to Whittemore. Cash and notes taken together in 1830 had
amounted to just over 17 percent of all credits in Whittemore ledgers; by
1850 they made up more than 38 percent of such credits.[14]

2.2. *Dollar Values of Various Credits Recorded in Whittemore Accounts,*
*1830 and 1850*

| Type of Credit | 1830 | 1850 |
|---|---|---|
| Hat credits | $20.57 | $20.74 |
| Agricultural goods | 6.82 | 3.46 |
| Third-party payments | 3.41 | 2.09 |
| Miscellaneous credits | 3.91 | 1.45 |
| Cash payments | 2.83 | 12.06 |
| Notes (IOUs) | 4.51 | 5.73 |
| Textiles, clothing | 1.10 | 0.66 |
| Total credits | $43.15 | $46.19 |
| Total cases | 298 | 971 |

We have, by now, some sense of the kinds of economic transactions carried out at the Whittemore store and the dollars and cents involved, but what can we say about the individuals who traded with Whittemore and made his palm-leaf hats? Who were these people and how did they change over time? Unfortunately, we cannot answer these questions as well as we might like because of the way Whittemore kept his accounts. We know the names of individuals holding accounts but not of the actual hatmakers. In 1830 about 64 percent of account holders were males; almost 72 percent were heads of households in Fitzwilliam or nearby towns. These figures remained about the same twenty years later: 66 percent of account holders were male and 65 percent were household heads. At both dates wives and daughters, though clearly the makers of the hats, had few accounts in their own names. In 1830, for instance, only eight wives and forty-one daughters had their own accounts. Together they comprised about 20 percent of account holders in these two decades. For the antebellum period male household heads predominated among Whittemore's customers.

Contemporary observers indicated that women and children made palm-leaf hats. In most cases, however, their hats were credited to family accounts in the names of their fathers or husbands. Yet this very practice tells us something about the workings of the putting-out system, in sharp contrast to factory wage labor in nearby Lowell and Lawrence. The putting-out system operated for the most part as a family labor system in which the contributions of several individuals helped to support the family as a whole. In this family economy a distinct minority of accounts were held in the names of individuals not heading households. In 1830 unmarried sons and daughters made up about 22 percent of account holders and their proportion remained steady at almost 21 percent in 1850. Apparently daughters made hats for the family account for a number of years and then, when they reached a certain age, their parents allowed them to make hats on their own account, perhaps to generate dowries.

Because hatmaking appears to have been family economic activity, it makes sense to analyze the accounts at the family as well as at the individual level. To do this, I have aggregated the individual ledger entries into family accounts using family information derived from genealogies and local censuses. My linkage was much more complete for Fitzwilliam than for neighboring towns so I have limited my analysis to local families. In the early ledger, 178 individuals from 142 different Fitzwilliam families had accounts and 123 of these accounts had hat credits. This is a substantial number of hatmaking families, about 55 percent of Fitzwilliam families enumerated in the 1830 census. The proportion increased over the next two decades, and by 1850 fully 69 percent of Fitzwilliam families were making hats for Whittemore.[15]

What is the typical profile for one of these family accounts in 1830? On average each account had about $67 worth of credits over a two-year period. Hats accounted for about $31 of this figure, and other credits for about $36. After palm-leaf hats, agricultural products accounted for almost $12 on average, IOUs about $7, and cash payments another $4. In all, palm-leaf hats constituted somewhat more than 46 percent of all credits. Clearly hats represented the primary "cash crop" produced by these farming families, at least in terms of their exchanges with the leading local storekeeper. The existence of this ready market for hats meant that even though these farms probably yielded a very small agricultural surplus above immediate family needs, farmers could still buy goods they needed at the local store.

To understand the place of hatmaking in the larger family economy we must examine family accounts in more detail. What distinguished hatmaking from nonhatmaking families, and what factors influenced the relative amount of hatmaking in a given family? To begin with, let us consider demography. On average there were 5.9 members in hatmaking families and only 4.9 in nonhat families. More than two-thirds of this difference was due to the number of females in these families, and this difference was concentrated within the ten-to-nineteen year-old age group. Families making palm-leaf hats had twice as many teenage daughters as nonhat families. Younger girls and married women undoubtedly made hats as well, but the figures on household composition suggest that hatmaking was concentrated in the teenage years.

Analysis of the ledger accounts confirms this finding. For all Fitzwilliam families in the 1830 ledgers the mean value of hats made in a year came to $18.62, but this figure varied according to the number of daughters between the ages of ten and nineteen. Families with no daughters in this age

2.3. *Annual Hat Credits for Fitzwilliam Families in Whittemore Accounts*

| No. of Daughters Aged 10–19 | Mean Hat Credits per Year | |
|---|---|---|
| | 1830 | 1850 |
| 0 | $12.01 ( 75) | $ 7.57 (160) |
| 1–2 | 24.69 ( 57) | 17.35 ( 76) |
| 3 + | 33.58 ( 10) | 30.69 ( 11) |
| Overall | $18.62 (142) | $11.61 (247) |

group averaged about $12 of hat credits each year; families with one or two daughters averaged almost $25; and families with three or more teenage daughters averaged more than $33 in hat business. The concentration of hatmaking in families with teenage daughters became even greater over the next two decades. By 1850 Whittemore families with three or more teenage daughters made four times as many hats annually as families with no teenage daughters (see Table 2.3).[16]

The level of hatmaking activity was also affected by the level of other kinds of transactions a family made at Whittemore's store. As one might expect, the use of cash to purchase goods was inversely related to hatmaking. In 1830, those families using some cash to purchase goods from Whittemore made only about $13 worth of hats on average in a year; families using no cash, on the other hand, averaged almost $24 worth of hat credits per year.[17] In other words, families with a source of cash for store purchases made fewer hats than families without such a source.

Patterns of hatmaking in 1830 are reinforced by evidence available two decades later. In 1850 we can draw a more convincing picture because of the availability of local tax assessments, the manuscript census of agriculture, and a more comprehensive population census.[18] Two findings are particularly striking: Hatmaking families were far poorer than nonhat families, with an average real property valuation of $1,336 compared to $2,276. In addition, the heads of hatmaking families were much more likely to be employed principally in agriculture. More than 67 percent of heads of hatmaking families were farmers or laborers compared with slightly over 47 percent of men heading nonhat families. Initially, I assumed that the property differences might have been largely a function of the occupations of household heads, but even when we control for occupation, the differences persist. Looking separately at the real property holdings of farmers and nonfarmers, we find that within each group hatmaking families had considerably less real property than families not making hats (see Table 2.4). Hatmaking seems to have been a by-occupation carried on primarily by

2.4. *Real Property of Hat and Nonhat Families in Fitzwilliam in 1850*

| Families | Value of Real Property | | |
|----------|---------|-----------|---------|
| | Farmers | Nonfarmers | Overall |
| Hat families | $1,394 (123) | $1,216 (60) | $1,336 (183) |
| Nonhat families | 2,499 (36) | 2,071 (40) | 2,274 (76) |
| Missing cases: | | | 38 |

farming families in Fitzwilliam, and by the poorer families within this group.

The agricultural census confirms the evidence on real property holdings presented in the population census. Nonhatmaking Fitzwilliam families among Whittemore's account holders in 1850 owned an average of nineteen head of livestock valued at $464, compared with only sixteen head worth $368 for hatmaking families. The former group's yields that year for corn, oats, peas, potatoes, and wool were all greater than those of their hatmaking neighbors. In terms of the production of butter and cheese and the value of animals slaughtered, nonhatmakers outdistanced hatmakers by a considerable margin (see Table 2.5). In sum, hatmakers were relatively poorer farmers whose land holdings and agricultural production were well below average for this particular community.

As in 1830, families who made palm-leaf hats at mid-century were generally larger than nonhat families. Hatmaking families averaged 2.8 children, while nonhat families averaged only 1.9. This difference seems relatively modest, but becomes significant when we look separately at farming and nonfarming families. Among farming families in Fitzwilliam in 1850, hat families averaged 3.1 children, and nonhat families only 1.2 children. For nonfarming families there was no significant difference in the number of coresident children in hatmaking and nonhatmaking families. Thus the difference in the numbers of children in hatmaking and nonhatmaking families was concentrated entirely among farmers, where hatmaking families had two and a half times the number of children of nonhat families (see Table 2.6). On the whole, hatmaking was carried on in the larger, poorer farming families in a rural community moving steadily away from the agricultural economy that had predominated earlier.

III

Although hatmaking was a family economic activity we can gain insights into women's place in the local economy by looking at specific groups of

2.5. *Average Agricultural Holdings and Production for Whittemore Account Holders in 1850*

| Product | Nonhat | Hat |
|---|---|---|
| Livestock, number | 19.0 | 15.8 |
| Livestock, value | $464 | $368 |
| Animals slaughtered, value | $ 77 | $ 64 |
| Corn, bushels | 48.3 | 46.7 |
| Oats, bushels | 63.6 | 21.6 |
| Peas, bushels | 2.3 | 2.0 |
| Potatoes, bushels | 173 | 122 |
| Butter, lbs. | 257 | 159 |
| Cheese, lbs. | 309 | 217 |
| | (12) | (97) |

individual accounts. In this respect, the accounts of male household heads, and of wives and widows are particularly instructive. First, as a statement of who controlled the family economy it is significant that in 1830 more than 150 male household heads had accounts with Whittemore, compared with only 17 widows and 8 wives. We get some sense of the variety of assets at the disposal of individuals in these groups by comparing the kinds of credits in the accounts. Male household heads averaged $11.53 worth of agricultural credits; widows mustered only $6.53 worth of such credits; wives brought up the rear with a trifling $1.13 in farm products on average. Furthermore, household heads had more access to cash than did wives. More than 58 percent of accounts for male heads and for widows had some cash credits; no wives' accounts had cash payments. Similarly, wives did not give Whittemore notes to cover their purchases, while 17 percent of widows and 35 percent of male household heads had notes listed among their credits. The evidence in wives' accounts reveals the continuing legacy of the legal doctrine of *feme covert* well into the nineteenth century.[19]

These differences are all reflected in the proportion of credits for each group that were accounted for by hatmaking. For husbands in control of a diverse family economy, hats accounted for only 37 percent of all credits; for widows, hats composed 69 percent of store credits; finally, for wives, hats made up more than 88 percent of credits in Whittemore's accounts. For Fitzwilliam families, the hatmaking activity of married women was generally subsumed within a family economy controlled by their husbands. In the rare cases in which wives traded in their own names, they bought goods with the proceeds from their own and their children's hatmaking.

Purchases, recorded as debits in the Whittemore ledgers, showed less

2.6. *Coresident Children of Hat and Nonhat Families in Fitzwilliam in 1850*

| Families | No. of Children | | |
| | Farmers | Nonfarmers | Overall |
| --- | --- | --- | --- |
| Hat families | 3.08 (123) | 2.27 (60) | 2.81 (183) |
| Nonhat families | 1.17 (36) | 2.52 (40) | 1.88 (76) |
| Missing cases: | | | 38 |

variation than did credits in the accounts. Husbands, wives, and widows all concentrated their spending on sewing goods and food supplies for their families. Between 60 and 67 percent of their purchases in 1830 were for items in these two broad categories. Here we see relatively uniform family needs determining how the proceeds from family economic activities were spent. There was considerably more variation in how individuals earned their credits, reflecting the differences in the places of men and women in the local economy.[20]

Just as husbands' and wives' accounts were fundamentally different from one another, so too were the accounts of their children. Unmarried sons and daughters had accounts in their own names; comparison of these two groups reveals much about their respective places in the rural family economy. Sons handled slightly larger accounts than did daughters, with total credits in 1830 amounting on average to almost $32 compared with less than $29 for their sisters (Table 2.7). The sources for these credits, however, were very different. Hats accounted for only 6 percent of sons' credits; but for 89 percent of daughters'. The ages of sons and daughters with their own accounts are also telling. In 1850 (when information about the number of children and their age distribution is adequate to permit generalization), we find many more teenage daughters than sons among account holders. Only 20 percent of sons—six of thirty—were under twenty years of age, while more than 49 percent of daughters were in their teenage years. Tracing unmarried children in the 1850 ledgers back to their earliest appearance in Whittemore's store records indicates that daughters opened store records on average at 18.4 years of age, whereas sons did so only when they were twenty-two. Together the age and gender differences gave cash credits a greater place in sons' accounts. In 1850 sons' cash credits averaged almost $27, while for daughters the comparable figure was under $6. Cash amounted to more than half of all credits in sons' accounts, but only 17 percent of credits for daughters. Sons had far greater access to wage-earning jobs in Fitzwilliam and these opportunities were clearly reflected in the nature of their accounts at Whittemore's store.

Because they had so few opportunities for wage work in town, however,

2.7. *Average Credits in Whittemore Accounts of Sons and Daughters in 1830*

| Credits | Sons | Daughters |
|---------|------|-----------|
| Nonhat | $30.00 | $ 4.32 |
| Hat | 1.92 | 24.31 |
| Total | $31.92 | $28.63 |
| | (13) | (41) |

daughters put much more of their time and energy into hatmaking activity than did other account holders. This pattern held true for the entire period of Whittemore's ledgers. The 1830 data are informative here. The median earnings on hats for daughters with their own accounts in 1830 came to $19.38; for all other accounts the comparable figure was only $8.19. Daughters evidently put in more time making hats than did other account holders, and their median output of ninety-one hats per year was almost double the figure of forty-seven for others. Given the fact that a woman could complete a hat in about three-fourths of a day, this meant that even the most conscientious hat producers in Fitzwilliam were only putting in about seventy full days of hat work a year. Clearly they would also have been helping on the family farm, taking care of poultry and cows, making butter and cheese, and perhaps weaving and sewing as well. Hatmaking was a by-occupation, not a full-time job for these rural women.

Of all Fitzwilliam residents, daughters obviously put the greatest effort into hatmaking. Still, their returns were slim when compared with the earnings of young women in New England textile mills in this period. Their total hat earnings averaged $20 a year for what amounted to about seventy days of work. They earned 25 to 30 cents a day, while mill women earned twice that figure. Of course, outworkers did not have to pay their own room and board out of their earnings, so one might want to reduce the differential somewhat. It would not have been unusual for a young woman working in a textile mill for nine months or a year to earn about $2 a week above room and board, or about $75 to $100 a year. Finally, the mill worker would be paid in cash while the outworker had to settle for credit at the local store.

What, then, prevented all the young women in Fitzwilliam from hopping on the first stage heading for Lowell? There were stagecoaches passing through town in this period, and some young women from Fitzwilliam and neighboring towns did find their way to Lowell.[21] Their number appears to be small, however, much smaller than for the towns in central Merrimack County, New Hampshire, for example. The situation in Fitzwilliam involved far less out-migration than occurred in other New Hampshire towns, probably because the growth of palm-leaf hatmaking and woodworking provided occupations for young women and men coming of age. In addition, it seems that some fathers, taking into account subsidiary earnings made possible by the growth of these rural industries, were willing to subdivide their farms to help several children settle within the bounds of the town. Between 1830 and 1850 the number of households in Fitzwilliam increased from 222 to 297, a gain of more than one-third. It was only the existence of these by-employments that permitted farmers to work smaller plots and yet maintain their customary standard of living.

What did women themselves have to say about palm-leaf hatmaking? This question remains difficult to answer. Because hatmakers generally lived at home and because all their neighbors were making hats as well they rarely wrote about the work. Roxanna Bowker Stowell was an exception. Her letters offer some insights into one woman's motivations. She traded with Whittemore as a single daughter living at home in 1830 and 1831. During a seventeen-month period Roxanna made eighty-two hats, which after deducting for the cost of split leaf netted her just over $17. After Roxanna married Leander Stowell and moved to St. Johnsbury, Vermont, her account was held in her husband's name, although she continued to braid hats.[22] She wrote to Dexter Whittemore asking him to send some split leaf to her by stagecoach and indicated her motivation at several points in the correspondence. In one letter she wrote, "money is so very scarce and we must have some." And in another letter she noted, "I had rather braid hats for 15 cents than to spin and there is no danger of my hurting myself Braiding for my Husband is unwilling I should braid more than one a day. . . ."[23] Perhaps because the Stowells lived some distance from Fitzwilliam, Whittemore paid them largely in cash rather than in store credit.

Roxanna Stowell's comments clearly place hatmaking within the framework of the family economy. She noted that "we must have some" money, and indicated as well that her husband was setting limits to her hatmaking activity. In addition, hatmaking was only one of a number of outwork alternatives open to Roxanna Stowell and she explicitly stated her preference for making hats over spinning yarn. She did not entirely give up spinning and weaving, for her husband's account included credits for 28 yards of fulled cloth. We know a little more about Roxanna Bowker Stowell than we do about Whittemore's other palm-leaf hatmakers, but her motivations were probably not very different from those of others. The need to earn money (or, for most families, its equivalent in store credit) and the need and preference to combine paid labor with domestic duties were probably the main incentives bringing farm women into outwork occupations in the antebellum decades.

IV

The putting-out system was just as much the product of the industrial revolution in this country as were the textile factories in Lowell or the central shoe shops in Lynn. Unlike those new institutions, however, the outwork system grew up in rural communities and seemed to lend direct support to the traditional economy of the family farm. In an earlier era farmers brought eggs, butter, cheese, and poultry to sell to their country storekeeper; as the sale of these products of New England women's labors declined in the nineteenth century, palm-leaf hats and other manufactured goods took their place. Outwork permitted young women to contribute to their families and, as they took accounts in their own names, to earn something for themselves.

Yet the institution played a contradictory role in the lives of farming women and in the development of the countryside itself. On the one hand, outwork offered supplementary income to farmers' daughters by permitting them to remain at home as contributors to a traditional family economy increasingly unable to hold its own. In this respect, outwork gave women an alternative to migration and urban factory employment, hence delaying the population decline of rural New England. On the other hand, outwork drew rural residents into broader economic networks and steadily, if more subtly, undermined the semisubsistence and barter practices that distinguished rural economies from urban markets. In the end, migration and outwork were two aspects of a multipronged attack on traditional values and practices. Both strategies permitted women significant roles in the resulting economic and cultural transformation of rural New England.

APPENDIX: Sources and Methods

My reconstitution of the families of palm-leaf hatmakers is based on the extensive records of the firm of D. Whittemore and Son in Baker Library, Harvard Business School. Surviving store records include chronological daybooks noting all purchases and sales made at the store and bills, receipts, and correspondence relating to wholesale purchases of goods and to the finishing and sale of hats. Finally, there are bound ledger volumes in which Whittemore reorganized daybook entries into separate accounts clearly noting all the credits and debits of individual customers. Ledgers survive for the period 1826–57; I have chosen two ledger volumes for detailed analysis. The first volume covers roughly 1829–31 and the second 1850–55—periods chosen to permit analysis of changes over time and also to facilitate tracing of account holders in the federal manuscript censuses of 1830 and 1850.[24]

The population discussed in this study consists of all account holders who had one hat transaction or at least two nonhat transactions recorded in the ledgers. I excluded from analysis a limited number of individuals who worked for Whittemore as teamsters, leaf splitters, or clerks, and whose ledgers represented what today we would consider payrolls rather than store accounts. These criteria led me to include 298 individual accounts from the early ledger and 971 from the later.

For individuals in either of the two groups I recorded summary data on the various credits appearing in the ledgers. These included agricultural goods, textiles, IOUs, cash payments, payments by third parties, and credits for miscellaneous goods and services. I then recorded the date of each hat transaction and number and value of palm-leaf hats sold. In addition, I linked account holders in the published genealogies and manuscript censuses of Fitzwilliam and of all adjacent towns to add family information to each record.[25] I have been able to locate more than 80 percent of all account holders in either genealogies or censuses for each ledger, giving me confidence that the demographic characteristics reported for linked individuals are reasonably representative of account holders as a whole. Finally, for the 1850 ledger I have linked account holders to surviving tax assessments and agricultural census returns for that year, facilitating a detailed reconstruction of the economic assets of families trading with Whittemore.

Two additional studies rounded out my work with the Whittemore records. To examine store purchases I coded the debit sides of customers' accounts for a sample drawn from the 1830 ledgers. Unfortunately, Whittemore's accounting grew less detailed by 1850 and the vague terms "sundries" and "miscellaneous" made it impossible to carry the analysis into the later ledgers. For the 1830 coding I used a stratified sample to insure adequate numbers of male and female household heads, spouses, widows, and sons and daughters among account holders studied. In all, I recorded data on debits for 78 of 298 accounts in 1830, grouping the disparate purchases into a limited number of broad categories to permit comparison among groups. Finally, to permit a fuller discussion of the place of hatmaking in the life cycle I traced back through ledger volumes to determine the starting dates for accounts held by unmarried sons and daughters in 1850. This procedure enabled me to move beyond the "snap-shot" cross-sectional data found in a single ledger volume.

NOTES

1. Percy Bidwell, "The Agricultural Revolution in New England," in L. B. Schmidt and E. D. Ross, eds., *Readings in the Economic History of American Agriculture* (New York, 1925); see also Harold F. Wilson, *The Hill Country of Northern New England* (New York, 1936).

2. John F. Norton, *The History of Fitzwilliam, New Hampshire* (New York, 1888), 414; William Bassett, *History of the Town of Richmond, Cheshire County, New Hampshire* (Boston, 1884), 178.

3. There is no general treatment of the organization of the manufacture of palm-leaf hats; this paragraph is based on correspondence and account books in the Dexter Whittemore Collection, Baker Library, Harvard Business School, and in Fisher, Blashfield, & Co. Collection, New York Public Library.

4. Louis McLane, Report of the Secretary of the Treasury, 1832. *Documents Relative to the Manufactures of the United States*, House Executive Documents, 22d Cong., 1st sess., Doc. 308, 2 vols. (Washington, D.C., 1833), 1:474–577; John P. Bigelow, *Statistical Tables Exhibiting the Condition and Products of Certain Branches of Industry in Massachusetts for the Year Ending April 1, 1837* (Boston, 1838), 31, 181.

5. Bigelow, *Statistical Tables*, 169. My figures assume that Massachusetts hatmakers worked a similar number of days each year as did the Fitzwilliam, N.H., outworkers in my 1830 sample.

6. Bigelow, *Statistical Tables*, 169, 181.

7. Franklin Mendels, "Proto-Industrialization: The First Phase of the Industrialization Process," *Journal of Economic History* 32 (1972):241–61; Hans Medick, "The Proto-Industrial Family Economy," *Social History* 3 (1976): 291–315; see also Peter Kriedte, Hans Medick, and Jürgen Schlumbohm, *Industrialization before Industrialization: Rural Industry in the Genesis of Industrial Capitalism*, trans. by Beate Schempp (Cambridge, Eng., 1981), esp. ch. 2; David Levine, "The Demographic Implications of Rural Industrialization: A Family Reconstitution Study of Shepshed, Leicestershire, 1600–1851," *Social History* 2 (1976):177–96; Rudolph Braun, "Proto-industrialization and Demographic Changes in the Canton of Zurich," in Charles Tilly, ed., *Historical Studies of Changing Fertility* (Princeton, N.J., 1978), 289–334.

8. The Whittemore Collection at the Baker Library includes more than ninety manuscript volumes and seven wooden cases of daybooks, ledgers, and correspondence for the period 1826–57. Additional account books have survived in the Fitzwilliam Historical Society, Fitzwilliam, N.H., and in the private collections of Allison Williams of Alfred, Maine, and Joel Whittemore of Stoneham, Massachusetts, whose cooperation is gratefully acknowledged. For more on the ownership of the store and information on Whittemore family members, see Norton, *History of Fitzwilliam*, 400, 776–79.

9. *Sixth Census, or Enumeration of the Inhabitants of the United States . . . 1840* (Washington, 1841), 27; *Compendium of the Enumeration of the Inhabitants and Statistics of the United States, From the Returns of the Sixth Census* (Washington, 1842), 7; Norton, *History of Fitzwilliam*, 369, 419–22.

10. Whittemore Collection, vols. 3, 4, 87, 88, Baker Library. Because more than one family member may have made hats credited to the same account, it is impossible to determine exactly how many individual hatmakers worked for Whittemore during each of these periods.

11. Data in Whittemore Collection, vols. 88, 93, Baker Library, on hat consignments and correspondence permit one to follow hatmaking in its final years at the store. See also the relevant daybook, vol. 41.

12. There were a number of stores in Fitzwilliam during these decades and it is important to stress that the unit of analysis here is the Whittemore account. Indi-

viduals undoubtedly sold hats and farm products to other storekeepers. For neighboring stores that accepted palm-leaf hats for credit, see the *New Hampshire Sentinel*, 5 February 1840 and 13 October 1841. Records of one other local store have survived and one set of ledgers actually overlaps the 1829–31 Whittemore ledger that I have used. The Spaulding & Perkins accounts were generally smaller than those in the Whittemore ledgers. In all, thirty-seven individuals had hat credits in both accounts, with Whittemore credits outweighing the others by about five to one. Another thirty individuals had hat credits in the Whittemore ledgers and only nonhat credits and purchases with Spaulding & Perkins. It is evident from comparisons of the ledgers that Whittemore did the lion's share of the palm-leaf hat business in town, though individuals evidently used hats to finance purchases at other stores. I have made no systematic effort to aggregate the two sets of accounts as they cover slightly different time periods and still do not entirely account for all store business in Fitzwilliam in this period. Spaulding & Perkins, ledger no. 2, Old Sturbridge Village, Sturbridge, Mass.

13. For an important theoretical consideration of the implications of this sort of network of exchanges see Michael Merrill, "Cash Is Good to Eat: Self-Sufficiency and Exchange in the Rural Economy of the United States," *Radical History Review* 3 (1977):42–71.

14. Credit figures reported here differ from actual credit entries in several respects. First, I have subtracted the cost of split palm leaf from hat credits to approximate actual hat earnings. Second, there are occasional notes and cash payments recorded on the debit side of the ledgers and the dollar figures reported here and in Table 2.2 reflect *net* credits for cash and notes.

15. It is very likely that some families tentatively recorded as nonhat families made hats for Whittemore either earlier or later than this period, so we should view these proportions as minimum estimates.

16. For the 1830 breakdown $F = 7.05$ with a significance of .009. For 1850, $F = 20.29$, with significance .0001.

17. The figures here are the result of a multiple classification analysis in which I considered the value of hats per year the dependent variable, all other kinds of account credits as independent variables, and the number of teenage females in the household as a covariate. The $11 difference between accounts with and without cash payments is based on controlling for the influence of the other independent variables and of the covariate.

18. The 1850 Fitzwilliam tax inventories are in the town hall in Fitzwilliam, while the volumes of the Federal Manuscript Census of Agriculture are at the State Library in Concord. The 1850 Population schedules are available at the State Library and on microfilm from the National Archives. This census was the first to enumerate all household members and to provide age, occupation, and the value of real property for all male residents. These additional data contribute to an understanding of the place of palm-leaf hatmaking in the rural economy.

19. Linda Kerber, *Women of the Republic: Intellect and Ideology in Revolutionary America* (Chapel Hill, N.C., 1980), ch. 5.

20. See Appendix for a discussion of the nature of sampling for the study of debits among 1830 account holders.

21. Hamilton Manufacturing Company Records, vols. 481–89, passim, in Manu-

script Division, Baker Library. For a fuller comparison of mill employment and rural outwork, see Thomas Dublin, "Women's Work and the Family Economy: Textiles and Palm Leaf Hatmaking in New England, 1830–1850," *Toqueville Review* 5 (1983): 297–316.

22. Whittemore Collection, vol. 44, Baker Library; Norton, *History of Fitzwilliam*, 485, 740.

23. Roxanna Stowell to Dexter Whittemore, June 1835 and 23 May 1832, Whittemore Collection, box 6, Family Papers, Baker Library.

24. The specific ledgers employed were vols. 44 and 55.

25. Norton, *History of Fitzwilliam*, 453–803. I also used published genealogies in town histories for Richmond, Rindge, Jaffrey, Troy, and Marlboro, New Hampshire; and Royalston, Winchendon, and Ashburnham, Massachusetts at New Hampshire Historical Society. For census links I utilized microfilms of the Federal Manuscript Census, M19 (1830), rolls 68 and 74, and M432 (1850), rolls 340–45, 427–28. Also particularly valuable were published indexes of the New Hampshire and Massachusetts censuses for 1830 and 1850 available from Accelerated Indexing Systems, Bountiful, Utah.

JONATHAN PRUDE

# 3. Town–Factory Conflicts in Antebellum Rural Massachusetts

I

Let us begin with a Yankee fantasy.* In his strange and gloomy romance, "The Tartarus of Maids," Herman Melville conjured up an antebellum paper mill. "It lies," he wrote, "not far from Woedolor Mountain in New England," in a hollow (the "Devil's Dungeon") amid "bleak hills," pressed "against the sullen background of mountain-side firs, and other hardy evergreens, inaccessibly rising in grim terraces for some two thousand feet." The tale proceeds to recount a brief visit to this factory by a businessman and his response to witnessing "blank-looking girls . . . blankly folding blank paper" or tending intricate water-driven machines (one of them an "iron animal") which transformed rag into paper (in "only nine minutes") for waiting customers. Indeed, through much of the factory, "Machinery— that vaunted slave of humanity—. . . stood menially served by human beings, who served mutely and cringingly as the slave serves the Sultan."[1]

This is an extraordinary story. It is remarkable, in part, because its grim inversion of sentient and mechanical vitalities (its deployment of people cast as automatons and machines billed as "animals") succeeds in projecting upon the reader the same "strange dread" that Melville's businessman-narrator experiences as he tours the paper mill.

To the historian, however, the tale is notable in other ways as well. In the first place, Melville's story underscores the fact—too often glossed over amid casual conflations of "urbanization" and "industrialization"—that America's industrial revolution had rural origins. In New England, where large-scale water-powered manufacturing first became widespread in this country, early factories were commonly located not in coastal entrepôts (which usually lacked adequate water power) but outside cities in hamlets (like Pawtucket, Rhode Island) or in communities scattered along hinterland streams. And this was true not only of paper mills, but also of America's vanguard manufacturing establishment: the textile mill. As late as the

*I would like to thank Cambridge University Press for permission to reprint portions of previously published material.

71

mid-1850s, most cotton and woolen factories in Massachusetts, as well as most textile operatives, were located in small "villages" which were in turn situated in townships dispersed through the countryside.[2] Melville's evocation of Woedolor Mountain usefully draws attention to such rural factory villages.

It also, of course, draws attention to the way Americans responded to these villages—but here Melville's story seems at first glance not to reflect the historical record so much as to offer an entirely anomalous vision. For the scholarly literature would clearly suggest that the "dread" braided through "The Tartarus of Maids,"—the general sense that the machine was not entirely compatible with the garden—was exceptional in antebellum America. There exists, in fact, a substantial scholarly tradition that most early nineteenth century Americans found the rustic setting of manufactories so reassuring that they were unable to give critical consideration to what industrialization might mean. The factory under the elms (so this argument runs) encouraged the premise that in the United States industry would not yield the evils commonly ascribed to the manufacturing cities of Europe (and especially of Britain)—and thus that industrialization would not threaten America's self-image as a pastoral republic.[3] So compelling has been this perspective that even those recent historians who have stressed the significant antagonisms stirred up by antebellum industrialization have tended to explore manufacturing centers that were, or became, cities. These scholars too thus leave the impression, if only implicitly, that rural industrialization was essentially placid.[4]

But is that an accurate picture? Is Melville's portrait really so lacking in historical resonance? What follows is a case study that explores the difficulties that emerged during the early 1800s following the construction of textile factories in the contiguous Massachusetts farming townships of Dudley and Oxford in southern Worcester County. (See Map 3.1.) The focus here is less on labor-management tensions sparked by the full-time mill operatives who lived and worked within the factory compounds (and who remained generally isolated from the currents and institutions of town life) than on the controversies developing between the mills and their host townships.[5] For the question we are addressing is this: How did antebellum rural communities surrounding large-scale manufacturing establishments come to feel about them? Did the distress experienced by Melville's protagonist (who, after all, was only visiting Woedolor Mountain) find some counterpart in the unease felt by actual Yankee residents of the towns in which factories took root?

We should not, of course, expect an exact fit. Melville was not writing social history and the concerns evinced by Dudley and Oxford residents centered on issues considerably more concrete than the densely symbolic technology unleashed in "The Tartarus of Maids." Moreover, we should

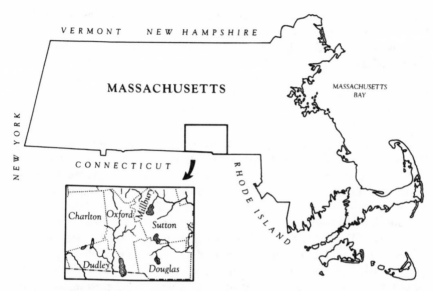

3.1. *Massachusetts, ca. 1822, with detail of Dudley and Oxford (based on map in* A Complete Historical, Chronological, and Geographical Atlas, *Philadelphia, 1822; courtesy of the Map Collection, Harvard College Library)*

not exaggerate the malaise that did develop in Dudley and Oxford, for in the final analysis a measure of ambivalence surrounded local mills. After all, the fifteen cotton and woolen factories that started operation in these townships during the early decades of the nineteenth century palpably strengthened community economies and anti-mill feelings were consequently neither continuous nor altogether unanimous.

What is significant, however, and what would seem to require consideration, is that despite the demonstrable benefits textile mills brought to the two communities, town–factory relations were anything but calm. Indeed, beginning in 1812, when textile establishments first appeared in this area of southern Massachusetts, town–factory tensions arose repeatedly, grew gradually more rancorous, and finally, after twenty years, led to a literal carving up of Dudley and Oxford. In 1832, Samuel Slater—proprietor of factories in both communities and the same famous English expatriate who some forty years earlier had helped introduce water-powered spinning technologies to America—resolved to end once and for all his long record of difficulties with Dudley and Oxford. In a decision provoking bitter controversy throughout the two towns, Slater "set off" his three local mill villages into the entirely new community of Webster.[6]

Webster's incorporation provides the proper termination for this investigation. In effect, our project is to explain what happened between 1812 and

1832 to make Webster possible and, in some ways, even unavoidable. But we must also understand that this episode is important because it is representative of the frictions intrinsic to the industrialization of antebellum rural New England.


II

Our first step must be to explore the difference between town and factory life. For the rising curve of ill will between the communities and their factories was ultimately rooted in the qualitative gap that existed between, on the one hand, the overall social system of Dudley and Oxford and, on the other hand, the social system of local mill villages.

Consider first the two towns. Located just north of the Connecticut line, in an area of Worcester County known widely in the 1780s for its support of Shays' Rebellion, Dudley and Oxford underwent numerous alterations during the early decades of the nineteenth century. Farmers, who remained the largest single occupational group in these towns, were growing more dependent on store-bought goods and the services of skilled craftsmen, and more inclined to produce salable surpluses (mainly dairy products) to finance their purchases. But nonagricultural activities were themselves also shifting. Quite aside from the influx of textile factories, small business ventures increased in both volume and variety during this period, and some of these establishments (the local stores, for example, and the new boot and shoe manufacturers) were linked to producers and markets considerably removed from Dudley and Oxford.[7] Then, too, although many workshops quickly succumbed to bankruptcy, the overall expansion of nonagricultural opportunities offset the relatively fixed availability of farm land and permitted substantial demographic growth in both communities. Dudley and Oxford maintained roughly equal populations throughout the period, but their combined number of residents jumped from 2,503 in 1810 to 4,189 in 1830. Although both towns remained well below the Commonwealth's demographic standard of "municipality," the growth rate between 1810 and 1830 was substantially sharper than it had been during the previous twenty years.[8]

In such basic ways had Dudley and Oxford changed during the early antebellum era. Equally noticeable, however, and probably even more important, were the fundamental continuities characterizing life and work outside local factory villages. It is evident, for example, that while the number and range of nontextile business establishments were increasing, most of these ventures remained as small and structurally simple as stores and workshops standing in Dudley and Oxford when George Washington took office. In 1832 as in 1789, those enterprises typically required less than five employees (usually all male), demonstrated little division of labor, only occasionally used intermediary managers (such as overseers), and relied on hand-powered technologies or (in the case of gristmills and sawmills) water-powered technologies that ran only intermittently, as need arose.[9] The tools and techniques of husbandry also remained largely unaltered from what had prevailed in the late eighteenth century or, indeed, even earlier in the colonial era.[10]

But an equally important continuity lay in the basic economic rationale that prevailed outside the textile factory villages. For what we find characterizing most of early nineteenth-century Dudley and Oxford are local economies in which market transactions were frequent, in which a buoyant consumerism was taking root, but in which, at the same time, a commercial ethos—in the sense of a whole-hearted commitment to profit maximization—had only a limited constituency. Local yeomen, for all their mounting involvement with buying and selling, still retained many conventions of household production. Nearly always owning the land they cultivated, typically relying for help less on hired workers than on family members and on the custom of receiving (and giving) neighborly assistance during busy seasons, farmers generally ventured into the market not to get rich but simply to acquire the goods and services needed (as they saw it) to preserve their household "competencies." Not surprisingly, then, the surpluses they produced did not signify an exclusive commitment to cash crops. Although hardly self-sufficient in any literal sense, yeomen in 1832, just as in 1789, sought to raise much, if not all, of the foodstuffs they and their households required.[11]

The indications are that artisans, shopkeepers, and their small retinue of employees evinced similarly noncommercial perspectives, not only because they often farmed on the side but also because the character of the market exchanges in which they engaged tended to dampen profit expectations. In the first place, these exchanges were usually limited to direct encounters between local residents. Despite their widening connection with distant customers, handicraftsmen did most of their business with fellow townspeople; and though stores increasingly acquired merchandise from urban entrepôts, their customers were still almost always nearby inhabitants. Then too, payments for goods and services (and even wages to employees) were typically made in kind or in labor (and reflected customary valuations of various products and kinds of work) rather than in the more abstract medium of cash. And often there was no payment at all. Just as in colonial years, and just as in many other rural communities of the antebellum Northeast, Dudley and Oxford were crisscrossed by an elaborate web of credit agreements. A chronic shortage of currency, combined with generally restrained commercial ambitions, promoted a system under which people frequently ended up both owing and being owed by their neighbors, and in which debts ran on for months, even years, with no interest charged.[12]

None of this precluded an elite, for antebellum Dudley and Oxford contained contingents of farmers and shopkeepers (or farmer-shopkeepers) who were known and respected for their wealth. Nor did it preclude some local residents (especially among the affluent elite) from guiding their affairs by the polestar of profit. Indeed, it was not uncommon in these years to see people moving back and forth between activities with limited commercial commitment to others (such as boot and shoe manufacturing) overtly dedicated to healthy balance sheets. On the other hand, the concrete power that could be derived from wealth was limited. The relatively broad distribution of property, the ease of receiving extended credit, and the small number of wage laborers tied to even the larger agricultural and handicraft undertakings—all this meant that no established institutional mechanism existed by which richer residents could translate affluence into coercive, townwide economic leverage. Moreover, whatever the local involvement with profit-minded enterprises, the overall center of gravity of economic life in Dudley and Oxford—again, outside the mill villages—remained linked to different priorities. The form and logic of full-scale commercialism had simply not yet taken root.

Considered as a whole, the configuration of shifts and continuities conditioning local social and economic patterns was common among early nineteenth-century rural Yankee townships. Of particular importance here, however, is the framework of *political* norms and institutions this configuration fostered, for most of the conflicts arising between communities like Dudley and Oxford and the mills they contained focused on divergent notions of power and authority.

Retaining much the same formal administrative apparatus as in colonial years, governance in antebellum Dudley and Oxford rested on periodic town meetings combined with slates of officials (headed by selectmen) elected by those adult males eligible to vote in town meetings.[13] It is clear, however, that in the period we are considering this governmental structure functioned with limited power and jurisdiction. To some degree, this was because the relatively modest scale and aim of most economic activities meant that any "improvements" residents required for their enterprises (a new gristmill dam, for example) rarely necessitated communitywide funding. But it was also because a range of centrifugal pressures had begun to erode the allegiance local inhabitants felt toward their townships as a whole. The increasing dispersal of residents to the far corners of Dudley and Oxford as community populations grew, the mounting transiency resulting from the expansion and volatility of small business projects, the growing religious heterogeneity of local populations—such factors tended to vitiate the sense of corporate solidarity, of commitment to Dudley and Oxford as abstract civil entities, among town residents.[14]

The net result was that, while credit and labor exchanges continued to link individuals (indeed, partly *because* these links could be relied upon), the towns were reluctant to press their collective governmental authority too far. More specifically, they were wary of using local governments to define communitywide priorities or projects. Throughout these years the general understanding of the commonweal—an understanding repeatedly articulated in town meetings—was that whenever possible residents should help themselves before soliciting (or demanding) assistance from the entire polis. And this was as true for wealthy citizens as for the less affluent. Because richer inhabitants enjoyed only limited economic power over their neighbors, they had no base from which to secure privileged political influence. To be sure, both towns frequently recruited candidates for high town offices from among well-to-do residents. But even with their cadre of (often) wealthy town leaders, Dudley and Oxford rarely committed community resources to help this or that rich citizen. Quite plainly, it was the judgment of these towns that the common good involved discouraging anyone from assuming that satisfying *his* needs, meeting *his* notion of the common good, would necessarily serve the best interests of the whole community.[15]

The world of the factory villages was very different. In fact, these compounds even stood out from other Yankee textile manufactories. For the mills of Dudley and Oxford were demonstrably *not* like New England's famous "boardinghouse"-style enterprises—the mills that originated in Waltham in 1814 and spread to Lowell, Manchester, and other urban (or urbanizing) industrial centers; the factories typically owned by absentee proprietors and equipped from the outset to weave as well as spin by waterpower; and the mills known above all for hiring unmarried daughters of "respectable" Yankee yeomen and for billeting these "girls" together in tightly supervised boardinghouses.[16] Far from duplicating this model, local mills reflected the quite different "Rhode Island" or "family"-style arrangements. This format was actually inaugurated in Samuel Slater's first factories during the 1790s and, though less well-known than the boardinghouse organization, had subsequently been adopted by most country mills of antebellum New England. In keeping with this latter style, Dudley and Oxford factories were comparatively small, moderately financed, and subject to some direct proprietary control. They were involved up through the late 1820s and early 1830s in "putting out" certain tasks, including weaving, to outlying families working by hand or with hand-powered machines (such as handlooms). And although they hired mainly native-born New Englanders in this period, factories like those in Dudley and Oxford were given to employing poor as well as "middling" operatives, and households (including children) as well as unattached individuals. Moreover, this motley assortment of rural "hands," most of them recruited from the Yankee countryside but newcomers to the townships immediately surrounding the mills, were usually distributed through a largely unsupervised assortment of cottages and boardinghouses spread through the mill villages.[17]

In all these ways local factory enclaves exemplified a distinctive genre of pre–Civil War textile enterprise. What is equally important, they also stood out from their host communities. They were more densely populated (some villages contained as many as 550 individuals) than any residential clustering outside the mill compounds, and the daily laborforce inside the factory buildings was larger (often numbering up to 100 hands) than any employee rosters previously assigned to local workplaces.[18] The basic character of factory labor was new, as well. Textile mills—including small rural establishments—invariably organized production around elaborate divisions of labor; they also invariably imposed novel time and work disciplines to insure the punctuality and sustained attentiveness that cotton and woolen factories (with their "perpetual" water-powered technologies) supposedly required.[19] And then there was the emphatically commercial character of the mills. It was not just that factories depended heavily on nonlocal sources for their raw materials and customers; it was also that, despite frequent assertions of "kindly and paternal interest" in their operatives' "welfare," mill managers set factory policies (including work hours and wage levels) so as to maximize profits.[20] As we have seen, there were other local businesses in this period that stressed making money and that forged extralocal economic connections. The fact remains, however, that textile manufactories did depart from the values most typical of local economic life, and their size and visibility rendered their exceptionalism particularly noticeable.

On the whole these distinctive characteristics were at first viewed by local residents as a matter of interest rather than a cause for alarm. Indeed, we need to remember that the mills were *somewhat* tolerated all through the antebellum period. To the extent it existed, this acceptance unquestionably derived largely from the basic fact that most Dudley and Oxford mills were owned by town citizens. Except for the three factory compounds (two in Dudley, one in Oxford) controlled by Slater and his family, local manufactories were capitalized by partnerships of local (though often only recently arrived) inhabitants. Not surprisingly, the slate of industrial investors was dominated by the more wealthy and economically acquisitive residents of these communities. Yet there were also small contributions ($50 to $100) from many middling farmers and shopkeepers, people who clearly invested in textile mills not to get rich but to solidify their "competencies"—just as they bought a new dairy cow, or expanded their blacksmith shops, or involved themselves (for short or long periods) in boot and shoe manufacturing.[21] Nor were the dividends they paid out the only benefits mills offered residents outside the factory compounds. So long as they survived (and some did go bankrupt), cotton and woolen manufactories represented an important potential source of local tax revenues. Moreover, farmers in these towns could often sell foodstuffs to factory managers charged with feeding their operatives, and until the putting-out system was abandoned, several local households supplemented their incomes by doing outwork for the mills.[22] Like the returns flowing to middling investors, these revenues and payments served more to facilitate conventional economic norms than to fulfill (or create) ambitions for wealth. But the payments were still appreciated.

All of which explains why textile factories persistently received some measure of support from the townships. What then accounts for the even greater measure of hostility local manufactories confronted? The answer, to a large extent, lies in the final novelty of these establishments: the new kind of authority created and promoted inside the mill compounds. We should understand that proper administration of antebellum factories was commonly understood to require a managerial authority that was rigidly hierarchical. Each department (or room) in local mills was under an overseer, who in turn answered to a resident supervisor or agent. Agents occasionally held proprietary interest in the mills they oversaw, but in principle they answered to mill owners. As a result, local factory proprietors, simply by being proprietors, stood atop multitiered managerial structures unknown in shops and stores outside the mill compounds.[23]

And some mill owners played even more striking roles. Although many factory investors remained involved in other activities (such as farming), each cotton and woolen manufactory numbered among its wealthy and acquisitive proprietors a few individuals committed to supervising their mill holdings personally. Samuel Slater—a millionaire by the early 1830s and a man directly, almost obsessively, concerned in the daily affairs of his three local manufactories—exemplified these activist factory masters, and so did Aaron Tufts of Dudley, for example, and the DeWitts of Oxford. Such men comprised the real industrial entrepreneurs of the two townships.[24]

They also acquired the aura of a new kind of elite. For it seemed clear even to casual observers that within their own mill compounds such individuals typically fused affluence with an employer's economic power to hire, fire, and set wages—power that in this case extended not to a few workers but to many dozens of operatives. It did not matter that for the most part mill hands were left alone outside working hours. What mattered—and ultimately what played into town–factory tensions—was that activist mill masters could make decisions that so fundamentally affected so many people; that they exercised, if not total, at least substantial control over what amounted to small communities; and that their economic authority was thus not only more wide ranging than that of any nontextile proprietors, but covered so many people so extensively as to resemble a new, overweaning form of political power.

Even the behavior of local factory workers encouraged this view. Close study of available data reveals sustained and intricate efforts by operatives to resist the regimen governing the mill compounds. Yet for a number of reasons (their mixed social and economic backgrounds, for example, and their dispersed factory living quarters) operatives in Dudley and Oxford found it hard—considerably harder than the more homogeneous and residentially centralized Lowell workers—to forge the solidarity necessary for strikes or public petitions.[25] Among townspeople living outside the textile manufactories, and who were ignorant of the operatives' largely covert militancy, the absence of dramatic confrontations naturally fostered the notion that local mill hands were acquiescent, as thoroughly passive as Melville's "blank-looking girls." Men such as Samuel Slater and Aaron Tufts thus *appeared* to run their manufactories—appeared, in effect, to determine the common good for hundreds of factory village residents—as unchallenged rulers.[26]

It was above all this image of excessive authority that drew the attention of Dudley and Oxford residents. And it was this image that increasingly led local residents to regard the textile factories springing up around them as decidedly, disturbingly, strange.

## III

The strangeness of the mills created the context within which town–factory disputes developed. The notion that manufactories represented a qualitatively—and in certain ways worrisomely—new kind of economic institution fostered among townspeople a general readiness to believe that at some point these factories were simply bound to cause trouble. But how was this anticipation fulfilled? What were the specific concerns and issues that transformed the sense of strangeness surrounding the mills into outright conflict?

Part of the answer involved the grim reputation of textile mills, including small country mills. Despite its frequent invocation by mill supporters (and its equally frequent reiteration by later historians), the belief that Yankee rural factories would avoid the blight ascribed to Old World industrial metropolises did not quiet all fears. From the moment mills appeared in Dudley and Oxford, many local residents likely shared the widespread concern that even hinterland manufactories could attract operatives with "vicious propensities." Indeed, local townspeople may well have also believed (again in company with many of their contemporaries) that the demographically dense ("crowded") character of country manufactories would actually nurture these "propensities" until, like a "contagion," they infected surrounding townspeople.[27] Coupled with this (and probably also exacerbated by the "crowded" configuration of rural mill compounds) was the equally widespread worry that mills would leach away needed workers. Along with the inevitable exodus from Yankee farms caused by population pressure—so ran the logic of this anxiety—cotton and woolen mills might attract "every farmer's son and daughter" until homesteads would be left "run[ning] up to bushes." Given the region's chronic labor shortage during the early nineteenth century, the putative capacity of manufactories to attract employees could easily have aroused considerable local concern.[28]

Throughout rural New England, this linkage of mills with moral "contagion" and labor scarcity helped to underscore the disturbing distinctiveness of textile factories and to heighten community suspicion of mill policies and goals. But in Dudley and Oxford, at least, a more immediate cause of conflict lay in a cluster of contested issues that emerged between towns and factories.

Some of these issues related to direct and obvious ways in which the mills disturbed community equanimity. There were quarrels over water, for example. Requiring substantial energy for their machines, and desiring to operate as continuously as possible in order to maximize earnings, cotton and woolen mill owners often constructed dams far larger than those used by earlier gristmills and sawmills. On occasion, textile dams were fully capable of causing upstream flooding of fields and other mills, or downstream water shortages, or both. Despite the diminished importance of river fishing (whose late eighteenth-century practitioners had vehemently criticized mill dams for blocking the passage of herring and salmon) and despite the tendency of antebellum courts to support manufactories in riparian controversies, dams erected by Samuel Slater, Aaron Tufts, and other local mill masters were the target of frequent protests (and several lawsuits) by town residents. But it is important to note that the problem was deepened by what the communities evidently believed the dams revealed about the men who built them. The activist mill masters who blithely permitted their neighbors to be flooded or deprived of water were viewed as attempting to specify their need for steady water as the common good of all town residents—as attempting to transpose the unique hegemony they sought over their employees into the broader arena of town affairs.[29]

It was much the same with taxes. Although the possibility of taxing "improved" mill properties was a major reason some New Englanders favored textile mills, the fact was that factory masters often spent considerable energy trying to avoid local levies. The resulting tug-of-war had spurred friction in Rehoboth, Massachusetts, in 1799, and may have been the reason Woonsocket, Rhode Island, residents decided nine years later to "place all the obstacles which they could" before a local mill. Tax disputes certainly created problems in Dudley and Oxford. Samuel Slater rejected tax assessments from the former town in 1829 and 1830, and from the latter community in 1825.[30] But again the impact of Slater's refusals was sharpened by his identity as a leading mill owner. It was not difficult, after all, to detect in his unilateral opposition to town imposts an assumption of authority similar to what he claimed within his villages. Once more the fear was that the power factory masters aimed for inside the mill enclaves was extruding into mechanisms of town life.

These two issues—mill dams and taxes—produced continual friction from the appearance of the first local manufactory in 1812 until Webster's incorporation in 1832. Over time, however, a second, distinct category of grievances emerged. These later disagreements disclosed, not only the towns' distress with manufactories, but also the rising impatience of mill owners toward actions and attitudes taken by Dudley and Oxford. And these new disputes also revealed the capacity of town–factory squabbles to spill out into areas that at first blush seem arcane and of little direct relevance to dealings between hinterland communities and their textile compounds. They disclosed, in sum, the further stage into which town–factory friction evolved as time went on.

One such "remote" quarrel focused on the Oxford Bank. Incorporated in 1823 as a "convenience to the inhabitants" of Oxford and surrounding townships, the bank initially drew support from both local merchants and mill owners, including Samuel Slater. Factory proprietors did not control bank policy, however, and were in fact often frustrated by what they saw as the facility's distressing independence. In 1830 the Dudley Woolen Manufacturing Company was turned down flat for a loan; two years earlier Slater had been irritated to find his warnings against "over liberal" loans summarily ignored. Indeed, Slater grew so annoyed that in 1831 he launched an unsuccessful petition to block the renewal of the bank's charter.[31] To most local residents, of course, the mill proprietors' complaints were thoroughly inappropriate. Factory masters angry at the bank seemed to be merely acting out their (by now) familiar exercise of claiming substantial authority outside their mills and to be displeased when community institutions refused to play along.

A somewhat more elaborate and extended quarrel centered on schools. Beginning in 1815, but with greater insistence as years passed, a number of local manufacturers petitioned Dudley and Oxford town meetings for permission to "draw off" their school taxes from community coffers, institute their own prudential districts, and "school their children at their Factor[ies]."[32] The petitioning mill masters hoped in this way both to save money (since running their own classes would in the end likely cost less than their school taxes) and to gain firmer control over the content and schedule of their young operatives' instruction. The towns, however, resisted the ploy.

They did so in part for the same reason they resisted all efforts by mills to escape taxation. But there were signs that Dudley and Oxford also believed charging factory villages with educational responsibilities would create a worrisome precedent. Specifically (and looking ahead to language Dudley residents would later employ during debates over Webster's incorporation), it would infuse into the "corporate rights" textile managers already possessed the "municipal authority" of town officials.[33] The change would thus, precipitously, create a species of authority far denser than the decentralized character most town administrative structures (including school districts) would permit. From a slightly different angle, but again with familiar implications, manufactories seemed to be trying to exert more pressure in community life than many residents judged proper for private interests.

So the arguments passed back and forth—with Slater once more a leading proponent of the mill position. Ultimately, the two communities gave way, granting three Oxford factory compounds (one of them owned by Slater) and the Perry mill in Dudley permission to "draw their school money."[34] But this resolution failed to expunge the hostility the controversy had generated.

The final controversy was over roads. Here the core disagreement concerned how to finance construction and upkeep of thoroughfares that textile mills determined they needed. Reflecting their diffused sense of commonweal, post-Revolutionary Dudley and Oxford generally allocated the major cost of highways, not to the entire township, but to residents "more immediately benefitted" by a particular road.[35] For their part, mill masters (seemingly bent once more on imposing their notion of common good upon the whole community) began over the years to argue that even if a road "more immediately benefitted" their interests, it should still be supported by the township as a whole.[36] Whatever helped mills would help all of Dudley and Oxford. Debates over highways flared repeatedly—and with mounting acerbity—in the two decades after 1812. Occasionally manufactories got their way; often they did not. But as with other "remote" issues—indeed, as with all issues dividing towns and mills—squabbles over roads left in their wake heightened antagonisms between local factories and their host communities.

## IV

These were the issues and concerns promoting town–factory friction between 1812 and 1832. Thus far, however, we have treated only casually the more detailed texture of these disputes. Questions remain: Did all mill proprietors participate in every town–factory squabble? To what extent did factory advocates attract nonfactory proprietors to their side in these quarrels? Who were the "townspeople" opposing local textile compounds?

Surviving records, unfortunately, provide neither complete nor consistent lists of those carrying the mills' banner. Nonetheless, it is safe to suggest that among members of the partnerships owning Dudley and Oxford manufactories, it was above all men we have labeled activist investors—the (usually) wealthy proprietors personally involved in their industrial holdings—who championed the factory side. It is also true, however, that even these most engaged of proprietors typically stirred themselves only when *their* mills faced criticism or needed cooperation from the towns. In controversies unrelated to their own properties, such mill masters often remained aloof; occasionally (perhaps to curry favor with the towns) they even sided against fellow entrepreneurs. Yet by the same token factory supporters at times included others besides mill owners. In some instances factory operatives were dragooned into endorsing petitions favored by mills employing them. In other cases—cases underscoring the ambivalence characterizing town–factory relations—individuals who were neither employees nor proprietors of factories took the side of these establishments.[37] Certainly it was not unknown for residents scattered through Dudley and Oxford to feel that, just as they gained from occasional outwork and sales of farm products to mill managers, so also they might "benefit" from a particular factory-supported highway. To such inhabitants it could appear both sensible and advantageous that a road sponsored by a given manufactory should receive townwide support.

The configurations of factory proponents thus escape facile classification. On the one hand, in any given dispute, the mills' cause was argued by individuals clearly identified as leading factory proprietors. On the other hand, no single dispute ever united all mill masters in Dudley and Oxford, and several squabbles linked committed advocates of the Yankee textile industry with people who took the factory side only under pressure or out of pragmatic endorsement of particular factory-sponsored "improvements."

As for those ranged against manufactories, they too shifted according to issue and episode. By all indications, however, the constituency resisting mill masters (and their occasional allies) centered around large and broad samplings of local inhabitants. Taken together, the concrete expressions of antimill sensibilities in Dudley and Oxford—including threats of lawsuits, angry letters and petitions and, above all, repeated votes in town meetings opposing local factories[38]—taken together these ventings of suspicion and outright hostility were produced by sizable clusters of every major occupational group outside the mill villages. At one time or another, in one way or another, the local mills were challenged by storekeepers, by owners and employees of local handicraft shops, and—the largest, most frequently aroused, and thus in many ways most significant contingent—by yeomen.

Overall, as we have seen, antimill attitudes were sufficiently widespread that factory masters were frequently prevented from doing as they pleased with local banks, schools, and roads. But equally striking is the way opposition to manufactories thwarted efforts by mill owners to dominate town government. Despite repeated efforts by these often wealthy and prominent men to win election to important offices, only a handful of factory proprietors (or managers) were thus elevated.[39] Although perfectly willing to accept other affluent citizens in high position, local residents translated their far-reaching—if never quite unanimous—nervousness about textile factories into a marked reluctance to accept civic leadership from mill masters.

Along with the identity of protagonists lining up for and against manufactories, another factor affecting the chemistry of town–mill friction was ideology. We have already noted that assertions of rural exceptionalism to industrial blight were not always convincing. What we also need to understand, however, is that formalized arguments supporting and attacking textile mills kept circulating through antebellum culture, and in certain ways kept complicating local town–factory disputes.

Thus pro-industrial ideologues sought to counter critiques levelled against textile mills by stressing the tax revenues such establishments would bring (blithely ignoring the millmasters' resistance to paying such taxes) and by underscoring the "ready home market" for foodstuffs mill operatives provided Yankee husbandmen. Then too, factory enthusiasts maintained that, so far from consuming needed rural labor, textile mills provided jobs to people (especially women and children) usually lacking gainful employment.[40] Indeed, it was suggested that at a time of widespread social change and volatile transiency, the opportunity manufactories offered for "steady work"—and thus for anchored, predictable, and responsible social interactions—offered more encouragement "for the morals of society . . . than the clergy themselves." Coupled with the "kindly and paternal" concern that mill managers commonly claimed they held toward their employees, this stress on "steady work" helped to define the high moral ground textile factories sought to occupy.[41]

Spreading the news that textile factories were engines of economic and moral "improvement" may have offered some reassurance to rural communities such as Dudley and Oxford. It may even have at least partially deflected anxiety about the disturbingly extensive authority mill proprietors seemed bent on wielding. Paradoxically, however, this same profactory ideology could also heighten tensions. This was because, first, it gave mill owners engaged in specific disputes little reason to compromise. If they believed their own slogans, manufactories were good for the countryside and any concerns voiced by rural townships were specious. The logic of arguments supporting textile mills encouraged factory masters to dig in their heels.

Moreover, certain implications of profactory protestations could also produce intransigence among residents unconnected to manufactories. All Yankee factory masters claimed "regard" for operatives, but because they hired more "poor and destitute" workers, owners of family-style mills (and their supporters) tended to stress that they were *elevating*, rather than merely *preserving*, their employees' morality and "welfare." And this rhetorical emphasis among country mill apologists—a further consequence of differences between Waltham- and Rhode Island-style enterprises—inevitably led to questions about the hinterland society that yielded many of the "vicious, improvident, and indigent" laborers entering small rural factories. As a result, what advocates of family-style mills found themselves saying, and what rural Yankees would scarcely have enjoyed hearing, was that it was *only* textile factories that saved the countryside from "wretchedness." For example: without mills to buy goods, provide employment, and implement "moral . . . instruction," all of rural society would reveal (in Slater's words) "a retrograde movement . . . to ignorance, weakness, and barbarism."[42] It was thus not only that the celebrations of rural industrialization were sometimes unconvincing; by the 1820s and 1830s, such celebrations could encompass quite blatant contempt for rural life—an ironic twist hardly calculated to encourage cooperation from backcountry Yankees.

Yet it would distort the motives of these backcountry Yankees to suggest they merely responded to profactory slogans. Residents of communities such as Dudley and Oxford had their own ideological reasons for resisting manufactories. Specifically, they had reasons provided by the "republican" sensibility that had helped fuel the American Revolution, and which remained deeply compelling to many antebellum New Englanders. Derived from English political thought, American republicanism set "liberty" as the capstone of a just society, but held that liberty could exist only among citizens who lived in rough equality, whose "virtue" reflected both independence and respect for the common good, who avoided "corrupt" dependency by owning land or plying their own trades, and who both feared and loathed overreaching "power."[43] By the standard of these axioms, textile mills were bound to come up short, because here were establishments whose leading proprietors were often wealthy, sometimes (as in Slater's case) very wealthy. Further, here were institutions whose policies routinely seemed to violate community conventions of common good, and whose employees (again it seemed) were entirely dependent on factory work and entirely dominated by the authority of factory managers. For all their putative desire to help rural society and elevate operatives, cotton and woolen mills could easily appear unrepublican.

Factory advocates could of course ring their own changes on republican themes. Hamilton had argued as early as 1791 that America's "virtuous" independence required textile mills because only through manufacturing enterprises could the United States avoid "corrupt" dependence on European workshops.[44] In the nineteenth century, supporters of manufactories went further, suggesting that in principle both mill workers and mill entrepreneurs could be "virtuous" citizens: the former because their "daily earnings" constituted a kind of independence; the latter because their investments made them property owners. Never a strictly unified doctrine, republicanism—in one form or another—was in fact invoked by an increasing range of interests as America's antebellum economy grew in complexity and scale.[45]

Still, despite such ideological crosscurrents, it was significant that rural Yankees distressed by textile mills had access to America's republican heritage. Perhaps most obviously, it added luster to the antifactory stance of yeomen. The central role of independent (landowning) farmers in republican recipes for "liberty" naturally called attention to the various—and frequent—antimill stirrings of Yankee husbandmen. Indeed, for Dudley and Oxford residents, the melding of yeoman-activism against factories and an overall political culture resonant with republican sympathies—this combination may well have suggested a continuity of sorts between local town–mill squabbles in the twenty years after 1812 and the local support given to Daniel Shays' uprising in the 1780s. For Shays' Rebellion had also centered on yeoman grievances, and it had also repeatedly claimed for itself the thoroughly republican project of warding off "encroachments" of Eastern merchants against the "liberties [and] properties of the people."[46] The language of republicanism could thus connect local hostility to mills with emotions surrounding both the Revolution and New England's brief post-Revolutionary excursion into agrarian protest.

The explosiveness of republican language also bears notice. In the lexicon of this political tradition, mill masters imposing new factory disciplines were not simply disturbing; they were "aristocratical" and "monarch[s]." We may note, moreover, that because their personal authority was more obvious than the control exerted by absentee investors in boardinghouse factories, activist owners of small rural mills were especially likely to attract such labels. And should these same country entrepreneurs demand their way over public roads or school districts, they could be accused of far more than merely violating town norms: When mill masters "step out into the community with the same air" they evinced within their factory villages, intoned a Rhode Island newspaper of the period, "What is this but tyranny?"[47]

Such rhetoric exacerbated friction, encouraging townspeople to become just as stubborn and shrill as factory supporters. In fact, to republican-minded residents of townships such as Dudley and Oxford, the policies of textile mills—and to some extent even the paternalistic rationalizations mills used to justify their actions—could arouse the same righteous contempt previously directed at royalty. Thus a poem out of Woonsocket, Rhode Island:

> For liberty our fathers fought
> Which with their blood they dearly bought,
> The Fac'try system sets at nought. . . .
> Great Britain's curse is now our own,
> Enough to damn a King and Throne.[48]

Here, in effect, was Melville's nightmare in its more widely circulated *political* version. Here was an explanation for why mill operatives were reduced to "blank-looking" automatons, an explanation that singled out the liberty-crushing authoritarianism of factory managers and linked that authoritarianism with the monarchial enemy Americans had recently—but perhaps not definitively—vanquished.


V


This, then, was the situation in Dudley and Oxford as the 1830s opened: on the one hand, an appreciation among town residents of economic benefits offered by local manufactories; on the other hand, an extensive (and expanding) series of conflicts rooted in the differences between town and factory social orders, intensified by ideology, and played out between shifting, but clearly identifiable, clusters of pro- and antifactory advocates. This was how matters stood in June 1831 when Samuel Slater organized a petition to the Massachusetts General Court to create the town of Webster.

The evidence suggests that Slater took this step because he was fed up. Long-building frustration with Dudley and Oxford—a frustration probably aggravated in the late 1820s by personal difficulties with several business associates—propelled him into the new venture of town building. It is true that Slater did not himself sign the petition dispatched to the General Court. As part of his strategy to avoid Dudley and Oxford tax assessments, this leading local mill master was by 1830 claiming residence in Rhode Island,[49] which made it inappropriate for him to address Commonwealth legislators about a new Massachusetts township. But there was little doubt as to who was behind the document. Two of Slater's sons (in residence at his southern Worcester County manufactories) figured prominently among the signatories; and at least four-fifths of the remaining 172 other names on

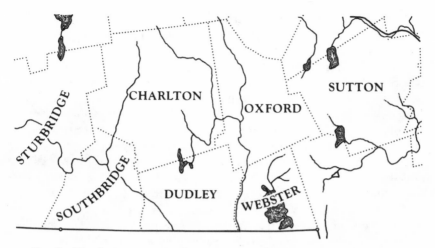

3.2. *Detail of South-Central Massachusetts, ca. 1842, showing the new township of Webster (based on "A Map Showing the Congressional Districts of Massachusetts as Established by the Act of September 16, 1842"; courtesy of the Map Collection, Harvard College Library)*

the petition belonged to operatives employed in Slater's local factories. Nor was there much mystery over Webster's purpose, for the territory of the proposed community (carved from southern Oxford and eastern Dudley) neatly encircled the three Slater villages. Webster was to be the new home for Slater's southern Massachusetts industrial holdings.[50] (See Map 3.2.)

The central argument presented by the Slater petition was shrewd. There was no mention of past disagreements with Dudley and Oxford. Instead, Webster was justified the same way Yankees had justified new communities for generations: by stressing geography, by reasoning that dispersed residential patterns left certain residents so "remot" as to require separate community status. "Most" of Webster's prospective inhabitants, the petition suggested, are "distant from [the center of] Dudley from three to four miles—from Oxford [center] from four to five miles, [and] it is burdensome and inconvenient to travel so great a distance to attend town meetings and for other town purposes."[51]

This argument, of course, was almost entirely disingenuous. Employees in Slater's three villages—those who would supply "most" of Webster's "remot" population, just as they had already supplied a majority of Slater's petitioners—had never received the slightest indication that management worried about their participation in town affairs. On the contrary, it was management's own policy of seventy-two-hour work weeks which, coupled with the operatives' transiency and their isolation, made it difficult for these workers to enter broader currents of town life. Still, however calculated and insincere, Slater's emphasis on the remoteness of "the premises prayed for" was tactically sound. He knew that Webster's incorporation would appear more acceptable to the General Court if articulated in terms the legislature was used to seeing in requests for new townships.

When we consider the number of names on his petition, it is apparent that Slater enjoyed support (or at least acquiescence) from several local constituencies. For these groups, however, the deciding factor was almost certainly not Webster's isolation. The operatives endorsing the new town had probably simply concluded there was little reason to fight management on this issue. While prepared to resist Slater over workplace conditions, Slater's employees would have seen little in Webster's incorporation that threatened them directly: so why not go along? The other significant group supporting Slater's petition was a contingent of roughly a dozen households living outside Slater's villages but within the area to be "set off." Such residents, doubtless aware that Webster's projected territory contained few paupers but numerous good roads, may well have assumed the new township would enjoy relatively low public expenses—and thus relatively low public taxes.[52]

To many, however, the incorporation of Webster was never acceptable. In sections of Dudley and Oxford beyond Webster's prescribed boundaries, resistance was broad enough that town meetings in both communities adopted strong remonstrances to the General Court opposing Slater's plan. The exact number and identity of residents joining these anti-Webster majorities are not known, but surviving evidence suggests they included a wide variety of occupational and economic groupings. There were merchants and—as usual—large numbers of yeomen. There were also some proprietors of local manufactories, men who often shared Slater's impatience with Dudley and Oxford but who, because they were not themselves petitioning for new towns, were in this case swayed by concerns of nonentrepreneurial neighbors.[53]

What could these concerns have been? After all, given their record of unease about textile factories, we might expect local residents to have applauded the secession of Slater's compounds. The answer to this puzzle is simple enough. The issue of Webster tapped powerfully the ambivalence with which rural Yankees commonly viewed manufactories—but it did so in a way that cast the prospective community as a thoroughgoing disaster. Thus, insofar as Dudley and Oxford inhabitants retained some hope of benefiting from Slater's mills, Webster represented a calamitous deprivation of valuable assets. Reckoning up the entire real estate package embraced by Slater's petition, Oxford put its loss at "about one-sixth portion of its taxable property" and a "considerable portion of [its] water power"; Dudley stood to lose "more than one-third of the population and more than one-quarter of the ratable property of the whole town [i.e., Dudley before the division]."[54]

Yet Webster's incorporation seemed equally ominous from an antimill perspective. For was it not apparent—was it not unavoidable—that the proposed community would cultivate precisely the kind of town–factory relations backcountry New Englanders so frequently found distressing? The remonstrances passed at Dudley and Oxford town meetings warned repeatedly that in Webster, where "Messrs. Slater" would employ most of the citizenry, nothing would stop the leading factory "interests" from having everything they wanted. Distorting the statistics somewhat in its excitement, Oxford's remonstrance noted that "in a large town various interests balance each other. But in the proposed town, there will be one interest—three-fourths of the property and one-half the population will be under one interest."[55] Dudley's residents pursued the same theme, using what were probably more accurate figures to drive the argument home: "Nearly two thirds of the real and personal estate, within the limits of the town prayed for by your petitioners, are in the possession and under the control of one individual; and two thirds of the population are in the service and employment, and in a great measure dependent on him." Because of its peculiar economic structure, Dudley's remonstrance continued, Webster would witness a peculiar centralization of government and a peculiar conflation of authority. Like a factory-run school district, the new town would be unprecedentedly dense, immune to the balancing "watchful influence of a large agricultural community." Explicitly raising the republican motif, Dudley held that Webster would emerge as an extreme example of a mill owner trying to "step out into the community": "To incorporate the town prayed for under circumstances like these, your remonstrants believe, would be impolitick, and contrary to the spirit of our free institutions and republican principles. It would be investing an individual, not merely with corporate rights, but with municipal authority—a power too great, your remonstrants apprehend, to be wielded by one man under a free government."[56]

Finally, the towns took up the character of the people who would constitute the bulk of Webster's inhabitants: Slater's employees. The evaluation was not flattering—but this is perhaps not surprising given how little townspeople knew about these (mostly) nonlocal workers. And we should note, too, that the controversy over Webster came shortly after a decision by the Slater mills to end their long-standing reliance on outworking handloom weavers and instead to produce cloth with operative-weavers laboring inside the factory compounds.[57] In a sense, the shift brought these Rhode Island-style factories closer to Waltham-style establishments (which had never used outworkers). But of greater immediate importance, this shedding of external weavers reduced links between Slater's mills and people living outside his three local manufacturing enclaves. In subtle but significant ways, the end of outwork heightened the isolation of these three textile ventures.

For all these reasons, then, the daily experience of Slater's employees and above all the covert forms of resistance they adopted were largely unknown to nonmill-working residents of Dudley and Oxford. (Such ignorance becomes the more—and more sadly—ironic when we realize that mill workers commonly grounded their antifactory stance in the same web of republican values as did many townspeople. There were factory employees who named their children "Liberty," for example, and the common aim of all their opposition strategies was clearly to curtail what they experienced as their employers' novel and arbitrary "power.")[58] As the Dudley and Oxford town meetings finished off their indictments against Webster, their naiveté about local factory hands encouraged what amounted to an uncritical marshaling of ideologically familiar postulates. Operatives (it was assumed) were passive and lacked key prerequisites for an "independent" citizenry. Ignoring even the presence of women and youngsters among the mill workers, Dudley announced that "Of the whole population now residing within the limits of the town prayed for, a vast proportion are transient and floating, men laborers from month to month, or year to year. Of the 115 of your petitioners within the limits of Dudley no more than 17 are freeholders."[59] This aimlessly restless population—so apparently inadequate by republican standards, so inert (perhaps even so "blank-looking") compared to virtuous yeomen—could not be expected to withstand the overwhelming "one interest" the Slater family would represent in Webster.

All these protests and concerns came to nothing. By January 1832 the Committee on Towns of the Massachusetts General Court had bowed to Slater's arguments (and very probably to his influence in the legislature) and granted permission to the "petitioners" to incorporate Webster.

Yet there had been one hesitation. The complaints raised by Dudley and Oxford about the economic losses they faced were dismissed out of hand. But the potential control of Webster by "one individual or . . . one family"—this, the members of the General Court conceded, required "serious consideration." In the end, they eased their minds by evoking the democratic mechanisms of New England town government. Although the logic and language of their position are murky, what the legislators appear to have suggested is that the capacity of Webster's residents—presumably including factory operatives—to elect their community leaders would "operate as a salutary check to any power which [the] present situation might give rise to in the hands of a few." Ignoring the various constraints (including persistently long work hours) that would almost certainly limit participation of factory workers in Webster's town meetings, ignoring the peculiar blend of public and private authority that the town of Dudley had warned would fall into Slater's hands—ignoring all this, the General Court declared its faith that "the subordinate employments of a part of the population in [the

Slater] business transactions" would be offset by a "permanent equality in municipal concerns."[60]

For these reasons, and propelled by this slender hope of democracy, Webster was created. The new community took its place among the incorporated townships of Massachusetts in March 1832.

## VI

The story changes after Webster's creation. Once Slater had his own town, Dudley and Oxford no longer had to contend with this prickliest of local mill masters. Moreover, for the rest of the antebellum period interaction between the two older communities and textile owners still within their boundaries also grew less stormy. An increase in the number, size, and complexity of nontextile businesses inside Dudley and Oxford reduced the distinctiveness of cotton and woolen manufactories, making these establishments appear less threatening.[61] At the same time, administrative pressures created by steadily growing populations produced a gradual increase in both the jurisdiction and the centralization of Dudley and Oxford town governments. There thus developed in the years after 1832 a local political leadership claiming much the same authority over town affairs that once only mill owners had asserted—again diminishing the distinctive aura surrounding mills. As a result, town–factory relations with Dudley and Oxford were calmer during the post-1832 years of the antebellum era than during the first two decades following 1812.[62]

And Webster was calmer still. But here a further antidote to tension was precisely the issue Dudley and Oxford had warned about: the Slaters' immense influence. Town–factory dealings were free of sharp conflicts in Webster between 1832 and 1860 largely because the Slater family—first Samuel, and then after his death in 1835, his sons—got most of what they wanted.[63]

Yet all this tranquillity existed only up to a point. Shortly after Webster's incorporation, during the elections of 1833 and 1834, residents of all three townships turned out in exceptionally large numbers to endorse the Commonwealth's newly formed Workingmen's party. Known for its attacks on the increasing " 'monopoly of wealth and income in the hands of the few,' " and especially for its criticism of those who manipulated " 'associated wealth' and, with it, affairs of public concern," the Workingmen's party polled only 6 percent statewide and soon faded away. But its relative success in Dudley, Oxford, and Webster (where it attracted over 20 percent of the aggregate vote) suggests that at least some local citizens remained concerned about the direction economic change was taking in their communities. Moreover, even though this economic change—and its attendant social and political consequences—in fact proceeded apace, it was never so rapid or so extensive that textile mills ever blended *entirely* into the landscape. Cotton and woolen factories—and the demands they made on local resources—still stood out sufficiently in Dudley and Oxford that their proprietors found themselves periodically ruffling local tempers (especially over the question of roads) well into the 1840s and 1850s.[64] Indeed, a close scrutiny of available records reveals that even Webster was not totally peaceful. Time and again between 1832 and 1860, residents of this township managed to register at least some measure of disagreement with their leading industrial family—over control of a Methodist church, for example, or over the schooling available to factory children, or (once again) over roads.[65]

But here it is important to stress again that the controversies depicted in these pages reflected more than the unique circumstances and personalities converging in early nineteenth-century Worcester County. For it is certainly safe to suppose that even had Slater never appeared on the scene, textile manufactories would have gone up in this area of southern Massachusetts and, having gone up, would have provoked arguments. Then too, Dudley and Oxford (as we have noted) were by no means the only communities in which—at one time or another—the construction of mills led to trouble. Cotton and woolen factories brought conflict to other Yankee towns as well.

In most cases, of course, mills continued to be built and do business despite such conflict. But the significance of town–factory disputes should not be discounted. Given the numerous advantages textile manufactories brought to rural communities, the fact that friction arose as much as it did requires attention. And beyond that, as we have seen, probing the antagonism that could develop between country mills and their host townships illuminates basic elements—or more accurately, basic tensions—within the process of early nineteenth-century rural industrialization. On the one hand, economic life in communities such as Dudley and Oxford was changing. A number of outright entrepreneurs had begun to emerge from (or move into) local populations. The economy as a whole was sufficiently dynamic and supple that even the majority of inhabitants still maintaining noncommercialized perspectives initially accepted the appearance of textile factories, frequently looked to benefit from mill-generated payments and revenues, and (in the case of the non-Slater compounds) sometimes actually invested in local manufactories. On the other hand, the fundamental texture of both social and economic life remained sufficiently traditional that the mills did seem exceptional. Moreover—and what was eventually quite important—prevailing social and economic patterns fostered a structure of political norms that directly conflicted with notions of authority embraced by the textile manufactories. The story we have been following thus rests on a rather grim paradox: Rural Yankees permitted, and in some instances actively encouraged, the development of manufacturing enterprises with which they soon found themselves in repeated and heated conflict.

The disaffection with factories explored in this essay was, of course, not entirely new to the nineteenth century. Mobilizing at least some of the same ideological weapons as antebellum Dudley and Oxford residents, some backcountry New Englanders had jousted with textile mills (especially over their dams) as early as the 1790s. Nor should we assume that, even within the antebellum period, textile mills were the only economic institutions to first attract support and then provoke concern from rural Yankees. The far-reaching penetration of market exchange already in evidence by the early 1800s did not always remain captive to traditional institutions and expectations. Farming households that willingly increased their dependence on store-bought goods and outwork were willy-nilly supporting a trajectory of economic development that, in the end, would undermine the very world of household production and modest "competencies" many of these farmers were trying to maintain by entering the market.[66]

But with all this understood, it remains true that early nineteenth-century town–factory tensions like those erupting in Dudley and Oxford are an important phase in the conflicted history of rural New England's economic transformation. Surfacing in a different context and evolving in different ways from their eighteenth-century antecedents, these disputes were among the earliest occasions in which antebellum residents of Northeastern hinterland communities—residents not tied to manufactories as operatives—expressed overt reservations about how a new economic order might affect them. Indeed, while such residents often showed little sympathy for those working inside factory compounds, the unease townspeople experienced was, in a broad sense, rooted in the same fundamental uncertainty that American political culture, including its wage-laboring constituencies, would puzzle over throughout the remainder of the nineteenth century: Could the progress of industrial capitalism (and especially its tendency to arm business leaders with unprecedentedly dense power) be reconciled to the nation's originating (and especially its republican) ideals?[67]

Inhabitants of the early nineteenth century Yankee countryside did not have any definitive answer to the problem of living with industrialization—any more than Melville had any final resolution to the disjuncture between man and machine that he discovered in a paper mill near Woedolor Mountain. But to understand the process of pre–Civil War industrialization—to tell the historical counterpart to "The Tartarus of Maids"—we must understand that the project of wrestling with the implications of an industrializing economy found early expression in the conflicts rippling through Dudley and Oxford, Massachusetts.

NOTES

1. Herman Melville, "The Tartarus of Maids" (published as part 2 of "The Paradise of Bachelors and the Tartarus of Maids") in *Selected Writings of Herman Melville* (New York, 1952), 195–96, 201, 202, 207.

2. *Statistical Information Relating to Certain Branches of Industry in Massachusetts for the Year Ending June 1, 1855* (Boston, 1856).

3. The classic text here is Leo Marx, *The Machine in the Garden: Technology and the Pastoral Ideal in America* (New York, 1964), esp. chs. 1, 3, 4. To Marx, Melville is representative of a "complex pastoralism" that found few adherents in an antebellum culture committed, for the most part, to wedding technology and pastoral ideals within a harmonious "middle landscape." As a result, "Americans had little difficulty in reconciling their passion for machine power with the immensely popular Jeffersonian ideal of rural peace, simplicity and contentment" (208). More recently, Thomas Bender, in his important study, *Toward an Urban Vision: Ideas and Institutions in Nineteenth Century America* (Lexington, Ky., 1975), has argued that Jefferson himself believed that rural industrialization was fully congruent with his notion of rustic republicanism (see ch. 2).

4. Thus the antebellum cultural antagonisms to industrialization illuminated by Bender's study and John Kasson's *Civilizing the Machine: Technology and Republican Values in America, 1776–1900* (New York, 1976) center around discussions of Lowell. For examples of urban industrial conflicts explored (often brilliantly) by labor historians of this period see Alan Dawley, *Class and Community: The Industrial Revolution in Lynn* (Cambridge, Mass., 1976); Paul G. Faler, *Mechanics and Manufacturers in the Early Industrial Revolution: Lynn, Massachusetts, 1780–1860* (Albany, N.Y., 1981); Susan E. Hirsch, *Roots of the American Working Class: The Industrialization of Crafts in Newark, 1800–1860* (Philadelphia, 1978); Bruce Laurie, *Working People of Philadelphia, 1800–1850* (Philadelphia, 1980); Sean Wilentz, *Chants Democratic: New York City and the Rise of the American Working Class* (New York, 1984).

5. For a detailed discussion of labor relations inside these mill villages see Jonathan Prude, *The Coming of Industrial Order: Town and Factory Life in Rural Massachusetts, 1810–1860* (New York, 1983), ch. 5.

6. Fairly accurate but thoroughly uncritical surveys of Slater's life and career may be found in George S. White, *Memoir of Samuel Slater, The Father of American Manufactures* ... (Philadelphia, 1836, repr. 1967); Edward H. Cameron, *Samuel Slater, Father of American Manufactures* (Freeport, Me., 1960); and Frederick L. Lewton, "A Biography of Samuel Slater," manuscript, 1944, Slater Mill Historical Site, Pawtucket, R.I. A less complete, but more balanced sketch is found in Carolina F. Ware, *The Early New England Cotton Manufacture: A Study in Industrial Beginnings* (Boston, 1931). Nineteenth-century accounts of Slater's role in Dudley and Oxford can be derived from George F. Daniels, *History of the Town of Oxford, Massachusetts, with Genealogies and Notes on Persons and Estates* (Oxford, 1892), 190–91, 198 (hereafter cited as *Oxford*); and Holmes Ammidown, *Historical Collections* ..., 2 vols. (New York, 1874), 1:461–97. For a recent treatment of this story, see Prude, *Coming of Industrial Order*, ch. 2–6.

7. Seventy percent of those men specifying occupations in 1820 cited "agriculture" as their vocation. See Manuscript Federal Censuses, Worcester County, Dud-

ley and Oxford townships, 1820, microfilm at Boston Public Library and National Archives. Shifts in farming and nonagricultural activities are derived from Worcester County Valuation Records, oversize vol. 2, Worcester County, Mass. Papers, 1675–c. 1954, American Antiquarian Society, Worcester, Mass. (hereafter cited as Worcester County Valuation); Daniels, *Oxford*, 148–49. For indications of increasing reliance on store-bought goods among families throughout Worcester County, see Rolla M. Tryon, *Household Manufacture in the United States, 1640–1860: A Study in Industrial History* (Chicago, 1917), 170, 314.

8. Town population: Dudley—1,114 in 1790, 1,240 in 1800, 1,226 in 1810, 1,615 in 1820, 2,155 in 1830; Oxford—1,000 in 1790, 1,237 in 1800, 1,277 in 1810, 1,562 in 1820, 2,034 in 1830. See *Return of the Whole Number of Persons Within the Several Districts of the United States* (Philadelphia, 1791); *Return of the Whole Number of Persons Within the Several Districts of the United States* (Washington, D.C., 1801); *Aggregate Amount of Persons Within the United States in the Year 1810* (Washington, D.C., 1811); *Census for 1820. Published by Authority of an Act of Congress Under the Direction of the Secretary of State* (Washington, D.C., 1821); *Fifth Census, or, Enumeration of the Inhabitants of the United States, 1830* (Washington, D.C., 1832).

9. The size and sex of this laborforce is inferred (somewhat indirectly) from Louis McLane, *Report of the Secretary of the Treasury, 1832. Documents Relative to the Manufactures in the United States, House Executive Documents*, 22d Cong., 1st sess., doc. no. 308, 2 vols. (Washington, D.C., 1833), 1:526–27 (hereafter cited as *Report*); Daniels, *Oxford*, ch. 8. For the organization and technology of nontextile enterprises like those in Dudley and Oxford, see Martha and Murray Zimiles, *Early American Mills* (New York, 1973), ch. 1; Anthony F. C. Wallace, *Rockdale: The Growth of an American Village in the Early Industrial Revolution* (New York, 1978), 147–48; Daniels, *Oxford*, 191, 197, 202. See also Feleicia J. Deyrup, *Arms Makers of the Connecticut Valley: A Regional Study of the Economic Development of the Small Arms Industry, 1798–1870* (Northampton, Mass., 1948), 100–102, 160–64; Merritt Roe Smith, *Harpers Ferry Armory and the New Technology: The Challenge of Change* (Ithaca, N.Y., 1977), 239–40, 273.

10. For resistance to adopting new farming methods see Prude, *Coming Industrial Order*, 103–4.

11. See Michael A. Bernstein and Sean Wilentz, "Marketing, Commerce, and Capitalism in Rural Massachusetts," *Journal of Economic History* 44 (March 1984): 171–73; Clarence H. Danhof, *Change in Agriculture: The Northern United States, 1820–1870* (Cambridge, Mass., 1969), 17; Christopher Clark, "The Household Economy, Market Exchange and the Rise of Capitalism in the Connecticut Valley, 1800–1860," *Journal of Social History* 13 (1979):169–89, esp. 176; James Parker Diary, Parker Family Papers, American Antiquarian Society, Worcester, Mass.; *Old Farmer's Almanack*, September 1837. Local agricultural production is derived from Worcester County Statistics, 1769–1837, American Antiquarian Society, and Worcester County Valuation.

12. Jeremiah Davis, Account Book, 1787–1822, Baker Library, Harvard Business School, Cambridge, Mass.; Josiah Dean, Account Book, 1820–1827, American Antiquarian Society. See also Michael Merrill, "Cash Is Good to Eat: Self-Sufficiency and Exchange in the Rural Economy of the United States," *Radical History Review* 3 (1977):42–71.

13. The right to vote in town meetings was limited to men over twenty-one years old, with twelve months' local residency, and with estates capable of generating a tax "equal to two-thirds of a single Poll tax" above a regular "Poll or Polls." See Oxford Town Meeting Records, 1800–1831, microfilm 859224, March 1809, 191, Genealogical Library, Boston and Atlanta branches (hereafter cited as Oxford Town Meeting Records III); Dudley Town Meeting Records, 1794–1845, March 1807, 131, Town Clerk's Office, Dudley, Mass. (hereafter cited as Dudley Town Meeting Records III).

14. Combined persistence rates of household heads in the towns fell from 59.5 percent between 1800 and 1810 to 48.9 percent between 1820 and 1830. Derived from Manuscript Federal Censuses, Worcester County, Dudley and Oxford townships, 1800, 1810, 1820, 1830, microfilm at Boston Public Library and National Archives. The geographical dispersal of local residents is revealed most clearly in the disputes it fostered. See for example Daniels, *Oxford*, 39–41, 53; Oxford Town Meeting Records III, April 1807, 73; May 1807, 76; October 1807, 80; Ammidown, *Historical Collections*, 1:419; Dudley Town Meeting Records III, January 1799, 72; November 1814, 216; January 1815, 220. On the increased religious heterogeneity of town residents, see Ammidown, *Historical Collections*, 1:221–25, 442–49; Daniels, *Oxford*, 53.

15. Derived from Dudley Town Meeting Records III, 1810–32 passim; Oxford Town Meeting Records III, 1810–31, passim. See also discussion in section III of this essay.

16. Boardinghouse mills are treated extensively in Hannah G. Josephson, *The Golden Threads: New England's Mill Girls and Magnates* (New York, 1949); Thomas Dublin, *Women at Work: The Transformation of Work and Community in Lowell, Massachusetts, 1826–1860* (New York, 1979); and Ware, *Early New England Cotton Manufacture*.

17. Prude, *Coming of Industrial Order*, xv.

18. The number of operatives is derived from McLane, *Report*, 1:484–85, 516–17, 576–77. The total populations of factory villages are estimates based on the ratio between, on the one hand, the known populations of two Slater villages and their roster of operatives in 1844 and, on the other hand, the number of operatives laboring in these compounds in 1832. See Slater and Tiffany, vols. 90–91, 178; Phoenix, vols. 24, 28; Union Mills, vols. 156, 144, Slater Collection, Baker Library (hereafter cited as SC).

19. Prude, *Coming of Industrial Order*, 127–28. Vols. 74, 78, Merino Records, ser. IV, part I, D, Old Sturbridge Village, Sturbridge, Mass. See also Slater and Tiffany, vols. 84, 88–91, SC.

20. McLane, *Report*, 1:577; Prude, *Coming of Industrial Order*, 57. For paternalistic rhetoric, see Erastus Richardson, *History of Woonsocket* (Woonsocket, R.I., 1876), 140; White, *Memoir of Samuel Slater*, 108; William R. Bagnall, *Samuel Slater and the Early Development of the Cotton Manufacture in the United States* (Middletown, Conn., 1890), 68–69.

21. Altogether, ninety individuals resident in these towns invested in local factories. Data on these investors are derived from Daniels, *Oxford*, ch. 8; Ammidown, *Historical Collections*, 1:435–38; McLane, *Report*, 1:484–85, 526–27, 576–77; 1815 Valuations, folio vol. 14, Worcester County, Mass. Papers, American Antiquarian

Society; and Oxford School Taxes in "Roads and Taxation," Town of Oxford, Mass. Records, box 7, Old Sturbridge Village.

22. Slater and Tiffany, Weave Books A and D; vol. 93, SC.

23. Henry A. Miles, *Lowell, As It Was, And As It Is* (Lowell, Mass., 1846, repr. 1972), 140; Slater and Kimball, vol. 3, SC.

24. Daniels, *Oxford*, ch. 8; Ammidown, *Historical Collections*, 1:435–38.

25. By the 1830s, operatives in Dudley and Oxford had mounted only one brief and unsuccessful strike (in one of Slater's villages). Slater and Howard to Major John Brown, 10 March 1827, Merino Records, ser. IV, part II, E, box 20, Old Sturbridge Village. On militancy in Lowell's boardinghouse-style mills, see Dublin, *Women at Work*, esp. ch. 6–7, 12. On the more covert resistance mounted by operatives like these in Dudley and Oxford, see Prude, *Coming of Industrial Order*, ch. 5.

26. A curious paradox is revealed here. The organization of managerial authority in the mills meant that, in certain respects, factory villages in antebellum southern Massachusetts offered closer parallels to the more firmly ranked and administered town society of 1750 than to the rather loosely structured social order that had developed in Dudley and Oxford by the early 1800s. The analogy, of course, is only suggestive. Overall, differences in social, economic, and technological organization between textile enclaves and mid-eighteenth-century townships obviously outweigh any similarities, and whatever similarities did exist were in any case not explicitly acknowledged by contemporaries. Yet on some level the anachronism of antebellum country factories may have been felt, and on some level may have contributed to the sense of "strangeness" surrounding these early industrial establishments.

27. Ware, *The Early New England Cotton Manufacture*, 7–8; Thomas Bender, *Toward an Urban Vision*, 21–29. White, *Memoir of Samuel Slater*, 116–17; Michael Ignatieff, *A Just Measure of Pain: The Penitentiary in the Industrial Revolution, 1750–1850* (New York, 1978), 60–62.

28. *New England Farmer* 17 (1838–39):406; *Old Farmer's Almanack*, April 1837. The concern (and these quotes) relate to a general tendency of youngsters to leave farming; the attractive power of textile manufactories simply contributed to this threatened exodus from husbandry. Specific reference to sons and daughters having "posted off" to factories, however, is found in *Old Farmer's Almanack*, 1850. Yet ironically, operators of country mills in the early nineteenth century frequently voiced concern about finding enough hands. See, for example, Phoenix Mill to Mr. James Cook, 30 June 1831, Webster Woolen, vol. 76, SC; Hedges to John Slater, 18 August 1834, Samuel Slater and Sons, vol. 236, SC; and S. H. Babcock to Mr. Clemons, 9 August 1834, Merino Records, ser. IV, part II, E, box 21, Old Sturbridge Village.

29. See Gary Kulik's essay in this book; Morton J. Horwitz, *The Transformation of American Law, 1780–1860* (Cambridge, Mass., 1977), 40–42. J. D. Van Slyck, *Representatives of New England Manufacturers* (Boston, 1879), 415; Dudley Town Meeting Records III, April 1826, 375; S. H. Babcock to John Clemons, 28 May 1834, Merino Records, ser. IV, part II, E, box 21, Old Sturbridge Village.

30. Rehoboth Town Meeting Records, vol. 5, 148, Town Clerk's Office, Rehoboth, Mass. William R. Bagnall, "Contributions to American Economic History...," 4 vols., manuscript, 2:998–99, Baker Library. Dudley Town Meeting Records III,

November 1832, 486; Samuel to John Slater, 7 February 1825, Samuel Slater and Sons, vol. 235, SC.

31. Petition for the Oxford Bank (n.d.) in Original Papers of Ch. 68, Acts of 1823, Mass. Archives, State House, Boston, Mass.; Daniels, *Oxford*, 232. S. Barton to Dudley Woolen Manufacturing Company, 4 June 1833, Merino Records, ser. IV, part II, E, box 23, Old Sturbridge Village; Samuel to John Slater, 11 April 1828, Samuel Slater and Sons, vol. 235, SC; Remonstrances of Samuel Slater et al. Against the Renewal of Charter of the Oxford Bank, 12 January 1831, in Original Papers of Ch. 73, Acts of 1830, Mass. Archives.

32. Dudley Town Meeting Records III, April 1815, 226.

33. See discussion in section V of this essay.

34. Oxford Town Meeting Records III, March 1829, 329; April 1829, 332; Oxford Town Meeting Records, 1831–1858, microfilm 859225, November 1831, 17, Genealogical Library (hereafter cited as Oxford Town Meeting Records IV); Dudley Town Meeting Records III, November 1831, 477.

35. Oxford Town Meeting Records, 1753–1799, August 1799, 348, Old Sturbridge Village; Oxford Town Meeting Records III, April 1810, 107; Dudley Town Meeting Records III, May 1794, 23; May 1821, 309.

36. Dudley Town Meeting Records III, May 1816, 241. Oxford Town Meeting Records III, May 1819, 197.

37. Derived from sources cited in nn. 32–36.

38. Van Slyck, *Representatives of New England Manufacturers*, 415; S. H. Babcock to Mr. Clemons, 28 May 1834, Merino Records, ser. IV, part II, E, box 21, Old Sturbridge Village; Oxford Town Meeting Records III, June 1829, 334. The quarrels over water, roads, and taxation mentioned earlier were all vented in town meetings.

39. Of the more than 100 individuals known to have had direct involvement—managerial or proprietary—in running local factories, only 8 became selectmen in either township between 1820 and 1830. Derived from Dudley Town Meeting Records III, 1820–30; Oxford Town Meeting Records III, 1820–30.

40. Alexander Hamilton, "Report on the Subject of Manufacturers, Dec. 5, 1791," *American State Papers: Finance*, 1:126. *New England Farmer* (1832):149.

41. Harriet Martineau, *Society in America*, 2 vols. (New York, 1837), 2:138.

42. McLane, *Report*, 1:71, 930–31.

43. See, generally, Bernard Bailyn, *The Ideological Origins of the American Revolution* (Cambridge, Mass., 1967); Gordon S. Wood, *The Creation of the American Republic, 1776–1787* (Chapel Hill, N.C., 1969); Sean Wilentz, "Artisan Republican Festivals and the Rise of Conflict in New York City, 1788–1837" in Michael H. Frisch and Daniel J. Walkowitz, eds., *Working-Class America: Essays on Labor, Community, and American Society* (Urbana, Ill., 1983), 37–77; Robert E. Shallope, "Republicanism and Early American Historiography," *William and Mary Quarterly* 3d ser. 39 (1982):334–56.

44. Hamilton, "Report on Manufacturers," 133.

45. Rowland Berthoff, "Independence and Attachment, Virtue and Interest: From Republican Citizen to Free Enterpriser, 1787–1837," in Richard L. Bushman, Neil Harris, David Rothman, Barbara Miller Solomon, and Stephan Thernstrom, eds.,

*Uprooted Americans: Essays to Honor Oscar Handlin* (New York, 1979), 99–124, esp. 106, 115–16. See also Wilentz, "Artisan Republican Festivals," 59–62.

46. David P. Szatmary, *Shays' Rebellion: The Making of an Agrarian Insurrection* (Amherst, Mass., 1980), 97.

47. See, for example, Seth Luther, *An Address to the Working-Men of New England* . . . (Boston, 1832), 24. *Pawtucket Chronicle*, 29 August 1829.

48. Sui Generis: Alias Thomas Mann, *Picture of a Factory Village: To Which are Annexed Remarks on Lotteries* (Providence, 1833), 8–9.

49. Samuel to John Slater, 7 February 1825, Samuel Slater and Sons, vol. 235, SC.

50. Petition of George B. Slater and 173 Others praying for the incorporation of a town to be formed of Oxford, South Gore and a part of the Towns of Oxford and Dudley, 3 June 1831, in Original Papers of Ch. 93, Acts of 1832, Mass. Archives.

51. Ibid.

52. There were enough roads in "that [eastern] portion [of Dudley] now sought to be taken off" to cause residents in this town's other, "western portion" to grow indignant; for they had (so they argued) contributed to the construction of these "improvements." Report of the Viewing Committee on petition of Geo. B. Slater and others, 17 January 1832, in Original Papers of Ch. 93, Acts of 1832, 4, 7, Mass. Archives. Dudley Town Meeting Records III, November 1831, 475.

53. Derived from Report of the Viewing Committee, 1; Dudley Town Meeting Records III, November 1831, 474. See also Oxford Town Meeting Records IV, September 1831, 13–14.

54. Oxford Town Meeting Records IV, September 1831, 13–14; Dudley Town Meeting Records III, November 1831, 474.

55. Report of the Viewing Committee, 6.

56. Dudley Town Meeting Records III, November 1831, 477.

57. Slater and Tiffany, Weave Book D, SC.

58. Slater and Tiffany, vols. 88–89, SC.

59. Dudley Town Meeting Records III, November 1831, 477. We may note in passing that the attitude of Dudley and Oxford residents toward local factory workers contrasts with the situation often characterizing small industrial communities in the late nineteenth century. In this latter period, workers (frequently members of the Knights of Labor) were on occasion known to take political control of their towns and, as town citizens and leaders, use local governmental mechanisms to limit company power. In other cases, employees received the support of town residents whose "traditional" values led them to pressure local business managers to follow "decent" labor policies. See Leon Fink, *Workingmen's Democracy: The Knights of Labor and American Politics* (Urbana, Ill., 1983); Herbert G. Gutman, "The Workers' Search for Power," in H. Wayne Morgan, ed., *The Gilded Age* (Syracuse, N.Y., 1970), 31–53.

60. Report of the Viewing Committee, 8.

61. Prude, *Coming of Industrial Order*, 188, 199–201.

62. Ibid., 239–47.

63. Ibid., 250–52.

64. See Arthur B. Darling, *Political Changes in Massachusetts, 1828–1848: A Study of Liberal Movements in Politics* (New Haven, Conn., 1925), 98; Clark, "The House-

hold Economy," 184. Dudley Town Meeting Records III, May 1841, 645; March–May 1845, 728, 734–39; Dudley Town Meeting Records, 1845–1860, November 1858, 230, Town Clerk's Office, Dudley, Mass.; Oxford Town Meeting Records IV, November 1836, 88, September 1851, 344.

65. Samuel to John Slater, 6, 19, 24, 27 January 1834, Samuel Slater and Sons, vol. 235, SC; Webster Town Meeting Records, 1832–1863, March 1855, 284–85; September 1854, 275–77, Town Clerk's Office, Webster, Mass.

66. See Kulik's essay, this volume; Clark, "The Household Economy," 180–85.

67. See Leon Fink, *Workingmen's Democracy*, chs. 1–4, 8; Sean Wilentz, "The Formation of the American Working Class: A Survey" (unpublished paper delivered to the conference on "The Future of American Labor History: Toward a Synthesis" held at Northern Illinois University, 10–12 October 1984), p. 3.

DAVID JAFFEE

# 4. One of the Primitive Sort

PORTRAIT MAKERS OF THE RURAL NORTH,

1760-1860

I

> I heard with pleasure that you had made some very clever attempts in portraits where you are and which had given much satisfaction.... Were I to begin life again, I should not hesitate to follow this plan, that is, to paint portraits cheap and slight, for the mass of folks can't judge of the merits of a well finished picture.... Indeed, moving about through the country ... must be an agreeable way of passing ones time ... it would besides be the means of introducing a young man to the best society and if he was *wise* might be the means of establishing himself advantageously in the world.[1]

Art historians have written extensively about the isolated "folk" artists and "primitive" painters found in rural New England during the late eighteenth and early nineteenth centuries.* John Vanderlyn's vision of a rich market for "cheap and slight" images, and the encouragement he gave his nephew to join the ranks of itinerant portrait makers, suggests a rather different experience.[2] Above all, Vanderlyn's experience was linked intimately to the steady commercialization of the Northeastern countryside.

For if the market economy transformed the lives of family farmers and limited the farming opportunities for their offspring, it simultaneously injected new vitality into at least some traditional rural handicrafts and turned several of those crafts into the carriers of commercial culture. The absence of a rigid artisanal system in the countryside, together with a growing population increasingly interested in consumer goods, enabled displaced farm boys to pick up a variety of trades and search widely for "the means of

*I would like to thank Fred Anderson, Joyce Appleby, Steve Botein, Christopher Clark, Christopher Jedrey, Gary Kulik, Roy Rosenzweig, Barbara Smith, Helena Wall, and especially Elizabeth Goss for their reading and comments on the numerous drafts of this essay.

establishing [oneself] advantageously in the world."[3] Using customary tools, experimenting with different techniques, and tapping available sources of power, they began to manufacture chairs, carpets, clocks, and books, as well as portraits, and to introduce rural denizens to products previously accessible only to urban dwellers and the local gentry. These rural artisans moved gradually but steadily toward the status of artisan-entrepreneurs: market-oriented purveyors of "cultural" goods who both anticipated and participated in the backcountry's industrial revolution.[4]

The life and work of portrait makers provide a compelling perspective on the process of commercialization in the countryside, for in their careers they followed the path of numerous other artisans emerging from the rural economy. Obtaining their artistic training from the pages of design books or from brief encounters with painters of the "primitive sort," portrait makers traversed the countryside, creating countless images from stark black-and-white silhouettes to colorful full-length oils. They pioneered the rapid (sometimes mechanically aided) manufacture of likenesses using stylized designs, which standardized their products but distinguished their subjects by the inclusion of personal items. Traveling the backroads of the rural North, they cultivated a ready market for their services among "middling" craftsmen, innkeepers, and farmers who sought symbols of middle-class identity.[5]

The experience was not without irony. Enterprising portrait makers seemed to welcome the new opportunities presented by the intensification of craft production; the progress some of them made toward becoming professional artists permitted certain individuals to stand out among other village artisans peddling wares along the same terrain. In their self-portraits these portrait makers reveal a newfound sense of status, and in their paintings they show the new domestic image of the Northern middle class: fathers and mothers surrounded by their children and their accumulating possessions. Some even embraced the daguerreotype after its invention in 1839, although few could have imagined that the very innovations they helped advance would eventually make their calling obsolete. Yet, in the meantime, they brought an era of mass production and consumption to the farmhouse door and stimulated a taste for a wide range of cultural commodities.

II

More than time separated the limner of the eighteenth century from his peripatetic counterpart of the early national era. There were few portrait painters in the northern British colonies, and fewer still sought a rural clientele. Those in Boston modeled themselves on European artists, and several successfully translated their training into commercial advantage with studies of the town's leading ministers and magistrates. In New York, a number of portraitists painted the Dutch gentry in their grand homes along the Hudson River.[6] Still, the portrait makers might make a rare appearance in rural villages and a local artisan such as Winthrop Chandler could stay close to home and keep busy painting his family and the town notables to supplement his decorative work. Chandler (1747–1790), a valued member of his village community, offered his sign, carriage, and house painting skills to rural neighbors whose farming background he shared. Most of his years were spent around Woodstock, Connecticut; only for a few years did he venture off, in part to receive formal training. Away from Woodstock he was sustained by the broad network of Chandler kin.[7]

Winthrop Chandler counted among his seventeenth-century ancestors several of Woodstock's founders. Both Chandler's grandfather and father pursued surveying as well as farming, and the Chandler family accumulated a large acreage in the town. But Winthrop's father, William, had ten children and his death in 1754 left his wife, Jemina Bradbury, with the difficult task of finding a niche for them all. When Winthrop, the youngest, came of age, his brother-in-law, who also served as guardian, apprenticed him to a Boston portrait painter. Returning to Woodstock in 1770, Winthrop's first commissions were the striking portraits of the Reverend Ebenezer Devotion and his wife Martha, who had the paintings done to celebrate Devotion's fifty-sixth birthday (see Figures 4.1 and 4.2). Devotion's ample library, with the titles and bindings meticulously detailed, offered one of the few opportunities for decorative display in this Puritan culture, testifying to his status as a professional and significant member of the community. So pleased was the Devotion family with Chandler's work that he was asked to paint five more Devotions in 1772.[8]

A versatile artisan in an isolated rural village, Chandler was called upon to paint portraits, landscapes, and houses as well as to serve occasionally as a gilder, carver, illustrator, and draftsman. When Chandler died in 1790, the *Massachusetts Spy* noted his important station in the community—although the tribute rested more on his skills in brightening the exterior walls of Woodstock homes than in providing portraits: "Died at Woodstock, Connecticut, Winthrop Chandler of this town, a man whose native genius has been serviceable to the community in which he resided. In profession he was a house painter, but many likenesses on canvas shew he could guide the pencil of a limner." Chandler had never traveled very far from his village; he painted only relatives and family friends. Although the strict social and economic hierarchy within village society gave Chandler limited scope for portrait work, the broad range of his abilities in allied crafts allowed him to earn a small surplus, which he invested in land, the most valued possession in a colonial rural community.[9]

4.1. *Winthrop Chandler*, Reverend Ebenezer Devotion, *1770*
*(courtesy of Brookline Historical Society, Brookline, Mass.)*

4.2. *Winthrop Chandler*, Martha Lothrop Devotion, *1770*
*(courtesy of Brookline Historical Society, Brookline, Mass.)*

A handful of limners were evidently sufficient to satisfy the demands for portrait making in eighteenth-century New England society. Winthrop Chandler served the gentry in his birthplace by offering them "correct" images, which followed the outlines of the academic art of the period. Another painter of Connecticut families, Ralph Earl, expanded the offerings available to a village elite anxious to satisfy their social designs. In the closing years of the eighteenth century Earl found the wealthy country set in New York, Connecticut, Massachusetts, and Vermont eager to have family portraits painted.[10]

The provincial elite wanted a family record, similar in purpose to, but grander in style than, the genealogies bound in treasured Bibles or hung on bare household walls. When the younger Reverend Mr. Thomas Robbins of East Haven, Connecticut, first commissioned limner Reuben Moulthrop to paint his parents' portraits in 1801, he had no idea that such an ostensibly simple undertaking would involve substantial delays or details. Moulthrop needed more than a decade to complete seven portraits, for which he received $30. He was continually in and out of the Robbins household. "My study was resigned up and looked like a painter's shop," the elder Reverend Mr. Ammi Robbins impatiently wrote his son, "he is constantly in the hall with all his apparatus & c.," but his work is "much admired." Completion of the portraits restored the sanctity of the Robbins home only temporarily; the popularity of the portraits brought a steady stream of curious visitors, "day after day as into a Museum—all agree are admirably drawn."[11]

Those able to afford the services of a Chandler or a Moulthrop were the magistrates and ministers: the established gentry in village society who found in such family icons the means to display their personal possessions and social status while decorating their homes in one of the few permissible modes in this still intensely Puritan culture. Just as the steady sequence of generations of Robbinses into the pulpit provided vocational continuity, so the portraits (the younger Rev. Thomas Robbins hoped) would yield visual evidence of family traditions. A "gallery" of notable Robbinses introduced into rural society the cosmopolitan images heretofore available only to the urban elite, and provided the village population with a model to emulate. Still, the rural portraitist remained on the periphery of a metropolitan culture in which the urban elite looked abroad and the local townspeople busied themselves with everyday concerns. Aspiring eighteenth-century limners, few in number and limited in influence, were the forerunners of later generations of portrait makers. Winthrop Chandler translated for his neighbors the available forms of "correct" portraiture into their own idiom. He profiled the severe New Englanders with bold lines and colorful design—the stock devices of the provincial artisan—and added individualizing details such as books, furniture, and clothing. The next generation would continue Chandler's quest to satisfy rural tastes with an artisan's training.

III

The transformation of the late eighteenth- and early nineteenth-century countryside accelerated with demographic growth and the rapid entry of village residents into commercial enterprise.[12] Pioneers of this era began to clear forests to make way for family farms. Crafts had always supplemented a farmer's livelihood, and a sizable number of artisans made a living in new frontier towns. One Vermont observer noted how these migrants exchanged their humble "necessaries": "The manufactures carried on in Vermont were, for many years, such only as the immediate wants of the people rendered indispensable, and in general each family were their own manufacturers.... The only trades which were deemed indispensable, were those of the blacksmith, and the shoemaker, and these were for the most part carried on by persons who labored a portion of their time upon their farms."[13]

The shift toward a more elaborate consumerism, which had taken several generations in the eighteenth century, advanced more rapidly on the nineteenth-century frontier: "As by the condition of the people improved, then by degrees, extended their desires beyond the mere necessaries of life; first to its conveniences, and then to its elegancies. This produced new wants, and to supply them, mechanics more numerous and more skilful were required, til at length, the cabinet maker, the tailor, the jeweller, the milliner, and a host of others came to be regarded as indispensable."[14] The absence of a commercial and cultural infrastructure adequate to the satisfaction of a growing population and new tastes meant that itinerants provided many of the practical and luxury items sought by village inhabitants.[15]

Chester Harding, for example, soon to be among America's most celebrated portrait painters, found his calling as an itinerant craftsman. In his *Egotistigraphy*, Harding recalled that in his childhood his family moved from Massachusetts to western New York, "then an unbroken wilderness." During those first difficult years, Harding noted, "my father and his other boys wielded the axe," and his older brother was a chair maker, "making common flag bottomed chairs for the neighbors." The family obtained extra provisions by these means, and Chester himself found employment during otherwise inactive winter months.[16]

But Harding's father had little taste for agricultural labor, being possessed of "a great inventive genius" which he turned to the search for perpetual motion. Chester had a more practical bent, if not greater enthusiasm for agriculture; when he reached nineteen he thought that "there must be an easier way of getting a living" than clearing the "heavily timbered forest." First he looked to chair turning with his brother. Then the War of 1812 erupted, giving Chester the chance to become "a distinguished drummer." At the close of hostilities he found work in drum making, but the urge to make his fortune persisted. Opportunity seemed to present itself when a local mechanic invented a spinning head and offered Harding the rights to sell the patent in Connecticut. So Chester "jumped into my wagon, whipped up my horse, and was soon out of sight of what, at that moment, seemed all the world to me." For the next few years Harding supported himself by plying a wide range of rural crafts and commerce along the country backroads: he peddled clocks, established a chair manufactory, and tried tavern keeping.[17]

None of these ventures proved very rewarding or held Harding's attention for very long. He did a stint as a house painter in Pittsburgh and in slow seasons painted signs, a skill allied with gilding, which he had picked up during his days as a chair maker. Next he fell in with a portrait maker named Nelson, one of "the Primitive sort." Nelson and his counterparts often entered the revered world of art without the rigorous apprenticeship of their provincial predecessors or the solemnity of academic painters. James Guild, another frontier peddler of notions and profiles, recalled his first portrait commission:

> Now I went to canadagua. Here I went into a painters shop, one who painted likenesses, and my profiles looked so mean when I saw them I asked him what he would show me one day for, how to distinguish the colours and he said $5, and consented to it and then I went to Bloom-field and took a picture of Mr. goodwins painting for a sample on my way. I put up at a tavern and told a Young lady if she would wash my shirt, I would draw her likeness. Now then I was to exert my skill in painting. I operated once on her but it looked so like a rech I throwed it away and tried again. The poor girl sat niped up so prim and look so smileing it makes me smile when I think of while I as daubing on paint on a piece of paper it could not be caled painting, for it looked more like a strangle cat than it did like her. However I told her it looked like her and she believed it.[18]

Enthusiasm, rather than experience, served to encourage this generation of pioneer portrait makers. There existed "a decided disposition for painting in this Country," John Neal, America's first art critic, wrote in 1829; "you can hardly open the door of a best room anywhere, without surprizing or being surprized by the picture of somebody plastered to the wall, and staring at you with both eyes and a bunch of flowers." Such portraits, "wretched as they are," flourished "in every village of our country," not as luxuries for the rich but as familiar household furniture, embellishing the homes of ordinary people. Neal, born in Portland, Maine, recalled his first experience in art. As a child he had never seen "a good picture . . . nor what I should call a decent drawing." So when he discovered a pen-and-ink drawing of a head pasted upon a wall over a shoemaker's bench, he was "delighted beyond measure," and thought this mere profile a "marvel." The shoemaker presented it to Neal, who carried it home, perched on an old leather trunk in a garret, and went to work, making copy after copy "until I had every scratch of pen daguerrotyped upon my memory."[19]

Wonder and a sense of mystery came over these "farmer's boys" when they encountered works of art. Chester Harding's mentor, Nelson, used a copy of the "Infant Artists" of Sir Joshua Reynolds for his sign, incongruously inscribed with "Sign, Ornamental and Portrait Painting executed on the shortest notice, with neatness and despatch." Harding wrote that "painting heads" was the real marvel; after seeing the painter's work, Harding commissioned likenesses of himself and his wife, "and thought the pictures perfections." Taking home what was in fact a rather crude representation, he pondered by day how it was possible for a man to produce "such wonders of art," and dreamed by night of commencing such a project. Finally, "I got a board; and with such colors as I had for use in my trade, I began a portrait of my wife. I made a thing that looked like her. The moment I saw the likeness, I became frantic with delight; it was like the discovery of a new sense. I could think of nothing else. From that time sign-painting became odious, and was much neglected."[20] Higher commissions and growing confidence accompanied Harding on each stage of his journey.

Artist and audience shared in the "discovery of a new sense." When fledgling efforts fell short of "real painting," and, in Guild's words, looked more "like a strangle cat," the painter often left his customer with "a profile if not a likeness." James Guild continued on his way, drawing likenesses, and teaching school, and touting himself as a professor of penmanship. He served, in short, as an itinerant instructor in the useful and elegant arts for a new rural clientele that did not yet demand from retailers of culture either specialized knowledge or fixed residences.[21] Quickly picking up what training they needed, Guild and others capitalized on both rural folks' passion for self-culture and their relative lack of sophistication.

Encouraged by a receptive public, some of these venturesome portraitists undertook more advanced training, and gradually began assuming the mantle and calling of the professional artist. They sought further instruction from academic artists in the cities and returned to the rural regions to ply their trade. James Guild closed his journal with the words, "he Commences his Profession as an Artist," and described his entry into a circle of London artists, where he sketched nude models and learned "the human figure": a far cry from his earlier painting of a country maiden in rural New York.[22] Yet, despite middle-class aspirations and achievements, village painters' country origins were still detectable in their likenesses. In his self-portrait, for example, Jonathan Adams Bartlett, farmer and house carpenter in Rumford, Maine, wore his Sunday best and proudly displayed the colors of his palette (see Figure 4.3), but the painting exhibits the same flat perspective

4.3. *Jonathan Adams Bartlett,* Self-Portrait, *1841 (courtesy of Abby Aldrich Rockefeller Folk Art Center, Williamsburg, Va.)*

with which he served his rural clients. Nathan Negus, son of a sign and carriage painter in Petersham, Massachusetts, assumed a regal pose in his depictions of himself, and planned to tour the South, making his fortune by painting. Yet he and his brother, Joseph, also a painter, were none too fussy over what they would paint. Joseph wrote to Nathan from Georgia in 1819 and proposed that they meet in New Orleans and "travel to all the most considerable places in the United States, working in each place, as we found encouragement. I think we would make money very fast in the southern states a year or two at portrait painting together with painting some rooms for wealthy men who would pay an extravagant price. We could probably obtain in many places hereabouts from $75 to $100 for an 18 foot room in style."[23]

Culture in the countryside grew out of pioneer soil. However inexpert the early efforts, an inexperienced audience's amazement and the enterprising artisan's enthusiasm fortified the pursuit of professional status. When Fitchburg, Massachusetts, was visited in 1832 by a practitioner of "the noble art of painting" there was great cause for rejoicing among its citizenry. An entire generation had grown up admiring portraits and venerating the vocation of painting likenesses. The anonymous author in the *Fitchburg Gazette* noted in his article the uplifting effects of popular portraiture on rural folk. The mysteries of painting no longer involved the mere copying of features but went well beyond to "transferring to canvas . . . the feelings of the heart." The appearance of gentility was available to all from this "gentleman now stopping in our village." Paintings that could produce such results were created in a standardized manner. By the 1830s, the visitor to a painter's studio remarked that the "some half dozen or more" likenesses resting along the walls of the rural salon, "tho' unfinished," would clearly represent in their final form the distinguished visages of their intended patrons. Families were invited to the painter's village salon to obtain "a valuable picture" as well as "a correct likeness," for there would rarely be such an opportunity "in a village like ours" to participate in what Neal called the "craze" for household decorations.[24]

The so-called Village Enlightenment in Fitchburg and other communities was thus no simple diffusion of urban goods but a wider cultural movement in a new age of abundance. The provincial limner of the eighteenth century gave way to artistic pioneers such as Harding, who, by their geographic and social mobility, banished local isolation and conservatism in the rural North, and promoted a culture of consumption.

IV

As the demand for portraits spread through various social strata, itinerant artists began to appear throughout the United States. By the 1820s and 1830s, portraitists of every description and skill level produced images at every price. If their earlier efforts represented mere copies of "the primitive sort," these cultural pioneers at least created a widespread desire for their offerings. Stylistic developments also had a place in their repertoire. The villager's purse and the painter's promise combined to permit significant innovation in rural design.

Some artists used mechanical devices to produce crudely composed profiles. These mass-produced images were promoted with immense zeal and imagination. Other artisans offered more elaborate (and more expensive) representations based upon some urban training and an acquaintance with academic models. Although they stylized designs and conventions to facilitate production, these latter portraitists were better able to display their sitters' features and surroundings to satisfy the desires of an emerging rural bourgeoisie for the various emblems of their newly won status.

Innovations in mass production made available to rural residents a greater number of portraits, whether inexpensive profiles or more expensive portraits. Indeed, this cycle of consumption was part of a general "cultural revolution" marked by a remarkable expansion not only of paintings, but in the number of ideas and items of all kinds that found their way to the farmhouse door during the Village Enlightenment. Previously isolated rural Americans discovered new access to information when almanac makers, newspaper editors, and book publishers marketed their wares to a farm population eager for self-improvement. And this diverse "schooling" produced a new look in rural design that made use of an artisan's training and an itinerant's experience.[25]

Some city-based artists, such as Samuel Morse, were shrewd enough to take advantage of the consumerism of this vast rural terrain. But the most successful artisans tapping this market were the locals. They included village handicraftsmen who began mass producing luxury items (for example, the Willard Brothers' banjo clocks) at a reasonable price, and village entrepreneurs who promoted an eclectic design (such as Lambert Hitchcock's painted chairs) influenced by current urban styles and old rural standards. All these artisans revealed the rural craftsmen's heavy reliance on colorful paint.[26] Stencils and design manuals may have offered the tools to imitate the imported elegance of Europe, but rural folk made their influence felt in all of their decorative efforts.[27]

In 1825, an anonymous rural *Encyclopedia* came off the presses in Concord, New Hampshire. Entitled *A Select Collection of Valuable and Curious Arts, and Interesting Experiments Which are Well Explained, and Warranted Genuine, and May be Prepared, Safely and at Little Expense*, this work covered various topics in the arts, manufactures, and science of interest to "improving" country craftsmen. The author, Rufus Porter, painter and promoter, represents in his far-reaching travels and speculations an example of the artisan-entrepreneur's critical role in the changes penetrating the countryside during this period. Porter's own "schooling" displayed the full scope of formal and informal possibilities available to mobile rural residents. Born in

Boxford, Massachusetts, in 1792, Porter moved as a child with his family to the frontier settlement of Pleasant Mountain Gore in Maine. He left the farm for six months' tuition at Fryeburg Academy, ending his formal education at age twelve. At this point machines caught his attention, and for the next two years he preferred dealing with water wheels, windmills, and lathes to performing agricultural chores. His family, concerned to provide him with a secure vocation, sent Rufus back to Boxford to serve an apprenticeship in shoemaking under his eldest brother. Within a few months he gave this up and returned to Maine to play "fife for military companies and the violin for dancing parties." Then he began to paint, becoming in 1810 a house and sign painter in Portland, Maine, where he came up with the idea of covering the walls of ordinary rooms with inexpensive landscape paintings. The outbreak of the War of 1812 found Porter painting gunboats and playing the drum. Soon Porter was in print with his first instruction manual, *The Martial Musicians Campanion containing Instructions for Drum and Fife, together with an Elegant Collection of Beats, Airs, Marches and Quick Steps* (1814).[28]

Rural residents welcomed the wide range of talents itinerant instructors and inventors brought to their villages. Over the next few years, Porter taught school, got married, and built wind gristmills, all the while acquiring a reputation as a professional portrait painter and "professor of dancing." By his early twenties Rufus Porter had demonstrated expertise as author, artist, and inventor. He began publishing *Scientific American* and a series of other journals, pamphlets, and instruction manuals; he painted sleighs, houses, signs, and landscape frescoes; and he continued the profitable portrait making that sustained his other ventures. He counted a "camera obscura" among his innovations; other inventions were more fanciful—for example, a "horseless carriage" and an "airship." Porter remained the inveterate itinerant and kept alive his early interest in mechanics. For Porter, like the readers of his *Select Collection*, the "arts," "experiments," and "expense" were not just words incongruously collected into an eye-catching title. This artist-inventor was the rural counterpart to Robert Fulton, promoter of the steamboat, and Samuel F. B. Morse, creator of the telegraph. These individuals moved easily between the worlds of art and science, finding their spatial and mechanical imaginations to be thoroughly compatible with their creative and entrepreneurial efforts.[29]

Porter found his greatest success on the road. Accompanied by a young relative named Joe, he strolled into villages with his brightly decorated camera box and hawked his handbill of reasonably priced portraits (see Figure 4.4). The artisan-entrepreneur sketched his subjects with the aid of his invention, the camera obscura, a dark box fitted with a lens and mirror to throw the sitters' image onto a sheet of paper and mounted on a handcart festooned with flags. Porter and Joe traveled from village to village, offering the public a full range of "correct likenesses," produced with Porter's mechanical aids and guaranteed to provide satisfaction. A typical Porter announcement of 1821 promised

> *Painting*
> The Subscriber respectfully informs the Ladies and Gentlemen of Haverhill and its vicinity, that he continues to paint correct Likenesses in full colours for two Dollars at his room at Mr. Brown's tavern, where he will remain two or three Days longer.
> (No Likeness, No Pay.)
> Those who request it will be waited on at their respected places of above.

He advertised his profiles at 20 cents apiece, producing perhaps twenty silhouettes in an evening by the use of a profile machine for the features (see Figure 4.4 for an illustration of a silhouette); or the popular side view, in which "full colours" were added to the stark profile (the construction of ears and clothes was skimpy); or his most detailed full view (see Figure 4.5) in which the camera obscura reduced his artistic labors to a mere fifteen minutes. These last images cost three times as much as the side view, but still showed the subject's ears in full profile, a shortcut preserved from his side views. Copies came cheap. Porter's *Select Collection* gave instructions for "the construction and use of a copying machine" or pantograph, which reduced, enlarged, or copied images. The client could choose an affordable original along with as many copies as desired. Porter created a standardized product with the aid of his mechanical inventions and labor-saving techniques; the rural client got just as much "art" as he or she was willing to pay for.[30]

As a publicist for ideas of rural design, Porter transmitted the rules necessary to paint landscapes on walls or to achieve the color of animals. These were no idle speculations of academicians but specific recipes garnered from Porter's experience and reading. In his work—both writing and painting—Porter placed repetition and rule at the very heart of the country vernacular. He made sure-footed suggestions for introducing into every American home the "embellishments" that John Neal thought would eventually improve American art. Porter emphasized color and line, both accessible to precise measurement in careful proportions. The farmhouse frescoes he envisioned had no room for the romantic shadowing or sublime scenery of the cosmopolitan set. Indeed, "improving" villagers wanted working farms and practical details on their walls. Just as some rural artisans used machines (such as lathes) to produce ever-greater quantities of chairs and clocks, enterprising artists like Porter experimented with new machines and techniques (such as stencils) to mass produce images. It was the same basic process of accelerating the manufacture of consumer

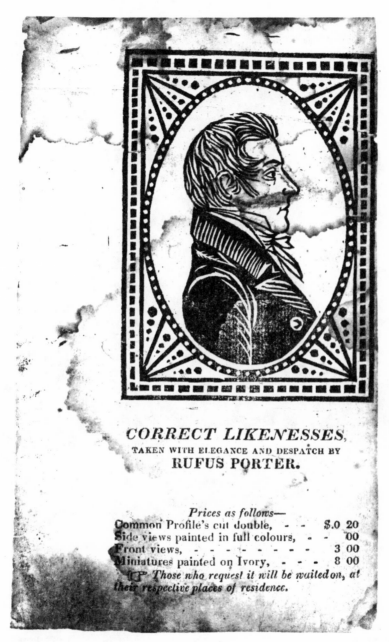

4.4. *Rufus Porter*, Handbill, *ca. 1818–1820, (courtesy of American Antiquarian Society, Worcester, Mass.)*

4.5. *Rufus Porter,* Portrait of a Man, *ca. 1830–1835 (courtesy of Abby Aldrich Rockefeller Folk Art Center, Williamsburg, Va.)*

goods.[31] And these goods found ready customers. As both producers and consumers, residents of rural America were attracted to, rather than alienated by, the standardized and homogeneous products that were becoming increasingly available in the countryside.[32]

In the final analysis, Porter's mass-produced images catered to the lower ends of the rural market. But rural communities (as we have seen) were also familiar with artists evincing at least some urban influence and some knowledge of academic models. These portraitists offered more elaborate likenesses; there were even a few who, without forgetting their village origins or audience, pushed the possibilities of rural design to their furthest form. Erastus Salisbury Field was one such artist. Boasting a career spanning nearly fifty years and encompassing several states, Field passed through a number of significant stylistic stages. He moved from farm to metropolis and back again, and finally matured into the painter of a richly embellished though still standardized product—the most "correct likeness" one could buy in rural America.

Field's talents had been discovered early in his childhood sketches of relatives made on the family farm in Leverett, Massachusetts. His parents encouraged these efforts, first by providing him with paints to experiment on scraps of cardboard and then, in 1825, by sending him to New York to study with Samuel Morse. The sudden death of Morse's wife ended Field's brief period of formal study and he returned to Leverett. There, in his first known portrait, he completed a somber-toned likeness of his grandmother Elizabeth Ashley.

Shortly after finishing this painting, Field left his birthplace. He turned up next in Hudson, New York, writing to his father that his great aunt there was helping him "in the prospect of retaining business." He claimed that his artistic prowess accounted for his excellent prospects; those who had seen his portraits "think that they are good likenesses." The itinerant reported, "I like it here very much so far," adding he would return home only when trade slackened: "I think I shall tarry here as long as I can obtain business."[33]

Traveling artists such as Field were keenly aware of the relationship between trade fluctuations and their own success. Another painter, Joseph Whiting Stock, carefully recorded in a journal his daily activities, the weather, his sitters, and business prospects. Stock relied upon the advance notice of friends and the welcome patronage of village notables to advise him on local conditions before his arrival. Once established in "his room" or by "boarding myself" he would paint portraits as long as the demand continued. Business was usually brisk; when it flagged Stock moved on. One of the most prolific painters traveling in the North, Stock reported after he finished a stint in New Bedford, Massachusetts, that

I have been as liberally patronized in this town, as could be expected. Considering the great depression of business the last three months I have had as much work as I could conveniently attend to and were I disposed to stay no doubt, there would be enough to keep me untill winter. So far as I am able to judge my work has given good satisfaction and if disposed to return next Spring I am assured that I can recommence business with better prospects as . . . money will be more plenty, and business more busy.

Over his five-month stay, Stock painted thirty-seven portraits and eighteen miniatures "to order," along with several landscapes, making a substantial profit before returning home.[34]

Erastus Field was destined to leave far behind his early and crude efforts at painting hometown kin. In the 1830s he found a means of portraying the rural bourgeoisie's expectations of elegance at a low price while relying on stock poses to increase volume. By displaying their personal possessions, Field evolved a formula that simultaneously individualized his sitters and emphasized their status. He opened the decade with a portrait of his brother stiffly seated on a hard wooden chair; his later portraits of country gentlemen adopted grander poses amid more lavish surroundings. Field always added small personal details of his sitters to their general outlines, which he quickly sketched by employing a large dark frock coat that occupied much of the commissioned space. By 1835 he could depict Eleazer Bullard (see Figure 4.6) in measured tones, subtly suggesting knuckles with dabs of paint applied in the same stippling technique as that used in the modeling of the face. Bullard's features were personalized by his ruddy complexion and unshaven cheeks, a number of props, and a dramatic juxtaposition of light and dark tones.

Field's formulation of individual likenesses achieved fullest development when he painted *Nathaniel Cook* in 1838 with an extended range of personal details and tonal coloring (see Figure 4.7). This same process is revealed in his portraits of women; Field found a comfortable pose for his sitters, arranged their hands naturally, added props to the foreground and details to the background, until his efforts teemed with color and decorative display. Field's new command of technique and color satisfied his audience's desire to proclaim their prosperity, for the artist's craft could now surround his subjects with consumer goods and sentimental domestic scenes.[35]

In 1839 Field combined these aesthetic and economic motifs in his masterpiece, *Joseph Moore and His Family*, one of the great images of nineteenth-century American life (see Figure 4.8). In the year this portrait was made Field had moved with his family to the home of his wife's parents in Ware, Massachusetts. Living across the street with his wife and children (two of which were the orphans of his wife's sister) was Joseph Moore from Windham, Maine, hatmaker in winter, itinerant dentist in summer, and professor of religion all year round. No one figure or piece dominates; the viewer's eye jumps from the black-and-white-clad subjects to the numerous, profusely painted possessions. The Moores' furnishings arrest attention with their exuberant colors and prominent position; the children Field carefully balanced around the adults. The tilted perspective and bright col-

4.6. *Erastus Salisbury Field*, Eleazer Bullard, *1835 (courtesy of Abby Aldrich Rockefeller Folk Art Center, Williamsburg, Va.)*

ors of the carpet draw the eye downward from the symmetrical windows at the top of the picture. Field successfully juggles all these items around the stenciled furniture—chairs, stands, and mirror—that completes his study of the Moores' decor.[36]

Decorative display predominated over geometric perspective in rural portraiture. Porter's flat but faithful likenesses gave rural residents elegant items with which to adorn their walls. Whereas the academic artist valued

4.7. *Erastus Salisbury Field*, Nathaniel Cook, *1838 (courtesy of Collection of Edgar William and Bernice Chrysler Garbisch, National Gallery of Art, Washington, D.C.)*

profound psychological insight and varieties of shadows and shading, the rural portrait maker aimed at a plain style in which simplicity and even stark linearity accompanied broad expanses of color and texture. Field's artisan training in house and sign painting lingered in his reliance upon repetition and two-dimensionality, but he was able to achieve enormous success within the confines of such rural rules of design.

In 1835, country editor William Stoddard reflected in his bimonthly journal, *The Rural Repository* in Hudson, New York, on the state of the arts in

4.8. *Erastus Salisbury Field*, Joseph Moore and His Family, *1839*
*(courtesy of M. and M. Karolik Collection, Museum of Fine Arts, Boston, Mass.)*

America and the hinterland's progress toward a national culture. In the traditional hierarchy of the fine arts of portrait, landscape, and history painting, Stoddard viewed "portrait painting [as] . . . the pioneer of the more exalted arts," the forerunner of "an elevated taste." This process of cultural elevation was influenced by masters such as Erastus Field, who integrated the lessons of the academic elite with the homespun ingenuity of village artisans. *The Rural Repository*, a mix of craft traditions and elite aspirations representing a unique document of American culture, closed with a ringing appeal for a new national canon based on the most traditional form of ancestor worship. "Need I say more for the art," wrote Stoddard, that "permits posterity to stand in the presence of Washington [as painted by Gilbert Stuart] . . . and in this vast household of liberty, makes the remotest descendants familiar with the forms and faces of those who laid down all for their country, that it might be dear to their children."

Aspirations for identity came from the nascent middle class of the villages, a class only gradually forging its social configuration and still wedded to a rural artistic idiom that stenciled its "elegant" ornamentation and flattened its subjects' features.[37] But in 1839 when Field recorded his celebration of the itinerant artisan's achievement—his striking portrait of rural craftsman Moore and his family—a new era was beginning. It was also in 1839 that Samuel Morse returned from Paris with Daguerre's invention.


V


The year 1839 marked a great divide in portrait making. Daguerre's invention of photography allowed some artisan-entrepreneurs to consolidate changes in production and consumption that they had initiated during their itinerant days. Building upon the labor-saving techniques and marketing methods developed by traveling craftsmen, some portraitists of the 1840s advanced into the full-scale industrialization of image making by building "the daguerreotype factory."[38] In portrait making, as in a host of other crafts, the new industrial order had rural origins.

A whole generation of artisan-entrepreneurs had promoted this change. Rural artists who had begun their careers painting a few stolid Puritan faces in the late antebellum era were offering, to Victorians still demanding family paintings in oil, a new sentimentalized image of playful children. Once introduced to the wonders of personal likenesses, however, much of the rural audience demanded ever-greater realism at ever-more affordable prices. By the 1840s and 1850s, traveling portraitists had created an appetite only daguerreotypists could satisfy; as a result daguerreotypists soon began replacing portrait painters.

A few artisans, such as Robert Peckham (1785–1865), lived through this entire process. His career represented both a typical and unique confrontation with the commercial opportunities of the rural North and the changing ways of its emergent industrial order. Peckham, longtime resident of central Massachusetts, demonstrated over the course of his career the vast changes appearing in rural New England since the era of the earlier village craftsman and provincial painter Winthrop Chandler. Peckham departed quickly from his first efforts in the 1820s, flat but effective portraits of his kinsmen's children. Like Erastus Field he matured during the next decade into a painter able to record the wealth and position of the new commercial class forming in country villages. He passed through the popular phase of rural portraiture and, emerging as a mature artist, mixed stylized and realistic modes in his rural designs. Peckham also proved capable of crossing the technological divide into photography and entering into the services of a new industrial village aristocracy. Peckham found his clients among the rising manufacturing magnates of central Massachusetts.[39]

Robert Peckham had strong roots in village and craft traditions of New England. His ancestors had moved in the eighteenth century from coastal Rhode Island to central Massachusetts in search of new land. His grandfather, John Peckham, blacksmith and farmer, was accompanied by three sons who cleared farms near Petersham, Massachusetts. John Peckham left one grandson "all my tools of my trade"; he left the future painter his legacy as village craftsman. Robert Peckham moved with his family after the Revolution to the neighboring town of Westminster but continued within the artisan fold, painting signs and carriages. Widely known for his passionate involvement in reform causes, he remained in Westminster for fifty years. His home served as the headquarters for the town's antislavery movement and he was asked to compose and recite a poem when the town dedicated its Civil War memorial. Another village resident recalled that Peckham "was a medium sized man, rather stooped, and wore his hair long with the ends curled under, a stern looking man, and his wife a very small woman, but both were kind to children." Peckham was best known as a painter of portraits, especially of local children. He traveled some distance during his career, painting full oil portraits of families around central Massachusetts and shifting from stylized, two-dimensional images to more realistic efforts.[40]

In 1822, the children of his brother-in-law, Oliver Adams, were cast by Peckham in two-dimensional likenesses in which the youngsters' wooden poses matched their furniture and toys. The flat features and the sparse detail of this painting identify Peckham firmly as a country limner. By 1831, he was capable of rendering group portraits, such as *The Children of Oliver Adams* (1831). Here Peckham pays greater attention to detail. The children's frocks are carefully painted, and the composition is graceful, with the figures grouped in the center, comfortably flanked by the window on the left and the "family record" on the right. In this portrait both Peckham and Adams were able to display their new acquisitions. The painter's greater command of perspective and detail allowed him to include his kinsman's growing possessions: the children's colorful clothing, the wooden trunk and cradle, and the bright carpet. Peckham had found his metier in the 1830s by offering vibrant portraits of children of the rising commercial class. The subject of *Mary Edgell* (1830), for example, was related to the innovative chair maker in Westminster who pioneered the popular cane-seated chair; Mary's uncle operated the local stage, a mercantile undertaking he subsequently abandoned to pursue a new career as insurance agent. The painting shows Mary Edgell with flat, stylized features, but her surroundings and accessories—four-poster bed, locket, and ceramic mug—show new realism and richness.[41]

In 1839 the daguerreotypist's art replaced the "correct likeness" with "perfect likenesses." When T. S. Arthur, author of the best-selling temperance tract *Ten Nights in a Barroom*, considered the enthusiasm for photography in 1850, he observed,

> If our children and children's children to the third & fourth generation are not in possession of portraits of their ancestors, it will be no fault of the Daguerreotypists of the present day; for verily, they are limning faces at such a rate that promises to make every man's house a Daguerrean Gallery. From little Bess, the baby, up to great-grandpa!, all must now have their likenesses; and even the sober Friend, who heretofore rejected all the vanities of portrait-taking, is tempted to sit in the operator's chair, and quick as thought, his features are caught and fixed by a sunbeam. In our great cities a Daguerreotypist is to be found in almost every square; and there is scarce a county in any state that has not one or more of those industrious individuals busy at work catching: "the shadoe" ere the "substance fade." A few years ago it was no every man who could afford a likeness of himself, his wife, or his children; those were luxuries known to those only who had money to spare; now it is hard to find a man who has not gone through the "operator's" hands from once to a half-a-dozen times, or who has not the shadowy faces of his wife & children done up in purple morocco and velvet, together or singly, among his household treasures. Truly the sunbeam art is a most wonderful one, and the public feel it a great benefit.[42]

A "Hall of Portraits," formerly the exclusive province of kings and nobility, was now priced to suit every pocketbook and fit comfortably in any room. Daguerreotypes appeared in every corner of the cluttered Victorian household. (See Figure 4.9.) Although their diverse subjects assumed poses that paralleled the homogeneity of the new national culture, their owners— especially the members of the new elites emerging in village society—were members of a generation that expected continual change, returning to the "operator's" chair several times over their lifetime for up-to-date "perfect likenesses." The speed of the photographic process, "quick as thought," matched their desire to record a vanishing set of individuals, places, and modes of life.

The unabated rage for portraits led several painters into attempts to incorporate the new technology. Some, like Joseph Whiting Stock and John Toole, simply offered daguerreotypes at their studios in addition to their efforts in oil. These painter-daguerreotypists were often uncomfortable in their new callings. At first John Toole worried little about the competition of the daguerreotype factories. Daguerreotype establishments quickly outnumbered the painters, but Toole remained confident in his abilities as a "face maker." He entered into an alliance with a photographic entrepreneur,

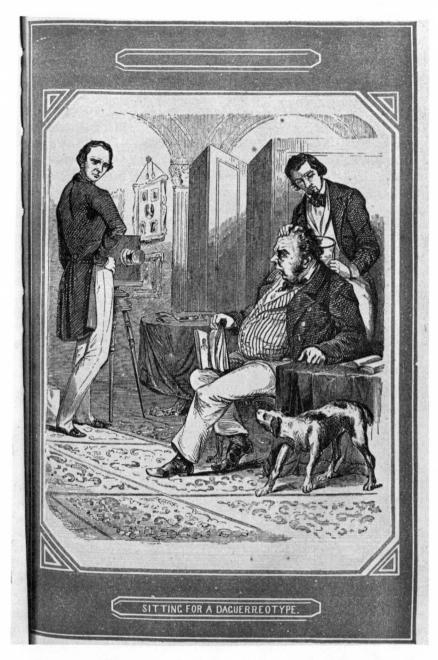

SITTING FOR A DAGUERREOTYPE.

4.9. Sitting for a Daguerreotype, *Engraving in T. S. Arthur,* Sketches of Life and Character, *50 (Philadelphia, 1850), Library of Congress, Washington, D.C.*

Mr. Munn of Petersburg, hoping to balance the two modes of portrait making. But his new partner demanded more from Toole than a change in design.

> Minis wants me to work by the year, but such an arrangement would not suit *me*. Were I to bind myself for a year he might be grumbling whenever I would go home, or take any recreation. I prefer working by the piece, and if he should not have the constant employment, I could work on *my own* engagements. I am willing to paint all he wants done so long as it suits me to stay, but not to bind myself whether it suits me or not. He knows he cannot do better than employ me on my own terms. He is to furnish a room for me to work in and give me twenty-five dollars for each large size portrait I paint for him and fifteen for head size, besides paying me extra for hands.[43]

The two planned to set up a complete portrait-making establishment or "factory," where residents were offered a full range of technologies and sizes to suit their tastes and budgets. Others, like Erastus Field, initially tried to copy the photograph's appeal and attempted a more realistic likeness. But the photograph's cheaper price and greater verisimilitude put the ordinary portrait maker at a severe disadvantage. A daguerreotypist's broadside from western Massachusetts in 1841 argued that "The value of a portrait depends upon its accuracy, and when taken by this process it must be accurate from necessity for it is produced by the unerring operation of physical laws—human judgement and skill have no connection with the perfection of the picture ... it is evident that the expression of the face may be fixed in the picture which are too fleeting to be caught by the painter."[44] As the availability and portability of the photograph fueled the "craze" for portrait making sweeping the North, the changes in technology caused shifts in artistic techniques.

The work of Robert Peckham offers a compelling example of how daguerreotypes could affect rural painters. His portraits from the 1840s, all depicting children of newly established central Massachusetts manufacturing magnates, are lavish canvases in the academic fashion. In them he assembled a new image of children and consumption. The cavorting youth of the industrialists were featured without their parents, in rooms filled with toys, carpets, tables, and chairs: the very products that spilled from their fathers' factories.[45] In *Rosa Heywood* (1840), a portrait of the only child of chair manufacturer Walter Heywood, Peckham gave little hint of the farm family or country furniture in the recent Heywood past. Born into a comfortable middle-class home, Rosa enjoyed her parent's success in producing many of the cheap wooden seats or plush Victorian upholsterings beginning to fill American homes.[46] The artisan-entrepreneur no longer journeyed among villages of the North to offer his wide range of likenesses to a popu-

4.10. *Robert Peckham,* The Hobby Horse, *ca. 1840 (courtesy of Collection of Edgar William and Bernice Chrysler Garbisch, National Gallery of Art, Washington, D.C.)*

lar market. Stylistically Peckham did travel some distance from his original wooden Adams children and even farther from Chandler's Devotions. He featured a new three-dimensionality in *The Hobby Horse* (1850), a work in which both painter and patron tried to conceal their rural upbringing. This massive canvas is dominated by its centerpiece, a toy produced by the Crandall clan (see Figure 4.10). The Crandalls were a Rhode Island family of rural farmer-craftsmen whose successful toy business led them to move, in the 1840s, to Brooklyn, New York. There they built one of the largest toy factories in the United States, using this facility to mass produce this elegant rocking horse, copied from a German hand-made model.[47]

Robert Peckham surmounted the challenges that faced the village portrait maker after his craft's industrialization. He abandoned the itinerant life with its popular promotions and left the market to the newest entrepreneurs—

the daguerreotypists. Instead Peckham ventured along the path set by Erastus Field and celebrated the changing social configuration in the countryside. He painted increasingly lavish portraits with such realism and depth that his village origins were barely visible. By taking the career of Robert Peckham as our "text," we can see the critical place of the artisan-entrepreneur in the transition from craft to industry in rural America. Peckham and his fellow portraitists, the farm generation that grew up after the Revolution, began as village craftsmen, pioneered efforts at painting domestic scenes, matured within the rural idiom, and finally confronted the popular taste for photographic "perfect likenesses," which they themselves had fostered in their faithful depictions of the village scene.

## VI

Artisan-entrepreneurs, like portraitists, were crucial in transforming the economic order of rural New England. They promoted a desire for personal likenesses and generated a taste for scarce commodities in the countryside. Drawing on their training as artisans, and using the power sources and labor organization already at hand to develop simple, time-saving inventions, these country craftsmen facilitated the manufacture of mass consumer goods directed toward widening circles of customers. No isolated set of "folk" artists bereft of communal traditions, these village artisans were often aspiring entrepreneurs, leading the charge for consumption in the countryside.

This critical change—the commercialization of the countryside—took place when the village scene was the active site of innovation and enterprise.[48] Adding up the evidence from our second set of "texts," the portraits themselves, we can see one path this new commercialization took in the rural North. Antebellum Americans in the countryside, especially those of middling status, bought family portraits to confirm their status in the village community and to consolidate their position as a new bourgeoisie.[49] The minister and merchants of colonial America were joined by the growing middle class of the nineteenth century. Manufacturers of various sorts came to sit for the portraitist, along with innkeepers and middle-class farmers, all key participants in the greater commercial activity that connected backcountry towns and regional markets. Meanwhile, the desire for "cheap and slight" portraits, ranging from paper silhouettes to framed daguerreotypes, allowed the rest of the town to join in this search for cultural identity. More and more faces were recorded in an increasing variety of poses with softer tones. Severe expressions turned sentimental.[50]

Neither the progress of our rural portraitists nor the overall process of commercialization to which they contributed proceeded in an inevitable, straight line. Itinerant artisans, such as Chester Harding, fled the farm, only to pick up a profusion of skills on their picaresque travels. Enterprising peddlers, such as Rufus Porter, promoted a variety of arts, crafts, and manufactures to rural residents. If the careers of such men led them to assume both greater professional status and an increasing artistic ability, their position never precluded decorating a sign or leaving a landscape on a wall. The relationship between individual and social change is always complex; during this era of developing cultural tastes it is a particularly difficult problem to untangle. Enterprising rural residents at this critical juncture encountered a lack of clearly defined career paths and a wealth of diverse commercial opportunities. When observed at close range, the innovative techniques of these entrepreneurs were often the result of a chance encounter on the road or a determined effort to earn a livelihood, rather than part of a sustained design. But viewed in the broadest perspective, portrait makers forged a new culture of commerce, providing the link between provincial farmers and future manufacturers and consumers. They prepared the way for the mass production and consumption of household commodities. This generation experienced a unique passage: Born into surroundings of scarcity, they left as their legacy paintings celebrating the abundance of a new business elite. Peddlers and promoters worked hard, long hours plying their trade in the hinterlands of nineteenth-century America. Only after the effects of industrialization had irrevocably swept away the village culture that had nurtured their efforts did these portraitists take on the aura which now romanticizes their lives and works.

When Erastus Salisbury Field died in the opening year of the twentieth century a local journal celebrated his achievement in an article entitled "Old Folks of the Country": "Although Mr. Field was an all-around painter of the old school the work which had been most highly appreciated is that of portrait-painting—his likenesses of people of past generation are as nearly correct as can well be made in oil, and give to posterity faithful ideas of the personal appearance of their ancestors."[51] Field and "the Primitive sort" of portrait makers had constructed a new commercial order and sanctioned a new cultural code of consumption that changed the face of rural America.

NOTES

1. John Vanderlyn to John Vanderlyn, Jr., 9 September 1825, in Barbara C. Holdridge and Lawrence B. Holdridge, *Ammi Phillips: Portrait Painter, 1788–1865* (New York, 1968), 14. On the problem of finding a "vocation" in the early republic see Joseph Kett, *Rites of Passage* (New York, 1977), and Donald Scott, "The Popular Lecture and the Creation of a Public in Mid-Nineteenth-Century America," *Journal of American History* 66 (1980): 791–801. Joseph Ellis, *After the Revolution* (New York,

1979), profiles several artist-entrepreneurs and the contradictions of classical culture in a commercial republic. Also see Neil Harris, *The Artist in American Society* (New York, 1966), esp. ch. 3.

2. The question of whether these itinerant portrait makers in rural America were "folk artists" or not is a hotly debated topic among art historians and folklorists. I found the vast literature on folk artists to be useful for its thorough scholarship on the great number of individuals traveling through the countryside and painting likenesses in this period. See Beatrix T. Rumford, ed., *American Folk Portraits: Paintings and Drawings from the Abby Aldrich Rockefeller Folk Art Center* (Boston, 1981) for its valuable introduction, which places the artists in their proper context and contains biographical sketches on particular portraitists. See also Jean Lipman and Tom Armstrong, eds., *American Folk Painters of Three Centuries* (New York, 1980); Ellen Miles, ed., *Portrait Painting in America: The Nineteenth Century* (New York, 1976). Clara Sears, *Some American Primitives: A Study of New England Faces and Folk Portraits* (Boston, 1941) is an account of a collector's search for these forgotten portraits and uncovers details about their production. The richest monographs were also collections of sources: Juliette Tomlinson, ed., *The Paintings and the Journal of Joseph Whiting Stock* (Middletown, Conn., 1976); William B. O'Neal, *Primitive into Painter: Life and Letters of John Toole* (Charlottesville, Va., 1960). I am indebted to Ellen Miles for the last reference.

3. See Robert Darnton's essays on the printers, pamphleteers, and booksellers of the Enlightenment in France, *The Literary Underground of the Old Regime* (Cambridge, Mass., 1982), where he states that "the study of careers, old-fashioned and merely biographical as it seems, may provide a needed correction to the more abstract study of ideas and ideologies" (69–70).

4. The literature on early industrialization has been most recently surveyed by Thomas C. Cochran, *Frontiers of Change* (New York, 1981), with an exhaustive bibliography. In our understanding of this process we still rely upon the textile paradigm and the factory experience. For some alternative models, see Peter Kriedte, Hans Medick, Jürgen Schlumbohm, eds., *Industrialization before Industrialization: Rural Industry in the Genesis of Industrial Capitalism*, trans. by Beate Schempp (Cambridge, Eng., 1981), which advances the "proto-industrialization" thesis with European materials; the essay by Thomas Dublin on rural outwork in this volume and his collection of letters portraying the rural backgrounds of New England textile workers in *From Farm to Factory* (New York, 1981); Christopher Clark, "Household, Market and Capital: The Process of Economic Change in the Connecticut Valley of Massachusetts, 1800–1860," Diss., Harvard University, 1982; and Maxine Berg, Pat Hudson, and Michael Sonenscher, *Manufacture in Town and Country Before the Factory* (Cambridge, Eng., 1983); William M. Reddy, *The Rise of Market Culture: The Textile Trade and French Society* (Cambridge, Eng., 1984).

5. Thomas Schlereth provides a useful guide through the thicket of material culture studies in his introduction "Material Culture Studies in America, 1876–1976," in *Material Culture Studies in America* (Nashville, 1981), which contains statements of theory, method, and practice. I found contemporary folklorists most useful for making one's way past the work of romantic antiquers; Kenneth Ames, *Beyond Necessity: Art in the Folk Tradition* (New York, 1976) is the place to begin, along with the Winterthur Conference papers edited by Ian Quimby and Scott Swank, *Perspectives*

*on American Folk Art* (New York, 1980). See also several contributors' work for case studies on craftsmen in their context: Michael Owen Jones, *The Handmade Object* (Berkeley, Calif., 1976), and John Vlach, *Charlestown Blacksmith* (Athens, Ga., 1981). Art historians have been slowest in taking up the challenge of confronting cultural change, but see Jules Prown, "Mind in Matter: An Introduction to Material Culture Theory and Method," *Winterthur Portfolio* 17 (1982): 1–20; Michael Baxandall, *Painting and Experience in Fifteenth-Century Italy* (Oxford, 1972); and Michael Baxandall, *The Limewood Sculptors of Renaissance Germany* (New Haven, Conn., 1980) and Karal Ann Marling, *Wall-to-Wall America: A Cultural History of Post-Office Murals in the Great Depression* (Minneapolis, Minn., 1982).

6. Early American art is surveyed by John Wilmerding, *American Art* (New York, 1978), and Joshua Taylor, *The Fine Arts in America* (Chicago, 1979). On early American portraiture see Ian M. G. Quimby, ed., *American Painting to 1776: A Reappraisal* (Charlottesville, Va., 1971); Mary C. Black, "Contributions Toward a History of Eighteenth-Century New York Portraiture: The Identification of the Aetatis Suae and Wendell Limners," *The American Art Journal* 12 (1980): 4–31.

7. For Chandler, see Nina Fletcher Little, "Winthrop Chandler," in Lipman and Armstrong, eds., *American Folk Painters*, 26–34; Nina Little, "Winthrop Chandler," *Art in America* 35 (1947): entire issue.

8. Little, "Winthrop Chandler," 77–78, 80–81.

9. *Massachusetts Spy*, 19 August 1790; Little, "Winthrop Chandler," 79.

10. See Laurence B. Goodrich, *Ralph Earl: Recorder for an Era* (Albany, N.Y., 1967).

11. "Reuben Moulthrop, 1763–1814," *Connecticut Historical Society Bulletin* 20 (January 1955): 50–51; see Christopher Jedrey, *The World of John Cleaveland: Family and Community in Eighteenth-Century New England* (New York, 1979) for the mental world of a village minister; also see Karen Calvert, "Children in American Family Portraiture, 1670 to 1810," *William and Mary Quarterly* 3d ser. 39 (1982): 87–113.

12.

*Population Growth, 1790–1840*

| Year | Massachusetts | Vermont | New Hampshire | Maine | New York | Total |
|------|------|------|------|------|------|------|
| 1790 | 378,787 | 85,425 | 141,885 | 96,540 | 340,120 | 1,042,747 |
| 1800 | 422,845 | 154,465 | 183,858 | 151,719 | 589,051 | 1,501,938 |
| 1810 | 472,040 | 217,895 | 214,460 | 228,705 | 959,049 | 2,092,149 |
| 1820 | 523,287 | 235,981 | 244,460 | 298,335 | 1,372,812 | 2,674,875 |
| 1830 | 610,408 | 280,652 | 269,328 | 399,455 | 1,918,608 | 3,478,451 |
| 1840 | 737,699 | 291,948 | 284,574 | 501,793 | 2,428,921 | 4,244,935 |

Source: John L. Andriot, *Population Abstract of the United States* (McLean, Va., 1980), 346, 370, 526, 562, 834.

The rates of growth on the northern frontier from 1770 to 1790 were spectacular: Maine and Vermont both had populations of less than 10,000 in 1770, but due to massive migration by 1776 they had reached 20,000. See United States Bureau of the Census, *A Century of Population Growth* (Washington, D.C., 1909). These population patterns had only slowed to growth rates of about 80 percent from 1790 to 1810, but the point is that a vast region of the rural North opened up for agricultural expansion and commercial development. For a general history of this migration by one of Turner's students, see Lois K. Mathews, *The Expansion of New England* (Boston, 1909). Malcolm Rohrbough, *The Trans-Appalachian Frontier: People, Society, and Institutions, 1775–1850* (New York, 1978) provides an overview of the experience of the "newest" frontier residents, many from New England. The slow process by which agriculture became commercialized is best captured by reading local histories of New England; an exemplary account is Ernest L. Bogart, *Peacham: The Story of a Vermont Hill Town* (Montpelier, Vt., 1948). Howard Russell, *A Long, Deep Furrow: Three Centuries of Farming in New England* (Hanover, N.H., 1976) is a mostly descriptive account; for more analysis see the works cited in n. 4 above, especially C. Clark.

13. Zadock Thompson, *History of Vermont, Natural, Civil, and Statistical: in Three Parts* (Burlington, Vt., 1853), 213–14.

14. Ibid., 214.

15. The basis for this statement is formed by my reading of autobiographies of farm boys of this period.

16. Chester Harding, *My Egotistigraphy* (Cambridge, Mass., 1866), 12. The debate on the subsistence or commercial orientation of the early rural American family is now a heated one. The "traditionalists" and the "entrepreneurialists" rage on; for a sample of the polemics see James A. Henretta, "Families and Farms: *Mentalité* in Pre-Industrial America," *William and Mary Quarterly* 3d ser. 35 (1978): 3–32; Christopher Clark, "The Household Economy, Market Exchange and the Rise of Capitalism in the Connecticut Valley, 1800–1860," *Journal of Social History* 13 (1979): 169–90; James T. Lemon, "Early Americans and Their Social Environment," *Journal of Historical Geography* 6 (April 1980): 115–32; and Robert Mitchell, "The Formation of Early American Cultural Regions: An Interpretation," in James R. Gibson, ed., *European Settlement and Development in North America* (Toronto, 1978), pp. 86–90.

17. Harding, *Egotistigraphy*, 10, 17–18.

18. Ibid., 21–26; James Guild, "Journal," *Proceedings of the Vermont Historical Society* 5, no. 3 (1937): 267–68.

19. John Neal, "American Painters and Painting," *The Yankee: and Boston Literary Gazette* 1 (1829): 45; John Neal, *Wandering Recollections of a Somewhat Busy Life* (Boston, 1868), 108. The literature by and about the "Yankee" is voluminous. Autobiographies such as *Barnum's Own Story* (New York, 1927) attest to the entrepreneurial bent of these itinerant Yankees. The traveling "pedlar" stories of Seba Smith, *The Life and Writings of Jack Downing* (Boston, 1833) and H. C. Haliburton, *The Clock Maker* (Philadelphia, 1837) contain valuable social history about nascent capitalism in the nineteenth-century countryside; also see Walter Blair, *Native American Humor* (New York, 1937); Richardson Wright, *Hawkers and Walkers in Early America* (Philadelphia, 1927); and Jay Dolan, *The Yankee Peddlers of Early America* (New York, 1964).

20. Harding, *Egotistigraphy*, 26–28.

21. Guild, "Journal," 227, 281.

22. Ibid., 312–13.

23. J. E. Bartlett, *Jonathan Adams Bartlett (1817–1902): Folk Artist from Rumford Center Maine* (Rumford, Me., 1976); Joseph Negus to Nathan Negus, 28 December

1819, in Agnes Dods, "Nathan and Joseph Negus, Itinerant Painters," *Antiques* 76 (1959):435–37.

24. "Painting," *Fitchburg Gazette*, 14 February 1832.

25. On the concept of "Village Enlightenment" see David Jaffee, "Culture and Commerce: The Village Enlightenment in the Rural North, 1770–1820," paper presented at annual meeting of the Organization of American Historians, Cincinnati, April 1983. The changes taking place at the town center during the Village Enlightenment are merely hinted at in the standard works on education. Lawrence Cremin, *American Education: The National Experience, 1783–1876* (New York, 1980) discusses the explosion in the number of schools and students or newspapers and readers. See Carl Kaestle and Maris Vinovskis, *Education and Social Change in Nineteenth-Century Massachusetts* (New York, 1980), and David F. Allmendinger, Jr., *Paupers and Scholars: The Transformation of Student Life in Nineteenth-Century New England* (New York, 1975) for studies that follow further into the rural areas; Richard D. Brown, "The Emergence of Urban Society in Rural Massachusetts, 1760–1820," *Journal of American History* 61 (1974): 29–51, traces the process from a different direction. See case studies of the following entrepreneurs of culture in the countryside for shifts in techniques and taste: On the almanac publisher R. B. Thomas, see George Lyman Kittredge, *The Old Farmer and his Almanack* (Cambridge, Mass., 1920); for an itinerant bookseller, see Marcus Allen McCorison, *Amos Taylor, Sketch and Bibliography* (Worcester, Mass., 1959); and for the village printer-editor John Prentiss, see "Autobiographical and Historical Recollections of Eighty-eight years," manuscript, Prentiss Family Papers, American Antiquarian Society, Worcester, Mass. We need more of the type of studies on "information flows" in rural areas comparable to the work of Allen Pred, *Urban Growth and the Circulation of Information: The United States System of Cities, 1790–1840* (Cambridge, Mass., 1973).

26. See Edward L. Morse, ed., *Samuel F. B. Morse, His Letters and Journals* (Boston, 1914); Chris Bailey, *Two Hundred Years of American Clocks and Watches* (Englewood Cliffs, N.J., 1975), 54–60. John T. Kenney, *The Hitchcock Chair* (Rutland, Vt., 1971), and Leah Lipton, "William Dunlap, Samuel F. B. Morse, John Wesley Jarvis, and Chester Harding: Their Careers as Itinerant Portrait Painters," *American Art Journal* 12 (1981): 34–50.

27. On the concept of rural style and vernacular design in provincial America see Henry Glassie, *Folk Housing in Middle Virginia* (Knoxville, Tenn., 1975), and the ambitious essay by Robert St. George, " 'Set Thine house in Order': The Domestication of the Yeomanry in Seventeenth-Century New England," in Jonathan L. Fairbanks, ed., *New England Begins: The Seventeenth Century*, 3 vols. (Boston, 1982), 2:159–351. For settlement and consumption patterns, see Cary Carson, "Doing History with Material Culture," in Iam Quimby, ed., *Material Culture and the Study of American Life* (New York, 1978), 41–64. Although Robert St. George, *The Wrought Covenant* (Brockton, Mass., 1979), and Robert Trent, *Hearts and Crowns: Folk Chairs on the Connecticut Coast, 1720–1840* (New Haven, Conn., 1977) study earlier materials, their discovery that craftsmen supplied regional patterns of culture by their training and design motifs bears comparison with work on nineteenth-century artifacts. See Neil Larson, "The Politics of Style: Rural Portraiture in the Hudson

Valley in the Second Quarter of the Nineteenth Century," M.A. Thesis, Winterthur Museum, Winterthur, Del., 1979; Nina Little, *Country Arts in Early American Homes* (New York, 1975).

28. Rufus Porter, *A Select Collection* . . . (Concord, N.H., 1825), iii–iv. See Jean Lipman, *Rufus Porter, Yankee Pioneer* (New York, 1969, rev. ed. 1980) for analysis of Porter's varied career, and "Rufus Porter, Founder of the Scientific American," *Scientific American*, 6 September 1884, for the details of Porter's early life.

29. See *Scientific American*, 6 September 1884, for Porter's biography. Artisan-inventors of antebellum America are discussed by Brooke Hindle, *Emulation and Invention* (New York, 1981); Eugene S. Ferguson, "The Mind's Eye: Nonverbal Thought in Technology," *Science* 197 (1977): 827–36; Otto Mayr and Robert C. Post, eds., *Yankee Enterprise* (Washington, D.C., 1981); Anthony F. C. Wallace, *Rockdale* (New York, 1980); and Merritt Roe Smith, *Harpers Ferry Armory and the New Technology: The Challenge of Change* (Ithaca, N.Y., 1977).

30. *Scientific American*, 6 September 1884; advertisement in Lipman, *Rufus Porter*, 5. See Rumford, *American Folk Portraits*, 169–72, for details of Porter's production of portraits. See Alice Carrick, *Shades of Our Ancestors* (New York, 1928) on silhou-ettists. One prodigious silhouette maker claimed a lifetime total of 30,000 likenesses (Rumford, 107).

31. See Lipman, *Rufus Porter*, 89–158, on his farmhouse frescoes; also his own series of articles, "The Art of Painting," published in 1847 in *Scientific American*.

32. David Pye, *The Nature and Art of Workmanship* (Cambridge, Eng., 1968) sug-gests a general theory of design, based on his own construction of objects, which is consistent with this account of the enthusiasm that greeted the introduction of stan-dardized products during the early days of industrialization. For contemporary ac-counts start with Horace Bushnell, "The Age of Homespun," *Work and Play* (New York, 1864), originally delivered at the Litchfield County Centennial in 1847.

33. Field quoted in Mary Black, "Rediscovery: Erastus Salisbury Field," *American Art Journal* 59 (1966): 50; also on Field see Rumford, *American Folk Portraits*, 93–99; Mary Black, *Erastus Field, 1805–1900* (Williamsburg, Va., 1963); Mary Black, "Erastus Field," in Lipman, ed., *American Folk Painters*, 74–80. Compare Baxandall's *Limewood Sculptors* for another case study of a group of artists innovating within a well-defined artisanal tradition (see n. 5, above).

34. Tomlinson, ed., *Joseph Whiting Stock*, 37. Stock's prices ranged between $5 and $10; Field charged about $5 for his large portraits and $1.50 for smaller ones of children. Field produced about one portrait a day (Black, "Erastus Field," 77).

35. Rumford, *American Folk Portraits*, 93–99.

36. Black, "Erastus Field," 77; Laura C. Luckey, "Family Portraits in the Mu-seum of Fine Arts, Boston," *Antiques* 110 (1976): 1008. See also Thomas N. May-tham, "Two Faces of New England Portrait Painting: Erastus Field and Henry Darby," *Bulletin, Museum of Fine Arts* (Boston, Mass.) 61, no. 323 (1963): 34.

37. William B. Stoddard, *Rural Repository*, 11 (1835), quoted in Ruth Piwonka, *Painted by Ira C. Goodell* (Kinderhook, N.Y., 1979), 3. I am indebted to Ruth Piwonka for this and several other references on rural portraiture. See Ruth Pi-wonka and Roderick H. Blackburn, *Ammi Phillips in Columbia County* (Kinderhook, N.Y., 1975), and *James E. Johnson: Rural Artist* (Kinderhook, N.Y., 1975). For the

high-style variant of this familiar refrain on the quest for a national culture, see Harris, *Artist*, and Lillian B. Miller, *Patrons and Patriotism* (Chicago, 1966).

38. On the early history of photography see Robert Taft, *Photography and the American Scene* (New York, 1938); William F. Robinson, *A Certain Slant of Light: The First Hundred Years of New England Photography* (New York, 1980); Floyd Rinhart and Marion Rinhart, *The American Daguerreotype* (Athens, Ga., 1981); and for an excellent case study of the reception of the new technology by local entrepreneurs, Margaret Denton Smith and Mary Louise Tucker, *Photography in New Orleans* (Baton Rouge, La., 1982).

39. On Robert Peckham: Stephen Farnum Peckham, *Peckham Genealogy* (New York, 1922), 267–69, 315–17; William S. Heywood, *History of Westminster, Massachusetts* (Lowell, Mass., 1876); and Dale T. Johnson, "Deacon Robert Peckham," *American Art Journal* 11 (1979): 27–36.

40. Peckham, *Peckham Genealogy*, 267–68; Johnson, "Deacon Robert Peckham," 27–28; Robert Peckham, *Historical Poem to be Read at the Dedication of the Soldiers' Monument, in Westminster, Mass. July 4th, 1868* (Fitchburg, Mass., 1868); Westminster resident quoted in Sears, *Some American Primitives*, 84.

41. Johnson, "Deacon Robert Peckham," 29; on the Adams and Edgell families, see Haywood, *History of Westminster*, 514, 632.

42. T. S. Arthur, "American Characteristics: No. V. The Daguerreotypist," *Godey's Lady's Book* 38 (May 1849): 352–53. This nostalgic impulse registered in other media: in the oratorical wave of centennial festivities that overtook New England at this time, and in the popular iconography of the period, Walter Rawls, *The Great Book of Currier & Ives America* (New York, 1979).

43. O'Neal, *Primitive into Painter*, 35–36. By 1848 Toole decided to stick to his old ways, even forsaking politics for painting: "I asked my self whether I could throw away my independence and self reliance, by asking J. H. Polk, Henry Clay or Lewis Cass for a living at such price, and I came to the conclusion that I would rather flatter people upon canvas than bow, fawn, and cringe to people in fine 'White Houses,' or flatter them with the subservient tongue of 'Office Seeker'!" (38).

44. Broadside by Anson Clark reproduced in Edna Bailey Garnett, *West Stockbridge, Massachusetts, 1774–1974* (Great Barrington, Mass., 1974), 109. Compare Field's *The Smith Family* painted twenty years after *The Moore Family* and after Field began painting from photographs; see Rumford, *American Folk Portraits*, 100–102. See Richard Rudisill, *Mirror Image* (Albuquerque, N.M., 1971), and Peter Galassi, *Before Photography* (New York, 1981), for discussions of the artistic scene before the new technology of the daguerreotype arrived. Both authors suggest that developments in design and form anticipated the realism of the photograph, which presents a more continuous and less revolutionary process in the history of perception.

45. Some of these Peckham portraits are unsigned. They have been attributed by Dale Johnson in "Deacon Robert Peckham" to Robert Peckham of Westminster. I have found convincing the argument that all these paintings of children from the 1840s are by the same hand. See Johnson for biographical information about the sitters.

46. Rumford, *American Folk Portraits*, 271–73; Heywood-Wakefield Company, *A Century Completed* (Boston, 1926); Richard Greenwood, *The Five Heywood Brothers*

(New York, 1951).

47. Inez McClintock and Marshall McClintock, *Toys in America* (Washington, D.C., 1961), 147–51.

48. The historical literature on the "consumer revolution" involved in industrialization is a recent and expanding one, mostly European. See Neil McKendrick, John Brewer, and J. H. Plumb, *The Birth of a Consumer Society: The Commercialization of Eighteenth-Century England* (Bloomington, Ind., 1982); Stuart Ewen and Elizabeth Ewen, *Channels of Desire: Mass Images and the Shaping of American Consciousness* (New York, 1982); Michael B. Miller, *The Bon Marché: Bourgeois Culture and the Department Store, 1869–1982* (Princeton, N.J., 1981); Rosalind H. Williams, *Dream Worlds: Mass Consumption in Late Nineteenth-Century France* (Berkeley, Calif., 1982). Rémy G. Saisselin, *The Bourgeois and the Bibelot* (New Brunswick, N.J., 1984). For the anthropologist's view see Mary Douglas and Baron Isherwood, *The World of Goods* (New York, 1979).

49. See the following for studies of the place of objects in the home: Mihaly Csikszemihalyi and Eugene Rochberg-Hatton, *The Meaning of Things: Domestic Things and Self* (New York, 1981); Joan Kron, *Home-Psych: The Social Psychology of Home and Decoration* (New York, 1983); and especially Pierre Bourdieu, *Distinction: A Social Critique of the Judgement of Taste*, trans. Richard Nice (Cambridge, Mass., 1984).

50. I draw these generalizations from the complete checklists of painters such as Earl, Toole, Phillips, and Stock along with those other artists authenticated in Rumford, *American Folk Portraits*, where the sitters' occupations were identified. Again, other craftsmen, including chair makers and clock makers, were following a similar process of commercialization, see n. 29, above.

51. *Greenfield Gazette*, 9 June 1900, quoted in Black, *Erastus Field*, n.p.

PART II

# The South

JOHN SCOTT STRICKLAND

# 5. Traditional Culture and Moral Economy

## SOCIAL AND ECONOMIC CHANGE IN

## THE SOUTH CAROLINA LOW COUNTRY,

## 1865–1910

I

Time and historical experience lent a distinctiveness to African-American life in the Low Country of South Carolina that the Civil War years extended and emphasized.* On 7 November 1861, barely seven months after the carnage between North and South had begun, Yankee gunboats sealed access to the islands around Port Royal Sound and brought the 150-year enslavement of the region's vast black majority to a close. Although the eastern portion of old Beaufort District remained the only part of South Carolina under direct Union control before General William Sherman cut through the state in early 1865, the presence of Northern forces and the transformation of black life under federal protection acted as a magnet of freedom for slaves residing between the Santee and Savannah rivers. Indeed, the prospect of sanctuary rendered plantation agriculture chaotic throughout eastern South Carolina.[1] But even more important, the early Northern successes created an environment that, when combined with the

*I am grateful to Lacy K. Ford, Vernon Burton, James Roark, Robert McMath, Donald G. Mathews, John F. Kasson, Gaines M. Foster, and David L. Carlton for reading and discussing the paper with me. I especially appreciate the criticisms of Craig Calhoun and Edward Ayers. As always, my greatest debt is to Jeannee P. Sacken. The Rockefeller Foundation generously supported the research for this and other work. Special mention should be made of the incalculably valuable advice, direction, and assistance provided by Ira Berlin, Leslie Rowland, and Joseph P. Reidy of the Freedmen and Southern Society Project of the University of Maryland and the National Historic Publications and Records Commission. Their work stands as a model and their openness and generosity is an example to scholars regardless of field.

traditional culture of Low Country African-Americans, initiated a struggle of unparalleled intensity between blacks and whites for control of the coastal lands.

That struggle suggests some of the unresolved problems in the literature on emancipation, for the efforts of African-Americans to shape their social and economic destinies in the rice and long-staple cotton growing Low Country differed dramatically from those of blacks elsewhere in the state and the South. Drawing upon a cultural heritage forged under slavery, Low Country blacks resisted the emergent capitalism of the postwar South. They rejected market agriculture and attempted to maximize their ability to determine the production of surplus. They waged these struggles by relying on long-standing work traditions. Their success can be measured by the great drops in production of the region's two commercial crops. Before emancipation, the Low Country had raised over 80 percent of the nation's rice and the majority of its luxurious long-staple cotton. By the turn of the twentieth century, both crops had fallen to virtual economic insignificance. While much of the state and the South had moved closer to the industrialized world, coastal South Carolina was to a large extent cut adrift.

The distinctiveness of the Low Country's experience has received insufficient attention from even the most careful students of the postwar South. Despite innovative methodologies and probing new questions, scholars have focused chiefly on the short-staple cotton areas of the Southern interior, and thus have continued to homogenize what was in fact a very diverse battle over the transition from slavery to freedom.[2] And, in their efforts to generalize, most tend to understate the active role played by blacks in that transition.[3] In coastal South Carolina the African-American drive for freedom with social and cultural integrity was just as influential as the visions, expectations, and power of Northern and Southern whites in directing the vectors of change.


II


Emancipation had destroyed the South's mode of production, but it had not determined the type of economy or labor that would emerge thereafter. Although Northern and Southern whites held very different views as to the solution of such fundamental issues, both could readily agree upon the need for bringing order out of the chaos that seemed to reign over the Low Country during the spring and summer of 1865. With few exceptions, whites believed that some form of disciplined and routinized labor had to replace slavery, and that plantation-based agriculture was the best means to organize it. Thus, in each of the districts supervised by the newly created Freedmen's Bureau Northern officials appointed labor commissioners who

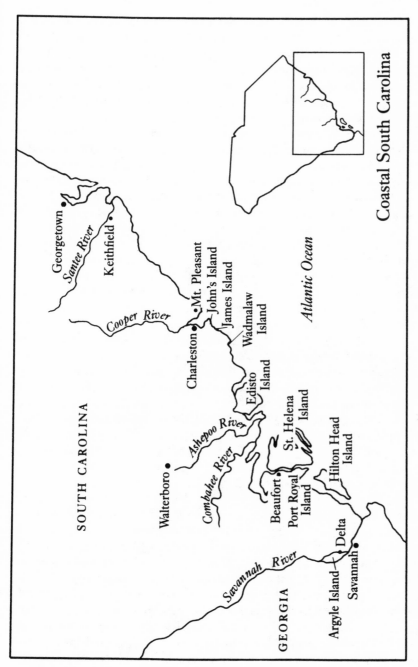

5.1. *Coastal South Carolina*

were to fashion a system of contracting that would prevent the reinstitution of slavery and, at the same time, protect the interests of Southern capital. As one of the officials observed, the balance was one that had to tip in favor of the white plantation owners, for if too much was given the former slaves, "the relation between capital and labor would be disturbed, and an undue value placed upon the latter, to the prejudice and disadvantage, in the end, of the laborers themselves."[4]

Throughout the South, blacks vigorously resisted the white drive to control their labor. They fought for self-determination and against a return to the plantation-based economy so reminiscent of slavery. But in the Low Country, African-Americans drew upon a collective experience that bolstered their struggle. For a century and a half they had known an intense social and cultural solidarity rooted in large, stable plantation communities, in the intergenerational continuity of slave families, and in the long-established practice of absenteeism on the part of their owners. Taken together, these traditions made for what E. P. Thompson has called a "moral economy": an explicit understanding of the correct economic roles of groups within a society based upon an integrated "view of social norms and obligations." The values of the community defined what was and what was not acceptable behavior for its members. Thus, the freedpeople relied upon what one author has in another context called a "material web of social relations," which placed individuals within the network of their communities as well as within the wider world. This network created "an enduring basis to collective action which did not have to be formally defined or mobilized on each new occasion."[5]

The freedpeople of coastal South Carolina appealed to their past, to their traditional moral economy, to denote the limits of "social justice, of rights and obligations, of reciprocity."[6] The system of values that developed over a century and a half inspired a defense of customary social and cultural patterns while embracing the very texture of the patterns themselves.

The moral economy of Low Country African-Americans manifested a multifaceted historical experience, but two aspects of it were particularly important in supporting the postemancipation quest for liberty and self-determination. Preeminent was the task system of labor that characterized both rice and long-staple cotton cultivation. The task system differed considerably from the gang labor system normally used in the production of tobacco, sugar, grains, and short-staple cotton. Under the gang system, hands worked as a unit, side-by-side in the crop rows, performing the same jobs, with an overseer or driver setting the pace. Labor was therefore regimented, supervised, and closed to nearly all personal initiative. The task system, on the other hand, offered more flexibility. And it had a long history.

When the first settlers of the Carolina Low Country claimed their plantations from the wilderness, they found swamps and lowlands crisscrossed by dozens of rivers and streams. After experiments with numerous crops, they discovered the swampy environment particularly hospitable to rice. Their planting techniques evolved from a relatively primitive method of sowing rice in inland swamps to the sophisticated grid of dams, dikes, canals, trunks, and gates that was in evidence by the third quarter of the eighteenth century and prevailed until the collapse of rice culture over 100 years later. Just when and how task labor emerged is not quite clear; but we do know that the distinguishing feature of the task system—a rigid demarcation between periods of field work and periods left entirely to the slaves' disposition—characterized Low Country life as early as the first decades of the eighteenth century. As rice culture then became more elaborate, task work became more entrenched, so that by the 1750s it was the principal form of labor for rice, indigo, and other less commercial crops. That rice fields were marked off into plots of one-fifth to one-quarter of an acre made task work all the more sensible, and the periodic flooding and draining of fields typical in tidal cultivation made tasks a reasonable way to define seasonal jobs. By the time of the Revolution, task labor had become so dominant that it served to organize long-staple cotton culture, which commenced in the 1780s, as well as almost every other plantation chore.[7]

The fields worked by task labor were divided into standard-sized plots. For rice, the trunks and ditches performed this function; for long-staple cotton and other crops, poles and stakes were employed. One quarter-acre comprised a task, and the number of tasks executed in a day depended upon the crop and time of the season. During the year, slaves received assignments dictated by the necessary jobs and by the individual's physical strength. The duties of full hands were considered to be the maximum, and other hands were rated as three-quarters, half, and quarter, with assignments scaled to their abilities. A given day's work, then, was clearly defined, individually controlled, and predictable.

But the real social and cultural significance of the task system lay in the fact that a slave could finish the day's work at his or her own chosen rate; a hand could focus all energies so that the jobs could be completed quickly or stretch out the tasks for the entire working day. Slaves who worked quickly often assisted others who were slower, thereby making task labor a collective experience.[8] Planters normally permitted hands who had finished their basic tasks to do additional work for compensation in cash or kind and usually provided extra ground beyond the customary garden plots on which truck crops or even rice and cotton were grown and sold to the whites. Furthermore, many blacks raised fowl and livestock while others fished the bays and streams of the coastal areas. The experience of task work thus helped to fashion a moral economy that prized the virtues of independence, self-determination, and personal achievement, while encouraging collective responsibility for the completion of assignments. Moreover, the system accustomed its practitioners to rely on nonplantation sources of subsistence, to accumulate small amounts of property if they wished, and thereby to raise their standard of living. Consequently, when Northern and Southern whites attempted to establish a free wage-labor system, they encountered a workforce used to exerting considerable leverage over the pace of production.[9]

The significance of the task system for traditional patterns of labor and its role in forging black social and cultural solidarity were not lost on Union officials during the first years of Reconstruction. Although very much committed to a market economy based upon an orderly, efficient laboring population, the Yankees acknowledged the futility of challenging an institution so deeply rooted in Low Country life. When confronted with disputed claims, Freedmen's Bureau representatives often found in favor of the hands, obstructing the planters' efforts to reestablish control over their black laborforce by eliminating task labor. As A. J. Willard, the Georgetown District agent, observed in 1865, blacks on rice plantations "have been accustomed to working by task which has always given them leisure to cultivate land for themselves, tend their stock, and amuse themselves, and therefore, very correctly, I think, that with such a change in the march of labor all their privileges will go and their condition will be less to their liking than when they were slaves." Willard knew he would face violent opposition if he supported the planters in this regard.[10] Indeed, many blacks did more than simply resist a break with the task system: they also protected their traditions from inquisitive whites who sought to gain the upper hand by probing task labor's intricate detail. A plantation supervisor from Port Royal expressed his acute frustration when he reported that "Billy would never give a straightforward answer how long it took him to do a task, or how many tasks he could do in a day. Nor would any of the others."[11]

For Low Country African-Americans, work and the relations of production constituted the fundamental elements of life. Over a century had passed since the task system emerged, and blacks had shaped much of their world around its structure and rhythms. Like working people everywhere, they had struggled to mold labor as much to their own benefit as possible, and they were not about to relinquish the power they had derived. So, despite planter efforts to the contrary, the majority of plantation work agreements in the first years of Reconstruction recognized the tenacity of established ways and included tasks in their stipulation of the laborers' responsibilities.[12]

Through their insistence on working by the task, blacks forced both planters and Union officials to accept far less control over the rate of production than they wished to have. One bureau agent echoed many others when he complained that "the Freedpeople generally do not perform more than ten compasses daily getting through their tasks at or before noon and nothing can induce them to perform more." In this manner, blacks spurned the market-oriented goals of the planters and refused to turn a large profit for their employers; instead, they worked just enough to provide the necessities of life. The same agent ruefully noted, "the crop will be small, probably just sufficient to subsist them for the year."[13]

The passage of time saw the task system's influence over the rate of production expand. Low Country blacks set strict limits to the labor they performed and the surpluses they produced. Another bureau agent complained bitterly in 1867 that although a full task worker generally had a season's responsibility set at eight acres, "a smart hand can cultivate nearly twice that amount."[14] Ralph Izard Middleton, one of South Carolina's major rice planters, rued the day he found it necessary to work his former slaves by tasks; his plantations were only half as productive as before emancipation.[15] The coercive measures available to Middleton under slavery no longer applied as he struggled to plant under free labor. And as time wore on, his problems were only compounded. Over three years after his return to the Low Country, Middleton concluded that direct white supervision and a factorylike time book were the only means to exert some control over his task laborers.[16] Although they tried continually, whites never succeeded in replacing tasking as the primary mode of work among the freedpeople; the system was thus fundamental to black life throughout the nineteenth century. In fact, T. J. Woofter recognized its significance as late as 1930 when he explained that contemporary methods of farming on St. Helena Island "were learned under the task system of slavery."[17] By insisting on task labor, former slaves preserved cultural components of their moral economy. But they accomplished more than that; they used tasking to press beyond their customary influence over labor time to seize even greater, if not total, control of production.

Together with the distinctive task method of labor, another traditional characteristic of Low Country slave communities helped blacks shape their social and economic futures. Unlike the freedpeople in short-staple cotton regions, those on the coast could, in 1865, trace their roots on home plantations to the first half of the eighteenth century. For owing to the high level of specialization required in raising Low Country crops, slave owners viewed workforce stability and intergenerational continuity as means to facilitate the transmission of essential knowledge. In fact, many rice and long-staple cotton skills were so specific to those crops that planters believed their practitioners were ignorant of more general farming duties.[18] When slaves were sold during the eighteenth and nineteenth centuries, they normally remained in the Low Country, and most often appeared on the market in whole plantation lots or in large groups representing a significant portion of the entire community.[19]

Coastal African-Americans realized the special nature of the customs and traditions upon which they relied for solidarity and distinction. As one Northern observer reported from Port Royal, "There are about a hundred people on this 'plan'shun,' almost all of them born on it. It was not the custom on these islands to sell the negroes. . . . The consequence is that there is a very strong feeling of locality, and jealousy of strangers. Phoebe, our cook . . . was bought about twenty years ago, but her family is still regarded as 'interlopers' to this day."[20] Freedpeople continued to depend on their membership in a particular community defined by plantation alliances and lineages stemming from slavery days.[21] This was so much the case that, as E. L. Pierce put it, the children were "regarded as belonging to the plantation rather than to a family."[22] When faced with leaving their Low Country homes after emancipation, many blacks preferred forgoing better material opportunities in order to maintain old ties. One man, offered the chance to buy land elsewhere, "seemed suspicious of it, as if he were going to be made to buy, and thought it as bad as slavery if they had to leave their old homes."[23]

Identification with locality and lineage remained uniquely strong in the Low Country well into the twentieth century. Woofter commented in 1930 on the significance of membership in communities traceable to antebellum plantations.[24] A more recent anthropological study has demonstrated that alliances with a group demarked by old plantation boundaries formed a central component of personhood for blacks on St. Helena Island as late as the 1970s.[25] Like labor patterns, ties on plantations—and between plantations by virtue of intermarriage—fostered a collective identity that encouraged considerable loyalty to the black moral economy. Responsibility to the local group was paramount in the system of values arising from coastal society. As one visitor to the Low Country during the early years of emancipation noted, "there is a great unwillingness among the people to testify against each other or do anything to incurr each other's ill will."[26]

III

As slaves, Low Country blacks had never known ownership of or control over the means of production. Nonetheless, the elaborate system of task labor fundamental to all types of work had accustomed the newly freed African-Americans to having considerable leverage over the productive processes of coastal plantations. And however limited their direct control over land and tools, they were at least able to determine the pace of work and the amount of surplus. As whites pressed for regular, orderly labor with high agricultural yields, freedpeople resisted, reaching for even greater control over production. So it was that they drew one of the first battle lines over the performance of postharvest and preplanting tasks.

Some of the most unpleasant jobs associated with rice culture came shortly after the harvesting and milling of one year's crop and before the planting of the next. Hands had to work in mud and water during the coldest parts of the year to repair ditches and canals and to create whatever new squares might be built. During freedom's first autumn, a Bureau official from Georgetown frequently complained that blacks abstained from any tasks not directly related to the 1865 crop. Many had signed contracts that included such work and yet, according to this agent, they steadfastly proclaimed "they never intended to contract for anything beyond the harvesting and division of the growing crops. . . ." The agent easily saw what Carolinians must have understood: Blacks knew they could be forced into labor arrangements that dispensed with the task system once they invested time in a future crop.[27] Planters and agents tried all manner of contrivances, but few if any rice workers agreed to enter the cold, wet fields.[28] In February 1867, for example, Kiawah Island planter Arnoldus Vanderhorst received some disturbing reports from the overseer of his estate, Chickessee. It seems that the hands there "positively refused" to renovate any of the ditches in the rice fields.[29] Although Vanderhorst managed to bargain for an agreement, it did not prove very durable. Whenever rice planters tried to find a way to incorporate postharvest tasks into contracts they met stiff opposition.[30]

Winter work in the rice fields was certainly unpleasant, but the unpleasantness of cold water and mud were not the major sources of resistance. If they had been, hands working the long-staple cotton plantations would have been more amenable to chores on the land between crops. It was control over labor and production, not just the conditions of work, that became the key issue in this struggle. Cotton workers emphatically joined their rice-producing counterparts in refusing jobs not directly connected to crops in which they held an interest. As 1866 came to an end, blacks laboring on the cotton plantations around Mount Pleasant refused to perform work unrelated to the harvest at hand. As a local bureau official reported, "most of the crops are now 'laid by,' and the freedmen suppose that they are not obliged to make fences, repair roads, etc."[31] One planter was so confounded by the behavior of Low Country cotton workers that he resorted to fabrication and trickery, assuring recalcitrant hands "that by doing in the Fall, the work mentioned, they who contracted another year, would be better off than they were this year."[32] The hands were not fooled. Nor were their peers on the Georgetown rice plantations where whites tried to urge them into the wet fields after harvest by insisting that public health was at stake. Workers throughout the region frustrated landowners by hiring their time for cash before a new contract season, and by hunting, fishing, and traveling to visit family and friends.[33] Mount Pleasant planters resolved the matter only when they agreed to pay additional wages for noncrop work.[34]

The resistance of Low Country blacks to maintenance work in rice and cotton fields continued throughout Reconstruction. However unschooled they were in a free labor economy, they understood quite clearly that such work contributed nothing directly to the value and quantity of the crops they grew. If ever they were to exert control over production, they had to draw the line at maintenance labor. Each fall and spring saw the emergence of new battles and the resurgence of old ones over noncrop work. The efforts of one group of freedpeople near Georgetown serve as a striking example of the style of resistance. Francis S. Parker, manager of the Santee River rice plantation Keithfield, found his hands reluctant to do any work after harvesting the 1867 crop. Rather than learning from a similar situation eighteen months earlier when his attempt to invest a particular black foreman with extra authority provoked a pitched battle between laborers and white Union soldiers, Parker again sought to assert his power. And he encountered an enraged plantation community under the leadership of Israel Lance. When Parker threatened the freedpeople with expulsion if they failed to repair the rice fields, Lance took charge and asserted that "no more mud work was to be done." Parker again solicited the aid of the Union army and had Lance and other leaders at Keithfield arrested.[35] Although the outcome of this dispute is unknown, skirmishes of this sort cut deeply into the efficiency of plantation agriculture.[36] African-Americans continued to refuse jobs they believed would reduce their control over production and surplus; their resistance was so effective that whites eventually capitulated. After the mid-1870s, rice planters relied on white migrant labor from Northeastern cities to work in the ditches and fields after the harvest was in.[37]

Although noncrop work constituted their first line of struggle, the freedpeople strove for control over every stage of plantation labor and fought for sovereignty over the land they worked. Many planters, for example James Ferguson of the Cooper River area, discovered the strength of the freedpeople's resolve when trying to make contracts with blacks occupying their estates in early 1866. The hands on Ferguson's estate bluntly told him "they would not work for any rebel son of a bitch"; and when he sought to drive them off, the workers fought back, claiming through their representatives that Northerners had granted them the land and "there they would stay if they had to fight for it."[38] Actions such as this spread beyond the boundaries of individual plantations and consumed whole areas of the Low Country. One sympathetic Bureau agent captured the spirit of the moment when he wrote, "It is really wonderful how unanimous they are, communicating like magic, and now holding out, knowing the importance of every day in regard to the welfare of the next crop, thinking that the planters will be obliged to come to their terms."[39]

Each new growing season witnessed large gatherings of freedpeople meeting in various locales to find a way to forge standard contract terms for the year. They understood intuitively that if they all bargained for the same arrangements, they all would benefit. In some cases, as on James Island in early 1867, the feelings at these meetings were so strong that the participants threatened reprisals against anyone who worked for less favorable terms.[40] Like labor leaders at other times and places, they knew their unity had to be absolute. Indeed, on other occasions committees went to plantations where contracts had already been made to encourage the freedpeople to renege.[41] For example, Kingstree-area blacks seized a potent symbol when they gathered and marched 200 strong through the town, carrying a red flag at the fore.[42] If whites or fellow laborers ever had doubts about the solidarity of these emancipated workers, such demonstrations abruptly dispelled them.

Even when there was little coordination between plantations, the refusal to enter into work agreements nevertheless was widespread and constituted a major threat to white control of agricultural production. When the first year of freedom neared its end, blacks throughout the Low Country showed their resolve to determine the disposition of their labor. As one agent noted in late 1865, there had never been any conception of the worth of rice and cotton tasks under slavery and the terms for the present crop were merely a negotiated stopgap to economic collapse and starvation. Planters and hands had very different ideas of the value of tasks, and hence, there was "little progress . . . towards contracts for the coming year."[43] Reports from other parts of the coast confirmed the general reluctance to sign contracts.[44] The end of March 1866 found the same situation from the Savannah River to north of Georgetown.[45] Many planters discovered that the hands occupying their estates refused "to contract for any white man."[46] Still others were warned against coming "on the plantation for any reason."[47] And when they finally settled on contracts, the planters were forced to concede more to the freedpeople than they had planned. "Planters who for a long time insisted on giving a third [of the crop in pay]," the bureau official from Georgetown observed, "have yielded and close their contracts for one half."[48] More than a few landowners were thoroughly frustrated because the blacks could subsist by hunting, fishing, raising food crops, and bartering. Such spheres of economic independence proved troublesome for planters and federal agents throughout Reconstruction.[49]

The freedpeople resisted making contracts again in 1867 and 1868, but in neither year was resistance as intense as in 1866.[50] For in that year, blacks avoided contracting because they believed they would be given land. And not without some reason. The wartime Sea Island experiment suggested that freedom might well include freeholds, and Sherman's Special Field Order No. 15, issued on 16 January 1865, reserved the coastal islands south of Charleston together with the rice plantations on tidal rivers up to

30 miles inland for exclusive black settlement. In March, Congress provided further cause for optimism when it authorized the newly established Freedmen's Bureau to divide abandoned lands into 40-acre plots and lease them to "loyal refugees and freedmen," with an option to purchase after three years.[51] Such developments nurtured a millennial expectation that the conquering Yankees would truly turn the Southern world upside down; it made little sense for freedpeople to sell their labor for cash or shares. Once the federal government's real intentions became apparent, the hope for land subsided, although it remained an important factor in Low Country labor relations.[52]

Freedmen's Bureau agents could not help but recognize that the desire to have land and control their own labor lay behind the freedpeople's rejection of contracts and postharvest tasks. Individual plantations and whole areas of the Low Country intermittently erupted into violence between blacks and whites, which threatened to tip the balance of power into the hands of the black majority. Along the Santee River in 1865 and 1866, for example, whites were so slow in returning to their homes that the freedpeople established virtual control over numerous plantations—and were not about to relinquish it when their former masters ultimately appeared. Francis Parker of Keithfield was just one of many Santee planters who failed to break the solidarity of black laboring communities.[53]

Langdon Cheves's Savannah Back River plantation, Delta, was the scene of violent struggle for quite some time. In 1865 and 1866, the hands seized control of Delta and refused to work for whites on any terms. They divided the plantation into plots farmed by family units. When the Cheveses had their ownership restored, blacks demanded and received the right to continue farming as renters. But the Cheveses tried to make further encroachments in 1867 and, after meeting resistance, moved to drive the blacks off. Matters only worsened as freedpeople promised to dig in, asserting that they preferred death to eviction. One leader proclaimed that "we have but one master now—Jesus Christ—and he'll never come here to collect taxes or drive us off." Ensuing gun battles left blacks and whites, including bureau agent O. T. Lemon, severely wounded. The freedpeople retained their hold on Delta, and the next year organized military companies for protection.[54]

Other Low Country areas periodically exploded as well. Harriet Beecher Stowe's younger brother, Col. James C. Beecher, found his humanitarian sensibilities sorely tested by blacks he supervised around the Combahee River. Their refusal to behave as he thought workers should drove Beecher to acts of coercion.[55] On nearby islands, blacks fended off white dominance with remarkable shows of strength. Former Governor William Aiken encountered an armed force when he tried to regain control of his plantation, Jehossee. On Edisto, Johns, Wadmalaw, and James islands, black sentries prevented Northern and Southern whites from landing. And along the Cooper and Ashley rivers, and north to Georgetown, troops had to be called out to subdue rebellious plantation communities.[56]

## IV

In the face of a socially and culturally rooted black solidarity, Northern and Southern whites joined in an attempt to tip the developing free labor economy toward the interests of capital. When potentially dangerous circumstances arose, the Union army consistently came to the aid of the planters and normally forced a compromise that supported white goals while significantly undercutting the objectives of black labor. The failure of the federal government to confiscate and redistribute rebel land choked the freedpeople's drive to become an independent yeomanry. Although coercion and intimidation were basic tools for the construction of the new order, planters and government agents found that widespread destitution and starvation in the Low Country often served the same purpose.

From the very beginning of the era, blacks found their progress toward independence jeopardized by critical shortages of the basic material necessities of life. And federal policy exploited these conditions to preserve, at least for a time, large-scale productive units. In the tumultuous summer of 1865, the South Carolina Freedmen's Bureau Assistant Commissioner Rufus Saxton made an important decision that discouraged independent black agriculture. He authorized his subordinates "to issue rations to white refugees and freedmen in case of extreme destitution, when the plainest dictates of humanity demand it. To those who are able to work and provide for themselves and fail to do it no rations should be issued."[57] At the same time, military officials ordered a cessation in emergency aid to all workers "able to earn their food by labor."[58]

When the 1865 harvest proved insufficient for the Low Country population, federal relief policy took on added significance for blacks trying to escape the plantation system. In 1866 Union authorities amended their regulations, further circumscribing black alternatives. Their policy now permitted the issuance of rations on credit to "special cases" of "resident freedmen on Plantations through the owner thereof."[59] Such action very clearly favored the former masters. As one agent claimed, "this arrangement will enable many planters to carry on their plantations more extensively and some to plant crops who could not have done so without such assistance."[60] Coupled with the retreat on land reform, federal relief practices thus had a major impact on the Low Country economy, especially after the disastrously small crops of 1866 and 1867.[61]

The quest for simple survival may have pushed large numbers of coastal blacks back into plantation agriculture, but material exigencies could not prevent them from shaping patterns of work to their own advantage. Freedpeople sought innovations to define the boundaries of work and minimize the surpluses extracted from them. These innovations were evident as early as 1865 and continued to evolve throughout the nineteenth century. One of the most powerful was known as the "two-day system," under which hands "paid" the landowner two to three and one-half days of labor in return for an allotment of land to be farmed as they chose. Sometimes the land was granted in plots of between 2 to 10 acres per family, and sometimes in larger parcels to the entire laborforce. The hands were free to plant subsistence or cash crops—or any mixture of the two—and work them without direction from the whites. And when they worked for the planter, freedpeople always relied on the task system. So it was that they had the benefit of subsistence security because of the provisioning and housing that came with work on the plantation, as well as the independence that accompanied tasking and the tilling of their own plots. It is difficult to comprehend how radical this change was, for the two-day system transformed customary plantation work, but not in the direction evident in the free labor economy of the North. Instead, the changes encouraged the type of ethos fundamental to a subsistence economy, fostering much more independence than workers knew under market capitalism. Again, both tradition and innovation shaped the postwar landscape.[62]

Northern and Southern whites alike understood the implications of the two-day system, and opposed it vigorously from the first. For those sympathetic to the freedpeople's plight, it was argued that terms could be stated so vaguely that planters could exploit the blacks through both work demanded and compensation offered. What struck most observers, though, was that the system allowed blacks greater independence than Northern capitalist ideologues thought reasonable. The freedpeople, they believed, would shirk plantation tasks for their own crops, and thus avoid regimented labor. It was also widely assumed that the blacks would prove far less diligent on the planters' crops than on their own. One bureau agent expressed a common opinion when he said that the two-day system led only to "idleness and distress."[63]

Despite steady opposition, freedpeople played their advantages and saw to it that the two-day system became as much a foundation of postwar plantation life as the task system. Indeed, blacks continually pressed the limits of the system so that it changed and adapted to an economically fluid world. By 1870, cash payments for task work, together with the standard land grant, were fixed parts of two-day labor.[64] With small amounts of money, blacks were able to participate, however marginally, in the cash economy. More significantly, the money augmented the subsistence security afforded by individual and family plots, thus providing additional breathing room. Cash compensation for tasks should in no way be confused with wage labor; the primary objective was increased reliance on the subsistence derivable from the workers' plots. Two-day labor spread throughout the Low Country as it evolved, becoming by the mid-1870s the characteristic mode of work organization for the large plantations that continued to operate. When Harry Hammond compiled his survey of agricultural conditions in South Carolina in 1883, he concluded that coastal blacks either owned or rented land, or, failing that, worked plantations under the two-day system. Even Hammond, the Edgefield planter, understood that the system prevailed because the freedpeople wanted it. They prefer it, he said, quite simply because "they are more independent."[65]

Two-day work, like the task system, became rooted in the black moral economy. Distinct notions of economic obligations, of limits and responsibilities between landowner and laborer, developed around this form of plantation agriculture after emancipation. Blacks clearly understood the terms of the bargain under which they had returned to the estates, and they did not shrink from demanding that these terms be upheld. Thus, Hammond could lament that two-day hands were not "so easily controlled as when cash wages are paid."[66] The extremes to which the blacks would go to protect the advantages they received under task labor and the two-day system were never so dramatically demonstrated as in the great rice strike of 1876.

In the spring of that year droughts throughout coastal South Carolina inflicted widespread suffering upon all classes. Whites still in possession of plantations saw in the chronic famine an ideal opportunity to break black solidarity and redefine the terms of two-day work. They wanted both to exert greater control over the way blacks farmed plantation crops and to enlarge the margin of surplus thereby extracted. After much meeting and consultation, planters agreed to begin their offensive by reducing the compensation per task from the generally accepted 50 cents to 35 cents.

Had they stopped there, the black response might not have been so explosive. But the planters were determined to restrict the freedpeople's independence further, and so decided next to make payments in vouchers redeemable only at their plantation stores. Most of the vouchers indicated that if the employee preferred cash, he or she could not get it until 1880. A scheme such as this virtually assured that any wages paid out would be promptly returned. The freedpeople readily understood that the arrangement would restrict the means by which they obtained goods they could not produce themselves. They also understood that the system of rights and obligations so firmly grounded in the black moral economy, and based on bargains inherent in the mode of plantation work, was no longer operative. Not only were freedpeople threatened with reduced control of production if whites could alter agreements at will; they were also rendered more vulnerable to natural disasters, such as the recent drought. Their very subsistence became precarious and, like agrarian people in other times and places, Low Country blacks revolted.

As early as the first of May, plantations all over the Low Country came to a virtual standstill. Even more important, squads of blacks, sometimes 200 to 300 strong, traveled from plantation to plantation forcing any hands who continued to work to leave the fields. Any resistance was punished with public scorn, or, if necessary, a sound thrashing. As with many incidents during the early years of Reconstruction, the moral economy of coastal blacks provided a social solidarity that thoroughly subverted white authority. Agricultural production for 1876 became highly problematic, and the spirit of resistance even spread beyond the Low Country, infecting workers on short-staple cotton plantations. The strike-related turmoil waxed and waned and waxed again, lasting well into the fall. Only the intervention of the prominent black political leader Robert Smalls and the willingness of the planters to return to previous rates and methods of payment defused the crisis and allowed for a meager harvest.[67]

While many Low Country blacks struggled to determine the social and economic shape of plantation labor through the extension of the task and two-day systems, others opted for the type of independence available in sharecropping and cash tenancy arrangements. And numerous freedpeople made even firmer claims to yeoman status by purchasing a few acres. Indeed, land tenure patterns in the Low Country provide excellent indication of the success of coastal blacks in confronting white efforts to determine the contours of freedom.

Throughout the postwar South, former slaves had a variety of alternatives in their relationship to the land. The most independent obtained fee simple title either through federal confiscation and redistribution, or through purchase or gift, although a good many of them moved into and out of the status of landownership as economic conditions changed. Besides these individuals, those closest to proprietors in terms of independence from white control were blacks who rented land for a fixed sum payable in cash or kind. Like owners, they normally determined what and how much they grew; they also carried heavy risks, however, for if the harvest was poor they owed the landlord the same amount as they would had the harvest been abundant.

Most of the blacks ended up farming as sharecroppers, the status we have come to see as characteristic of the postbellum South. Others became agricultural laborers who worked the undivided plantation land. Sharecroppers usually worked a portion of the owner's land, planting what they were told except in their truck gardens, and receiving a fraction of the crop as pay. The size of that fraction depended on the extent of provisions, housing, implements, and seed distributed by the landlord. Sharecroppers did have some leeway in bad years, for they would at least receive a percentage of what was produced. But the advantage was minimal at best. Because they could not choose the kind and amount of cash crop they grew, sharecroppers were always more vulnerable to white authority than were either owners or renters.

The contracts approved by the Freedmen's Bureau are the best source for comprehending the nature of Low Country land tenure during the first years of freedom (see Table 5.1). They do not, of course, tell us anything about blacks who had gained land titles, but they do offer important information about the other three groups of agricultural workers along the Carolina coast. Except for the Beaufort District (where Sherman's Field Order had maximum impact), most freedpeople who contracted with whites in 1865 worked as part of a large plantation laborforce. Only about 18 percent of those contracting were either sharecroppers or renters.

After struggling through that year, Low Country blacks were, as we have seen, determined to improve their circumstances. And they did. Again, the gains were most apparent in the Beaufort District, where over 19 percent of the blacks signed on as renters, and another 23 percent as sharecroppers. In the Berkeley District, 23 percent of the blacks sharecropped, and in Colleton 15 percent either sharecropped or rented. Even Georgetown blacks, who had lived among the largest plantation communities under slavery, made some progress along the road of sharecropping. Given the overwhelming dominance of plantation agriculture in the Low Country before emancipation, the move toward individual or family farming was quite remarkable. Nonetheless, undivided plantations remained the norm for most of the Low Country.

The 1867 contract year saw an expansion of sharecropping and renting in some districts and a contraction in others. Beaufort freedpeople continued to steer away from plantation agriculture; although sharecropping increased at the expense of renting, 60 percent did one or the other. In short, almost two-thirds of Beaufort blacks who did not own land at least worked small parcels without the direct supervision of a white manager. And we must remember that this transition occurred in just a year and a half.

The final year of bureau-supervised labor agreements was in 1868. Drought had plagued the Low Country during the previous season and undercut the independence of black farmers. As a result, only 34 percent of the Beaufort freedpeople who signed contracts did so as renters or croppers, a substantial drop from 1867.

Although coastal blacks struggled and faltered in their drive for independence, the evidence suggests that success increased with time. Census data, for example, show increasingly favorable tenure arrangements: In 1880 only 9 percent of Low Country farm units were operated by sharecroppers, who fell subject to the greatest white supervision, while over one-quarter were

### 5.1. *Labor Terms in the South Carolina Low Country, 1865–1868*

| Freedmen's Bureau District | Cash Wages (%) | Wages in Fixed Kind (%) | Share Wages ("Gang") (%) | Share cropping (%) | Tenancy (%) | Total (N) |
|---|---|---|---|---|---|---|
| Barnwell |  |  |  |  |  |  |
| 1865 | 12 | 20 | 68 | — | — | 25 |
| 1866 | 8 | 8 | 76 | 8 | — | 25 |
| 1867 | 4 | 8 | 80 | 4 | 4 | 25 |
| 1868 | — | 3 | 68 | 26 | 3 | 31 |
| Beaufort |  |  |  |  |  |  |
| 1865 | 68 | 4 | 11 | 14 | 4 | 28 |
| 1866 | 30 | — | 28 | 23 | 19 | 43 |
| 1867 | 4 | 2 | 33 | 49 | 11 | 45 |
| 1868 | 10 | 7 | 45 | 24 | 10 | 29 |
| Berkeley |  |  |  |  |  |  |
| 1865 | — | — | — | — | — | — |
| 1866 | 14 | — | 63 | 23 | — | 56 |
| 1867 | 10 | 7 | 57 | 27 | — | 30 |
| 1868 | 11 | 64 | — | 25 | — | 28 |
| Charleston |  |  |  |  |  |  |
| 1865 | — | 5 | 95 | — | — | 20 |
| 1866 | 7 | 7 | 83 | 3 | — | 29 |
| 1867 | 9 | 31 | 47 | 9 | 3 | 32 |
| 1868 | — | — | — | — | — | — |
| Colleton |  |  |  |  |  |  |
| 1865 | — | 4 | 96 | — | — | 26 |
| 1866 | 15 | 4 | 67 | 11 | 4 | 27 |
| 1867 | 13 | 16 | 71 | — | — | 32 |
| 1868 | — | — | — | — | — | — |
| Georgetown |  |  |  |  |  |  |
| 1865 | — | — | 98 | 2 |  | 45 |
| 1866 | 4 | 2 | 83 | 11 |  | 47 |
| 1867 | 14 | 2 | 83 | — |  | 42 |
| 1868 | — | 5 | 91 | 5 |  | 22 |

Note: Data were drawn from a sample of the over 13,000 labor contracts extant for the period 1865–68 in South Carolina. Lacy Ford and I took a stratified random sample based on the total universe of contracts for each district. The total sample comprises 10 percent of the 13,000 contract universe. Ralph Shlomowitz, "The Transition from Slave to Freedman Labor Arrangements in Southern Agriculture, 1865–1870," Diss., University of Chicago, 1978, also samples the South Carolina contracts; he makes, however, a serious mistake in drawing his approximately 600 contracts from the total universe of contracts available in the bureau records. This leaves him with only about 60 from the Low Country and almost 550 from what he calls "the upland region." It is our belief that such a method seriously distorts the reality of labor arrangements in the years immediately following emancipation. Taking a farmed by cash renters, who had to contend with only limited white interference. Most remarkable, almost two-thirds of the farms were cultivated by owners. And when we disaggregate the regional data into counties, a striking portrait emerges. In Charleston, Colleton, Georgetown, Horry, and Williamsburg counties at least 90 percent of black farmers were cash tenants or landowners, and in Beaufort the figure reached a staggering 99 percent. A comparison of the 1880 Low Country tenure pattern with that for the entire state demonstrates how extraordinary the patterns of Low Country blacks were, for throughout South Carolina fewer than half of the farms were owner operated and over one-quarter were worked on shares.

Data for 1890 show that the patterns persisted. Although the incidence of owner cultivation in the Low Country declined slightly, from about 63 percent to just over 55 percent, small-scale black farmers did not find themselves forced into the lower status of sharecropping; the increase in the number of cash renters accounts for all of the contraction in landownership. In some coastal counties, the number of owner-farmers actually grew between 1880 and 1890, and in Beaufort it grew by more than half, from 47 to 72 percent. Some other counties saw a pronounced drop in real property holding, but only two saw a commensurate rise in sharecropping. In the state as a whole, meanwhile, landownership became less prevalent, and both renting and sharecropping more prevalent.

The census of 1900 was the first to distinguish land tenure by race, and it provides some striking evidence. In that year, only 8 percent of coastal black farmers were sharecroppers, in contrast to over 27 percent in the rest of the state. African-Americans in the Low Country owned land twice as frequently as their peers in other parts of South Carolina. Indeed, nearly three-quarters of the black farmers in Beaufort and almost two-thirds in Georgetown had property titles. During the next decade the number of coastal African-Americans who were owner-farmers continued to increase, while the number who were owner-farmers elsewhere declined slightly. Every Low Country county except Williamsburg saw growth in this group of black agriculturalists. Coastal blacks did enter into sharecropping agreements more often in 1910 than at any earlier time, but they did so at half the rate of all the state's blacks (see Table 5.2). In Beaufort, where a black yeomanry was most firmly established, sharecroppers composed less than 1 percent of the population.

---

sample on a district basis rather than from the total population allows greater sensitivity to geographical and historical forces.

Source: Records of the Subordinate Field Officers for South Carolina, Bureau of Refugees, Freedmen and Abandoned Lands, Record Group 105, National Archives, Washington, D.C. The labor contracts for Barnwell, Beaufort, Berkeley, Charleston, Colleton, and Georgetown districts provided the data.

5.2. *Low Country Land Tenure Rates, 1880–1910*

| County | 1880 | 1890 | 1900 | 1910 |
|---|---|---|---|---|
| **Barnwell** | | | | |
| Owner cultivated | 55.1 | 34.9 | 8.4 | 12.7 |
| Cash rental | 21.0 | 35.8 | 64.4 | 46.3 |
| Share rental | 23.9 | 29.3 | 25.9 | 40.9 |
| Total N | 3,474 | 4,991 | 2,870 | 2,235 |
| Percentage black-operated farms | — | — | 62.3 | 64.6 |
| **Beaufort** | | | | |
| Owner cultivated | 47.5 | 72.0 | 70.7 | 74.5 |
| Cash rental | 51.2 | 27.3 | 28.9 | 25.1 |
| Share rental | 1.3 | 0.6 | 0.2 | 0.4 |
| Total N | 3,593 | 3,762 | 5,241 | 4,002 |
| Percentage black-operated farms | — | — | 95.7 | 93.1 |
| **Berkeley** | | | | |
| Owner cultivated | — | 53.4 | 56.4 | 65.7 |
| Cash rental | — | 43.9 | 40.1 | 29.0 |
| Share rental | — | 2.6 | 4.8 | 5.2 |
| Total N | — | 5,999 | 2,846 | 2,720 |
| Percentage black-operated farms | — | — | 75.1 | 78.6 |
| **Charleston** | | | | |
| Owner cultivated | 44.6 | 23.7 | 35.7 | 48.9 |
| Cash rental | 48.8 | 75.9 | 57.0 | 49.6 |
| Share rental | 6.6 | 0.3 | 6.8 | 1.6 |
| Total N | 4,586 | 632 | 3,470 | 2,700 |
| Percentage black-operated farms | — | — | 91.3 | 90.3 |
| **Colleton** | | | | |
| Owner cultivated | 65.9 | 71.6 | 49.3 | 53.9 |
| Cash rental | 27.1 | 22.1 | 46.3 | 30.3 |
| Share rental | 6.7 | 6.4 | 4.3 | 15.7 |
| Total N | 3,216 | 3,872 | 2,947 | 2,416 |
| Percentage black-operated farms | — | — | 63.1 | 55.1 |

5.2. *(continued)*

| | | | | |
|---|---|---|---|---|
| **Dorchester** | | | | |
| Owner cultivated | — | — | 52.4 | 53.1 |
| Cash rental | — | — | 41.1 | 33.6 |
| Share rental | — | — | 6.0 | 13.1 |
| Total N | — | — | — | 1,192 |
| Percentage black-<br>operated farms | — | — | 55.2 | 55.2 |
| **Georgetown** | | | | |
| Owner cultivated | 79.7 | 52.3 | 66.5 | 76.2 |
| Cash rental | 13.8 | 24.1 | 24.1 | 15.1 |
| Share rental | 9.1 | 23.4 | 7.1 | 8.5 |
| Total N | 627 | 1,208 | 941 | 517 |
| Percentage black-<br>operated farms | — | — | 66.5 | 50.0 |
| **Hampton** | | | | |
| Owner cultivated | 63.6 | 44.7 | 34.5 | 43.6 |
| Cash rental | 17.2 | 50.2 | 62.6 | 46.1 |
| Share rental | 19.1 | 5.1 | 2.6 | 10.3 |
| Total N | 1,605 | 2,542 | 2,024 | 1,900 |
| Percentage black-<br>operated farms | — | — | 62.6 | 62.8 |
| **Horry** | | | | |
| Owner cultivated | 85.8 | 86.8 | 61.9 | 62.8 |
| Cash rental | 7.1 | 6.2 | 14.9 | 6.5 |
| Share rental | 7.1 | 6.9 | 22.7 | 30.9 |
| Total N | 1,637 | 2,097 | 687 | 662 |
| Percentage black-<br>operated farms | — | — | 21.0 | 18.4 |
| **Williamsburg** | | | | |
| Owner cultivated | 63.6 | 58.1 | 36.4 | 34.2 |
| Cash rental | 33.3 | 37.3 | 61.9 | 54.8 |
| Share rental | 3.1 | 4.5 | 1.4 | 11.0 |
| Total N | 2,488 | 3,267 | 2,772 | 3,383 |
| Percentage black-<br>operated farms | — | — | 60.5 | 60.3 |
| *Mean* | | | | |
| Owner cultivated | 63.6 | 55.3 | 47.1 | 52.5 |
| Cash rental | 27.4 | 35.9 | 44.1 | 33.7 |

5.2. *(continued)*

|  | *1880* | *1890* | *1900* | *1910* |
|---|---|---|---|---|
| Share rental | 9.7 | 8.8 | 8.2 | 18.5 |
| Percentage black-operated farms | — | — | 65.3 | 62.8 |
| *State* |  |  |  |  |
| Owner cultivated | 49.7 | 44.7 | 22.1 | 21.9 |
| Cash rental | 23.4 | 27.8 | 49.7 | 39.6 |
| Share rental | 26.9 | 27.5 | 27.9 | 38.5 |
| Total N | 93,864 | 115,008 | 85,401 | 92,695 |
| Percentage black-operated farms | — | — | 55.0 | 54.9 |

Source: U.S. census statistics for Agriculture. See Appendix.

This brief outline of work and land tenure patterns in the postwar Low Country demonstrates that neither whites nor blacks unilaterally determined the shape of the emerging order. During the four decades that followed emancipation, the contours of society were forged through struggle. One group aimed for complete control of labor and production in order to regain a large measure of their lost wealth and power, while the other fought for an independence believed to be the just companion of freedom. Although coastal blacks were not entirely successful in achieving their goals, they relied upon their traditional culture and moral economy to attain more of their objectives than did most of their peers across the South. That said, we must now consider the nature of the Low Country production ethic and explore its impact on economic change in what had been one of the world's richest agricultural regions.

V

When we examine the economic behavior of Low Country blacks—whether as laborers under the two-day system, or as sharecroppers, renters, or small landowners—it becomes apparent that neoclassical or other models predicated on market responsiveness afford little insight. To be sure, coastal blacks sold and bought goods through the market networks linking them with the outside world, and the importance of crossroads stores and cash crop factors in the development of the postbellum economy cannot be denied. Still, this does not mean that the chief goal of the freedpeople's economic activity was exchange.

Rather, the goal of production among the former slaves was domestic consumption. The social and cultural experiences of the blacks had prepared them to behave as traditional rural peoples throughout the world who remain on the periphery of market economies. Like other peasantries, Low Country blacks tried to strike a balance between domestic needs and the arduous demands of work, and thus they failed to respond to market incentives. One scholar has labeled this the "domestic mode of production," claiming that it "harbors an anti-surplus principle. Geared to the production of livelihood, it is endowed with the tendency to come to a halt at that point."[68] Economic needs were counterposed by a nonmarket appreciation of leisure and time away from labor. The primary objective was to insure basic subsistence from year to year, not to maximize profit. And this was the prevailing *mentalité* among Low Country blacks well into the twentieth century.[69]

Black economic attitudes and the success of the freedpeople in gaining control over production transformed the coastal economy. The rise of small farming and the impact of the two-day system set plantation agriculture on the road to irreversible decline. Harry Hammond observed that, as a result, much of the best land had fallen out of use. He thought that as many as 2 million acres of the finest rice land were no longer being cultivated. Furthermore, Hammond showed that the number of acres tilled per capita in the Low Country was less than half the state average. These great changes he attributed to "that condition of the industry which favors small enterprises, and discourages accumulation of capital in large investments and the organization of labor into large masses."[70] The consequence was a system of small-scale, family agriculture unparalleled in other parts of South Carolina.[71]

A great deal of work in the manuscript census schedules must be done before we can explore fully the domestic orientation of agriculture in the postbellum Low Country. There is, however, sufficient evidence in published returns to support the conclusion that a distinct black economic ethic emerged, and to plot its impact on the development of the region. Indeed, reference to the average size of coastal farms shows that Hammond correctly identified one of the prominent characteristics of the postemancipation Low Country. In what had once been the epitome of a plantation society, farming was so reduced in scale that between 1880 and 1910 the average size of farms on the coast and in the rest of the state became almost identical. Moreover, in an area that had once been farmed intensively, the amount of land not in use increased dramatically.[72]

The declining size of Low Country farms and the decreasing intensity of land usage were part of the emerging dominance of domestically oriented production. If the freedpeople were to grow crops principally for their use rather than for the market, then smaller agricultural units were a natural consequence. But so, too, was the significant change in the volume of the region's major crops. Rice, the economic foundation for the princes and patriarchs of the antebellum Low Country, suffered most from the postwar changes. Some districts had produced as much as 55 million pounds during the 1850s. Georgetown District had alone cultivated over 3,000 pounds for every black man, woman, and child living there in 1859. Throughout the rice districts in 1849, nearly 1,000 pounds of rice were raised per slave, and though there were dips over the next ten years, in 1859 a still incredible 709 pounds of rice per slave were produced.

During the 1860s rice production dropped by as much as 90 percent in some areas. Georgetown rice plantations grew just over 5 million pounds in 1869, and farm units in other districts were only slightly more productive when pre- and immediately postwar volumes of rice are compared. While the industry struggled and recovered somewhat over the next three decades, the overall trend was decisive decline. Between 1850 and 1910, for example, mean per capita rice production dropped from 950 to just over 100 pounds.[73] In the process, South Carolina fell from leadership in rice culture to a weak third; by 1920, the state grew barely 3 percent of its prewar crop. A long-term slide in rice prices undoubtedly contributed to this trajectory, as did increasing competition from western rice producers. But most important was the desire of Low Country blacks to balance economic needs with goals unrelated to the market-affected rice crop.[74] Faced with this assertion of the freedpeople's independence, large landowners had little choice but to take their land out of production. Unlike the developing dry culture regions of Louisiana and Arkansas where mechanization permitted planters to reduce their laborforce and increase their crop tenfold over what had been the norm in South Carolina, the structural skeleton of the old tidal fields prevented the introduction of new technology.[75] In the last decades of the nineteenth century, rice virtually ceased to be a market crop in the Low Country: Not only were far fewer pounds grown but most of what was grown remained in the domestic economy (see Table 5.3 and Figure 5.2).

Because the region's other major commercial crop, long-staple cotton, had always been produced on a smaller scale, one might expect it to have increased in importance as emancipation reduced the size of plantation agriculture. And this might well have been the case had the black economic ethic not achieved preeminence. For the domestic orientation of production cut deeply into the amount of long-staple cotton cultivated. During the final decade of the antebellum era, long-staple cotton, worth sometimes as much as $2 per pound, had been produced at sharply increasing rates. Plantations between the Santee and Savannah rivers, the geographical limits of Sea Island cotton in South Carolina, grew almost twice as many bags in 1858 as in 1850. But the first long-staple crop after emancipation was nearly 90

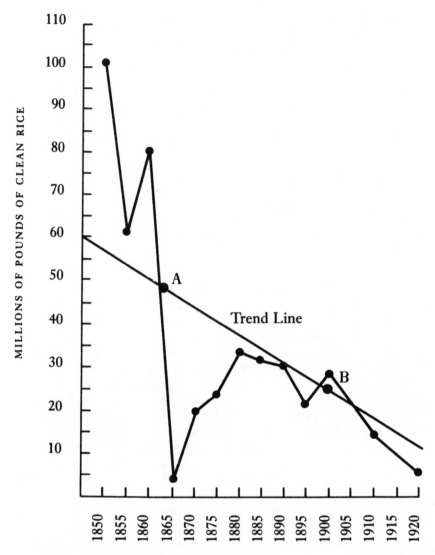

5.2. *Aggregate Rice Production in South Carolina, 1850–1920 (see Appendix for sources and methods of calculation)*

5.3. *Aggregate South Carolina Rice Crops, 1850–1920*

| Year | Clean Rice (lb.) | Year | Clean Rice (lb.) |
|---|---|---|---|
| 1850 | 101,540,000 | 1890 | 30,338,951 |
| 1855 | 59,415,060 | 1895 | 22,364,800 |
| 1860 | 77,212,800 | 1900 | 29,836,881 |
| 1865 | 1,977,120 | 1910 | 15,353,510 |
| 1870 | 20,352,040 | 1920 | 3,471,882 |
| 1875 | 22,688,640 | | |
| 1880 | 32,808,834 | | |
| 1885 | 32,366,700 | | |

Source: For sources of these data and the method of their calculation, see Appendix. These data are the basis of Figure 5-1.

percent smaller, falling from 47,500 to just over 5,000 bags. By 1869 the crop had made some recovery, but the harvest was still a mere 25 percent of its heyday. And during the last third of the century, the rate of its decline was even sharper than that for rice. After 1900, the boll weevil ushered in the end: The center of world production shifted to Egypt where a more reliable laborforce could be found.[76] (See Table 5.4 and Figure 5.3.)

The story of short-staple cotton in the Low Country is quite different. This crop, which could be grown more effectively on small units with low capitalization, showed an almost steady increase between 1870 and 1910. Average production for each black resident rose from just under three-tenths of a bale in 1850 to over one and two-tenths bales in 1910, amounting to a per capita surge of nearly 400 pecent. We should not conclude, however, that this represented either a decisive step into the market economy or significant economic growth. Short-staple cotton production increased as long-staple production decreased; this was simply because short-staple cotton was the cash crop of choice in the postbellum South. Coastal blacks came to depend on the crop for the money they needed, and the short-staple variety was hardier and easier to grow on small parcels of land.

One final measure of the domestication of agriculture is the ratio of commercial to subsistence crops. Comparing, for example, short-staple cotton with food corn should give us an accurate index of the degree to which increasing cotton production affected the market orientation of the Low Country. Thus, while the cotton to corn ratios for the Low Country and the state at large were roughly similar during the antebellum era, between 1870 and 1910 the statewide ratio ranged from 50 to over 100 percent higher. In

5.4. *Aggregate South Carolina Sea Island Cotton Production, 1850–1900*

| Year | Clean Cotton (bags) | Year | Clean Cotton (bags) |
|------|------|------|------|
| 1850 | 28,362 | 1873 | 11,703 |
| 1852 | 32,814 | 1875 | 8,188 |
| 1854 | 40,841 | 1877 | 11,106 |
| 1856 | 45,314 | 1879 | 9,966 |
| 1858 | 47,592 | 1881 | 15,971 |
| 1865 | 5,503 | 1883 | 9,397 |
| 1867 | 9,266 | 1886 | 7,327 |
| 1869 | 13,049 | 1900 | 9,209 |
| 1871 | 11,585 | | |

Source: For sources of these data and the method of their calculation, see Appendix. These data are the basis of Figure 5-2.

fact, the coastal cotton to corn ratio was lower than the aggregate ratio for any of the five major cotton states in the period.[77] Combined with other evidence, this clearly indicates that short-staple production along the coast was geared more toward use than toward exchange.

## VI

As the South Carolina Low Country entered the twentieth century, its social order stood in great contrast to the plantation system only forty years before. Once part of the most productive agricultural region in the state, the coastal counties had by 1900 traveled far down the path of economic fragmentation and decline. Conversely, districts above the fall line rushed headlong into the industrializing modern economy. But the prevailing interpretations of postwar Southern agriculture do not adequately account for the particular direction taken by the Low Country. Deriving their evidence chiefly from short-staple regions, most studies do not throw enough light on the traditional culture of Low Country blacks. Yet African-Americans in that area struggled hard for control over the means, pace, and nature of production. In so doing, they drew their strength from a moral economy rooted in a century and a half of social life that led them to resemble more peasant peoples throughout much of the world than commercially oriented farmers elsewhere in America. Barely a generation removed from slavery, they succeeded in exerting great influence on the society in which they lived. And they transformed a region of enormous plantations into one of

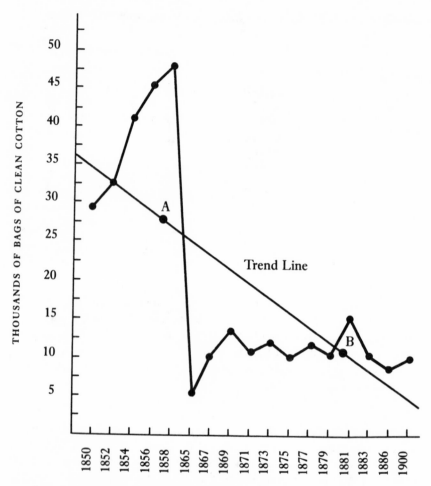

5.3. *Aggregate South Carolina Long-Staple Cotton Production, 1850–1900 (see Appendix for sources and methods of calculation)*

small farms operated by freeholders and renters. If the process ultimately resulted in economic underdevelopment, the freedpeople nonetheless acted both to preserve a familiar world and to expand their freedom and independence. It is in this context that we must consider their triumphs and failures.

APPENDIX: Sources and Methods

The sources for Table 5.2 and notes 72, 73, and 74 are as follows: J. D. B. DeBow, *The Seventh Census of the United States, 1850* (Washington, D.C., 1853); Joseph C. G. Kennedy, *Agriculture of the United States in 1860 Compiled from the Eighth Census* (Washington, D.C., 1864); Francis Walker, *The Statistics of the Wealth and Industry of the United States Compiled from the Ninth Census* (Washington, D.C., 1872); Department of the Interior, Census Office, *Report of the Production of Agriculture as Returned by the Tenth Census* (Washington, D.C., 1883); Department of the Interior, Bureau of the Census, *Report on the Statistics of Agriculture in the United States at the Eleventh Census: 1890* (Washington, D.C., 1895); Department of the Interior, Bureau of the Census, *Twelfth Census of the United States Taken in the Year 1900: Agriculture, Part II, Crops and Irrigation* (Washington, D.C., 1902); and Department of the Interior, Bureau of the Census, *Thirteenth Census of the United States taken in the Year 1910; Agriculture, 1909 and 1910; Reports by the States with Statistics for Counties, Nebraska-Wyoming, Alaska, Hawaii and Porto Rico* (Washington, D.C., 1913). The rates for land tenure in Table 5.2 were calculated in a straightforward manner for 1880, 1890, and 1900. For 1880 and 1890, the data are for all farms; for 1900 and 1910, the figures represent only black farmers. The tenancy data for 1910 are not so clearly derived as those for the other three intervals. The census reports tenancy in two ways for that year: all share and all cash renters irrespective of race; or all black tenants without regard for type. I estimated the numbers for black share and cash tenants using the percentage of black farmers in each county. When the number of black sharecroppers and renters was totaled, it was in every case less than 1 percent different from the reported number of black tenants of all types.

The cotton to corn ratio was calculated using Stanley Engerman's method of pounds of cotton divided by bushels of corn. This is a more direct calculation than that used by other scholars. See note 77 for a full citation of this literature.

The statistics for rice production presented in Table 5-3 and graphically represented in Figure 5.2 were derived from two sources: the Agricultural Census in decennial years and S. A. Knapp, "The Present Status of Rice Culture in the United States." *U.S. Department of Agriculture Division of Botany Bulletin no. 22* (Washington, D.C., 1899) for intervening years. These two sources did not, however, provide comparable data; the census reported rice in pounds of rough rice and Knapp used clean rice figures. According to John Hetrick, "Treatise on the Economics of Rice Production in Georgetown County, South Carolina: The Middle Period, 1786 to 1860," M.A. Thesis, University of South Carolina, 1979, it took 945 pounds of rough rice to make 600 pounds of clean, a difference of approximately 37 percent. This statistic was used in converting rough rice data in the census. Knapp's figures were reported for both North and South Carolina through 1880. As available information shows that South Carolina consistently produced between 78 and 82 percent of that amount, Knapp's reports to 1880 were reduced by 20 percent to obtain South Carolina data. After 1880, he disaggregated his information.

The data for Sea Island cotton presented in Table 5.4 and portrayed in Figure 5.3 were taken from *The Charleston Yearbook* for 1880, 1883, and 1887 and from the 1900 census, the only one to report this information.

The calculation of the trend line in Figures 5.2 and 5.3 is based on the method of Ya-Lun Chou, *Statistical Analysis with Business and Economic Applications* (New York, 1969), 540–42.

NOTES

1. See Willie Lee Rose, *Rehearsal for Reconstruction: The Port Royal Experiment* (Indianapolis, 1964) and George C. Rogers, *The History of Georgetown County, South Carolina* (Columbia, S.C., 1970) for discussions of the Low Country during the Civil War.

2. The literature in journals and books is far too extensive to cite in full here. The principal econometric contributions are Roger Ransom and Richard Sutch, *One Kind of Freedom: The Economic Consequences of Emancipation* (New York, 1977); Robert Higgs, *The Transformation of the American Economy, 1865–1914: An Essay in Interpretation* (New York, 1971); Robert Higgs, *Competition and Coercion: Blacks in the American Economy, 1865–1914* (New York, 1977); Stephen DeCanio, *Agriculture in the Postbellum South: The Economics of Production and Supply* (Cambridge, Mass., 1974); and Jay Mandle, *The Roots of Black Poverty: The Southern Plantation Economy after the Civil War* (Durham, N.C., 1978). The main works of social history are Jonathan M. Wiener, *Social Origins of the New South: Alabama, 1860–1885* (Baton Rouge, La., 1978); Dwight Billings, *Planters and the Making of a "New South": Class, Politics, and Development in North Carolina, 1865–1900* (Chapel Hill, N.C., 1978); Leon Litwack, *Been in the Storm So Long: The Aftermath of Slavery* (New York, 1979); and Lawrence Powell, *New Masters: Northern Planters During the Civil War and Reconstruction* (New Haven, Conn., 1980). Useful as a survey of the econometric literature is William N. Parker, "The South in the National Economy, 1865–1970," *Southern Economic Journal* 46 (1980):1019–48. The most thoughtful treatment of the literature is Harold D. Woodman, "Sequel to Slavery: The New History Views the Postbellum South," *Journal of Southern History* 48 (1977):523–54. The major literature on postwar South Carolina tends, also, to underplay variations within the state. See Francis Butler Simkins and Robert H. Woody, *South Carolina During Reconstruction* (Chapel Hill, N.C., 1932); Joel Williamson, *After Slavery: The Negro in South Carolina During Reconstruction, 1865–1872* (Chapel Hill, N.C., 1965); Martin Abbott, *The Freedmen's Bureau in South Carolina, 1865–1872* (Chapel Hill, N.C., 1967); and Thomas Holt,

*Black Over White: Negro Political Leadership in South Carolina During Reconstruction* (Urbana, Ill., 1977).

3. Notable exceptions to this are Wiener, *Social Origins*; Litwack, *Been in the Storm*; and Holt, *Black Over White*.

4. See the discussions in Simkins and Woody, *South Carolina During Reconstruction*; Williamson, *After Slavery*; Abbott, *Freedmen's Bureau*; and George R. Bently, *A History of the Freedmen's Bureau* (Philadelphia, 1955). The quotation is from Captain Charles Soule to General O. O. Howard, 12 June 1865, Records of the Subordinate Field Officers for South Carolina (hereafter cited as SFO), Columbia Office, Miscellaneous Records, series 3129, Bureau of Refugees, Freedmen and Abandoned Lands, Record Group 105 (hereafter cited as BRFAL), National Archives, Washington, D.C. A fuller version of this quotation can be found in the Registers and Letters Received by the Commissioner of the Bureau of Refugees, Freedmen, and Abandoned Lands, Record Group 105, microcopy 752, reel 17, National Archives (hereafter cited as Howard Records, with reel number).

5. E. P. Thompson, "The Moral Economy of the English Crowd in the Eighteenth Century," *Past and Present* 50 (1971):76–136. See also E. P. Thompson, *The Making of the English Working Class* (New York, 1963, repr. 1968). The second quote is from Craig Calhoun, *The Question of Class Struggle: Social Foundations of Popular Radicalism during the Industrial Revolution* (Chicago, 1982), 46. Calhoun offers a brilliant critique and, ultimately, extension of Thompson's notion of moral economy on pp. 34–57 of his important book. He maintains that Thompson was heading in the right direction in emphasizing the importance of traditional culture in popular, radical responses to social change but that he expounded his notions without reference to "sociological context." The people of the Low Country provide an excellent opportunity to see the interactions of culture and society in the time of major social change.

6. James C. Scott, *The Moral Economy of the Peasant: Rebellion and Subsistence in Southeast Asia* (New Haven, Conn., 1976), vii, 10. Scott's argument came to me after I formulated the argument presented here; even though it deals with a completely different cultural and historical context, the book was very helpful in refining my ideas as I revised this essay. I also found Jeffery M. Paige's *Agrarian Revolution: Social Movements and Export Agriculture in the Underdeveloped World* (New York, 1975) and Michael T. Taussig's *The Devil and Commodity Fetishism in South America* (Chapel Hill, N.C., 1980) to be very helpful and provocative. Samuel L. Popkin in *The Rational Peasant: The Political Economy of Rural Society in Vietnam* (Berkeley, Calif., 1979) attempts a systematic refutation of "moral economy" when applied to peasant societies. Although Popkin should be read by those interested in the concept, I do not feel he successfully counters the notion of moral economy as a cultural force in shaping social and economic change.

7. Citations to the task system in primary sources are numerous, the first dating from the early eighteenth century. There is sufficient evidence to conclude that by this time, task labor was firmly established in the Low Country. As the antebellum period progressed, discussion of the ins and outs of tasking became commonplace in agricultural literature and from plantation records it is very clear that the mode of labor constituted the backbone of coastal agriculture. The best early appreciation

and description of the importance of task work in comparison with gang labor can be found in Lewis C. Gray, *History of Agriculture in the Southern States to 1860*, 2 vols. (Washington, D.C., 1933), 1:550–56. U. B. Phillips also discussed task labor in *American Negro Slavery* (New York, 1918). Two essays came to my attention after I had formulated the argument of this paper. Thomas F. Armstrong, "From Task Labor to Free Labor: The Transition along Georgia's Rice Coast, 1820–1880," *Georgia Historical Quarterly* 64 (Winter 1980):432–47, raises some of the issues I address, but because of the focus of his work he does not develop them fully. Philip D. Morgan, "Work and Culture: The Task System and the World of Low Country Blacks, 1700–1880," *William and Mary Quarterly* 3d ser. 13 (1982):563–99, is first-rate and should be referred to as the most complete exploration of the origins of the task system we have. He has mined the sources and presents them faithfully. I disagree with him rather strongly, however, about the implications of task labor for the black moral economy and for the economic behavior of freedpeople. Our differences should be apparent in the final section of this essay. Morgan goes over much of the same material and most of the same arguments in "The Ownership of Property by Slaves in the Mid-Nineteenth Century Low Country," *Journal of Southern History* 49 (1983):399–420.

8. For the origin and development of the task system see the two articles by Morgan, cited in n. 7, above.

9. Morgan emphasizes the aspects of the task system that encouraged accumulation. Our differences should be apparent.

10. A. J. Willard to George W. Hooker, 7 November 1865, Letters Received, series 4112, Departments of the South and South Carolina and the Second Military District, Record Group 393, part I, National Archives (hereafter cited as DOS).

11. William Allen Diary, 1 June 1864, microfilm of the original at the Wisconsin Historical Society, South Caroliniana Library, Columbia, S.C. (hereafter cited as SCL).

12. The labor contracts for the Low Country in SFO/BRFAL provide excellent evidence of the tenacity with which freedpeople held to the task system after emancipation.

13. S. F. Smith to H. W. Smith, 25 April 1866, Letters Received, series 4112, DOS.

14. A. J. Willard to H. V. Smith, Georgetown District, Letters Sent, SFO/BRFAL.

15. Ralph Izard Middleton to "General," December 1867, series 4111, box 11, DOS.

16. Ralph Izard Middleton to H. A. Middleton, 1869, Middleton Papers, Cheves Collection, South Carolina Historical Society, Charleston, S.C.

17. T. J. Woofter, *Black Yeomanry: Life on St. Helena Island* (New York, 1930), 133.

18. See for example the comments in Edward Barnwell Heyward to Allen C. Izard, 16 July 1866, Heyward Family Papers, SCL. Thomas B. Chaplin, a St. Helena cotton planter, frequently made references to the differences between Low Country and Upcountry blacks. See the Thomas B. Chaplin Plantation Diary, South Carolina Historical Society.

19. Planters' papers are replete with references to coastal blacks being sold in lots. See, for example, the R. F. W. Allston Papers and the Alonzo White Papers,

both at the South Carolina Historical Society. The former gives the planter's perspective on the matter, as he bought, sold, transferred, and oversaw the transferal of whole lots of slaves over a forty-year period; the latter, a major Charleston slave trader's records, allows a broader indication of how plantation groups were often kept intact.

20. William Allen Diary, 25 November 1863, SCL.

21. Examples of the significance of identification with a particular community can be found in many places. See, for instance, Rufus Saxton to E. M. Stanton, 16 August 1862, Saxton Papers, Yale University Library, New Haven, Conn.; G. S. Bryan to Williams Middleton, 7 May 1865, Middleton Family Papers, Middleton Place Archives, Charleston, S.C.; William Nearland to William Stone, 12 July 1867, Barnwell District, SFO/BRFAL.

22. E. L. Pierce to S. P. Chase, 2 June 1862, Port Royal Correspondence, Records of the Treasury Department, Record Group 56, National Archives.

23. William Allen Diary, 25 November 1863, SCL.

24. Woofter, *Black Yeomanry*, 8.

25. Patricia Guthrie, "Catching Sense: The Meaning of Plantation Membership Among Blacks on St. Helena Island, South Carolina," Diss., University of Rochester, 1977.

26. William Allen Diary, 16 June 1864, SCL.

27. A. J. Willard to George W. Hooker, 7 November 1865, Letters Received, series 4112, DOS.

28. Ben Allston, F. S. Parker, and others to Col. Williams, 20 October 1865, series 2392, Records of the United States Continental Commands, Record Group 393, part II (hereafter cited as Continental Commands), National Archives; A. J. Willard to G. W. Hooker, 20 October 1865, Continental Commands; and Charles Devens to W. L. Burger, 13 November 1865, Letters Received, series 4112, DOS.

29. J. M. Hucks of Chickessee to "Sir," 4 February 1867, Arnoldus Vanderhorst Papers, South Carolina Historical Society.

30. E. W. Everson to E. L. Deane, 31 October 1867, Georgetown District, Letters Sent, SFO/BRFAL. See also Ralph Izard Middleton to E. W. Everson, 22 November 1867, Georgetown District, Letters Received, SFO/BRFAL; J. A. McCall to G. E. Pinegree, 26 November 1867, Darlington District, Letters Received, SFO/BRFAL; and J. E. Lewis to G. E. Pinegree, 30 November 1867, Marion District, Letters Sent, SFO/BRFAL.

31. E. F. O'Brien to A. M. Crawford, 10 August 1866, Mount Pleasant District, Letters Received, SFO/BRFAL. See, for example, F. H. Whittier to Lt. Fillebrown, 4 October 1865; and J. J. Upham to J. W. Clous, 14 November 1865, Letters Received, series 4112, DOS.

32. R. Y. Dwight to H. W. Leidtke, 18 August 1866, Moncks Corner District, Letters Received, SFO/BRFAL.

33. H. W. Leidtke to "Major," 31 August 1866, Records of the Assistant Commissioner for South Carolina, microcopy 869, reel 34, Records of the Bureau of Refugees, Freedmen, and Abandoned Lands, Record Group 105, National Archives (hereafter cited as AC/BRFAL, with reel number).

34. R. K. Scott to O. O. Howard, 22 October 1866, AC/BRFAL, reel 1.

35. The material on Keithfield is extensive and is, in conjunction with events

elsewhere, worthy of an article in itself. The major outlines of the situation in 1867 can be found in Francis S. Parker to E. W. Everson, 11 November 1867, Georgetown District, Registered Letters Received, SFO/BRFAL; Everson to Parker, 24 November 1867, and Everson to W. H. Read, 11 November 1867, Georgetown District, Letters Sent, SFO/BRFAL.

36. See, for example, W. C. Daniels to H. C. Brandt, 10 February 1868, Rice Hope District, Letters Received, SFO/BRFAL; and R. I. Middleton to H. A. Middleton, 24 August 1869, Middleton Papers, Cheves Collection, South Carolina Historical Society.

37. Henry W. Ravenel, "The Last Days of Rice Planting," in David Doar, ed., *Rice and Rice Planting in the South Carolina Low Country*, Contributions of the Charleston Museum, vol. 8 (Charleston, S.C., 1936), 45–46.

38. H. F. Hawkins to Commander of the Military District of Charleston, 1 January 1866, Heyward Ferguson Papers, Southern Historical Collection, University of North Carolina at Chapel Hill.

39. H. W. Smith to "Lieut.," 21 January 1866, Letters Received, series 4112, DOS.

40. R. K. Scott to O. O. Howard, 25 January 1867, ibid.

41. W. H. Holton to J. S. Guenther, 31 January 1867, Columbia District, SFO/BRFAL.

42. James W. Johnson to A. M. Crawford, 4 February 1866, Governors' Papers, South Carolina Department of Archives and History, Columbia, S.C.

43. A. J. Willard to W. H. Smith, 13 November 1865, Georgetown District, Letters Sent, SFO/BRFAL.

44. F. H. Whittier to C. B. Fillebrown, 20 November 1865, Letters Received, series 4112, DOS.

45. H. S. Hawkins to Charleston District Headquarters, ibid.

46. W. H. Wesson to A. B. Andrews, 7 February 1866, A. B. Andrews Papers, Southern Historical Collection.

47. B. T. Sellers to Williams Middleton, 15 February 1866, Middleton Papers, Middleton Place Archives.

48. B. F. Smith to H. W. Smith, 20 February 1866, Grahamville District, Letters Sent, SFO/BRFAL.

49. B. F. Smith to M. N. Rice, 20 February 1866, Letters Received, series 4112, DOS; H. W. Leidtke to H. W. Smith, 15 May 1866, Columbia District, Letters Sent, SFO/BRFAL; R. K. Scott to O. O. Howard, 21 May 1866, AC/BRFAL, reel 1; R. K. Scott to O. O. Howard, 20 May 1868, AC/BRFAL, reel 2; W. C. Daniel to H. C. Brandt, 20 July 1866, Rice Hope District, Letters Received, SFO/BRFAL.

50. See, for example, A. J. Gonzales to Emmie, Summer 1867, Elliott–Gonzales Papers, Southern Historical Collection; James R. Sparkman to Ben Allston, 23 November 1866, in J. Harold Easterby, ed., *The South Carolina Rice Plantation as Revealed in the Papers of Robert F. W. Allston* (Chicago, 1941), 224–25; R. K. Scott to O. O. Howard, 25 January 1867, Letters Received, series 4112, DOS; J. D. Waring to G. A. Williams, 13 January 1867, Summerville District, Letters Received, SFO/BRFAL; William Nearland to William Stone, 27 February 1868, Barnwell District, Letters Sent, SFO/BRFAL; F. E. Irving to F. W. Leidtke, 14 January 1868, Moncks Corner District, Letters Sent, SFO/BRFAL.

51. The best brief discussion of land policy is still LaWanda Cox, "The Promise of Land for the Freedmen," *Mississippi Valley Historical Review* 45 (1958–59):413–40; on South Carolina see, Carol K. R. Bleser, *The Promised Land* (Columbia, S.C., 1970); and on the general question, Claude F. Oubre, *Forty Acres and a Mule: The Freedmen's Bureau and Black Land Ownership* (Baton Rouge, La., 1978).

52. For a discussion of the problems inherent in overemphasizing the importance of landownership, see Herman Beltz, "The New Orthodoxy in Reconstruction Historiography," *Reviews in American History* 1 (1973):106–13.

53. The Santee area remained unsettled for much of 1866 and after; discussions of many incidents appear throughout the Bureau and Military Records at the National Archives. See, for example, William B. Pringle to General D. Sickles, 18 January 1866, series 2392, Continental Commands; D. T. Corbin to H. W. Smith, 1 February 1866, AC/BRFAL, reel 9; and C. V. J. Wilson to Major O'Brien, 18 July 1866, Kingstree District, Letters Received, SFO/BRFAL. Typical of the troubles encountered on the Santee is the comment of E. J. Parker to D. W. Jordan, that in trying to get the blacks on the plantation to contract and then to work, one Isaac Reid "would not do it. . . . He cut up all sorts of Shines—said he would suffer to be shot down before he would sign it—That he did not intend to do anything for any man that he had been under all his life," 29 September 1865, D. W. Jordan Papers, Duke University Library, Durham, N.C.

54. The material on Delta is more extensive than on any other single plantation in the Low Country. It can be found in the Bureau and Military Records for South Carolina and Georgia at the National Archives. Newspapers also carry frequent reports of the incidents. See, for example, the Savannah, Charleston, and Beaufort papers for 1865–1868.

55. The Beecher correspondence is the most extensive and expressive of a single opinion of any of the federal agents in South Carolina. It can be found in the James C. Beecher Papers, Duke University Library; in DOS and Continental Commands; and in SFO/BRFAL for Summerville District, AC/BRFAL, and in the Records of the Commissioner of the Bureau of Refugees, Freedmen, and Abandoned Lands, Record Group 105, microcopy 759, National Archives.

56. For example, on Jehossee see James P. Roy to W. L. M. Burger, 1 February 1866, series 4109, DOS; on Edisto, D. H. Whittemore to A. P. Ketchum, 30 January 1866, AC/BRFAL, reel 9; on Johns, T. A. Beckett to James C. Beecher, 13 March 1866, Letters Received, series 4112, DOS; on Wadmalaw, James C. Beecher to Major Smith, 31 January 1866, James C. Beecher Papers; on James, E. J. Daniels to G. S. Burger, 13 January 1866, series 4109, DOS; on Cooper, J. N. Low to R. K. Scott, 8 February 1866, AC/BRFAL, reel 10; and on Georgetown, F. Weston to Col. Smith, 17 February 1866, series 2392, Continental Commands.

57. Rufus Saxton to James C. Beecher, 17 August 1865, AC/BRFAL, reel 1.

58. E. H. Jewett to James C. Beecher, 3 August 1865, series 2421, Continental Commands.

59. W. L. Burger to W. P. Richardson, 24 January 1866, series 2264, ibid.

60. B. F. Smith to M. N. Rice, 4 February 1866, series 2389, ibid.

61. See, for example, Charles Devens to R. K. Scott, 4 April 1866, AC/BRFAL, reel 9. At every juncture, the authorities tried to exclude individuals they felt were undeserving, forcing many destitute to turn elsewhere for support. Discussions of

the measures taken to withhold provisions during 1866, 1867, and 1868, in the wake of droughts and floods, are too numerous to cite. In the face of destitution, Bureau policy changed very little from that promulgated in 1865 and 1866. For an outline of the policy see Abbott, *Freedmen's Bureau*, 37–51.

62. Discussions of the two-day system during Reconstruction are to be found in many private papers and in the Bureau and Military Records. See, for example, E. F. O'Brien to M. C. Crawford, 1 March 1867, Mount Pleasant District, Letters Sent, SFO/BRFAL; J. E. Lewis to H. B. Clitz, 29 February 1868, Grahamville District, Letters Sent, SFO/BRFAL; and James Hemphill, *Climate, Soil, and Agricultural Capabilities of South Carolina and Georgia* (Washington, D.C., 1882), 12–13.

63. E. W. Everson to A. M. Crawford, 30 June 1867, Mount Pleasant District, Letters Sent, SFO/BRFAL.

64. It seems that cash wages for tasks had become common practice by 1868 and represented an effort on the part of planters to "buy" productive labor from the hands who were all too willing to subsist on their gardens and small cash crops grown on the land provided in compensation. The evolution of this added wage in the bargain for labor power can best be traced through the labor contracts in the Bureau papers. As we shall see, this transaction in the ongoing exchange between capital and labor had become an established custom by the mid-1870s.

65. Harry Hammond, *South Carolina Resources and Population* (Columbia, S.C., 1883), 29; Harry Hammond, "Report on the Cotton Production of the State of South Carolina," in *Tenth Census of the United States, 1880* (Washington, D.C., 1884), vol. 6, pt. ii, 61.

66. Hammond, *South Carolina Resources*, 30.

67. The very brief narrative of the events of the rice strike is compiled from a variety of sources. I am currently working on a paper that focuses almost exclusively on the strike, straying from the incident only to place it in the context of the struggle to control labor and production. Scott, *Moral Economy* and Paige, *Agrarian Revolution* have informed my interpretation here; their emphasis on the violation of a "moral economy" and its understood structure of rights and obligations in prompting agrarian revolt is a powerful way of understanding the rice strike and other events in Low Country South Carolina.

68. A. V. Chayanov, *The Theory of Peasant Economy*, trans. and ed. by Daniel Thorner (Homewood, Ill., 1923, 1966); Marshall Sahlins, *Stone Age Economics* (New York, 1972), esp. ch. 2 and 3. The quote is from p. 86.

69. In *Stone Age Economics*, Sahlins argues that economics organized on the basis of the domestic mode of production are inherently underproductive and that still, all the people's wants are met. Production is "not merely 'production for use' but production for *use process*, even through the acts of exchange, and as opposed to the question for exchange value. . . . Even with exchange, the domestic mode is cousin to Marx's 'simple circulation of commodities,' . . . the manufacture of commodities . . . for sale in the market in order to obtain wherewithal [money] for the purchase of other, specific commodities. . . ." Sahlins notes that " 'Simple circulation' is . . . more pertinent to peasant than to primitive economies. But like peasants, primitive peoples remain constant in their pursuit of use values, related always to exchange with an interest in consumption, so to production with an interest in provisioning. And in this respect the historical opposite of *both* is the bourgeois entrepreneur with

an interest in exchange value" (83). Sahlins's book and its use of Chayanov are brilliant, provocative, and, for historians as well as anthropologists and other social scientists, programatic. It has spawned a great deal of literature. My understanding of Chayanov has been influenced by some imaginative books: Scott, *Moral Economy*; Taussig, *Devil and Commodity Fetishism*; Claude Meillassoux, *Maidens, Meal and Money: Capitalism and the Domestic Community* (London, 1981); Stephen Gudeman, *The Demise of a Rural Economy: From Subsistence to Capitalism in a Latin American Village* (London, 1978); and Gregor Dallas, *The Imperfect Peasant Economy: The Loire Country, 1800–1914* (London, 1982).

70. Hammond, *South Carolina Resources*, 56.

71. Ibid.

72. Low Country agriculture during the antebellum era saw ever-increasing returns to scale. In rice culture, particularly, there was essentially no optimum size for a plantation; as the units grew larger, they grew more productive. See Dale Swann, "The Structure and Profitability of the Antebellum Rice Industry, 1859," Diss., University of North Carolina, Chapel Hill, 1972. The agricultural census statistics for 1880 report the Low Country mean farm size to be 199 acres and that for the state 143 acres; for 1890, 118 versus 115 (excluding outsized Horry County, 107 versus 115); for 1900, 107 versus 90 (excluding outsized Georgetown County, 98 versus 90); for 1910, 101 versus 76 (excluding Georgetown again, 88 versus 76). See Appendix for sources.

73. These data come from the agricultural censuses for 1850 through 1910. For full citation, see Appendix. The mean per capita rice production (calculated with total output for the crop and total black population) for the Low Country was at its highest in 1850 with 954 pounds being grown for every man, woman, and child. This figure fell slightly to 709 pounds in 1860 and declined dramatically in the postwar years. The figures for 1870, 1880, 1890, 1900, and 1910 were 219, 250, 138, 210, and 107, respectively. The decline in the biggest rice districts was even greater. In 1850, blacks in Georgetown District grew 2,534 pounds per person; by 1910, the amount declined to only 115 pounds. Clearly, commercial production of the grain had essentially ceased in the Low Country.

74. For rice products see Frederick Strauss and Louis H. Bean, "Gross Farm Income and Indices of Farm Production and Prices in the United States, 1869–1937," *U.S. Department of Agriculture Technical Bulletin* no. 703 (Washington, D.C., 1940). They provide an estimate of *farm prices* based on New York wholesale prices. Scattered data in other sources indicate that Charleston prices were slightly lower than the national estimate.

75. See S. A. Knapp, "The Present Status of Rice Culture in the United States," *U.S. Department of Agriculture Division of Botany Bulletin* no. 22 (Washington, D.C., 1899) and S. A. Knapp, "Rice Culture," *U.S. Department of Agriculture Farmer's Bulletin* no. 417 (Washington, D.C., 1910).

76. Woofter, *Black Yeomanry*, offers a discussion of the impact of the boll weevil on the longer maturing Sea Island cotton.

77. Stanley Engerman, "Economic Aspects of the Adjustments to Emancipation in the United States and the British West Indies," unpublished paper, subsequently published in *The Journal of Interdisciplinary History* 13 (1982):191–220, provides the evidence for the South as a whole. The data for South Carolina come from the

agricultural censuses for 1850 to 1910. The mean cotton to corn ratio for those years compared with that for the state was 6.2 to 7.4; 6.4 to 9.4; 8.0 to 13.3; 10.1 to 20.1; 15.0 to 25.9; 11.6 to 24.2; and 19.6 to 30.7. For an introduction to the issue of consumption and cash crop ratios, see Gavin Wright and Howard Kunreuther, "Cotton, Corn and Risk in the Nineteenth Century," *Journal of Economic History* 35 (1975):526–51; Robert McGuire and Robert Higgs, "Cotton, Corn, and Risk in the Nineteenth Century: Another View," *Explorations in Economic History* 14 (1977): 167–82; Gavin Wright and Howard Kunreuther, "Cotton, Corn, and Risk in the Nineteenth Century: A Reply," *Explorations in Economic History* 14 (1977):183–95; DeCanio, *Agriculture in the Postbellum South*, 240–61; and Ransom and Sutch, *One Kind of Freedom*, 157–70.

STEVEN HAHN

# 6. The "Unmaking" of the Southern Yeomanry

## THE TRANSFORMATION OF

## THE GEORGIA UPCOUNTRY,

## 1860–1890

I

At one time, the great European debate over the transition from feudalism to capitalism was only of peripheral interest to American historians.* The colonization of North America, after all, grew directly out of European commercial expansion, quasi-feudal relations took hold in but few areas, and colonists, for the most part, appeared to exhibit many traits of individualism and acquisitiveness normally associated with capitalism. If capitalism did not quite find passage on the "first ships," as one historian wryly suggested it had, the obstacles it encountered in its march to hegemony seemed less structural and cultural than organizational and technological.[1] The transition was, so the story goes, largely temporal, and far more given over to the building up of new relations and institutions than to the breaking down of old ones.

This story, with varying degrees of modification, continues to command interpretive preeminence among most historians. But there are some new issues and questions with which they must contend. Recent scholarship on early American labor systems is beginning to show that precapitalist formations may have been more significant and more resilient than once assumed. Slavery and indentured servitude have come forth most conspicuously, as we now know that the majority of immigrants who arrived on these shores during the first century and three-quarters did so in some condition of unfreedom.[2] Yet there were other formations as well—craft production in towns and cities, and, for our purposes, household production in the coun-

---

*I would like to thank Oxford University Press for permission to reprint portions of previously published material.

tryside—which predated and subsequently resisted the full penetration of the marketplace.[3]

The evidence, it should be noted, is still far from overwhelming and certainly subject to conflicting assessments. Nonetheless, it suggests that farm families in a variety of geographical settings well into the nineteenth century relied upon their own labor, looked to household subsistence before marketing "surpluses," and were reluctant to embrace improved methods of tillage and animal husbandry. "The concept of agriculture as a market-focused, profit-making business was by no means universally accepted even in 1850," historian Clarence H. Danhof has observed, pointing to widespread "indifference or hostility . . . to new ideas and techniques."[4] The "market-focused concept of agriculture," to be sure, would never win "universal" acceptance, but it clearly came to dominate the rural sector during the second half of the nineteenth century. The problem, then, is to analyze and comprehend the dynamics of this transformation—to analyze and comprehend how farm households were invaded and conquered by the logic and relations of commodity production. American historians, in short, have a transition question of their own with which to grapple, one that draws this nation into a larger world experience.

Nonplantation areas of the South offer particularly interesting case studies of the American "transition." On the one hand, they were situated within a wider slave society and thus provide a new vantage point from which to consider the changes effected by the abolition of unfree labor. On the other hand, they were dominated by yeoman farmers, not planters, and had an agricultural economy before the war similar in important respects to what prevailed in many parts of the rural North. Like their Northern counterparts, moreover, these Southern yeomen became increasingly involved in the export market thereafter. The transition was unquestionably more dramatic, more wrenching, and more politically inspired than was true in the North and West; its trajectory was defined by the peculiar place of the entire postwar South in the national political economy. Yet it forces us to ponder the larger parameters of the development of capitalist relations in the countryside. The Upper Piedmont, or Upcountry, of Georgia was one such nonplantation area (see Map 6.1), and it may be fruitful to explore some aspects of the transition there.

I I

The antebellum South with which we are most familiar was a region of rich lowlands and rolling, fertile loams, of planters and slaves, cotton and commerce. It was the Black Belt and the networks and institutions linked vitally to it. The Georgia Upcountry was part of another South—a South about which we know far less but which also suggests that dual economies, if not dual societies, emerged in the Southern states. The Upcountry was a region of hilly and broken terrain, an overwhelmingly white majority, relatively small farms, and semi-subsistence agriculture. As late as 1860, on the eve of the Civil War, more than six of every ten free household heads owned land, although their land holdings usually included fewer than 100 improved acres. Indeed, most of the cropland in the Upcountry fell into farms of this size, quite unlike in the Black Belt where most of the cropland fell within the boundaries of large plantations.[5] Slave holding, of course, was hardly unknown in the Georgia Upcountry, or in most other nonplantation areas: nearly one-quarter of the population was black and, with a handful of exceptions, unfree. But again unlike the Black Belt, relatively few farm families owned slaves, and those who did seldom owned more than five.[6]

At the center of economic life in the antebellum Upcountry stood the household, for the relations of production were mediated principally by ties of kinship rather than by the marketplace. Very much in the manner of rural people in the North and in many other areas of the world, farm families in Upcountry Georgia organized the basic tasks of social sustenance and reproduction, attempting to produce most of what they needed.[7] And it appears that they could have reasonable hope of success. Statistics compiled by the Federal Census Bureau suggest that yeoman farmers normally raised surplus food crops together with considerable numbers of livestock, especially hogs.[8] They also normally raised a little cotton, usually possessed spinning wheels and looms, and occasionally owned tools for blacksmithing, carpentry, and furniture making.[9] To be sure, this household economy had its own division of labor, one based chiefly on sex and age. Husbands, older sons, and perhaps the few slaves did most of the field work. Wives and older daughters by and large attended to spinning, weaving, cooking, and other domestic chores. Younger children filled in when able and called upon. It was, in fact, relations of legal and customary dependency—slavery being the extreme and absolute representation—that linked household members to the male head, although a variety of social and economic interdependencies and the self-exploitation of the household as a whole gave these relations a distinctive cast.[10]

If the household embraced the dominant social division of labor, it was part, too, of a larger and more intricate grid of production and exchange, spreading out through the Upcountry settlements, hamlets, and villages. Neighboring farm families, some tied by kinship, often "swapped work" when labor demands proved most arduous and imperative. As one local farmer recalled, "If Willis Howell's fodder was ready to pull before Ernest Cowart's both families pulled fodder together on the Howell farm . . . [and] after a farmer gathered his corn, he invited his neighbors to come to a corn shucking."[11] When such exchanges were not feasible or sufficient, yeomen

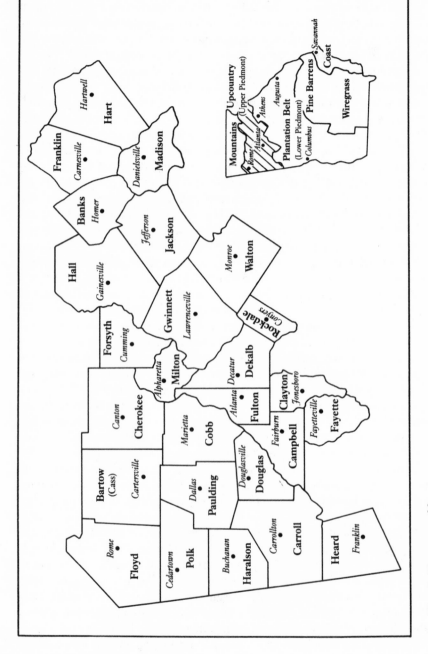

6.1. *Georgia Upcountry, 1880s*

hired slaves or, more frequently, other whites—usually for short stints and specific tasks—at a customary rate in cash or kind. Some of these white laborers were freeholders themselves looking to supplement incomes and make ends meet; many more were the sons of freeholders who hired out in the hope of eventually acquiring farms or as they waited to inherit them.[12]

Communitywide relations of production and exchange such as these created dense social networks, but they ramified further still. Although most of the free household heads worked chiefly in agriculture, at least 10 percent were artisans and craftsmen, more than a few claiming farms or a few acres of their own, who provided essential goods and services for their neighborhoods. The spectrum of craft occupations was, in fact, rather considerable, as millers, blacksmiths, carpenters, coopers, wagon makers, shoemakers, tailors, and hatters—among others—found niches in the Upcountry economy.[13] And to the trade that they encouraged may be added a local demand for foodstuffs occasioned by the denizens owning no land and the newly arrived settlers who needed provisions until they could plant and harvest their crops giving the yeomen a ready, albeit limited, outlet for surplus produce. Court and market days, during which rural families made their way to the county seat, saw brisk rounds of buying and selling.[14]

It is clear, therefore, that Upcountry yeomen were not isolated cultivators plying a rude self-sufficiency. Yet it should also be clear that the economic relations into which they entered were quite distinct from those characterizing a market society. These petty producers generally owned basic productive resources or were related to those who did; they devoted their energies principally to family subsistence, supplementing it through local exchanges of goods and labor; and the exchanges cast a net that brought producers face-to-face in a market very much governed by local custom. Probated inventories recorded in two Upcountry counties during the 1850s show that upwards of seven decedents in ten had debts owed to their estates, while fewer than half had any hard cash or currency.[15] The extension of low-interest credit and eventual payment in kind or labor typified a great many transactions. Thus, a Hart County blacksmith could be reimbursed variously for services he rendered with "100 lbs seed cotton," "fifteen pounds of flour," "100 split rails," "buttons," "four bushels of corn," and small amounts of cash.[16]

The handful of mercantile establishments scattered across the Georgia Upcountry carried only small stocks of goods and did a decidedly limited business. But they too followed these practices, accepting, as they often announced, "all kinds of country produce" to settle bills.[17] Although farmers normally purchased on credit, interest accrued only if accounts remained open at year's end. And obtaining that credit rarely necessitated mortgaging, for Georgia's homestead exemption shielded a substantial amount of real and personal property from levy for debt.[18] Merchants could therefore exert little influence over farming operations, and commonly found themselves in a perilous position. Small wonder that those who managed to keep their heads above water combined farming with trading, as did craftsmen.[19]

A number of factors placed a lid on the commercialization of agriculture in the antebellum Upcountry: a hillier, less fertile topography and a cooler climate than in the plantation districts; poor and undeveloped transport facilities; a shallow market for foodstuffs offered by either the Plantation Belt or the comparatively few Southern cities and towns. Still, Upcountry yeomen were by no means isolated from the staple economy. By 1860, most farm families grew some cotton for sale, and, amid an upturn in prices, the 1850s had witnessed some particularly notable increases in production.[20] Such ventures into the market were, in large part, nurtured by the very dynamics and priorities of the household economy. As the antebellum era wore on, the population increased, the size of farms gradually diminished, and the value of land rose. Added security for the household and offspring under the prevailing system of partible inheritance thus made accumulation desirable, and accumulation required a cash crop. Indeed, under historical conditions of limited economic integration, limited demand for labor-power, and limited vulnerability for productive property, participation in the market here, as in many peasant societies, could serve to reinforce, rather than jeopardize, the household's claims on the means of production.[21] And in the Upcountry, general farming and a "security-first" orientation left the decisive imprint throughout.

Southern yeoman households were not alone among rural producers of early nineteenth-century America in pursuing this economic logic. Large numbers of rural households in the North and West did much the same, responding to market pressures and incentives by intensifying customary forms of production—especially during slack season—instead of shifting in a clearly commercial direction.[22] But the rapid economic development of the free states, which created conditions for an expanding domestic market, greater specialization, and a wider range of nonagricultural alternatives, subjected rural areas to the pulls of the market more quickly and more powerfully than was true in the South. In the South, slavery severely circumscribed the emergence of a market for labor-power, and thus obstructed regional economic integration and the developmental possibilities of staple-generated profits.[23] Commercial and industrial capital remained weak, and the decentralization of civil society, which ultimately rested on the master–slave relationship, was accentuated by the federal political system established in 1787. Upcountry yeoman households could then enter and withdraw from the cotton market with relative ease, sustaining and reproducing themselves, as it were, on the market's periphery. If the acquisition of slaves and plantations increasingly fell beyond their reach, the existence of slavery and plantation agriculture buffered their economic integrity, making it feasible for them to dip into the market in order to avoid subjection to the market—to preserve their own independence and that of their heirs.

The planter class appeared to recognize as much, for the proslavery argument, especially as directed toward Southern non–slave holders, proclaimed that the enslavement of blacks secured the independence of all whites by restraining the growth of market relations. Even those spokesmen for "*Herrenvolk* democracy," for white egalitarianism, insisted that free labor in the North reduced poor folk to the status of "wage slaves," and they predicted identical consequences in the South should emancipation be effected.[24] Yeomen may have had their own understandings of the connection between slavery and independence—and ones that likely rejected the paternalist resonances of proslavery theory. But the connection was unmistakably glimpsed by a wide spectrum of Southern whites, and it served as the foundation of the slave holders' political hegemony.

III

It may be argued that the increases in cotton production during the 1850s signaled the beginnings of an economic trajectory that would carry the Georgia Upcountry ever deeper into commercial agriculture whether or not the Civil War had intervened. That decade did in fact bear witness to a more general surge of Southern commercial activity and to some growth in the market for white labor-power both in cities and towns and in some rural districts.[25] But even where a transition to capitalist relations appeared most auspicious, as for example in parts of the Upper South, those relations remained encased, however uneasily, within the political economy of slavery.[26] In the Georgia Upcountry, where the boundaries established by the slave regime were firmer still, such a transition could only have been a dim and distant glint. So it was that the Civil War, and the swift, uncompensated emancipation it brought with Confederate defeat, ushered forth a new order throughout the South and lent that order distinctive contours.

The war very much strained the resources of the yeoman household economy while initiating a process that would integrate the Upcountry into a national economic system based on market relations. Four years of war-related privation and dislocation—especially severe in nonplantation areas dependent on family labor—reached a climax with the ravages of Federal troops, Confederate cavalry, and bands of deserters. Homes and barns were razed, fields were trampled, livestock were slaughtered, and destitution was widespread. Agents of the federal Freedmen's Bureau stationed in north Georgia spent much of their time in 1865 and 1866 distributing needed rations among whites, not blacks.[27] Several years of drought only made matters worse. The 1870 federal census, although of questionable reliability, at least suggests the magnitude of economic disruption: the Upcountry produced 40 percent fewer bushels of corn and had 35 percent fewer head of livestock than in 1860. Per capita grain production dropped by almost 40 percent during this period. Settlements previously able to achieve a basic self-sufficiency now had to depend on purchasing goods from the outside.[28]

Hoping to recoup their losses and to repay debts contracted for necessary provisions, Upcountry yeomen looked to cotton as a reasonable means to recovery. Although no longer at heady wartime levels, cotton prices nonetheless remained quite high in the late 1860s and early 1870s, and, as one Upcountry newspaper noted, cotton did "not cost one half [of what corn cost] to carry" to market. Thus, farmers began to expand their cotton planting, so much so that the local Carroll County *Times* could marvel at a "considerable revolution" taking place. "Cotton, formerly cultivated on a very limited extent, has increased rapidly," the *Times* observed, "so that if the ratio continues, the county will, ere long, take rank among the foremost cotton producing counties of the state."[29]

The "revolution" so touted by the Carroll County *Times* was evident through most of the Upcountry, and it received additional stimulus from the construction of rail lines—financed by localities, state Reconstruction governments, and Northern investors—and from the ensuing availability of commercial fertilizers, which helped surmount the Upcountry's shorter growing season.[30] As early as 1875, cotton covered more than one-quarter of the cropland on white-operated farms, and the trend continued apace. By 1880, the Upcountry could boast almost 180,000 bales, three times the harvest of 1860, and by 1890 cotton truly reigned as king, surpassing even corn in total acreage (see Table 6.1).[31]

Yet, although the initial impulse may well have come from yeoman farm families, this agricultural revolution was not entirely of their own making. However favorable cotton prices were, there was no quick abandonment of the traditional "security-first" disposition. So a Plantation Belt newspaper found, reporting in 1873 that many "farmers of Upper Georgia" attended to "their grain, provender, and provisions and then bestowed their surplus labor on cotton."[32] As cotton prices then continued on what turned out to be a long and steady decline, a heightened concern for food crops would be expected, for this had been the response to downward shifts in prices before the war. But now the story was otherwise: Yeomen moved ever further along the road of staple agriculture, as significant changes in the relations of production and exchange—linked directly to the abolition of slavery—transformed the local marketplace, fastened it to an expanding capitalist nation-state, and recast the household economy. They were changes that "unmade" the yeomanry while remaking Southern society. New lines of

6.1. *Cotton and Corn Production in the Upcountry, 1860–1890*

|  | 1860 | 1870 | 1880 | 1890 |
|---|---|---|---|---|
| Cotton (bales) | 63,094 | 34,789 | 179,892 | 215,500 |
| Cotton acres | — | — | 348,921 | 596,947 |
| Corn (bushels) | 5,009,639 | 3,336,385 | 6,122,499 | 6,349,307 |
| Corn acres | — | — | 399,707 | 475,695 |
| Per capita cotton production (bales) | 0.3 | 0.2 | 0.6 | 0.6 |
| Per capita corn production (bushels) | 26.0 | 16.6 | 20.9 | 19.0 |

Sources: *Eighth Census of the United States, 1860* (Washington, D.C., 1864), Agriculture, 23–27; *Ninth Census of the United States, 1870* (Washington, D.C., 1872), Agriculture, 120–127; *Tenth Census of the United States, 1880* (Washington, D.C., 1883), Report on Productions of Agriculture, 183–84; *Eleventh Census of the United States, 1890* (Washington, D.C., 1894), Agriculture, 200–204, 360–61, 393–94.

transportation and communication, a new system of credit, and new definitions of property rights set the foundation for the transition; merchant capital served to organize and mediate it.

As railroads began pushing into the Georgia Upcountry during the 1870s, mercantile establishments sprang up in proliferating towns and hamlets. Carroll County, in northwest Georgia, provides a useful illustration. In 1870, thirteen stores serviced the entire county, five of which had survived from the antebellum era. By 1875, however, the county had thirty-six stores, by 1880 forty-nine stores, and by 1885 seventy. Most of the storekeepers were native Georgians with little capital and small inventories, many had arrived only recently in Upcountry locales, and few initially owned land. One merchandiser in Maysville, Jackson County, for instance, began business in 1875 with "a respectable little stock of goods" but "no property only paying poll tax."[33] What attracted him and his counterparts to the region and enabled them to establish a foothold was the crop lien system.

The rise of the lien system in Georgia, as elsewhere in the South, reflected both the direct economic impact of the Civil War and the developing political economy of postwar America. Among the casualties of the sectional conflagration were the Southern financial institutions that had previously sustained the principal networks of credit, marketing, and supply. Planters had been accustomed to shipping their cotton to factors in the ports or interior market towns; the factors, in turn, sold it and purchased provisions required on the plantation, financing the transactions with the help of cotton brokers and bankers. Once the war broke out, soaring cotton prices and less-than-patriotic dealings enabled some of the factorage houses to reap windfalls, but by 1865 most faced trying circumstances. Confederate currency was worthless, many state banks had closed their doors, land had plummeted in value, and emancipation had eliminated the planters' traditional form of collateral.[34]

The federal government did take steps to prevent the wartime and postwar disintegration of the plantation economy, committed as it was to the maintenance of Southern cotton production: The contract labor system, initiated in Union-occupied Louisiana in 1862, put refugee slaves to work on abandoned estates under the supervision of Northern or loyal Southern lessees; the Freedmen's Bureau, created in the spring of 1865, oversaw the transition to free black labor; and Congress, after much deliberation, scotched Radical hopes for Southern land confiscation and redistribution.[35] Yet, any chance of rejuvenating familiar financial and marketing arrangements dissipated in the face of Republican-inspired legislation establishing a national currency and banking structure that severely limited the number and operations of Southern banks.[36] Although the full ramifications remain to be explored, it is clear that this new economic edifice kept much-needed rural credit in short supply in the South, and thereby made that credit increasingly costly. The balances of finance came to favor creditors over debtors, industry over agriculture, and the East over both the South and the West—a shift that the historian Robert Sharkey calls "*the* momentous change" between 1850 and 1873.[37]

Filling the vacuum left by the factors and the banks were the country merchants and the crop lien. In an effort to remedy the financial crisis almost every Southern state quickly passed laws enabling suppliers to obtain mortgages, or liens, on the crops of their customers to secure advances of money and provisions. At the earliest stages, these suppliers were overwhelmingly small merchandisers who had accounts with Northern wholesalers or Southern commission houses and who set their sights on the plantation districts where cotton culture and the black laborforce were concentrated. It could hardly have been otherwise, for most resident planters simply lacked the capital, experience, and temperament to move into the provisioning business themselves.[38] Still, the planters did not rest comfortably with the new arrangements. With gang labor rapidly giving way to tenancy as the mode of staple production, their surpluses—and thus their economic fates—came to depend as much on controlling the ex-slaves' crops as it did on controlling the ex-slaves' labor time. And however essential the merchants may have been to the revitalization of the cotton economy, the merchants' use of the crop lien very much threatened that control.

Taking on the duties of merchandising offered the planters one solution to the dilemma; tailoring the lien laws to their advantage offered them another. The late 1860s and early 1870s saw a series of legislative skirmishes as planting and mercantile interests fought for the upper hand. The outcome in Georgia was fairly typical: Planter-landlords won superior lien rights for both rent and advances to tenants, shouldering merchants with the greatest risks of default.[39] In theory, this should have relegated Plantation Belt storekeepers to the status of minor functionaries; in actuality, the result was more complex. The lien laws often were ignored in practice, and merchants still could furnish smaller planters and farmers as well as tenants indirectly through the landlord.[40] Yet, the resolution of the lien conflict did have an unintended, though important consequence. It made nonplantation areas, where the majority of potential customers were yeomen, more alluring, and provided merchants in those areas with new economic leverage. As one landowner in the Georgia Upcountry recalled, "When the lien law was passed the town merchant became an important factor in farming."[41]

## IV

The lien system began the work of altering traditional exchange relations in the Upcountry. But beyond this, it afforded merchants a role in the productive process. The legacy of wartime devastation and short food crops, as may be expected, offered merchants a more extensive clientele than they would have had in antebellum years, a clientele that purchased goods on credit as a matter of course. Within the framework of the postwar political economy, however, credit became a rather costly necessity. Merchants obtained their stocks on consignment and sought to buttress their finances, and then some, by substantially marking up items bought on time. Although we still know very little about the transactions between merchants and wholesalers, we do know that the markups added at least 25 percent to the cash price, with additional interest then charged.[42] To secure operations further, merchandisers demanded a lien on their customers' crops. Yet the lien did not simply serve as collateral to buffer the risks of default; it also gave merchants influence over farming operations. While the liens did not specify the acreage to be planted in particular crops, merchants preferred that cotton be grown because it was the easiest crop to market and the most likely to bring a return. It is, in fact, quite difficult to find any evidence of liens executed on grain crops alone.[43] Of course, yeoman farmers probably required little prodding. Saddled with mounting debts and high interest rates, they needed a substantial commercial crop if they hoped to come out ahead at year's end. Either way, the merchants drew yeomen decisively into the cotton market.

The growing power of merchants in the Upcountry derived only to a limited extent from what economic historians Roger Ransom and Richard Sutch have termed "territorial monopolies": small geographical zones, perhaps a few miles in radius, dominated by individual merchandisers as a result of the scattering of crossroads stores and the workings of the crop lien. A variety of local records shows that stores normally clustered in and around the few county towns having railroad depots, and that farmers might have traded with more than one concern.[44] Competition for customers, together with the exactions of wholesalers, put quite a number of mercantile establishments on the short road to failure.[45] The growing power of Upcountry merchants as a class, nonetheless, did stem from a near monopoly —a near monopoly over the sources of essential credit in an economy increasingly dependent on staple agriculture. Whether or not a farmer dealt with more than one merchant, he had almost no alternative to the country store for advances, and thereby entered into a vicious cycle. The acquisition of credit demanded the expansion of cotton production; the expansion of cotton production meant proportionately shorter food crops; and shorter food crops sent the farmer back to the merchant's door for provisions.[46] Merchants as a class, in short, helped turn cotton from one part of a crop mix, from a market-oriented expedient in a system of general farming, into an enduring and, indeed, defining feature of the Upcountry economy.

The increasing dependence of yeoman households on storekeepers for foodstuffs was only one sign of the changing pattern of exchange, for the erosion of household self-sufficiency was wider in its impact. Probated inventories reveal, for example, a dramatic decline in the capacity for home manufactures. Whereas seven decedents in ten had spinning wheels and looms in the 1850s, only two in ten did by the 1880s.[47] Farmers therefore turned to local merchants who took advantage of newly constructed rail lines and arrangements with wholesalers to undercut craftsmen in stocking a greater variety of goods at lower cost. Wealthier storekeepers soon had extensive assortments. As one firm put it, "We deal in Gen'l Mdse, consisting in part DG (dry goods), B&S (boots and shoes), Hats, Notions, Clothing, Hardware, Bagging, and a gen'l stock of groc[eries] &c."[48] Thus, when the Jackson County seat saw a railroad enter its limits for the first time in 1883, the prospects of its merchants brightened considerably. In 1882, about $40,000 of "general merchandise" had been sold in the town; by 1885, the figure approached $300,000 annually.[49]

Once they had established a viable business, merchants often diversified their enterprises. To strengthen their position and to bolster surpluses from agriculture, many moved directly into the ginning and marketing of cotton. The postwar era, in both the Upcountry and Plantation Belt, saw not only the disintegration of the factorage system, but also the shift of ginning facilities from the countryside to town. Especially in nonplantation districts, where landlords and farmers alike normally had limited means, prospering storekeepers were best able to afford expensive steam gins.[50] And when they had the gins, they could add to their clientele by insisting that custom-

6.2. *Occupational Groups in Upcountry Georgia, 1860–1880*
*(Jackson and Carroll Counties)*

| Occupational Group | 1860 | | 1880 | |
|---|---|---|---|---|
| | No. | % | No. | % |
| Farmers and farm laborers[a] | 2,496 | 83.3 | 3,858 | 78.6 |
| Artisans | 320 | 10.7 | 230 | 4.7 |
| Merchants and retailers | 43 | 1.4 | 108 | 2.2 |
| Professionals | 109 | 3.6 | 130 | 2.6 |
| Unskilled | 9 | 0.3 | 159 | 3.2 |
| Others | 21 | 0.7 | 425 | 8.7 |
| Total | 2,998 | 100.0 | 4,910 | 100.0 |

[a]Category includes tenants and overseers.

Source: Manuscript Census, Georgia, Jackson and Carroll counties, Schedule I, 1860, 1880, Georgia Department of Archives and History, Atlanta.

ers sell them the cotton as well. With profits accumulated from the trade, moreover, merchants began to invest in an array of local businesses. Together with general stores, they soon could be found operating hotels and taverns, flour mills, sawmills, shingle machines, fertilizer outlets, and livery stables.[51] Merchants came to dominate the Upcountry marketplace.

Such dominance over exchange relations is evidenced, in part, by a great contraction in the presence and variety of Upcountry artisans. In 1860, about 10 percent of the white household heads reported craft occupations, and those ranged over quite a spectrum. By 1880, about 5 percent of the white household heads reported craft occupations (see Table 6.2), and they were disproportionately blacksmiths, millers, and carpenters—trades that could not be replaced in an agricultural economy with proliferating small towns. Horses had to be shod, farm tools repaired, grain processed, and buildings constructed. Other skilled craftsmen who made clothing, furniture, and sundry goods fell victim to the emerging system of mass production and distribution.[52]

The changing structure of debt further highlights the new dimensions of the Upcountry marketplace and the merchants' power within it. The antebellum network of exchange linking farmers, artisans, and laborers found expression in a pattern of widespread indebtedness, as over seven of ten inventories probated during the 1850s showed debts owed to the estate. By the 1880s, only half of the inventories showed debts and, more important, the control of debts became extremely concentrated. If, for example, decedents are ranked by the value of debts owed to their estates, the top 10

6.3. *Debt Structure in Upcountry Georgia, 1850s–1880s:*
*Distribution of Debts Owed Estates (Jackson and Carroll Counties)*

| Rank (Decile) | 1850s | | 1880s | |
|---|---|---|---|---|
| | Value of Debts | % Total Debts | Value of Debts | % Total Debts |
| Top | $33,584.88 | 52.1 | $121,200.16 | 72.9 |
| Second | 15,454.19 | 24.0 | 27,619.89 | 16.6 |
| Third | 7,881.01 | 12.2 | 10,619.74 | 6.3 |
| Fourth | 3,897.46 | 6.0 | 5,051.59 | 3.0 |
| Fifth | 2,347.33 | 3.6 | 1,800.32 | 1.1 |
| Sixth | 1,021.12 | 1.6 | 39.80 | 0.1 |
| Seventh | 281.53 | 0.4 | 0.00 | 0.0 |
| Eighth | 24.75 | 0.1 | 0.00 | 0.0 |
| Ninth | 0.00 | 0.0 | 0.00 | 0.0 |
| Tenth | 0.00 | 0.0 | 0.00 | 0.0 |
| Total | 64,492.27 | 100.0 | 166,331.50 | 100.0 |

| | | |
|---|---|---|
| Number of inventories | 159 | 257 |
| Number of inventories with debts owed to estate | 115 (72.3%) | 132 (51.4%) |

Sources: Ord. Est. Recs., Inv. and App., Carroll County, vol. C–D, 1850s; Court of Ord., Inv. and App., Jackson County, vol. A, 1850s; Ord. Est. Recs., Inv. and App., Carroll County, vol. A, 1880s; Court of Ord., App., Adminis., Guardians, Executors, Jackson County, book A, 1880s.

percent increased their share of the value of total debts from about 50 percent to over 70 percent during this period (see Table 6.3). And the most substantial debt holders were merchandisers like J. W. Adamson of Bowdon in Carroll County, who held notes and accounts amounting to $9,254.65 in 1888, or S. M. Shankle of Harmony Grove in Jackson County, who claimed notes worth $17,505.92 in 1885. The Adamsons and the Shankles—merchants, not producers—held sway over postbellum exchange.[53]

Yet the merchants did more than assume a commanding role in local trade. They also helped to transform the very terms of trade. Although transactions in the antebellum Upcountry were influenced by external markets, those transactions commonly involved some sort of barter and thus bore the stamp of local custom. Corn, wheat, shoes, and other goods, rarely shipped out of the region, could all serve as "money." With the taking hold of commercial agriculture, however, an important change soon occurred. It was not that the currency supply expanded; given the virtual absence of banking facilities in the Upcountry and the nationwide monetary contraction, the shortage remained chronic. Rather, it was that cotton became the preeminent money commodity. Storekeepers advertising goods for "all kinds of country produce" were becoming the exception. By the late 1870s, and certainly by the 1880s, mercantile establishments expected to conduct business in "cash or cotton."[54] And with far-reaching consequences; for when "cash or cotton" emerged as the basic medium of exchange, notions of a "just price" deriving from community standards and interdependencies no longer could define the boundaries of the Upcountry marketplace. Trade henceforth would be regulated by a market over which producers had little or no control, a market subordinating countryside to town and agriculture to industry.[55]

## V

The transformation of exchange relations, which tied the Upcountry and its producers to commercial agriculture and the fluctuations of a national and international market, was accompanied by a serious weakening of the claims yeoman households had on productive resources, and thus by the beginnings of a significant transformation in the relations of production themselves. If the lien system opened the way, even more important, albeit less well recognized, was the dismantling of Georgia's homestead exemption. However much liens enabled merchants to lay hold of growing crops and encourage the cultivation of cotton, the homestead exemption prevented them from laying hold of the means of production, for it secured a substantial amount of real and personal property against levy for debt. Property mortgaging and legal dispossession were, therefore, quite uncommon. Then, in 1877, mercantile interests won major concessions from a state constitutional convention: The homestead exemption's coverage was sliced and, of greater consequence, debtors were permitted to waive its protection.[56] From that point, waiving the homestead and mortgaging property in addition to crops became the conditions for obtaining credit. As one Upcountry farmer complained, "Merchants now demand that the homestead be waived [even] if the farmer wants to buy $20 worth of supplies."[57]

The effect of homestead reform became apparent with remarkable rapidity, as evidence from Carroll County attests. In 1875, before reform, the county court recorded 18 individual mortgages. By 1882, the annual number recorded exceeded 150, and by 1885 it surpassed 900, a staggering 5,000 percent increase within the span of a decade.[58] Mortgages on personal property far outnumbered those on real estate—farmers who viewed landownership as the foundation of their independence sought to circumscribe their liability. Yet the amount of land coming under mortgage was by no means inconsiderable. In 1885 alone, Carroll County farmers mortgaged over 7,500 acres.[59]

The growth of various forms of farm tenancy throughout the Georgia Upcountry during the 1880s came largely as a product of such credit arrangements. Encumbered property, high interest rates, and declining cotton prices made the auction block the resort for the hopelessly indebted. "Sheriffs advertisements," in the words of one county newspaper, were "as long as your arm," and as another county paper observed, "sale day" brought heavy trafficking in real estate. One such day in Jackson County in November 1883 saw nearly 2,300 acres change hands.[60] And merchants became prominent beneficiaries. By virtue of foreclosure or bidding at public auction, they began to accumulate substantial acreage. Some of the wealthiest, to be sure, had antebellum roots in the Upcountry or had acquired land early in the postwar era. But they and other prosperous merchandisers clearly capitalized on the woes of their land-holding customers. Between 1885 and 1890, for instance, twelve merchants in two Upcountry counties engrossed almost 8,000 acres among them.[61]

Impressive as it was, however, merchant accumulation of Upcountry land did not lead to the emergence of large-scale plantations. Their holdings, for the most part, consisted of relatively small units scattered over a district or two and farmed by tenant and sharecropper families.[62] If anything, merchants seem to have avoided indiscriminate foreclosures and the relentless engrossments made famous by the English rural bourgeoisie. It was the better-quality land that they really wanted, and for reasons befitting their social class. Attracting "hands" proved a perpetual problem for Upcountry landlords, the more so when farm units contained rocky, sandy soil with little promise of decent yields. Nothing would be gained by taking outright possession of a farm that remained vacant for a stretch of time, and there were no guarantees that a new tenant would be more successful than the hapless yeoman. It made more sense, and required less risk, to run the debt and maintain a flow of surplus than to chance an extended search for a replacement. "Carrying" a farmer for years was not at all unusual.[63]

Indeed, in a manner characteristic of merchant capital's role historically,[64] Upcountry merchandisers intensified the exploitation of, rather than reorganized, the prevailing household form of production, chipping away at its protective hedges and subsistence base while continuing to rely on the labor and consumption of the unit as a whole. However prosperous some had become by the standards of the postwar South, the merchants generally lacked the resources and disposition to refashion agricultural enterprises along the classically capitalist lines of land consolidation, wage labor, and mechanization. And however powerful merchants had become as a class locally, their inroads met resistance from yeoman and tenant farmers attempting to fend off deeper dependency and proletarian status. The political turbulence of the 1880s and 1890s to a large extent reflected such struggles.[65]

Yet, although the household remained the central form of production, the structure and dynamic of the yeoman household economy were being steadily recast. Having once embraced the dominant social relations by virtue of its own division of labor, control of productive resources, and orientation to self-sufficiency, the household moved toward specialization through its growing reliance on a market mediated by merchant capital. In some degree, the process bore resemblance to what European historians have called "proto-industrialization." For with the decline of household manufactures, with the heavy mortgages on land, implements, and work animals, and with the influence of the credit system on the crop mix, the range of yeoman household economic activity narrowed—as was true among the affected peasant households in Europe, albeit for different reasons—and the labor time devoted to staple cultivation increased. And cotton was a preeminently industrial crop. Household production thus fell subject to a particularly ruthless logic of commercialization and to an ever-widening social division of labor. Customary exploitation within the household was burdened by exploitation of the entire household in the new market economy. Self-exploitation at the point of production was now intensified by outside exploitation in the sphere of exchange.[66] It was a transition that yeomen perceived as qualitatively different, disturbing, and unjust. One man, suffering under the strains of debt and encumbrance, explained his desperate flight from a hounding creditor: "I just got tired of working for the other fellow. I worked and toiled from year to year and all the fruits of my labor went to the man who never struck a lick."[67]

## VI

The experience of the Georgia Upcountry between 1860 and 1890 surely points to the critical role of the Civil War and Reconstruction, not only in toppling slavery, but also in promoting the absorption of nonplantation areas of the South into a developing national capitalist economy. The economic repercussions of the war, and the new relations that emerged out of the struggle over free labor, both pushed yeoman families into greater participation in the cotton market and dramatically changed the conditions under which that participation occurred. With the planters weakened financially and politically, and the South as a whole subordinated to the demands of the industrializing North, merchant capital assumed a leading part in the transition and depended on the increasing self-exploitation of rural households as the driving force of accumulation. Given the paucity of employment opportunities outside of agriculture—itself a product of slavery's legacy and the political economy of the postwar settlement—the increasing self-exploitation of rural households contributed substantially to widespread impoverishment. The long-standing debate over Southern poverty and underdevelopment might be reconsidered in this context.

The Upcountry experience points, as well, to a number of issues bearing on the process of agricultural commercialization generally. It suggests that the oft-drawn dichotomy between subsistence and commercial farming based on market exchange is analytically artificial and misleading. Instead, what we must begin to grapple with are qualitatively distinct patterns of exchange, each founded upon discrete sets of productive relations, and the way societies move from one to the other. Furthermore, we need to look more closely at the relations of the household economy over time. One of the striking features of American economic development is the persistence of the household as the dominant productive unit in agriculture. As late as 1970, the ratio of family to hired labor on farms stood at 3 to 1.[68] And yet, the involvement of family farms in commodity production has changed drastically since the early nineteenth century. In part, as we have seen, the effort to maintain the viability of the traditional, precapitalist household ironically thrust it out into the market. But equally, if not more, important was the erosion of the social division of labor within the household itself. All of these considerations point to the task of rethinking and redefining the questions we ask about the American transition—questions that will be sharpened by looking to Europe and other rural societies.

NOTES

1. Carl N. Degler, *Out of Our Past: The Forces That Shaped Modern America* (New York, 1970), 1.

2. Richard S. Dunn, "Servants and Slaves: The Recruitment and Employment of Labor," in Jack P. Greene and J. R. Pole, eds., *Colonial British America: Essays in the New History of the Early Modern Era* (Baltimore, 1984), 157–94.

3. See, for example, Michael Merrill, "Cash Is Good to Eat: Self-Sufficiency and Exchange in the Rural Economy of the United States," *Radical History Review* 3 (1977):42–71; James A. Henretta, "Families and Farms: *Mentalité* in Pre-Industrial America," *William and Mary Quarterly* 3d ser. 35 (1978):2–32; Eric Foner, *Tom Paine and Revolutionary America* (New York, 1976), 24–26; Sean Wilentz, "Artisan Republican Festivals and the Rise of Class Conflict in New York City, 1788–1837," in Michael H. Frisch and Daniel J. Walkowitz, eds., *Working-Class America: Essays on Labor, Community, and American Society* (Urbana, Ill., 1983), 37–77; Alan Dawley, *Class and Community: The Industrial Revolution in Lynn* (Cambridge, Mass., 1976), 42–72.

4. Clarence H. Danhof, *Change in Agriculture: The Northern United States, 1820–1870* (Cambridge, Mass., 1969), 22; Max Schumacher, *The Northern Farmer and His*

*Markets During the Late Colonial Period* (New York, 1975); Christopher F. Clark, "Household, Market, and Capital: The Process of Economic Change in the Connecticut Valley of Massachusetts, 1800–1860," Diss., Harvard University, 1982; Jonathan Prude, *The Coming of Industrial Order: Town and Factory Life in Rural Massachusetts, 1810–1860* (New York, 1983), 6–12. For dissenting points of view see James T. Lemon, *The Best Poor Man's Country: A Geographical Study of Early Southeastern Pennsylvania* (Baltimore, 1972); Joyce O. Appleby, "Commercial Farming and the 'Agrarian Myth' in the Early Republic," *Journal of American History* 68 (1982):833–49; Winifred B. Rothenberg, "The Market and Massachusetts Farmers, 1750–1855," *Journal of Economic History* 41 (1981):283–314. The emerging debate has suffered, in my view, from some lack of conceptual clarity on both sides, but particularly from the dissenters' tendency to equate exchange transactions with market social relations. For a concise and very perceptive elaboration, see Michael A. Bernstein and Sean Wilentz, "Marketing, Commerce, and Capitalism in Rural Massachusetts," *Journal of Economic History* 44 (1984):171–73.

5. In Carroll and Jackson counties, for example, 52 percent and 45 percent of the total improved acreage, respectively, were controlled by farms having fewer than 100 improved acres in 1860; well over 70 percent of the cropland was controlled by farms with fewer than 200 improved acres. In the southeastern Cotton Belt, which includes Georgia, over half of the total improved acreage was controlled by units with 500 or more improved acres. See Manuscript Census, Georgia, Carroll and Jackson counties, Schedule II, 1860, Georgia Department of Archives and History, Atlanta (hereafter cited as GDAH); James D. Foust, *The Yeoman Farmer and the Westward Expansion of United States Cotton Production* (New York, 1975), 110.

6. In Carroll and Jackson counties, 83 percent and 69 percent of the free household heads, respectively, owned no slaves; 69 percent and 62 percent of the respective slave-owning household heads owned five slaves or less. See Manuscript Census, Georgia, Carroll and Jackson counties, Schedule III, 1860, GDAH.

7. See Merrill, "Cash Is Good to Eat," 42–66; Teodor Shanin, "The Nature and Logic of the Peasant Economy," *Journal of Peasant Studies* 1 (1973): 67, 74; Florencia E. Mallon, *The Defense of Community in Peru's Central Highlands: Peasant Struggle and Capitalist Transition, 1860–1940* (Princeton, N.J., 1983), 15–41.

8. A calculation of food production and consumption on farms containing fewer than 200 improved acres in Jackson and Carroll counties in 1860 shows that almost three-fourths of the farms had surpluses.

9. See, for example, Ordinary Estate Records, Inventories and Appraisements, Carroll County, vol. C, 117, 119–20, 273–74, 282; vol. D, 588–89, GDAH; Court of Ordinary, Inventories and Appraisements, Jackson County, vol. A, 591–92, 635, GDAH. The probate records suggest that at least seven households in ten had spinning wheels and looms.

10. Excellent illustration of the household division of labor can be found in the Civil War questionnaires compiled by folklorist John Trotwood Moore from war veterans residing in Tennessee at the turn of the twentieth century. Many of the respondents had grown up and spent many years in other Southern states. The questionnaires are deposited in the Tennessee State Archives, Nashville. Also see Lawrence M. Friedman, *A History of American Law* (New York, 1973), 184–86; Anne Firor Scott, *The Southern Lady: From Pedestal to Politics, 1830–1930* (Chicago,

1970), 46–79; Elizabeth Fox-Genovese, "Antebellum Southern Households: A New Perspective on a Familiar Question," *Review* 7 (1983):224–26, 238–49.

11. Jess Hudgins quoted in Floyd C. Watkins and Charles H. Watkins, *Yesterday in the Hills* (Chicago, 1963), 103–4. Also see Lloyd G. Marlin, *A History of Cherokee County* (Atlanta, 1932), 83; Frank L. Owsley, *Plain Folk of the Old South* (Baton Rouge, La., 1949), 104–17.

12. Marlin, *History of Cherokee County*, 51; George B. Hudson Store and Farm Account Book, Gwinnett County, 1856, Mrs. Don G. Aiken Collection, GDAH; James Washington Watts Farm Diary, Cass County, 1854–55, GDAH; John S. Dobbins Papers, Habersham County, December 25, 1856, reel 2, Emory University Archives, Atlanta, Ga.

13. See Table 6.2.

14. Garnett Andrews, *Reminiscences of an Old Georgia Lawyer* (Atlanta, 1870), 73; James C. Bonner, *Georgia's Last Frontier: The Development of Carroll County* (Athens, Ga., 1971), 27; Lewis E. Atherton, *The Southern Country Store, 1800–1860* (Baton Rouge, La., 1949), 69.

15. See Table 6.3.

16. Job Bowers Account Book, Hart County, 1832–36, GDAH. Also see Foster and King Mill Account Book, Cherokee County, 1857–58, GDAH; Watkins and Watkins, *Yesterday in the Hills*, 59.

17. R. G. Dun and Company, Credit Reporting Ledgers of the Mercantile Agency, Baker Library, Harvard Business School, Cambridge, Mass., Georgia, V, 102–6, 110, 112, 116; XVIII, 19–24; XVI, 110, 112; Thomas Morris Store Ledger, Franklin County, 1847, GDAH; Fain Account Books, Floyd County, 1847–52, GDAH; Atherton, *Southern Country Store*, 49.

18. The homestead exemption entitled every household head to exempt from judgment 50 acres of land, and an additional 5 acres for each child under the age of fifteen; one horse or mule; ten hogs; $30 worth of provisions; one cow and one calf; beds and bedding for the family; one spinning wheel and loom; two pairs of cotton cards; 100 pounds of lint cotton; common tools of trade; ordinary cooking utensils and table crockery; and the family's clothing. See Thomas R. R. Cobb, *A Digest of the Statute Laws of the State of Georgia* (Athens, Ga., 1851), 389–90; R. H. Clark, T. R. R. Cobb, and David Irwin, *The Code of the State of Georgia* (Atlanta, 1861), 398–99. In Carroll and Jackson counties, the ordinary recorded twenty-one and twelve mortgages, respectively, in 1860. Most were held by merchants, involved real property and slaves, and secured substantial sums, the notes averaging $300. See Superior Court Deed Record, Carroll County, vol. I, 379–595, Carroll County Courthouse, Carrollton, Ga. (hereafter cited as CCC); Superior Court Deeds and Mortgages, Jackson County, vol. P, 236–427, GDAH.

19. In Carroll County, almost half of the stores opened during the 1850s failed to survive until the end of the decade, but in 1860 seventeen of nineteen merchants owned real estate.

20. Among farmers cultivating fewer than 200 acres in Carroll and Jackson counties in 1860, about 75 percent raised cotton for sale. More generally, the counties located near the recently completed Western and Atlantic Railroad saw two-, three-, and fourfold increases in cotton production during the decade. See *Seventh Census of*

the United States, *1850* (Washington, D.C., 1853), 210–16; *Eighth Census of the United States, 1860* (Washington, D.C., 1864), 23–27.

21. It is important to recognize that acquisitive behavior does not simply reside within the realm of capitalist social relations. Acquisitiveness is common in many different precapitalist societies, as anthropologists have long noted. The key historical point is not whether people are acquisitive, but what they seek to acquire, how they acquire it, and what they do with what they acquire. For a splendid discussion that focuses on Peru, yet should be required reading for American social historians, see Mallon, *Defense of Community*, 24–40. By "demand for labor-power" I mean, of course, demand for free labor.

22. Clark, "Household, Market, and Capital," 50–54, 131–43.

23. Eugene D. Genovese, *The Political Economy of Slavery: Studies in the Economy and Society of the Slave South* (New York, 1965), 13–39, 157–59; Barbara J. Fields, "The Nineteenth-Century South: History and Theory," *Plantation Society* 2 (1983): 8–17.

24. See, for example, Milledgeville (Georgia) *Federal Union*, 11 December 1860; J. D. B. DeBow, *The Interest in Slavery of the Southern Nonslaveholder* (Charleston, S.C., 1860); Cassville (Georgia) *Standard*, 26 November 1857.

25. Ira Berlin and Herbert G. Gutman, "Natives and Immigrants, Free Men and Slaves: Urban Workingmen in the Antebellum South," *American Historical Review* 88 (1983):1175–1200; Joseph P. Reidy, "Masters and Slaves, Planters and Freedmen: The Transition from Slavery to Freedom in Central Georgia, 1820–1880," Diss., Northern Illinois University, 1982, 64–74; William L. Barney, "Towards the Civil War: The Dynamics of Change in a Black Belt County," in Orville Vernon Burton and Robert C. McMath, Jr., eds., *Class, Conflict, and Consensus: Antebellum Southern Community Studies* (Westport, Conn., 1982), 146–65.

26. For a brilliant analysis focusing on Maryland see Barbara J. Fields, *Slavery and Freedom on the Middle Ground* (New Haven, Conn., 1985).

27. J. D. Harris to W. O. Bannon, Carrollton, 29 May 1867 (courtesy of Edna Lackey, GDAH); John Mills to Col. C. C. Sibley, Lawrenceville, 5 April 1867; W. J. Bryan to Col. C. C. Sibley, Cartersville, 15 May 1867, reels 15 and 16, Bureau of Refugees, Freedmen, and Abandoned Lands, Record Group 105, Records of the Assistant Commissioner, National Archives, Washington, D.C.

28. See Table 6.1. As a visitor to Jackson County wrote in 1869, "The farmers are very despondent and assume that the drought will cut down the yield . . . to about one third of a crop. I learn that a movement is on foot to organize an association to buy Western corn before it gets beyond their reach." See Athens *Southern Banner*, 3 September 1869.

29. Carroll County *Times*, 2 February 1872. Also see Columbus *Sun*, quoted in Carroll County *Times*, 12 September 1873; Cartersville *Standard and Express*, 29 February 1872.

30. On railroads see Athens *Southern Banner*, 4 December 1868, 1 January 1869, 17 June 1870, 25 November 1870; Grand Jury Presentments, Franklin County, Superior Court Minutes, April 1869, 273–74, GDAH; Henry V. Poor, *Manual of the Railroads of the United States, 1869–1870* (New York, 1870), 274; *Manual, 1871–1872*, 453; *Manual, 1875–1876*, 435–36; *Manual, 1877–1878*, xxiv, 512, 580;

*Manual, 1881*, 404; Peter S. McGuire, "The Railroads of Georgia, 1860–1880," *Georgia Historical Quarterly* 16 (1932):194–95. On the increasing availability and use of commercial fertilizers, see the testimony of M. A. Stovall in U.S. Senate, Committee on Education and Labor, *Report of the Committee of the Senate on the Relations Between Labor and Capital*, 5 vols. (Washington, D.C., 1885), 4:765–66.

31. Thomas P. Janes, *Annual Report of the Commissioner of Agriculture for the State of Georgia for the Year 1875* (Atlanta, 1875), 146–57.

32. Columbus *Sun*, quoted in Carroll County *Times*, 10 October 1873.

33. R. G. Dun and Company, *The Mercantile Agency Reference Books, 1870–1885* (New York, 1870–85); Dun and Company, Credit Ledgers, Georgia, XVIII, 37.

34. Harold D. Woodman, *King Cotton and His Retainers: Financing and Marketing the Cotton Crop of the South, 1800–1925* (Lexington, Ky., 1968), 199–294; Roger L. Ransom and Richard Sutch, *One Kind of Freedom: The Economic Consequences of Emancipation* (New York, 1977), 107–9.

35. The literature on federal policy regarding the ex-slaves and the plantation system is now quite large, but see especially Louis S. Gerteis, *From Contraband to Freedman: Federal Policy Toward Southern Blacks, 1861–1865* (Westport, Conn., 1973); Willie Lee Rose, *Rehearsal for Reconstruction: The Port Royal Experiment* (New York, 1964); William S. McFeely, *Yankee Stepfather: O. O. Howard and the Freedmen* (New Haven, Conn., 1970); Eric Foner, *Politics and Ideology in the Age of the Civil War* (New York, 1980), 97–149; Lawrence N. Powell, *New Masters: Northern Planters During the Civil War and Reconstruction* (New Haven, Conn., 1980).

36. Ransom and Sutch, *One Kind of Freedom*, 110–16; Robert P. Sharkey, *Money, Class, and Party: An Economic Study of the Civil War and Reconstruction* (Baltimore, 1959), 221–37.

37. Robert P. Sharkey, "Commercial Banking," in David T. Gilchrist and W. David Lewis, eds., *Economic Change in the Civil War Era* (Greenville, Del., 1965), 27.

38. Michael Wayne, *The Reshaping of Plantation Society: The Natchez District, 1860–1880* (Baton Rouge, La., 1983), 150–83; Jonathan M. Wiener, *Social Origins of the New South: Alabama, 1860–1885* (Baton Rouge, La., 1978), 77–102.

39. David Irwin, *Code of the State of Georgia* (Macon, Ga., 1873), 344; Robert P. Brooks, *The Agrarian Revolution in Georgia, 1865–1912* (Madison, Wisc., 1914), 32–33; Enoch Banks, *The Economics of Land Tenure in Georgia* (New York, 1905), 47.

40. For a detailed discussion, see Harold D. Woodman, "Post-Civil War Southern Agriculture and the Law," *Agricultural History* 53 (January 1979):326–31; Wayne, *Reshaping of Plantation Society*, 150–98.

41. Testimony of H. J. McCormick, Bartow County, 1912, in Robert P. Brooks, Inquiries Concerning Georgia Farms, I, University of Georgia Archives, Athens, Georgia.

42. Dun and Company, Credit Ledgers, Georgia, VI, 56; *Publications of the Georgia Department of Agriculture, 1883* (Atlanta, 1883), 350; *Supplemental Report of the Georgia Department of Agriculture, 1882* (Atlanta, 1882), 10–11; Jackson *Herald*, 4 November 1887; Ord. Est. Recs., Annual Returns, Carroll County, 3 January 1884, vol. I, 133, GDAH. Also see Ransom and Sutch, *One Kind of Freedom*, 237–43.

43. See, for example, Mortgage Book, Carroll County, vol. A, 110–11; vol. B, 346–47, CCC.

44. In Carroll County, for instance, the Dun and Company records demonstrate

that forty-six of forty-nine mercantile concerns in 1880 were located at or near one of four such towns. See Dun and Company, *Mercantile Reference Book, 1880*; Ransom and Sutch, *One Kind of Freedom*, 146–48. On farmers trading with more than one merchant, see Ord. Est. Recs., Annual Returns, Carroll County, vol. I, 133, 138, GDAH.

45. Dun and Company, Credit Ledgers, Georgia, XVIII, 23, 33.

46. Court of Ord., Inv. and App., Jackson County, vol. H, 260–61, 264–65, 279, GDAH.

47. In Carroll and Jackson counties, respectively, 66 percent and 77 percent of the probated inventories filed during the 1850s listed spinning wheels and looms. During the 1880s, only 19 percent and 22 percent of the respective inventories listed spinning wheels and looms. See Ord. Est. Recs., Inv. and App., Carroll County, vol. C–D, 1850s; vol. A, 1880s; Court of Ord., Inv. and App., Jackson County, vol. A, 1850s; Court of Ord., Appraisements, Administrators, Guardians, and Executors, Jackson County, Book A, Jackson County Courthouse (hereafter cited JCC).

48. Dun and Company, Credit Ledgers, Georgia, V, 116L; Thomas D. Clark, *Pills, Petticoats, and Plows: The Southern Country Store, 1865–1900* (Norman, Okla., 1944), 41–42.

49. Jackson *Herald*, 12 June 1885; Frary Elrod, *Historical Notes on Jackson County* (Jefferson, Ga., 1967), 130; Thomas G. Hardman, *History of Harmony Grove–Commerce* (Commerce, Ga., 1949), 64.

50. Dun and Company, Credit Ledgers, Georgia, V, 116A, 116E, 118–19, 134; Jefferson *Forest News*, April 1878; Jackson *Herald*, 3 June 1887; *Report on Cotton Production in the United States*, 2 vols. (Washington, D.C., 1884), 2:170; Clark, *Pills, Petticoats, and Plows*, 43–44; Woodman, *King Cotton*, 301–3.

51. Dun and Company, Credit Ledgers, Georgia, XVIII, 31; V, 116, 121, 138; Jackson *Herald*, 3 June 1887; Jefferson *Forest News*, 7 August 1875; Carroll County *Times*, 3 August 1888; Bonner, *Georgia's Last Frontier*, 101, 181–84.

52. In 1860, for example, millers, blacksmiths, and carpenters composed 51 percent and 41 percent of all craft occupations in Carroll and Jackson counties, respectively. In 1880, they composed 65 percent and 66 percent, respectively.

53. Ord. Est. Recs., Inv. and App., Carroll County, vol. A, 1888; Court of Ord., App., Jackson County, Book A, 1885, JCC.

54. Court of Ord., Inv. and App., Jackson County, vol. H, 295–96; vol. F–G, 20; Ord. Est. Recs., Inv. and App., Carroll County, vol. A, 163–66, GDAH; Lucius H. Featherston Papers, Heard County, 30 April 1873, box 1, folder 7, Emory University Archives.

55. For important comparative treatments of this process, see E. J. Hobsbawm, *The Age of Capital, 1848–1875* (New York, 1975), 176–77; Edward W. Fox, *History in Geographic Perspective: The Other France* (New York, 1971), 19–32.

56. *Proceedings of the Constitutional Convention Held in Atlanta, Georgia, 1877* (Atlanta, 1877), 463–64, 451; Henri H. Freeman, "Some Aspects of Debtor Relief in Georgia During Reconstruction," M.A. thesis, Emory University, 1951, 63–64. For complaints against the homestead exemption from Upcountry commercial interests see Cartersville *Express*, 14 April 1870; Gwinnett *Herald*, 16 July 1873; Carroll County *Times*, 3 August 1877.

57. Cartersville *Express*, 4 May 1876; Mortgage Book, Carroll County, vol. B, 331,

346–47, 362; vol. C, 28, 267–68; vol. I, 133, 138, 268, 325–27, CCC; Court of Ord., Inv. and App., Jackson County, vol. H, 39, 280, 299, GDAH.

58. Superior Court Deeds and Mortgages, Carroll County, 1875, GDAH; Mortgage Book, 1882, 1885, vol. B–C, CCC. In Jackson County, twenty-three mortgages were recorded in 1875, eighty-seven in 1880, and although concrete evidence is not extant for the 1880s, the county clerk claimed that he recorded more mortgages in 1891 than during a previous ten-year term. See Superior Court Deeds and Mortgages, Jackson County, vol. N; vol. T, GDAH; Jackson *Herald*, 10 April 1891.

59. Mortgage Book, Carroll County, 1885, CCC. The annual acreage mortgaged underrepresents the total county acreage under mortgage at any given time, for mortgages were often carried from year to year when debts remained outstanding. See *Eleventh Census of the United States, 1890* (Washington, D.C., 1894), Report on Real Estate Mortgages, 373, 380.

60. Jackson *Herald*, 9 November 1883; Gwinnett *Herald*, n.d. In 1880, 60 percent of Upcountry farms were owner operated; in 1890, only 48 percent were owner operated. Although these statistics are not distinguished by race, they point to a clear trend in a region with relatively few blacks and extremely few black landowners. See *Tenth Census of the United States, 1880* (Washington, D.C., 1883), Agriculture, 40–45, 183–84; *Eleventh Census*, Agriculture, 128–32.

61. Jackson County Tax Digests, 1885, 1890, GDAH; Carroll County Tax Digests, 1885, 1890; Dun and Company, *Mercantile Reference Books, 1885–1890*; James A. Furgeson, "Power Politics and Populism: Jackson County, Georgia as a Case Study," M.A. Thesis, University of Georgia, 1975, 39–40.

62. William A. Gilley, a Carrollton, Carroll County, merchandiser, for instance, owned 2,189 acres of land during the 1880s. Of this land, 260 acres were located in the sixth district of the county on three separate land lots; 186 acres were on a lot in the ninth district; 43 acres were on a seventh district lot; and the remaining 1,700 acres were on nine additional lots in the fifth district. Gilley, moreover, had a "dwelling house" and a "store house" in town. The tax digests show similar patterns for other substantial land-holding merchants. See Ord. Est. Recs., Inv. and App., Carroll County, vol. A, 511–13; Carroll County Tax Digests, 1880–90, GDAH.

63. Compared with the average county valuations, the holdings of merchandisers normally received higher assessments. In 1890, for example, Jackson County farm land averaged $5.80 per acre. But merchant I. T. Austin's real estate was valued at over $8 per acre, merchant L. G. Hardman's at over $7, merchants George and William Harbor's and S. M. Shankle's at over $6. See Jackson County Tax Digest, 1890, GDAH; Furgeson, "Power Politics and Populism," 40. On the practice of "carrying" farmers, see Michael Schwartz, *Radical Protest and Social Structure: The Southern Farmers' Alliance and Cotton Tenancy, 1880–1890* (New York, 1976), 65.

64. Elizabeth Fox-Genovese and Eugene D. Genovese, *Fruits of Merchant Capital: Slavery and Bourgeois Property in the Rise and Expansion of Capitalism* (New York, 1983), 3–25.

65. I have discussed this political contention at some length in *The Roots of Southern Populism: Yeoman Farmers and the Transformation of the Georgia Upcountry, 1850–1890* (New York, 1983), 204–68. The capitalist *reorganization* of Southern agriculture did commence during the late nineteenth century in rapidly developing areas of the Old Southwest (Louisiana, Mississippi, Texas, and Arkansas) as well as in the

relatively newly settled cotton lands of southwestern Georgia. But the major advance did not come until the 1930s and 1940s and it required large infusions of capital from the federal government.

66. The concept of "proto-industrialization" has, it should be said, come under recent attack. Among other things, critics have argued that many areas witnessing the emergence of merchant-organized rural outwork failed to continue along the road of industrial development. I am certainly not trying to suggest direct parallels between rural outwork in Europe and household-based staple agriculture in the South. Nonetheless, if we can overlook some of the misleading connotations of "proto-industrialization" (which historians, in any event, do not wish to overemphasize), a process of capitalist transition in the countryside, offering very useful comparisons, can be glimpsed. The comparisons should push us to learn much more about the size, composition, and changing division of labor within Southern rural households, black and white. For important theoretical treatments of the European experience, see Peter Kriedte, Hans Medick, and Jürgen Schlumbohm, *Industrialization before Industrialization: Rural Industry in the Genesis of Capitalism*, trans. by Beate Schempp (Cambridge, Eng., 1981); Hans Medick, "The Proto-industrial Family Economy: The Structural Function of Household and Family During the Transition from Peasant Society to Industrial Capitalism," *Social History* 3 (1976): 291–315.

67. Jackson *Herald*, 26 February 1892. Also see Cherokee (County) *Advance*, 5 December 1890; Schwartz, *Radical Protest*, 65; Rupert P. Vance, *Human Geography of the South: A Study in Regional Resources and Human Adequacy* (Chapel Hill, N.C., 1932), 190.

68. Carol MacLennon and Richard Walker, "Crisis and Change in U.S. Agriculture: An Overview," in Roger Burbach and Patricia Flynn, eds., *Agribusiness in the Americas* (New York, 1980), 25.

ROBERT C. MCMATH, JR.

# 7. Sandy Land and Hogs in the Timber

(AGRI)CULTURAL ORIGINS OF THE FARMERS'

ALLIANCE IN TEXAS

I

The Farmers' Alliance began in the late 1870s at the point west of Fort Worth, Texas, where the farming and ranching frontiers collided.* That much is clear, but *why* such a movement began there and then has been a matter of debate ever since. Scholars have addressed the question within the framework of a more general one—what causes protest movements to erupt in industrializing societies? Many have perceived such movements as by-products of "modernization": Inexorable forces disrupt familiar patterns of community life, leaving in their wake a "mass society" of discontented, culturally confused individuals. Confronted with this inevitable rush to modernization, so the story goes, protestors have either evoked a lost golden age to mount a comforting albeit anachronistic crusade, or adopted the techniques of the modernizers themselves in an effort to create a counter-vailing economic force. Thus, farmer and labor movements can be categorized as backward-looking and utopian (i.e., political), or forward-looking and "businesslike."[1]

Happily, our understanding of social protest in America has passed beyond these simplistic, and often false, dichotomies. We now know, for example, that in the nineteenth century labor politics and trade unionism went hand-in-hand, and that agrarian insurgency and farmer cooperatives were part of the same movement.[2] The notion that protest occurs because modernizing forces have severed bonds of community and culture has been challenged with regard to factory workers during the period of rapid industrialization. Studies of working-class culture and workers' organizations reveal persistent efforts by skilled workers to preserve a social vision that was

*An earlier form of this essay was published as "The 'Movement Culture' of Populism Reconsidered: Cultural Origins of the Farmers' Alliance in Texas, 1879–1886," in Henry C. Dethloff and Irvin M. May, Jr., eds., *Southwestern Agriculture: Pre-Columbian to Modern* (College Station, Tex., 1982).

neither a nostalgic anachronism nor a capitulation to industrial capitalism. Through trade and reform organizations, community institutions, and the social dynamics of the shop floor, workers kept alive a "movement culture" that looked to the establishment of a cooperative commonwealth in America and to the creation of a political economy more egalitarian and humane than that being shaped by industrial capitalism.[3]

So too with American farmers has the term "movement culture" been used to denote the democratic ethos at the heart of Populism in the 1890s —most notably by the historian Lawrence Goodwyn. In Goodwyn's usage, the concept suggests a sense both of group identity and of group will that enlivened the mass movement that Populism became. The agrarian movement showed "how people could generate their own culture of democratic aspirations in order to challenge the received culture of democratic hierarchy."[4] This "movement culture" was established, according to Goodwyn, when the Farmers' Alliance, with its cooperatives and Greenbacker ideology, spread from Texas across the South and Plains states in the late 1880s.

I share the view, expressed with great eloquence by Goodwyn, that the short-lived Populist movement had at its core such a purposeful, democratic spirit. The term "culture," when thus applied to the Populists, carries the active meaning that Giovanni Vico gave it over 250 years ago of "man making his own history." I question Goodwyn's explanation of the historical foundations and specific social boundaries of that culture, however. The movement culture of Populism (as an identifiable subculture within rural America) needs to be viewed not merely as the essence of a protest or as a concept synonymous with the movement itself (as Goodwyn comes close to doing) but, historically, as a set of practices, beliefs, and values that are linked to specific rhythms of work, relations of production, and patterns of community life. We would do well, in this instance, to remember that the term "culture" had first to do with the tilling of crops. The emergence of a protesting subculture—the movement culture of Populism—had to do with the traditional culture of cotton, corn, and hogs.

For Goodwyn, the movement culture of Populism was essentially a new political subculture born from the convergence of farmer cooperatives, labor radicalism, and Greenbacker ideology among Texas Alliancemen in the late 1880s. The forces being protested composed the "received" political culture of the Civil War–Reconstruction era, especially a party system that severely limited the range of debate about America's political economy. In the South (including Texas), the dominant vehicle of that received political culture was, of course, the Democratic party. The new movement culture, in Goodwyn's view, was transmitted to rural communities throughout the South and West by the traveling lecturer-organizer of the Farmers' Alliance. All members of those rural communities could potentially be drawn into the movement culture, regardless of class or race, for all were adversely affected by the financial system that held farmers in thrall.

It will be argued in these pages that an incipient movement culture embracing both communal solidarity and egalitarianism was widespread among small farmers of the South and West *before* the rise of the Farmers' Alliance and People's party, and that it mingled with labor radicalism on the Texas frontier *before* the establishment of the cooperative system that would become the Alliance's hallmark.

If, in fact, the movement culture of Populism was well defined in rural communities before the spread of the Alliance's program of cooperative marketing and purchasing (which, for Goodwyn, was the heart of the movement culture), then the dynamics of the Alliance's astonishingly rapid organizing campaign throughout the South and Plains, and even the basic nature of the movement, need to be reexamined.

In considering the Alliance's rapid, but uneven, spread across the rural South after 1886, Goodwyn's account of organizing campaigns in the various Southern states focuses entirely on the skills of the Alliance lecturer-organizers and their fealty to the Texas-based cooperative and political programs (e.g., a close adherence to the Texas model in Georgia, and, less so, in North Carolina). But we also need to examine the resonance between the message of the organizers (often men who returned to their home states from Texas) and the preexisting culture of protest within the particular farming communities they visited.

In analyzing the nature of the Alliance movement, Goodwyn equates evidence of a pre-Populist movement culture with romantic agrarianism or the alleged "status anxiety" of American farmers, and thus rejects it.[5] There can be no doubt that Goodwyn has done a great service in laying to rest the notion that Populism was an irrational evocation of a "lost arcadia." But in rejecting Hofstadter's version of the Populist revolt, we need not throw the baby out with the bathwater: We should not overlook the traditions of rural self-sufficiency and republicanism, dating back at least to the Revolutionary era, which formed an important part of the Alliance's movement culture.

In the South, such a movement culture had long flourished among the yeoman farmers both of the Upcountry and sandy land interstices of the Plantation Belt. It was grounded in what Steven Hahn has called the "moral economy" of small producers, in which "habits of mutuality" born of a premarket economy shaped a powerful and persistent sense of community. Embedded in the mentality of self-sufficient farm ownership, this culture in the post–Civil War era shared with labor radicalism a sense of outrage at the rapid concentration of economic power that threatened personal autonomy. The two cultures also shared a sense of community solidarity, which put limits on property rights, including property rights in land.[6]

Before the Civil War, the movement culture of the Southern countryside usually lay concealed within the social fabric binding planter, yeoman, and slave together in mutually dependent relationships. After 1865, the transformation of the slave plantation, the intrusion of cotton agriculture into the Upcountry, and the end of the boom in world cotton prices made visible the conflict between small farmers, on the one hand, and planters and merchants, on the other. The conflict came to light in several forms during the 1870s and 1880s—social banditry and arson, fence cutting, and a host of community-based political protest movements.[7]

On the Texas frontier labor and agrarian radicalism converged, creating a movement expressed institutionally in the Farmers' Alliance. To understand this convergence, it is essential to understand the community in which it all began. We need to know the lay of the land and the patterns of social organization that settlers brought with them to the frontier beyond Fort Worth, as well as the impact of a market economy on their lives.

II

The great Western historians Walter Prescott Webb and James C. Malin would urge us to begin a study of the Farmers' Alliance with soil, vegetation, and water. They knew, as did Marc Bloch, that rural history begins with the land itself.[8] Webb and Malin would also remind us that the birthplace of the Alliance was neither the Great Plains nor the grasslands, but the Cross Timbers region of Texas. After an abortive start in 1877 in Lampasas County, the Alliance reemerged in 1879 at Poolville, Parker County, just south of the Wise County line (see Map 7.1). For five years the Alliance operated almost entirely in Parker, Wise, and some surrounding counties. Most of that territory lay within the western Cross Timbers, one of two fingers of sandy, hilly land reaching down from the Red River toward central Texas. The Cross Timbers region is covered by post oak and blackjack, broken here and there by patches of open prairie and sliced by the rich bottom land adjoining the tributaries of the Trinity and Brazos rivers. The western Cross Timbers sits athwart the ninety-eighth meridian; it lies at the edge of a region that receives enough rainfall to support traditional agriculture.[9]

To settlers from the South, the Cross Timbers might well have looked like home. The trees were a little scrubby, but the region's soil, timber, and watercourses reminded them of eastern and central Texas, southern Arkansas, and even the Deep South. The soil was not as fertile as the Grand Prairie to the east, but in years of average rainfall this was good poor man's land. Here a Southern dirt farmer could raise corn and cotton in the bottoms and later on the upland slopes, and could let his hogs root for mast in

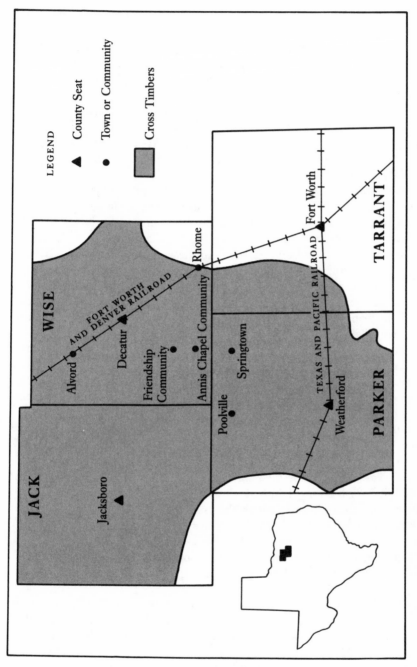

*7.1. The Cross Timbers Region of Texas*

the timber and his cattle graze on the open prairie as his forebears had done for generations.[10]

In the 1870s, as geographer Terry G. Jordan has demonstrated, the Cross Timbers and the "Heart of Texas" region immediately to the south marked the meeting point of two migratory streams of Southern farmer-stockmen. Over the course of a century, one stream had flowed through Georgia and the Pine Barrens of the Lower South into the coastal prairie of south Texas and thence to the Cross Timbers and Heart of Texas. The other had moved through Tennessee and Kentucky—even Indiana, Illinois, and Missouri—thence into northeastern Texas and then onto the frontier beyond Fort Worth. Both migratory streams had their headwaters in the South Carolina backcountry of the seventeenth and eighteenth centuries, where there had flourished a culture of open-range cattle and hog raising, mixed with subsistence farming—a culture brought to the New World by the English, Scots-Irish, and African settlers of Carolina.[11]

Along the way from South Carolina to Texas, this Anglo-Celtic, African culture of herding and farming absorbed elements of the Mexican cattle culture. As Terry Jordan shows, however, it was "Carolina's Children" who set the pattern of open-range cattle production and subsistence farming, which in turn shaped the Western cattle industry. The point of origin of the Great Plains cattle kingdom was the Cross Timbers/Heart of Texas—a tier of counties stretching from Lampasas in the south up through Erath, Parker, and Wise, to Montague on the Red River. This was, in addition, precisely the area from which the Farmers' Alliance would in the 1880s expand back to the southeast (retracing the steps of Carolina's children), and northward to Kansas and the Dakotas.[12]

In the early 1850s, Southern farmer-stockmen first began taking up small tracts of land in what would soon become Parker and Wise counties. The settlers, many of whom had trekked from Kentucky and Tennessee with stops in east Texas, made their way along the military roads extending west from Fort Worth on the Trinity River and from Fort Graham on the Brazos. Their farmsteads clustered along the creek bottoms in distinct communities, often made up of kinsmen and former neighbors, as was the case in the Deep Creek community of Wise County, established by Samuel Woody, Jr., and his Tennessee neighbors. Here these Southern emigrés combined stock raising with subsistence farming, producing very little in the way of cash crops.[13]

The settlements that dotted the watercourses and military roads during the 1850s were fragile outposts indeed, separated by miles of unsettled land, cut off from access to markets, and subject to raids from nearby Comanches. With the outbreak of the Civil War, this frontier area became a virtual no-man's-land, threatened by marauding deserters from both sides, as well as by Indians. The settled population of both Parker and Wise counties shrank during the war, and many of those who remained sought the relative safety of the county seats of Weatherford (Parker County) and Decatur (Wise). For a full decade after the war, frontier violence and isolation prevented the renewal of farm settlement.

Soon after the last Indian raid in 1875, however, vast tracts of land were thrown on the market; by the end of the decade two railroads were pushing into the Cross Timbers. The Texas and Pacific Railroad was built west from Fort Worth through Weatherford, and the Fort Worth and Denver Railroad ran through Decatur. By the late 1870s Fort Worth had rail service, which greatly reduced the cost of marketing commercial crops grown in the Cross Timbers.[14] In the late 1870s the great migration to Texas resumed, and now the Cross Timbers received a full measure of the new settlers.

Compared with before the Civil War, even more of the new arrivals were Southerners, mainly from Tennessee, Missouri, Arkansas, and Mississippi, as well as from east Texas. Almost all were white, and almost all were small-scale farmers.[15] The agriculture they practiced reflected an economic system in transition: like white yeomen of the Southern Upcountry before 1880, they raised cotton as part of a diversified crop mix essential to self-sufficiency.[16] By 1880, farmsteads were filling up the bottom and timber land of Parker and Wise counties. Crossroads settlements were popping up every few miles, and the county seats of Weatherford and Decatur were becoming bustling trade centers.[17]

The settlers brought with them more than bull tongue plows and seed corn. Like immigrants in other times and places, they also carried familiar patterns of culture and social organization. The values shared by Southern white yeomen prevailed as the collective sense of this new community. Socially, this was no undifferentiated mass of humanity. Immigrants often came with extended family groups and with neighbors from the Old South or east Texas. Like other settlers on the Western frontier, they immediately established churches, schools, fraternal lodges, neighborhood farming clubs, and even literary societies: in short, the making of a "voluntary community," which quickly created an interlocking web of social relationships.[18]

But before concluding that this region was peopled by one happy family, consider the persistent strain of violence in the Cross Timbers, a proclivity that involved more than the celebrated Indian raids and deserter lawlessness. When Texas joined the Confederacy the Cross Timbers saw the eruption of armed conflict between Confederate and Union sympathizers. In Wise County, which had narrowly voted against secession, five members of a pro-Union organization were hanged by vigilantes for supposedly participating in a plot to seize north-central Texas. In nearby Collin County, where Unionism was less strong, vigilantes hanged *forty* alleged participants in the plot.

After the war, various secret organizations operated in rural Parker and

Wise counties. The Union League actively promoted Republican candidates for office, and well-organized bands of settlers pursued horse thieves and cattle rustlers. In 1872, for example, vigilantes in Parker County killed a woman and five of her daughters whose home near Springfield was thought to be a center of prostitution and a rendezvous for horse thieves. The woman's husband, a Union sympathizer, had been killed by vigilantes near Springtown in 1863.[19] With the influx of farmers in the late 1870s, disputes over land titles led to more violence. By that time most of the "free" land had been preempted and was held by individual owners, land companies, and railroads, or by county school systems from the settled parts of the state. The confusion and outright venality of the land system engendered hatred for "land sharks" and land syndicates. Neighborhood bands enforced the principle that in a title dispute, occupancy counted for more than a piece of paper from the state land office.

In Wise County between 1874 and 1879, many land patents were issued by the state, most of them ranging from one-half to four sections. As this was much larger than the average farm size in the county, much of the land must have been held for speculative purposes. During the same time, land was sold in farm-sized lots (150–200 acres) by agents of the Matagorda and Van Zandt county school systems, which had been given large tracts of land in Wise County. By the end of the 1870s most of the state and school land had passed into private hands, and most real estate transactions were between private individuals. In southwestern Wise County, where the Alliance first entered the county, much of the land was deeded originally to Matagorda County schools and to the Texas and Pacific Railroad, which had received land there even though it did not build its line through Wise County.[20]

Popular opposition to the concentration of wealth and power also included support for "social banditry." Sam Bass, a transplanted Indiana farm hand, had a brief but spectacular career as a train robber in north-central Texas in the late 1870s. Between robberies, he and his gang hid out in the bottoms and woodlands of the Cross Timbers. Bass was known locally as the "Robin Hood of the Cross Timbers," and his exploits were celebrated in story and song. The fact that he stole gold from the Texas and Pacific Railroad rather than cattle from settlers helps explain his popularity. The telling and retelling of Sam Bass stories among families in the Cross Timbers gives us one more clue about the social consciousness of rural people in this region 100 years ago. Whatever Bass's personal motivation for robbing trains, the legends that surrounded his brief career place him squarely in the tradition of "social banditry" described by E. J. Hobsbawm.[21] These stories can be viewed as part of a tradition of "peasant" protest, resembling, in some respects, the peasant movements of Spain and southern Italy in the nineteenth century.

Violence and social conflict in these counties had a territorial dimension. In Wise County, Union sympathizers clustered in the Cross Timber section west of Decatur, while the eastern Grand Prairie and the town were Confederate strongholds. In Parker County, residents of Weatherford and the southern part of the county considered settlers around Poolville and Springtown to be low-living poor whites and agitators. These divisions predated the influx of Southern farmers in the 1870s, but they would continue to influence the social dynamics of these counties for years to come.[22]

One other manifestation of social conflict in the Cross Timbers was the struggle between Democrats and insurgent Greenbackers. Northern Parker and southwestern Wise counties were Greenback party strongholds in the late 1870s. Greenbackers on the north Texas frontier shared with their Northern counterparts a deep concern about the concentration of economic power. Their antimonopoly spirit was, of course, articulated in the soft-money ideas of Edward Kellogg and Alexander Campbell, but in the Cross Timbers it was expressed with equal force in ideas about land. Texas Greenbackers believed that land should be reserved for actual settlers and that ownership of a tract of land did not convey the right to restrict free access to grass and water. Antilandlordism and the cry of "land to the cultivator" were, moreover, part of the cultural heritage of west Texas settlers of Scots-Irish and Irish descent. The agitation of the land issue in west Texas in the 1870s and 1880s coincided with the rise of the American Land League among Irish-Americans. It is at least possible that some of the west Texas protestors were familiar with the Land League and its organ, the *Irish World.*[23]

Their opponents believed that Greenbackers in Parker and Wise counties did more than *talk* about land rights. Greenbackers led neighborhood associations which, it was reported, took the law into their own hands to oppose rustlers. Greenback associations were accused of other extralegal activities, including defending squatters' rights to their homes and farms and cutting fences put up by large land holders. J. J. McKinley, a leading Wise County Greenbacker and spokesman for one neighborhood protective association, denied published reports of a paramilitary band in his part of the county: "There is a stock association of all the citizens of this community for the legal and legitimate protection of our stock on the range. . . . We have never talked anything [illegal], only to be governed by the laws of our land."[24] To upstanding Democrats, the Greenbackers represented more than political adversaries. Working in secret and promoting objectives that challenged values dear to propertied Democrats, Greenbackers were, like Union sympathizers and marauding Indians, beyond the pale of civilization.

III

This, then, was the Cross Timbers in 1879: sandy land, white yeoman farmers, a stock-raising/small farming economy and Southern community in the making, and a deep-seated tradition of conflict and violence. The founding of the Alliance was part of the larger process of building a voluntary community and of protecting the culturally sanctioned rights of dirt farmers against all comers, regardless of legal niceties.

The Alliance's early days have been described in detail elsewhere.[25] Suffice it to say that a Farmers' Alliance began in northern Lampasas County in 1877. This neighborhood club of small farmers was steeped in fraternal rituals and secrecy, and its main economic activity involved livestock raising. In the Pleasant Valley community, cattle grazed freely in the open pasture and timberland. This traditional practice required cooperation in locating lost and stolen animals, a need the Alliance attempted to meet by concerning itself with returning strays and protecting the community against rustlers.

The founding of the Alliance coincided with the drive to establish local Greenback clubs in Texas. The Lampasas group was immediately drawn into Greenback politics, although some of its members remained staunch Democrats. The group could not resolve the problem of how to maintain its identity as a nonpartisan community organization and economic interest group while participating in political insurgency. Politics divided the infant Alliance, rendering it virtually moribund by 1879.[26]

In the spring of that year an itinerant rural teacher named William Baggett established a Farmers' Alliance based on the Lampasas constitution at Poolville, Parker County.[27] Like the Lampasas group, this club clothed itself in the ceremonial trappings of fraternal organizations and devoted much of its energy to locating strays and deterring rustlers. In its organizing efforts, the Alliance made use of rural teachers (such as Baggett) and preachers (such as S. O. Daws), men who could "get up a school" or sway a congregation. It recruited neighborhood notables for leadership positions, old settlers whose community standing derived more from their years of residence than from substantial accumulation of wealth. The Alliance also spread through kinship and trade networks extending northward from Poolville to Wise County and westward into Jack County.

In addition to Daws and Baggett, the early Alliance had the services of D. B. Gilliland, who taught school and farmed in Parker and Jack counties; William Garvin, who taught in various Wise County communities; and Garvin's neighbor, O. G. Peterson, a physician who was superintendent of a neighborhood Sunday school. Early sub-Alliance presidents included Matt Huff and C. J. Van Meter, pioneer settlers of the Black Creek and Bethel communities. Numerous family connections existed between early Alliancemen in northern Parker and southwestern Wise counties, and a number of them moved on to Jack County, forming a community of immigrants from the Poolville–Springtown–Annis Chapel area in the next county to the west. In the early days, Poolville and Springtown were isolated physically as well as culturally from the county seat of Weatherford. Mail and wagon routes ran from Springtown up into Wise County through the Friendship and Annis Chapel communities. The initial expansion of the Alliance followed that road.[28]

The Alliance fit comfortably into the interlocking collection of voluntary associations and neighborhood settlements that bound together frontier society. In that setting the ritualistic affirmation of community, the protection of livestock, and the organizing power of the voluntary associations were very important. Alliancemen took these associations and responsibilities seriously, and so should those who study the agrarian movement. But there is more to the story.

The Alliance formed in Poolville in a dry year, when the corn crop failed to meet even the subsistence needs of local farmers, and when foreclosures, as well as title disputes, were commonplace.[29] And it began amidst the climate of protest that fostered Greenback insurgency and farmer vigilantism in the Cross Timbers. There is, in fact, considerable evidence that the Alliance was, at its inception, directly involved in both.

In the first place, several of the early Alliance leaders unquestionably were active in the Greenback party. There was William Forster, for example, who edited the Greenback and Alliance newspaper in Wise County. Other figures, including S. O. Daws, the most influential leader of the Alliance in its early years, were probably Greenback party members.[30] At least as early as 1882, Alliancemen were supporting Greenbacker candidates for office in Cross Timbers counties, and in the decade of the 1880s there followed an unbroken string of Alliance-backed third-party efforts. In 1882 the Alliance declared that "we will not nominate or support any man or set of men for office *as a distinct party,*" but the very wording of their resolution suggests the kind of compromise with political activism that some Northern labor groups had already made and which would become, under Daws's leadership, the standard Alliance policy.[31] Given the familiarity of early Alliance leaders with Greenback labor politics, it seems more likely that the "Daws plan" was an *adaptation* from organized labor, rather than an Alliance *innovation*, as Goodwyn contends.

Evidence of Alliance vigilantism is less conclusive but still substantial. In 1884 a Fort Worth reporter was given this account of the organization's beginnings: Settlers had flooded into Parker and Wise counties during the 1870s, purchased homes and made improvements on them, only to discover that the titles to the land were in question, and ... a slip of paper in Austin and a well worked technical flaw somewhere in the chain of the title was, in the hands of skillful and expert landsharks, liable to turn them all out of house and home. ... A common necessity ... cemented them together in a common cause; so strong a front did they present that their phalanx was irresistible, and the landsharks were routed, horse and foot, in complete and admirable confusion.[32]

Newspapers in the county seats that took notice of the Alliance in the first years presented a similar picture, although stated somewhat differently. One called the Alliancemen "Molly Maguires, Anarchists, and Communists." Another said that the order harbored "thieves, robbers, and even murderers."[33] It must have seemed to these worried townsmen that the Alliance was just one more secret backwoods organization threatening to destroy the fragile veneer of civilization in the Cross Timbers.[34]

Here, then, was the beginning of Alliance radicalism and the emergence into public view of the movement culture that would animate Populism. Before the crop lien came to the Cross Timbers, before the cooperative stores and exchanges, before the joint campaign with the Knights of Labor, the Farmers' Alliance represented the convergence of agrarian and Greenbacker radicalism.[35] The initial point of convergence was a shared set of values about land—about the importance of landownership in the preservation of republican liberties, about the growing danger of land monopolies, and, as we shall see, about the preservation of traditional community obligations that accompanied landownership.

IV

Between 1883 and 1886 the Cross Timbers region was transformed by economic and social upheavals that compelled the Alliance movement to refocus its activities. Interpreted through the movement culture of the young Alliance, those upheavals were judged a consequence of growing monopoly power. And in response, the Alliance's organizational structure enabled its leaders to mobilize new recruits for the army of the cooperative commonwealth.

In the early 1880s, the rapid spread of barbed wire fencing touched off armed conflict in parts of Texas. Tens of thousands of acres were enclosed in a single fence, without gates, sometimes cutting off access to public roads, water, and even towns. By 1883, in vast sections of the state the open range had virtually disappeared.[36] In west Texas, fencing was typically done by large-scale cattlemen, to the disadvantage of small operators who combined open-range stock raising and general farming—for example, the dirt farmers of the Cross Timbers.

The point at issue was not the construction of barbed wire fences per se (census records show that Alliancemen themselves were investing in small quantities of fencing material), but rather whether the traditional practice of enclosing cultivated fields was to be replaced by extensive enclosures of pastures and woodlands. The former practice was part of the traditional cotton–corn–hog culture; the latter threatened that culture's existence.

In the summer and fall of 1883, night riders cut fences and conducted a guerrilla war against big landowners and their agents. Cattlemen met the challenge head on, denouncing the fence cutting as "a widespread communistic raid against private rights." Some prominent citizens tried to limit the fencing debate by acknowledging that ranchers should not restrict access to roads and water, simultaneously asserting the principle of fee simple land rights and an owner's prerogative to fence his property. But this, of course, was precisely what was being questioned. Fencing impinged on customary common rights to pasture and water. It threatened the independence of small farmer-stockmen, who were prepared to deal forcibly with the threat.[37]

The fence war that raged on the Texas frontier was part of a nationwide controversy over enclosure. The cultural, economic, and political ramifications of the fence controversy need further study. Scholars pursuing this topic might well consider parallels with earlier enclosure movements in England and elsewhere, if for no other reason than that fence-cutting vigilantes in the United States saw such a connection. As one group of night riders in west Texas warned: "We don't care to be made serfs of yet like poor Ireland and the majority of England [as a result of enclosure]. We are a free people and if we can't have protection we will protect ourselves and the least you can say the better it will be for your hide and neck." Texans were using arguments identical to those of Upcountry Georgians in the early 1880s. There, a Carroll County farmer wrote, "The woods . . . were put here by our Creator for a benefit to his people, and I don't think it right to deprive a large majority to please a minority." Another farmer from the same county declared, "The citizens of this county have and always have had the legal, moral, and Bible right to let their stock . . . run at large. We all knew this when we purchased our land."[38]

In the western United States, conflict between farmers and ranchers over fencing was commonplace in the 1880s. On the farming frontier, the fencing controversy was sometimes linked to the larger question of land monopoly. In New Mexico Territory, as in Texas, antimonopoly sentiments, directed toward large land and cattle companies, created among Alliance farmers a sense of solidarity with other working people in opposition to monopoly power of all sorts.[39]

But the fencing controversy was not simply a frontier matter: It was of major concern to farmers in the Southeast and even in New England. Steven Hahn has demonstrated that in Georgia the fence question was a major political issue in the 1870s and 1880s. Opponents of extensive fencing claimed, with justification, that the practice violated such traditional common rights as grazing, hunting, and wood gathering on unenclosed pasture and woodlands. The new practice threatened the "habits of mutuality," which bound their communities together. Supporters of enclosure, on the other hand, viewed themselves as promoters of modern, scientific agriculture, which required fencing of pastures for the upgrading of livestock herds as well as for protection of crops.[40]

How did the Alliance fit into this conflict? Jack County, the western outpost of the Alliance, was in the thick of the west Texas fence war, and Alliancemen were almost certainly involved. In Parker and Wise counties there were few large fenced pastures and thus not much fence cutting, although in Parker County a fence around one 700-acre pasture was cut repeatedly. A note was left on a pile of uprooted fences reading, "We understand you have plenty of money to spend to build fences. Please put them up again for us to cut them down again. We want the fence guarded with good men so that their mettle can be tested."[41]

Whatever the extent of direct Alliance participation in fence cutting, the episode heightened the antimonopoly spirit in the movement and brought forth demands for the Alliance to act politically. Throughout the Cross Timbers, Alliancemen viewed the fencing controversy through a cultural lens that brought the immediate issue into focus, identifying for them the line between friend and foe. Said one Alliance member, "let us give the monopolists and speculators [in the legislature] a full dose of private life. . . . We can be free men, and why not?"[42] In Jack County this spirit led to the creation of the Commonwealth Immigration Society, an Alliance-backed antifencing group and vehicle for political insurgency. Under the leadership of William Garvin and other Alliancemen, the society ran a full slate of nominees for county offices in 1884 and won most of the key positions.[43]

At the same time that the fencing controversy was forcing Alliancemen to defend traditional rights, the maturing of a cotton-based market economy in the Cross Timbers compelled them to seek new forms of economic cooperation. In the early 1880s, farmers working the sandy land of the Cross Timbers steadily increased their cotton acreage. The commercial crop in the eastern Grand Prairie sections of Wise and Parker counties was wheat, not cotton. Despite increasing their cotton production, Cross Timbers farmers in the 1880s seem to have been following the "safety-first" principle, which characterized subsistence farmers the world over and was likely familiar to yeomen of the late antebellum era. As a result, cotton acreage increased, but not at the expense of corn acreage, which remained adequate for local needs. Because drought diminished the crops in 1879, a comparison between cotton and corn *production* in 1880 and 1890 would be meaningless, but a comparison of acreage provides a good clue about the farmers' *intentions*. Based on the acres they planted in corn, these husband-men evidently aimed to be self-sufficient in food- and feedstuffs, and in good years were probably able to accomplish this goal.[44]

By 1883, however, these practices had changed. The Fort Worth and Denver Railroad, along with the Texas and Pacific line, had reached Deca-tur and Weatherford, introducing a new cotton-marketing system that put these interior towns in direct contact with Galveston, St. Louis, New York, and Liverpool.[45] Along with the greater commercial opportunity came greater risk and greater dependence on the world cotton market, which had already begun its long decline. Other, more distressing developments ac-companied the increase in cotton production. The percentage of owner-operated farms declined and sharecropping increased, as did the number of farmers who were dependent on merchant credit.[46] What was happening at that moment across much of the Upcountry South was happening in the Cross Timbers: The self-sufficiency of the yeoman was giving way to the uncertainty and potential dependency of the small-scale cotton farmer.

The Alliance responded with the establishment of cooperative marketing facilities, beginning in February 1884 when the state Alliance voted to "en-courage the formation of joint stock companies in Sub and County Alli-ances."[47] It is important to understand the climate in which the Alliance turned to cooperatives. Although the Greenback party was nearly dead, the fencing controversy still raged and helped keep frontier insurgency very much alive. The market economy, meanwhile, was intruding more and more on Cross Timbers farmers. The Alliance itself was growing under the leadership of special lecturer S. O. Daws, who had been reviving lapsed Alliances and organizing new ones, delivering stirring talks on "the condi-tion of American farmers as a class and their duties as American citizens," and reminding farmers of "their obligation to stand as a great conservative body against the encroachments of monopolies and in opposition to the growing corruption of wealth and power."[48]

At the February meeting, Daws himself made the motion that launched the Alliance into cooperative enterprise. He had spent the preceding month and much of the previous year visiting farming communities across north Texas, and he understood the problems of the dirt farmers. From the per-spective of Daws and others like him, the cooperatives were a logical exten-sion of the Alliance's earlier efforts to defend the community of indepen-dent farmers.

Several county Alliances quickly organized joint stock companies on the Rochdale plan (all transactions in cash, profits divided among stockholders), but the most dramatic of the early Alliance cooperative ventures were the efforts to market cotton, wheat, and cattle in bulk. With cotton buyers competing among themselves in interior towns along the railroads, the Alliance did have some leverage by selling in bulk. In the fall of 1884, a bloc of Wise County Alliancemen brought their cotton to Decatur to sell in bulk to the highest bidder. At one sale in October, 2,000 Alliance farmers from Wise and surrounding counties descended on the county seat with 3,000 bales. By "bulking" their cotton, they were able to command a price slightly higher than the going rate. Their solidarity took the buyers by surprise. Two weeks earlier Alliancemen had taken their cotton elsewhere rather than accept the prevailing street price in Decatur.[49]

In 1885 the Wise County Alliance hoped to repeat its triumph by selling cotton directly to textile manufacturers through the Alliance's cotton yards at Alvord, Decatur, and Rhome.[50] This time it was less successful. The Alliancemen failed to establish marketing agreements with manufacturers, and in Decatur local buyers boycotted the Alliance yard and finally forced members to sell at their price. There was talk of violence, including threats of burning cotton in the Alliance yard.[51] Under such circumstances the term "middleman" became more than an unpleasant abstraction; it embodied the "encroachment of monopolies" and "the growing corruption of wealth and power" against which Daws had warned.

By the summer of 1885, the Alliance had spread beyond its frontier home across most of north Texas and was continuing to attract new members at an astounding rate. By August 1885, the Alliance had organized in forty-nine counties and claimed 30,000 members. By the end of the year the number of sub-Alliances had doubled.[52] The promise of the cooperatives and the antimonopoly message that Daws and other lecturers proclaimed were giving organizational focus to a protest movement of major proportions.

This burgeoning movement's foundation in antimonopoly radicalism and Greenbacker insurgency raised the possibility of alignment with the Knights of Labor, which was then conducting an aggressive organizing campaign in the state. At its meeting in 1885, the state Alliance listened to spokesmen from the Knights and endorsed joint action with them, while resisting appeals to merge the two groups in an overtly political organization.[53] The idea that political insurgency killed the original Lampasas Alliance had already been enshrined in the written and oral accounts of the movement's brief history, and Alliancemen of 1885 did not wish to repeat the "mistake" of the founders.

In east Texas, the Knights of Labor organized railroad workers, and in the western coal fields of Palo Pinto and Erath counties organized miners; but all across north Texas the Knights also did heavy recruiting among farmers. In rural Wise County, for example, local assemblies sprang up in which members were also mostly Alliancemen.[54] Thus, in the Cross Timbers, the debate over amalgamation between the Knights and the Alliance was almost academic: Despite the Alliance's decision to remain separate, the two organizations had many members in common who were bent on political insurgency. The enthusiasm of these individuals was fueled, in particular, by the Knights' struggles against the Mallory steamship line and Jay Gould's railroad system (causes that many Alliancemen espoused as their own), and by Alliance struggles against fence builders and middlemen. Underlying both was an antimonopoly and Greenbacker ideology which, in 1886, could not be accommodated within the Democratic party.[55]

In Wise County the demise of the Greenback party after 1882 had left would-be insurgents without an organizational base other than the Alliance. Nevertheless, throughout the mid-1880s there were calls for political cooperation between farmers and laborers.[56] In the spring of 1886, while the Great Southwest Railroad Strike was raging, calls for farmer–labor cooperation became stronger and more explicit. All across the country, sub-Alliances organized "mass meetings" of Alliancemen and Knights. One after another they endorsed political demands "relative to farmers and laborers." The list included demands for settlers' rights to the land, Greenbacker monetary policies, and an end to convict leasing.[57]

In August, a "Laboring Man's Convention" made up of Alliancemen and Knights met in Decatur. Declaring that laborers were not represented in the old parties, they adopted a list of demands like those coming from the precinct meetings and nominated candidates for county offices. The slate included prominent Alliancemen and Knights, some of whom had been leading Greenbackers in Wise County six years earlier. The insurgent group aligned itself with the state Antimonopoly party and endorsed its slate, which included the popular Alliance lecturer "Stump" Ashby for state senator representing the Cross Timbers counties.[58]

Although the insurgents did not carry the day in November, they did make a fight of it. Moreover, the returns showed that many Alliancemen had supported the effort. Insurgents carried all the Cross Timbers precincts west and south of Decatur, while losing in the county seat and on the Grand Prairie to the east. In neighboring Parker County, Stump Ashby and other Antimonopoly candidates carried most of the precincts in the Alliance's original stronghold around Poolville.[59] In 1886 old patterns of community-based cultural cleavage, along with the political dynamics of rapid modernization, helped fuel Alliance energies.

V

By 1886 economic and political programs that would typify the Farmers' Alliance in its heyday were coalescing. And by that time the Alliance had developed the infrastructure that would facilitate its amazing organizational sweep across the Southeast and Great Plains. This essay has explored the cultural setting and the internal dynamics of that movement *before* it burst upon the national scene to catch the attention of contemporary observers (and most historians of agrarian protest). The evidence presented here suggests a rather different picture of the movement's origins than has been delineated in some recent scholarly reflections on Southern and Southwestern Populism.

The Alliance movement began in a rural setting that was, in a sense, precapitalist: small-holder semisubsistence farming coupled with open-range stock raising, isolated from sustained involvement in formal commodity markets or institutions of credit and tenancy. Most farm operators owned the land they worked, and there was no rigid class system in the modern sense. Lawrence Goodwyn is on far surer ground when he denies the applicability of Marxian class analysis to rural west Texas of the 1870s and 1880s than when he makes the same claim for the Deep South and Southeast.[60] And yet there existed in the Cross Timbers commonly held and deep-seated values about land—who should possess it and what should be the limits upon the rights of ownership—and about community obligations. When those values were threatened, there arose angry and sometimes violent confrontations between family farmers on the one side and "land sharks" and fencers on the other.

In their discussions of Populist land policy, both Lawrence Goodwyn and James R. Green have overlooked what was happening before the Alliance/Populist movement focused its attention on the market-related problems of landowners and tenants. Green did not push his investigation back far enough to see that Cross Timbers farmers, like the Southwestern socialists about whom he has written, questioned unlimited individual rights to land. And Goodwyn, by describing a rural setting in which the oppressive hand of the furnishing merchant was already on the necks of farmers (inappropriate for the Cross Timbers before 1890), has failed to notice an Alliance land policy addressing issues other than debt-peonage which gave rise to Alliance radicalism.[61]

When Cross Timbers farmers *were* drawn into the world market economy (at just the moment when the price of cotton began to decline sharply), and when they *did* begin to experience the misery of tenancy and the crop lien, they interpreted their new class status in terms of old values about land and community. What gives this particular frontier experience larger meaning is that it was being simultaneously replicated across the nonplantation South.

Family farmers from the Carolinas to Texas were, for the first time, staking their future on cotton. For many it was a gamble that failed, although the extent of their losses was not uniform.[62] Responding to their plight, farmers and stockmen throughout the South could turn to a tradition of common rights and community interdependence. It was to this *living* heritage (neither a dimly remembered romantic agrarianism nor a brand-new "movement" culture) that organizers of the Texas-based Alliance appealed in spreading the cooperative commonwealth across the South. And the organizers were most successful precisely in those parts of the South—Hill Country, Piney Woods, Wiregrass, and Upper Piedmont—which had only recently been integrated into the market economy, and in which the old culture was still strong.

The Alliance began among farmer-stockmen who possessed a culture of protest harking back to an earlier day and having its roots in community. Both Goodwyn and James Turner have underestimated the ties of kinship, neighborhood, and voluntary association among those who took the Farmers' Alliance from Poolville across the South. The Alliance was founded by rural people who were already part of a dense network of churches, schools, lodges, and extended family groups. When Turner asserts that "the primary cause of Populism was the impact of economic distress on socially isolated farmers," and when he describes the Populists as "farm families starved for social life," he is not describing the social reality of the Cross Timbers or of Southern farming communities to which the Alliance spread.[63] The Alliance organizers did their work in *communities*, not in a disorganized mass society.

In his classic study of Texas Populism, Roscoe Martin used anecdotes as well as statistics to analyze the social and economic origins of the People's party. Two of them apply equally well to this early wave of insurgency and the culture of protest it represented. While campaigning in Cooke County, just north of Wise County, in 1894, Lieutenant Governor M. M. Crane proclaimed: "I am proud that most Democrats live on the prairie and are well-to-do people. The Cross Timbers are full of Populists." A staunch old Democrat put it even more bluntly years later in an interview with Martin: "Where you found the hogs running loose, there were lots of Populists; where you found them penned up, the Democrats were in the majority."[64]

Sandy land, hogs loose in the timber, and a venerable culture of rural interdependence: these, too, were part of Populism's beginnings—along with cooperatives, the subtreasury, and the heroes of Alliance radicalism. The agrarian response to a new economic order was informed by an older culture, an older consciousness of people making their own history. The Alliance movement did not spread among people cut off from community and culture by the grinding forces of modernization. To understand their movement, not only on the Texas frontier but all across the South and

Midwest, we need to understand the social fabric of their particular communities. And we need to reckon with that venerable movement culture which was their birthright and which eased the task of the traveling lecturer who brought news of this Farmers' Alliance to rural people whose liberties seemed threatened with extinction.

NOTES

1. C. Wendell King, *Social Movements in the United States* (New York, 1956), 11–22; Richard Hofstadter, *The Age of Reform from Bryan to FDR* (New York, 1955), ch. 2; Samuel P. Hays, *The Response to Industrialism, 1885–1914* (Chicago, 1957), ch. 2; Robert H. Wiebe, *The Search for Order, 1877–1920* (New York, 1967), ch. 3; Gerald N. Grob, *Workers and Utopia: A Study of Ideological Conflict in the American Labor Movement, 1865–1900* (Evanston, Ill., 1961). For a cogent critique of the Parsonian social theory that underlies the work of Hofstadter and others and of the assumptions about community and modernization which that theory entails, see Thomas Bender, *Community and Social Change in America* (New Brunswick, N.J., 1978), ch. 2.

2. David Montgomery, *Beyond Equality: Labor and the Radical Republicans, 1862–1872* (New York, 1967); Lawrence Goodwyn, *Democratic Promise: The Populist Moment in America* (New York, 1976); Robert C. McMath, Jr., *Populist Vanguard: A History of the Southern Farmers' Alliance* (Chapel Hill, N.C., 1975).

3. David Montgomery, "Workers' Control of Machine Production in the Nineteenth Century," *Labor History* 17 (1976):485–509; Michael Hanagan and Charles Stephenson, "The Skilled Worker and Working-Class Protest," *Social Science History* 4 (1980):5–14; Alan Dawley, *Class and Community: The Industrial Revolution in Lynn* (Cambridge, Mass., 1976); Herbert G. Gutman, *Work, Culture, and Society in Industrializing America, 1850–1920* (Chicago, 1978), 40–45; Michael Cassity, "Modernization and Social Crisis: The Knights of Labor and a Midwestern Community, 1885–1886," *Journal of American History* 66 (1979):41–61.

4. Goodwyn, *Democratic Promise*, 547, 542.

5. Richard Hofstadter's interpretation of Populism as a romantic and reactionary movement has been challenged, on somewhat different grounds, in Norman Pollack, *The Populist Response to Industrial America* (Cambridge, Mass., 1962); and Goodwyn, *Democratic Promise*.

6. Steven Hahn, "Common Right and Commonwealth: The Stock Law Struggle and the Roots of Southern Populism," in J. Morgan Kousser and James M. McPherson, eds., *Region, Race, and Reconstruction: Essays in Honor of C. Vann Woodward* (New York, 1982), 51–88. Another view of this culture is found in Forrest McDonald and Grady McWhiney, "The Antebellum Herdsman: A Reinterpretation," *Journal of Southern History* 41 (1975):147–66.

7. Gavin Wright, *The Political Economy of the Cotton South* (New York, 1978), ch. 6; Albert D. Kirwan, *Revolt of the Rednecks: Mississippi Politics, 1876–1925* (Lexington, Ky., 1951), 45–46; William Warren Rogers, *The One-Galloused Rebellion: Agrarianism in Alabama, 1865–1896* (Baton Rouge, La., 1970), 19, 28, 52–54; Hahn, "Common

Right and Commonwealth." Hahn's work deals most explicitly with this cultural conflict.

8. Robert P. Swierenga has noted the pioneering contributions of Webb and Malin to the advancement of an American school of rural history comparable to the "total" history of Bloch and other French historians of the *Annales* school. Swierenga, "Towards the 'New Rural History': A Review Essay," *Historical Methods Newsletter* 6 (June 1973), 111–12.

9. William Garvin, *History of the Grand State Farmers' Alliance of Texas* (Jacksboro, Tex., 1885), 6–15. Gayle Scott and J. M. Armstrong, *The Geology of Wise County, Texas,* University of Texas Bulletin no. 3224 (Austin, 1932), 9–10; Leo Hendricks, *Geology of Parker County, Texas,* University of Texas Publication no. 5724 (Austin, 1957); Rupert N. Richardson, *The Frontier of Northwest Texas, 1846–1876: Advance and Defense of the Pioneer Settlers of the Cross Timbers and Prairies* (Glendale, Calif., 1963), 123–27. Most of the early settlements were built along these creeks. Poolville, for example, was located at the headwaters of Clear Fork of the Trinity beside a spring-fed pool, which silted over when the area came under cultivation. G. A. Holland, *History of Parker County and the Double Log Cabin* (Weatherford, Tex., 1937), 119.

10. Interview with Fred R. Cotten, Weatherford, Texas, 2 August 1971; interview with Mrs. Rosalie Gregg, Mrs. Mozelle Hudson, and Mr. Samuel B. Hudson, Decatur, Texas, 8 February 1980; Worth Ray, *Down in the Cross Timbers* (Austin, 1947), ch. 1; U.S. Census Bureau, *Cotton Production in the United States* (Washington, D.C., 1884), pt. 1, 681, 773–800. This last volume's descriptions of agricultural practices in all the counties of the Cotton Belt demonstrates clearly the similarity of the Cross Timbers and much of the South outside the rich plantation districts. For example, Kemper County, Mississippi, home of Alliance leader S. O. Daws, was predominantly sandy, timbered by blackjack, post oak, and shortleaf pine. Much of the farming was done in the creek bottoms, as was the case in the Cross Timbers in the 1870s (p. 249).

11. Terry G. Jordan, *Trails to Texas: Southern Roots of Western Cattle Ranching* (Lincoln, Neb., 1981), ch. 2, 5.

12. Ibid., ch. 6.

13. Richardson, *Frontier of Northwest Texas,* 116–17; Cliff D. Cates, *Pioneer History of Wise County, Texas* (Decatur, Tex., 1907), 37–38.

14. Richardson, *Frontier of Northwest Texas,* 293.

15. *Tenth Census of the United States* (Washington, D.C., 1883), 1:530.

16. Gavin Wright, *Political Economy of the Cotton South,* ch. 3.

17. On town development in Wise County in the 1870s and 1880s, see Rosalie Gregg, ed., *Wise County History: A Link with the Past* (1975), passim.

18. Cates, *Pioneer History of Wise County,* 38. The social networks in the Cross Timbers at the end of the 1870s were much more extensive than one would expect from a reading of McMath, *Populist Vanguard,* ch. 1. An excellent study of Midwestern town settlement that emphasizes the role of the "voluntary community" is Don Harrison Doyle, *The Social Order of a Frontier Community: Jacksonville, Illinois, 1825–1870* (Urbana, Ill., 1978).

19. Cates, *Pioneer History of Wise County,* 148–52.

20. General Index to Deeds and Deed Records, 1874–83, Wise County Clerk's Office, Decatur, Tex. A check of land purchases by identifiable Alliance members reveals acquisition patterns similar to those of other settlers in the 1870s and early 1880s, although some had rather extensive holdings. For example, Andrew Dunlap, president of the state Alliance in the mid-1880s, received a homestead from the state in 1877 and also purchased several other tracts of 100 to 160 acres each from various individuals and their agents.

21. Ray, *Down in the Cross Timbers*, 8–9. As his biographer noted, Sam Bass hideouts became "almost as numerous as George Washington beds in Virginia." According to one recurring story, Bass would spend the night with an unsuspecting farm family (often a widow and her children), behave as a gentleman, and repay their hospitality with a fistful of stolen $20 gold pieces. Wayne Gard, *Sam Bass* (Lincoln, Neb., 1961); E. J. Hobsbawm, *Primitive Rebels: Studies in Archaic Forms of Social Movement in the 19th and 20th Centuries* (New York, 1965), ch. 1.

22. Cates, *Pioneer History of Wise County*, 148–52; Cotten interview. Intracounty sectionalism seems to have persisted much longer in Parker than in Wise County, but in the post–Civil War era it was significant in both.

23. Eric Foner, "Class, Ethnicity, and Radicalism in the Gilded Age: The Land League in Irish America," in Foner, *Politics and Ideology in the Age of the Civil War* (New York, 1980), 156–60. A resident of Springtown reported that "there are Greenbackers by the 'wholesale' around here." Poolville and Veal Station precincts consistently returned majorities for Greenback and Independent candidates in the earliest elections for which intracounty returns are available (1882). Wise County also had a vigorous Greenback organization. In 1880 a Greenback rally at Crafton (named for Greenbacker and Allianceman George R. Craft) drew a crowd of 2,000. Paradise *Messenger*, 7 May; 16, 23 July 1880. Parker County Election Returns, book O, 1882, Office of County Clerk, Weatherford, Tex.

24. Paradise *Messenger*, 7 May 1880.

25. McMath, *Populist Vanguard*, ch. 1; Goodwyn, *Democratic Promise*, ch. 2.

26. McMath, *Populist Vanguard*, 5–8.

27. Information about this organization's earliest years is meager. We have the testimony of participants, as recorded in the order's official histories beginning in the mid-1880s (especially Garvin, *History of the Grand State Farmers' Alliance of Texas*), a handful of contemporary references in Fort Worth and Dallas newspapers, and a larger body of information in two local papers, the Jacksboro *Rural Citizen*, and the *Wise County Messenger*. The *Messenger*, published at several locations in the county, began in 1880 at Paradise, 15 miles from Poolville. It subsequently became the official organ of the Wise County Alliance, and its files give us our most detailed account of the fledgling Alliance and the community in which it began.

28. Gregg, ed., *Wise County History*, 474–76; Cates, *Pioneer History of Wise County*, 38.

29. U.S. Department of Agriculture, *Report of the Commissioner of Agriculture for the Year 1879* (Washington, D.C., 1880), 126. Deed records for Wise County in 1879, Wise County Clerk's Office, show scores of farms being deeded back to the Matagorda County school fund.

30. Files of the *Wise County Messenger* provide connections between individual

Alliancemen and the Greenback party for that county which are unavailable elsewhere. George R. Craft, a neighborhood Alliance leader in northwestern Wise County and later a county lecturer, was an official of the county Greenback party in 1880. William Forster established the *Messenger* in 1880 as a Greenback organ. He followed the career of the Alliance with interest, and his paper soon became the official organ of the county Alliance. In 1881, while the *Messenger* was still aggressively promoting the Greenback party, S. O. Daws served as agent and correspondent for the paper in Springtown. In his correspondence to the paper he spoke favorably of the Greenbackers. Paradise *Messenger*, 19 August; 18 November 1881.

31. The resolution quoted in the text is from the minutes of the state Alliance, 9 August 1882, quoted in Garvin, *History of the Grand State Farmers' Alliance of Texas*, 53–54. Italics added. In 1882 the Greenback gubernatorial and congressional candidates fared well in Alliance strongholds in Parker County. No Wise County precinct returns are available for 1882. For a discussion of similar political tactics used in the 1879s by trade unions and the National Labor Union, see Montgomery, *Beyond Equality*, 190–95. See, contra, Goodwyn, *Democratic Promise*, 67–70.

32. Fort Worth *Gazette*, quoted in Jacksboro *Rural Citizen*, 15 May 1884.

33. Statement of William Baggett in Farmers' State Alliance of Texas, *Proceedings ... 1888* (Dallas, 1888), 27; Garvin, *History of the Grand State Farmers' Alliance of Texas*, 13, 14.

34. Paradise *Messenger*, 19 August 1881.

35. For a quite different account, which links the origin of the "movement culture" to these developments in the mid-1880s, see Goodwyn, *Democratic Promise*, 26–33, 70–86.

36. R. D. Holt, "The Introduction of Barbed Wire into Texas and the Fence Cutting War," *West Texas Historical Association Year Book* 6 (1930):72–74.

37. Resolution of State Livestock Convention, quoted in Jacksboro *Rural Citizen*, 17 January 1883. Holt, "Introduction of Barbed Wire," 72–73; Decatur *Post*, quoted in Alvord *Messenger*, 10 January 1884.

38. Holt, "Introduction of Barbed Wire," 74. Cf. J. A. Yelling, *Common Field and Enclosures in England, 1450–1850* (Hamden, Conn., 1977), 227–32; E. P. Thompson, *The Making of the English Working Class* (New York, 1964), 216–19; Hahn, "Common Right and Commonwealth," 63.

39. T. A. Larson, *History of Wyoming*, 2d ed. (Lincoln, Neb., 1978), 148–50; Robert W. Larson, *New Mexico Populism: A Study of Radical Protest in a Western Territory* (Boulder, Colo., 1974), 13.

40. Henry M. Smith, *Barb-fencing and the Fence Question* (N.H., 1882); Hahn, "Common Right and Commonwealth."

41. William O. Witherspoon, "Populism in Jack County, Texas," M.A. Thesis, North Texas State University, 1973, 72–74; Letter from Annis Chapel (site of the first Wise County Alliance) in Jacksboro *Rural Citizen*, 20 March 1884; Alvord *Messenger*, 29 February 1884.

42. Jacksboro *Rural Citizen*, 13 September 1883.

43. Witherspoon, "Populism in Jack County," 75–82.

44. Wright, *The Political Economy of the Cotton South*, 62–74.

45. L. Tuffley Ellis, "The Revolution of the Texas Cotton Trade, 1865–1885,"

*Southwestern Historical Quarterly* 73 (1970):478–508; Harold D. Woodman, *King Cotton and His Retainers: Financing and Marketing the Cotton Crop of the South, 1800–1925* (Lexington, Ky., 1968), ch. 23.

46. The increasing dependence on merchant credit is inferred from the shift toward cotton monoculture and the increase in farm tenancy. I have found no evidence that the crop lien system was pervasive in Wise and Parker counties in the 1880s. In fact, the ability of Alliancemen to offer their cotton for sale cooperatively suggests that their crops were not bound by lien.

47. Garvin, *History of the Grand State Farmers' Alliance of Texas*, 67. The Alliance had attempted to market cotton through the Grange's cooperative association in 1882, but had failed to reach an agreement. On Grange cooperatives in the Southwest see Robert A. Calvert, "The Southern Grange: The Farmers' Search for Identity in the Gilded Age," Diss., University of Texas at Austin, 1969, ch. 7–10.

48. Jacksboro *Rural Citizen*, 21 February 1884. The quotation is from an address Daws gave, on request, at the state Alliance meeting, but the ideas he expressed then were undoubtedly contained in his standard organizing lecture as well.

49. Jacksboro *Rural Citizen*, 20 August 1885. Alvord *Messenger*, 17, 31 October 1884.

50. Wise County *Messenger*, 25 April 1885. The Rhome facility, in the wheat belt of eastern Wise County, was a combination cotton yard, grain elevator, lumber yard, and general store, organized on the Rochdale plan.

51. *Wise County Messenger*, 3, 10, 17 October 1885.

52. Ibid., 8 August 1885, 2 January 1886.

53. Jacksboro *Rural Citizen*, 13 August 1885; *Wise County Messenger*, 5 September 1885.

54. *Wise County Messenger*, 15 May 1886.

55. Goodwyn, *Democratic Promise*, ch. 3.

56. See especially the address of Assistant County Lecturer J. M. Thompson in Alvord *Messenger*, 4 April 1884.

57. In July a mass meeting at Alvord issued the following demands to potential legislative candidates:

1. A repeal of state lease laws
2. Land to be reserved for actual settlers
3. No railroad pooling or discriminatory freight rates
4. No hiring out of convict labor
5. Acceptable U.S. senatorial candidates must support free coinage of silver, abolition of national banks, circulating medium of $50 per capita, payment of national debt in any legal tender on hand.

The county Alliance adopted the same list of demands and forwarded them to the state Alliance meeting in Cleburne. *Wise County Messenger*, 10, 24 July 1886. During this political turmoil S. O. Daws was counseling a middle course, as he had been for years. The Alliance, he said, "will not be converted into a secret caucus" to further the ends of any party, but would educate its members to "understand what policies or principles are necessary to be carried into effect to secure to them the true reward of their toil." *Wise County Messenger*, 2 January 1886. Any veteran of trade union politics would certainly have recognized the "Daws formula" as standard procedure.

58. *Wise County Messenger,* 7 August, 25 September 1886.

59. Ibid., 13, 20 November 1886; Parker County Election Returns, book I, 1886.

60. Lawrence Goodwyn, "The Cooperative Commonwealth and Other Abstractions: In Search of a Democratic Premise," *Marxist Perspectives* 3 (1980):14–15.

61. James Green, "Populism, Socialism and the Promise of Democracy," *Radical History Review* 24 (1980):16; Goodwyn, "Cooperative Commonwealth," 22.

62. Both contemporaries and most students of the rural South have seen significant distinctions between the economic status of sharecroppers, cash renters, and landowners large and small. But see, contra, Goodwyn, "Cooperative Commonwealth," 15.

63. James Turner, "Understanding the Populists," *Journal of American History* 67 (1980):367.

64. Roscoe Martin, 65n, 70n.

# PART III

# The West

JOHN MACK FARAGHER

# 8. Open-Country Community

## SUGAR CREEK, ILLINOIS, 1820–1850

I

Over the past two decades historians from Daniel Boorstin to Michael Zuckerman have turned away from the study of "individualism" in American culture toward the study of "association." Some historians have even proposed a general reinterpretation of the sweep of American history that focuses on the course of community development.[1] Before accepting such a revision, however, we should think again about the meaning of "community" and its applicability to the American past.

A review of the vast literature on community suggests that it has never been a purely descriptive concept, but has included an important evaluative element. Nineteenth- and twentieth-century social thinkers employed the notion of community life to critique the bureaucratic and impersonal direction of modern social development. German critics—Herder, Schiller, and Hegel among them—proposed the Greek polis as the archetypal community. But English and American critics tended to look to the traditional rural village for their model of "man conceived in his wholeness." Oliver Goldsmith and George Crabbe lamented the decline of the village (and by extension the decline of English civilization), while Jefferson celebrated village yeomen as the backbone of the agrarian republic. A century later William Morris found models of community in feudal England, and Herbert Baxter Adams celebrated the genius of Teutonic villages and founded the professional pursuit of history in the United States with a series of community studies. In short, "community" was loaded with normative notions of a life that prevailed in the centuries before industrialization and the growth of modern cities.[2]

In the early 1970s, Kenneth Lockridge reasserted something of this normative interpretation in modern social history. *A New England Town: The First Hundred Years* described seventeenth-century Dedham, Massachusetts, and other New England communities, as "peasant utopias" with "a synthesis which looked to the past." In this important work, Lockridge promoted village communalism as a standard against which to evaluate what he called "the incoherence of individual opportunism." Emphasizing in this way the wholeness of life within a New England community, Lockridge's "good community" is very much in accord with the traditions of Anglo-American social thought.[3]

But the early New England village experience was unique in North America. By the mid-eighteenth century, in New England and elsewhere, open-country settlements—isolated farmsteads spread over relatively large rural areas, without nucleated villages or towns—were the typical form of rural development; open-country settlement characterized the agricultural development of the Trans-Appalachian and Trans-Mississippi wests. Lockridge proposes that those open-country settlers "abandoned the web of relationships created by residence in the villages." Because most rural Americans have not lived in towns, villages, or hamlets, but in the open country, one might conclude that "community" has had a rather limited existence in rural America. "Those who stress community generally do not take sufficiently into account the truly rural segment of the population," David Russo cautions; "until we know as much about rural people as we do about townspeople, there is a danger that we will stress to excess the role of community in American history."[4] We may ask, then, to what extent has the American rural experience been communal?

For Frederick Jackson Turner, the pioneer interpreter of frontier America, an important part of his "frontier thesis" was that the majority of settlers, those living outside rural towns, represented the force of individualism, not community. "The frontier is productive of individualism," he wrote. "Complex society is precipitated by the wilderness into a kind of primitive organization based on the family. The tendency is anti-social." Turner acknowledged the existence of rural cooperation, but he believed that the demands of settlement were destructive of corporate and communal ties. Recent historical work on rural demography seems to reinforce Turner's argument. American rural areas were characterized by dicennial persistence rates of about 30 percent; typically, after a ten-year period, over two-thirds of the residents were recent arrivals. In the words of Merle Curti, who, with a group of assistants, measured similar rates for Trempeleau County, Wisconsin, "it is always a minority that persists."[5] How could there be an effective community when the population "turned over" so frequently?

Turner and Lockridge, despite their opposing roles as celebrant and critic of individualism, both suggest the absence of the necessary "webs of relationships" that would constitute community in the American countryside. They would agree, first, that community depended on compact, nucleated settlements, with communal public institutions, such as churches, which had the authority to encourage or compel individuals to submit to the communal covenant. And second, they would agree that the West was individualistic.

Not all students of rural life have accepted this perspective. "Central place" studies of rural sociologists suggest that even dispersed farm families developed certain "webs." In 1915, Charles J. Galpin used survey data and mapping techniques to demonstrate that what appeared as dispersed and randomly scattered farms in southeastern Wisconsin were in fact settlements with a focus on a central place, a town, or village service center. Outlying farm families, constituting the majority of households in the trade zone, associated at a common "center" where they sold their farm commodities, purchased goods and services, and participated in community institutions. "It is difficult, if not impossible, to avoid the conclusion," Galpin wrote, "that the trade zone about one of these complete agricultural civic centers forms the boundary of an actual, if not legal community, within which the apparent entanglement of human life is resolved into a fairly unitary system of interrelatedness." Galpin's work was followed in the 1920s and 1930s by other studies demonstrating the wide applicability of trade zone/central-place theory. Of particular importance was a series of studies of rural areas in Wisconsin, Missouri, North Carolina, and New York, which showed patterns of association at an even more primary level. Galpin's trade zones were almost always composed of three or more neighborhoods, each consisting of from fifteen to thirty associating households in a more or less contiguous area. Central-place theory offered the possibility of investigating open-country districts, explaining the system of relations that linked dispersed farming families to each other and to the larger society.[6]

The working definition of community that these studies offered, however, was unabashedly deterministic: community was shaped by the forces of economic life and place. "Community" was a behavioral concept. In the language of sociology, "a community arises through sharing a limited territorial space for residence and sustenance and functions to meet common needs generated in sharing this space by establishing characteristic forms of social action."[7] Certainly any notion of community hinges on a behavioral specification, but in its classic formulations the concept also implies what might be called "community sentiment," an awareness of a shared way of life, of attitudes and values held in common. As students of rural society turned to the study of these more intangible phenomena they came up against the deterministic cast of central-place theory. The need to trade brought farmers to town, but within the trade zone what contributed to a sense of shared purpose? "Culture" is one answer, but one that fits most easily into the study of relatively close and nucleated settlements, partly because of the practical difficulty of interviewing "outlanders" and partly because of the continuing tradition of associating "wholeness" with "village."[8]

Another theoretical difficulty arose as rural sociology expanded its scope in the 1950s, studying other areas of the rural world. It became relatively clear that the trade zone provided only a limited explanation for central-place community. "As an economy changes from a self-sufficient to a communal or exchange system," one authority noted in the 1960s, "there appear on the landscape facilities for the collection, exchange and distribution of commodities (including goods and services) provided in a spatially separated specialized place."[9] The trading village as a focus for open-country community, in short, seemed less a universal than a specific historical phase. Many of the villages and towns studied by Galpin and his associates were products of transportation development in the second half of the nineteenth century, in many cases some decades after the actual process of settlement had begun. Moreover, with further shifts in the pattern of the economy by the 1950s, many of these same villages had been reduced to the status of mere crossroads.

There is much in the achievement of rural sociology to provoke historical exploration of community in the countryside. The notion of households dispersed through the countryside, but still bound together by common concerns and "webs of relations," was an important breakthrough in understanding the countryside. Yet with its final focus on the village as the source of community, rural sociology still leaves us where we began: consigning the majority experience of the open landscape of the American countryside to Turnerian individualism.

Equally important, both individualism and community in rural America remain abstractions. There are, as yet, no close studies of open-country settlements: studies that test them over time, as Thomas Bender suggests, for communal and noncommunal patterns. The question with which Galpin began his 1915 study of Delavan, Wisconsin, remains relevant: "Is there such a thing as a rural community? If so, what are its characteristics? Can the farm population as a class be considered a community? Or can you cut out of the open country any piece, large or small, square, or triangular, or irregular in shape and treat the farm families in this section as a community?"[10]

Turning Galpin's question around, to what extent does community depend on compact, nucleated settlement? Certainly other structures were at work that also pulled men and women together and helped them act not just as individuals or isolated families but as a social unit. The creation of a European landscape of fields, pastures, woodlots, roads, bridges, and mills quickly linked people's experience with a specific sense of place. A household economy—largely producing for local consumption, with few distinctions of wealth—required cooperation and a nonmarket system of exchange among the producers. A tendency toward endogamy, or patterns of intermarriage within the area, created and perpetuated "clans" that came to control an inordinate share of the lands, as well as the key positions of public authority.[11]

Open-country settlements, I believe, demonstrated the communal patterns usually attributed to nucleated villages alone. At least this was the case for the farming district of Sugar Creek, Illinois, examined here from its first Anglo settlement in 1817 to the coming of the railroad in the 1850s. Despite the absence of a village, the patterns of everyday life in Sugar Creek acted as constituents of community.[12]

II

Draining 200 square miles of prairie and timber land, Sugar Creek flows northeast some 25 miles through central Illinois to its mouth on the Sangamon River. (See Map 8.1.) In the second decade of the nineteenth century Anglo-Celtic pioneers from Virginia, Kentucky, and other areas of the upland South wrested Sugar Creek (then part of the Illinois country) from its native proprietors and resettled it. By 1830 the 100 square-mile area of the upper creek was home to a hearty, if primitive, pioneer settlement of over 100 households and homesteads, with a total of perhaps 650 residents.[13] The pattern of geographical mobility that had brought the settlers was a continuing and prominent feature of the first forty years of the creek's history. From 1830 to 1850, ten-year rates of persistence of heads of households were nearly 37 percent for 1840 and 32 percent for 1850, rates that were typical of North American rural settlements.[14] (See Table 8.1.) Despite this turnover, however, upper Sugar Creek's population grew; by 1850 almost 1,200 people lived in over 200 farm households along the creek.

These settlers organized the landscape into dispersed family farms spread along the margin of the timber and prairie.[15] Husbandmen almost never grouped their homesites, but separated them at intervals of 0.5 to 2 miles along the section lines—making it harder to visit each other, perhaps, but easier to work surrounding fields from the farmyard. Most of the service facilities of the settlement—mills, craft shops, taverns—were dispersed throughout the countryside, and there was no central village upon which the area focused. Developers were able to plan a successful town, Auburn, only when the Alton and Sangamon Railroad finally laid track south along the creek and built a depot in the 1850s. Until the 1850s, then, upper Sugar Creek was a typical open-country settlement, one of many established at about this time throughout the Old Northwest.[16]

Although settlers did not cluster their dwellings, they laid out their farms on adjoining claims. Pioneer families concentrated their settlement, improvement, and purchase of lands along the wooded margin of the Creek. By 1833, after sixteen years of settlement and ten years of land sales, several distinct neighborhoods had developed along Sugar Creek. (See Figures 8.2 and 8.3.) Moreover, surviving Sugar Creek diaries and account books

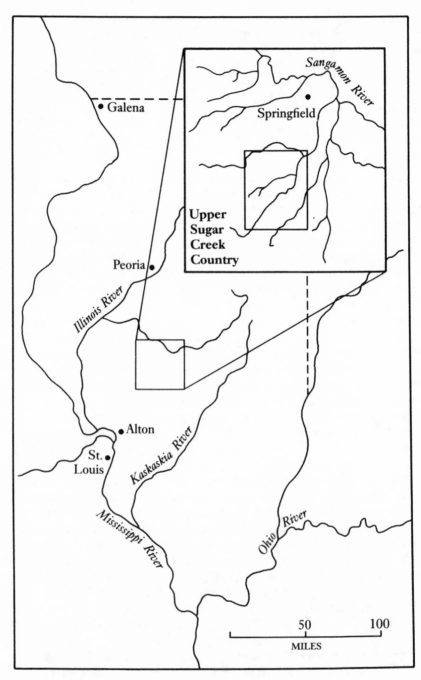

8.1. *The Illinois Country in the Early Nineteenth Century*

8.1. *Number and Persistence of Households in Sugar Creek*

| Year | N Households | N Continuing | % |
|------|------|------|------|
| 1830 | 113 | — | — |
| 1840 | 133 | 49 | 36.8 |
| 1850 | 208 | 66 | 31.7 |

Source: Manuscript schedules, reprinted in *Federal Census, 1830, Sangamon County, Illinois,* trans. Ruth Z. Marko (Springfield, Ill., n.d.); *Federal Census, 1840, Sangamon County, Illinois,* trans. Ruth Z. Marko (Springfield, Ill., 1980), and *Sangamon County, Illinois, 1850 Census and Mortality Schedule* (Springfield, Ill., n.d.) [hereafter cited as *Federal Census, 1850*].

suggest that the rounds of economic and social life within the settlement brought men and women into a good deal of contact with their neighbors, and that such relations constituted most of social life. During 1849, for instance, farmer Eddin Lewis recorded visits with over thirty people in his account book; the visitors lived an average of 3 miles from Lewis's farm. Lewis was a man of the world and a community leader, active in Whig politics, the Cumberland Presbyterian Church, and the local temperance society; yet his furthest visits from home in 1849 were trips 5 miles north and 4 miles south, and none of Lewis's recorded visiting included people from outside upper Sugar Creek. Twelve years later, in 1861, Job Fletcher, Jr., farmer and stock-raiser, recorded visits of forty-eight men and women who brought their mares to breed with his champion stallion Sampson. These people lived an average of 4 miles from Fletcher, and all but one were from within the upper Sugar Creek area. If Lewis and Fletcher were typical, and there is no reason to suspect they were not, the settlement was small enough that settlers at the southern end of the creek knew farmers 10 miles north, and it was inclusive enough that most of an individual's social relations occurred within the settlement.[17]

The deep concern with the land among farming folk fostered a strong sense of place. In 1825, Robert Crow established the first local water mill midway along the creek's course, raising a 6-foot dam and creating a large mill pond that became a favorite spot for fishing and swimming. Further north, near the junction of Lick and Sugar creeks, another water-powered saw and gristmill began operation in 1827. Known as Ball's mill, it continued operation under different owners until 1861 when William Crow, son of Robert, bought the site and added steam power. Six miles south of Crow's original mill, a bend in the creek and a drop in elevation created another opportunity to exploit waterpower; there, in 1830, Jacob Rauch established a gristmill and lent his name to the southern end of the creek. At the mills owned by Rauch, Crow, and Ball, men and boys waited their turn with bushels of corn or wheat; the mills became standard points of

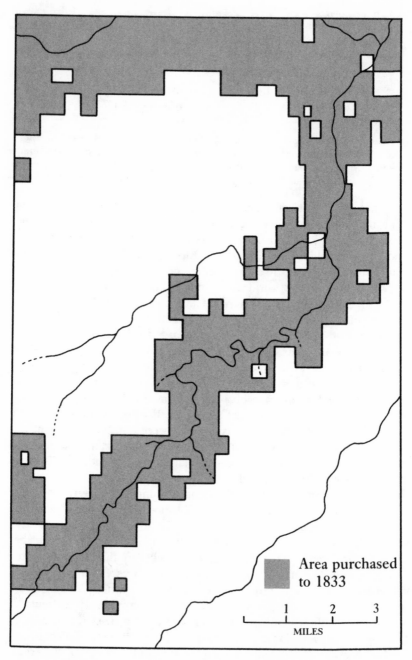

8.2. *Upper Sugar Creek Land Purchases to 1833 (Source: "Federal Law Claims in Sangamon County," list available at the Illinois State Archives, Springfield, Ill.)*

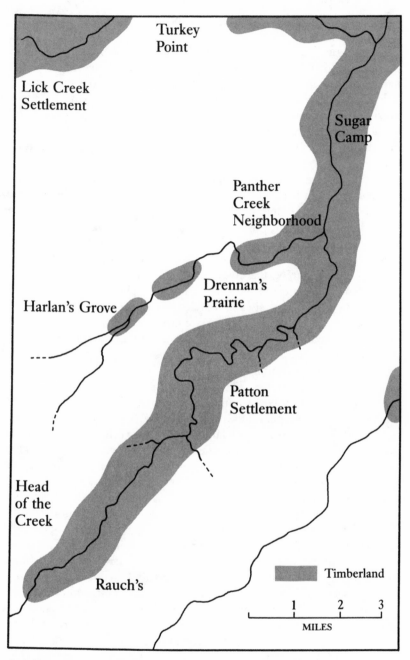

8.3. *Upper Sugar Creek Neighborhoods and Timberland, ca. 1840*

reference, defining the south, center, and north of the creek and the settlement.

Brooks, or "branches" in local parlance, feeding Sugar Creek, springs,
prominent groves, and prairies were named after their owners and those
names continued long after the families had passed from the scene. Even
individual trees were landmarks to these early settlers. Moses Wadsworth,
looking back over forty years in the 1880s, recalled a huge cottonwood that
stood on the east bank of Lick Creek to the west. "When a youth, in pursuit
of a fugitive horse," he wrote, "I found my way home over the trackless
prairie by keeping my eyes on that old landmark."[18]

As they ordered and named the elements of landscape, settlers appropri-
ated the environment as the site for a specific human habitation. "All human
events *take place*," writes geographer D. W. Meinig, and social scientists
have often noted the necessity of strong attachment to a specific place for a
sense of communal feeling to develop.[19] It is important to add, however,
that this sensibility was active, not passive. The settlers of Sugar Creek
participated in shaping the character of the landscape, molding it to their
own needs and future expectations. Through clearing or conservation of
timber lands; choice of sites and styles for houses, outbuildings, gardens,
and orchards; discovery of appropriate crops and their rotation for specific
fields; and fencing of fields and pastureland, the landscape became a complex, cumulative record of the work of men and women in a common place.

Some of this transformation took place at the level of the family farm, but
some was more collective. The laying out and construction of roads and
lanes, for example, was a community experience. J. B. Jackson, our foremost critic of landscape, reminds us, roads are "the most powerful force for
the destruction or creation of landscapes that we have." Crossing rolling
timber and prairie land, creeks, farming fields, fences, and homelots, as
well as working within the grid system of the federal survey—all this required that roads be the product of discussion, argument, and consensus
within the settlement. Public roads were maintained by the ancient system
of corvée: each male head of household was required to contribute five
days of labor annually to the repair of roads, and new roads were "thrown
up" by the collective action of farmers. Meanwhile, farmers tried to convince the county commissioners to declare the narrow passways bounding
their homesteads as county roads, as they could then count the maintenance
of lanes serving their own material interests as their community service.
The declaration of a county road, however, required collecting the signa-
tures of a significant number of householders. One may chart, in the files of
the County Commissioners Court, the petitions, surveys, and work reports
that signaled the creation of a Midwestern landscape through collective
effort. Here, then, was a dynamic between individual self-interest and collective action that contributed to the active communal life of farmers. The

landscape was not merely the setting for community; it was, more accurately, the community's product.[20]

## III

The struggle over internal improvements, long understood to have dominated legislative politics, clearly played an important role in the making of community at the local level. Otherwise, local, state, and federal government activity in central Illinois was minimal. Nonetheless, the public rituals of local democracy provided men, and sometimes their wives and children, an opportunity for communal activity. Beginning in 1827, the county commissioners established upper Sugar Creek as an election and judicial district. All householders of the district met at John Drennan's Stage Stand and Post Office, the common polling place and muster ground near the creek in the center of the district. At precinct and county elections in August the voting was viva voce with householders' names called off the voters' roll, men indicating their preference, and their votes announced publicly. Constables and justices of the peace were selected from within the ranks of Sugar Creek men. Those elected were among the most long-standing and substantial farmers of the community. The same family names—Drennan, Lockridge, Patton, Rauch, Nuckolls, Fletcher—recur in all the local positions. Before the 1850s it was rare for "new men" to contest the election of established residents for local office. But even in the 1850s, when social relations were more fluid, and men relatively new to Sugar Creek did enter the running, established families filled 62 percent of all local offices. Original settler families held a monopoly of local political power.[21]

Drennan's was also the site for monthly militia musters, Independence Day celebrations, elections, and camp meetings. The local militia, one Sugar Creek settler wrote, "was concerned not only with military affairs, but was inter-woven with the social life of the community. The company was composed of the active young and middle-aged men of the vicinity, in which the best citizens of the community took an active interest." The Sugar Creek militia, like others, elected its own officers. Men who wished to stand for office would present themselves on a makeshift platform, and electors would line up behind their favorite. These elections required public declarations of an individual's politics.[22]

There were other aspects to public community organization. By 1830 three separate subscription schools had been organized in northern, central, and southern sections of the Sugar Creek district. School was held during winter months. One resident recalled, "the first day of March found every able-bodied boy back on the farm whether school was out or not. School was of minor importance, while 'the call of the wild' or 'back to the farm' was imperative." For our purposes, however, schools were not "mere incidences," for they demonstrated the ability of the settlers to organize and control their own social institutions. The location of the three schools, moreover, points to the presence of distinct neighborhoods within the district.[23]

Similarly, by 1830 five congregations with separate facilities had been organized and were holding regular services. The Cumberland Presbyterian Church, an evangelical Calvinist body, was the strongest and largest. Established in 1825, it met at the centrally located farmhouse of William and Mary Drennan. Complete parishioner lists have not been preserved, but membership grew from the four founding families to sixty-six adults by 1830 and to ninety by 1864, a significant minority of the community that included several of the most prominent families. Although it certainly did not stand in the same relation to the community as Puritan churches in colonial New England, the Cumberland Church nonetheless demanded behavioral compliance with a strict code of morals. For example, on 30 May 1840, twenty-year-old Jane Nuckolls stood before the congregation that had witnessed her baptism and acknowledged her guilt of "immoral conduct." Later that year, in the same church, she and John Lockridge were married. The active role the Cumberland Church played in camp meetings, community revivals, and temperance reform suggests that its impact was larger than its parishioners' list would imply. Edgar Lee Masters, raised north of the Sangamon River in Menard County, commented on the relationship of the Cumberland Church to the rural lives we have been discussing:

> If there was a culture, a spiritual flowering and growth in the Sangamon River country it was among these Cumberland Presbyterians, these humble, generous souls, who in the days of Andrew Jackson followed him faithfully as their salvation from the evil plots of cities, from the scheme of selfish money-changers. They read the Psalms and the poetry of the Bible, and they sang the hymns of Watts and the Wesleys. Like primitive Christians they stood for moral virtue, good will, as the means of accomplishing what they regarded as the supreme object of life, the eternal salvation of the soul. Truthtelling, honest dealing, neighborly kindness were their religion.[24]

Four other churches also held services in Sugar Creek: a small group of Catholic families at the home of William Burtle; a Methodist flock in John French's cabin in Harlan's Grove; an "old school" or Presbyterian congregation at Samuel McElvain's tavern on the Springfield–Alton post road; and a "primitive" Baptist group of some thirty members in the timber near Ball's mill. As T. Scott Miyakawa has argued, these congregations created a "vital fellowship" where "hitherto complete strangers" could "establish close personal relations quickly." The churches were clearly a part of communal organization.[25]

I V

The farmers who moved to the Sangamon valley brought with them a tradition of self-sufficient farming. Cabins were located on high ground near the creek for access to water and to timber for fuel; nearby prairie land could be used for pasture or, after considerable effort spent breaking the sod, for crops. One acre produced vegetables, another acre or two yielded wheat or other small grains, with the remaining improved land—perhaps 50 acres after several years of invested labor—provided corn for family food and animal fodder. Livestock typically included a yoke of oxen, three or four horses, two or three milk cows and five to ten beeves, forty hogs, ten to twenty sheep, a brood of poultry, and a gaggle of geese. Sheep, flax, or even a cotton patch provided fiber for homespun. Some hay was made for livestock, but more commonly animals were allowed to forage on prairie grasses or timber mast. In addition to supplying most of their own food, an English immigrant wrote home, "an industrious family can manufacture most of their own clothing, soap, candles, and sometimes sugar. . . . In fact it is impossible to imagine a more independent style of life."[26]

Independent, perhaps, but not isolated or autonomous. Self-sufficiency should be understood as a community experience. Sharing work with neighbors at cabin raisings, log rollings, haying, husking, butchering, harvesting, or threshing were all traditionally communal affairs. Moreover, exchanges of labor, products, and tools, all outside the market, were part of the day-to-day operation of agriculture. In their account books farmers carefully recorded each exchange. Entries such as "six days work planting corn [$]3.00," "½ stack of hay .75," "¾ day harvesting .75," or "one day butchering hogs .50," recorded work performed, work or tools received in exchange, or other transactions. Accounts frequently ran for years without a tally. Monetary value was assigned to each exchange, but records of actual money transactions were rare. "Money is so scarce and hard to be got [that] we must live without buying much," Lucy Maynard wrote to her sister in Ohio, "but most people get along on what they produce or trade with others for." Farm families depended upon their neighbors to supply the variety of goods and tools, and the extra supplies of labor, that made economic life possible.[27]

An account book of Sugar Creek blacksmith John Smith documents the manner in which this exchange system produced a social division of labor. From July to March of 1837–38, for example, widow Sarah Smith ran up an account of $10.99 for shoeing, sharpening tools, and purchasing nails, hinges, and door latches. Over the next nine months she brought into the shop produce from her farm, including 15 pounds of veal, 110 pounds of beef, and over 250 pounds of flour. When balanced in late 1838 the account showed a credit to Mrs. Smith of $2.84. The Sugar Creek community included not only a smith but a wheelwright, a carpenter, a physician, and three millers; they probably conducted their operations in a similar manner. At the mills "they would not take any money," Lemira Gillett recalled, "everything was done 'on the halves,' there wasn't any money involved."[28]

Almost as soon as squatters began to claim Illinois lands in the 1810s, investors and merchants proposed schemes to link those lands with Eastern markets. Even before land sales officially began, potential investors in prairie lands proposed dredging the Sangamon River as a route for steam transport. Meanwhile, Congress subsidized the construction of an Illinois River–Lake Michigan canal. In the 1830s merchants in Springfield, some 15 miles north of Sugar Creek, solicited funds for the construction of a railroad to Alton on the Mississippi. A primitive rail line west to Meredosia on the Illinois River was actually laid in 1842. All these plans amounted to little; the first effective transportation line to outside markets awaited the completion of north–south rail links in 1852. Before the 1850s, the shortage of capital, the lack of effective demand, and the underdevelopment of agricultural productive forces kept capitalist transportation a vision in the minds of merchants. "Springfield was only a limited market," Moses Wadsworth remembered, its residents consuming only a small portion of the agricultural surplus; moreover, the costs of transport to more distant markets generally exceeded the value of what little surplus there was.[29]

Agricultural reformers continually complained about the unenlightened style of husbandry in the region. When the "deep snow" blizzard struck on Christmas Day 1830, the corn of Sugar Creek farms still stood on the stalk. "The fall had been so warm," one local man remembered, "that the farmers had a better reason than common to indulge the careless habit of leaving their corn in the field, to be gathered in winter when they wanted it." Solon Robinson, the noted agricultural reformer, scornfully joked that crop rotation along the Sangamon was "corn, weeds, hogs, mud, and corn." "The people are not given to experiments," Timothy Flint wrote, "they continue to farm in the beaten way. Agricultural improvement comes at a slow pace."[30]

Indeed, agricultural improvement was not a preeminent goal of the mode of production in Sugar Creek. With little or no possibility of surplus exchange, with little or no pressure to compete or accumulate capital, there was little incentive to innovate. Hence, traditional methods and hand-tool technology prevailed. Homemade plows, sometimes with iron or steel points, wooden harrows (often no more than a brush drag), cradles for reaping, hand flails for threshing determined a rate of productivity low by comparison with the mechanized farming to come. Before the 1850s there were few agricultural wage workers—most farmers simply had neither the means nor the need to hire them. The exponential increase in agricultural wage workers was a phenomenon of the "agricultural revolution" of the late 1850s, the 1860s, and beyond, when farms were converted, in economic terms, into units of capital. Until then, most labor was generated within the family, where gender- and age-specific divisions of labor assigned each family member his or her portion, all working for the support of the whole.[31]

For the most part, farming was, in these last decades of antebellum agriculture, a solitary occupation; farm operations succeeded, failed, or muddled through as a consequence of individual or family initiative and fortune. But the forces of economic life in what Michael Merrill has called the "household mode of production" required that farmers not only know and work with each other but trust each other as well. Economic relations were, of necessity, communal relations.

V

The forces and relations discussed so far produced a society rather more egalitarian than societies characteristic of commercial agriculture, merchant capitalism, or industry. (See Table 8.2.) In 1838, the wealthiest 20 percent of farm owners held a little more than 40 percent of the owner-operated acreage; by 1850, when commercial forces had developed further, the wealthiest fifth still owned only some 50 percent. The distribution of productive property did not reflect great inequities; these figures are low compared to other areas in the United States at the same time. In 1838 the median farm size was 120 acres of improved and unimproved land—almost precisely the same as the mean size when one disregards the richest and poorest tenths of real estate owners; in 1850 the average Sugar Creek farmer worked some 71 acres of improved land, and the modal and median farm included 80 improved acres. In other words, land was quite evenly distributed among property owners.[32]

There were, however, important material distinctions between those who owned their own lands and those who did not. (See Table 8.3.) The proportion of owner-operators in Sugar Creek remained at about one-half of the households over the twenty years from 1830 to 1850. Excluding nonfarm occupations, the other households must have worked land as tenants, renters, or, less frequently, as farm laborers. Though land was fairly evenly distributed among owner-operators, a few large-scale farmers owned enough acreage to require either hands or tenants. It is important to note

8.2. *Distribution of Farm Acreage among Household Heads in Sugar Creek*

| Wealth | 1838 (%) | 1850 (%) |
|---|---|---|
| Top fifth | 42.5 | 50.8 |
| 2d fifth | 21.8 | 19.3 |
| 3d fifth | 15.3 | 14.4 |
| 4th fifth | 10.6 | 8.5 |
| Bottom fifth | 9.7 | 7.0 |
| Totals | 100.0 | 100.0 |

Source: 1838 Tax List in "Taxable Lists for Sangamon County, 1832–1838"; Federal Census, 1850, Agricultural Schedules, both manuscripts at the Illinois State Archives, Springfield, Ill.

that Sugar Creek lands were also purchased by outsiders: men with capital who speculated on rising land values while renting their holdings to families with little means to buy. In 1840, when owner-operators held over a third of the total acreage of the upper Sugar Creek district and another third of local acreage (mostly outlying "wet prairie" land) waited for claimants, fully 30 percent of the land of the district, over 19,000 acres, belonged to some fifty absentee owners. In the mid-1830s the local agent of John Grigg, a wealthy Philadelphia publisher, bought nearly 10,000 acres of timber and prairie land along Panther Creek, a branch draining the west bank of Sugar Creek. Other speculators, including Nathaniel Ware of Natchez, Mississippi, and the Berry brothers of Bath County, Kentucky, bought up other huge tracts. During the 1840s and 1850s, speculators continued to purchase the remaining prairie away from the creek at $1.25 per acre, while more traditional and cautious farmers with capital or access to credit bought creek and timber land from other farmers or speculators at $3 to $5. Meanwhile, substantial numbers of households worked the land of outside capitalist investors, hoping to climb the agrarian ladder to eventual land-ownership.[33]

The foregoing may be the material basis of class distinction, but there is no evidence in the documentary record that antebellum tenants or renters saw themselves as a class. As Allan Bogue has written, some frontier tenants in fact managed to acquire their own property, and most of them probably believed the myth of free land and the opportunity of ownership in the West. But more important in understanding the lack of social tension between owners and tenants—at least in Sugar Creek—was the fact that these nonowning households did not persist. Lack of landownership seems to have been a significant factor in the turnover of population. (See Table 8.4.) In 1840 and 1850 about three in four persisting households were

8.3. *Occupational Status of Household Heads in Sugar Creek*

| Occupation | 1830 | | 1840 | | 1850 | |
|---|---|---|---|---|---|---|
| | N | % | N | % | N | % |
| Farmers | | | | | | |
|   Owner-operators[a] | 55 | 48.7 | 64 | 48.1 | 97 | 46.6 |
|   Tenants[b] | | | | | 20 | 9.6 |
|   Farmers without farms[c] | | | | | 38 | 18.3 |
|   Unknown[d] | 46 | 40.7 | 54 | 40.6 | 31 | 14.9 |
| Other | 12 | 10.6 | 15 | 11.3 | 22 | 10.6 |
| Totals | 113 | 100.0 | 133 | 100.0 | 208 | 100.0 |

[a]Heads of household for whom documentary evidence was found verifying farm ownership.
[b]Heads of household listed in the manuscript agricultural census schedules of 1850 as farming a specific farm, but not listed as having any cash value in that farm.
[c]Heads of household listing "farmer" as their occupation on the manuscript population schedules, but not appearing on the agricultural schedule list of farms and farmers.
[d]Heads of household not specifically identified as one of the above. Before 1850 there is no way to identify tenants and farm laborers. It is possible that some of these owned property, or were in the process of purchasing it, but as most of these included the least persistent residents, the bulk of these were surely nonowners.

Source: *Federal Census*, 1830, 1840, 1850; Federal Census, 1850, Agricultural Schedules, manuscripts, Illinois State Archives; Marilyn Wright Thomas and Hazelmae Taylor Temple, comp., *1835 Tax List, Sangamon County, Illinois* (Springfield, Ill., 1978); "Taxable Lists for Sangamon County, Illinois, 1832–1838," manuscripts, Illinois State Archives, Springfield, Ill.; *Early Federal Land Sales*; John Carrol Power, *History of the Early Settlers of Sangamon County Illinois* (Springfield, Ill., 1876); *History of Sangamon County* (Chicago, Ill., 1881).

owner-operators. By contrast, the vast majority of those who moved on were squatters, tenants, or renters. The Sugar Creek community—the group that lived together, worked together, and persisted—was mostly composed of small, self-sufficient farmers who owned their own means of production. Those who failed to enter into the ranks of this fraternity usually moved on.[34]

If we examine this persistent body of settlers—the families rather than the individuals—we find that family persistence was much higher than individual persistence. From 1830 to 1850, 44 to 47 percent of area families retained at least one household in Sugar Creek. (See Table 8.5.) In other words, although individuals died, moved, or otherwise disappeared from the record, family names continued. In Sugar Creek some thirty families, all of them settlers of the first fifteen years, were notably persistent. The chances that a second- or third-generation man or woman from one of these families would remain in the community was about three in four. (See Table 8.6.)

To a remarkable degree, moreover, these second- and third-generation

8.4. *Property Ownership of Persisting and Nonpersisting Households in Sugar Creek*

| Years | N Continuing | N Owners Continuing | % Owners Continuing | N Leaving[a] | N Owners Leaving | % Owners Leaving |
|---|---|---|---|---|---|---|
| 1830–40 | 49 | 35 | 71.4 | 61 | 8 | 13.1 |
| 1840–50 | 66 | 50 | 75.8 | 60 | 2 | 3.3 |

[a]Excluding confirmed deaths.

Source: *Federal Census*, 1830, 1840, 1850; Marilyn Wright Thomas and Hazelmae Taylor Temple, comp., *1835 Tax List, Sangamon County, Illinois* (Springfield, Ill., 1978); "Taxable Lists for Sangamon County, 1832–1838," manuscripts, Illinois State Archives, Springfield, Illinois; Power, *History of the Early Settlers*; *History of Sangamon County*.

men and women found marriage partners from within this limited number of persistent families. Although rates vary by sex and generation, anywhere from a quarter to nearly half of these descendants of the original settlers were married to other second- or third-generation settlers. (See Table 8.7.) By the 1840s, for those families who settled and stayed in Sugar Creek, relationships of work, of church, of politics, largely became relationships of kinship.

Kinship connections are evident in documented community relationships. The church congregations, for example, appear to have first coalesced around kin-related groups that moved into the area together and settled in a common section of Sugar Creek. Likewise, kinship connections were perhaps the most prominent relationships encouraging the work cooperation that contributed to economic success.

One example among many may make the point. In October 1841, faced with an unusual surplus of wheat, seven Sugar Creek householders filled their wagons and set out to make the week-long round trip to the St. Louis grain market. The six—Silas Elijah Harlan, Noah and Thomas Mason, George Eastman, Ezra Barnes, and William Crow—all lived on the west side of the creek, five of them within a mile of Crow's mill. As neighbors they were accustomed to swapping work, cooperating at harvests, and frequenting the same tradesmen. But although the account makes no mention of deeper kin connections, in fact these men were related in a complicated, but by no means uncommon, manner.

The Mason brothers' parents, Noah Sr. and Lucinda Mason, were among the few early immigrants to the Sangamon area from New England. Arriving in Sugar Creek in 1824, Lucinda corresponded with some female relations back home, and struck the spark for their husbands to emigrate. First, in the late 1820s, came the Eastman clan—father, mother, and chil-

8.5. *Persistence of Household Head Family Names in Sugar Creek*

| Years | N Family Names | N Continuing | % |
|-------|----------------|--------------|-----|
| 1830 | 78 | — | — |
| 1830–40 | 95 | 41 | 43.6 |
| 1840–50 | 137 | 64 | 46.7 |

Source: *Federal Census*, 1830, 1840, 1850.

dren; then, in the 1830s, the Wadsworths, Daniel, Margaret, and their children. The Wadsworths and the Eastmans were close; indeed, Daniel Wadsworth and George Eastman had married half-sisters, relatives of Lucinda Mason, and in 1840, when father Eastman died, his widow went to live with her sister Elizabeth, wife of Daniel Wadsworth. The connections continued. In 1841 Daniel's daughter Emily was being courted by Jehu Harlan; they would marry within the year. Jehu's aunt, Elizabeth Messick (Mrs. Silas Harlan), had a much younger sister, Julia, living in her household. Julia was seeing a lot of young William Crow; they would marry in 1843. Ezra Barnes, another New Englander who had tried life at sea before leaving the Atlantic for Sugar Creek, was married to Elizabeth Mason, sister to Noah Jr. and Thomas Mason.[35]

Marriage and blood ties linked their lives and fortunes. The ox-drawn wagons carried more than simply neighbors to St. Louis. The men were part of a rural community that adhered through the bonds of kinship—subtly turning neighbors into family, and anchoring community in something more firm than merely a desire to belong somewhere. Moses Wadsworth, who left us the story of the trip, referred to Silas Harlan—who had organized it—as "Uncle Si." Silas—actually the uncle of Moses's sister's husband—was an "uncle" to Moses because the lives of kin touched so regularly and so intimately. In the same way nearly every Sugar Creek child who belonged to one of the persistent families and who had grown up in the Sangamon region, could point to numerous other uncles and aunts.

## VI

In important ways communal elements retained much strength in the settlement of Sugar Creek, even in the context of a typically Turnerian environment. Intensive cooperation was required to shape a natural countryside into the patterns of a farming landscape. Economic life, too, demanded working relations among households; the underdevelopment of technology and commerce may have encouraged more sharing than competition. Com-

8.6. *Persistence of Members of the Thirty Most Persistent Families in Sugar Creek*

|  | Percent of Total Family Members | |
|  | Men | Women |
| --- | --- | --- |
| 2d generation | 78.1 | 79.5 |
| 3d generation | 77.5 | 75.0 |

Source: Family Reconstitution Forms compiled from Power, *History of the Early Settlers*; *History of Sangamon County*; *Federal Census*, 1830, 1840, 1850; and miscellaneous genealogical materials in the Illinois State Historical Library, Springfield, Ill.

munity institutions, such as churches and schools, bound people together in the common pursuit of goals and fostered common values. Finally, despite the transiency that by the next century would irreparably damage the kinship system, antebellum Sugar Creek kinship bonds were reasserted and, among the persistent, strangers were converted into family. From this perspective, Allan Bogue's assertion that the frontier may have been more productive of anomie than community appears too pessimistic.[36]

In an influential article written thirty years ago, Stanley Elkins and Eric McKitrick proposed a model of community building on the American frontier that seems to fit the Sugar Creek case. An initial period of settlement when relations had to be created and institutions built, fostered the creation of democratic community.[37] Elkins and McKitrick assumed a generalized equality within the frontier, and if we based our conclusions on the distribution of acreage among owner-operator heads of household, inequality would seem to have increased only slightly during the period. But as Bogue pointed out in his critique of this model, the frontier was a diverse and heterogeneous society. In Sugar Creek, community did not work to the benefit of all; rather, it was the device that allowed some men and women to succeed and prevail while others, the majority, failed and pushed on. The relative stability of Sugar Creek for the persistent owners was accompanied by high levels of mobility and "shiftlessness" for those who lacked the means to buy land. Depending upon one's viewpoint, depending upon which group among the settlers one studies, one may find either the geographic mobility and loss of community that have become the hallmarks of modern America, or the communal order of a traditional society.

NOTES

1. Daniel Boorstin, *The Americans*, 3 vols. (New York, 1958–73); Michael Zuckerman, *Peaceable Kingdoms: The New England Town in the Eighteenth Century* (New York,

*8.7. Endogamy of the Thirty Most Persistent Families in Sugar Creek*

|  | Percent of All Members' Marriages | |
|  | Men | Women |
| --- | --- | --- |
| 2d generation | 39.0 | 46.6 |
| 3d generation | 25.9 | 33.3 |

Source: Family Reconstitution Forms.

1970). Among other influential and provocative studies are Kenneth Lockridge, *A New England Town: The First Hundred Years, Dedham, Massachusetts, 1636–1736* (New York, 1970); Robert Gross, *The Minutemen and Their World* (New York, 1977); Alan Dawley, *Class and Community: The Industrial Revolution in Lynn* (Cambridge, Mass., 1976); Donald H. Doyle, *The Social Order of a Frontier Community: Jacksonville, Illinois, 1825–1870* (Urbana, Ill., 1978); Robert Dykstra, *The Cattle Towns* (New York, 1968). David J. Russo, *Families and Communities: A New View of American History* (Nashville, 1974) and Thomas Bender, *Community and Social Change in America* (New Brunswick, N.J., 1978) provide excellent critical reviews of the field and chart the outlines of a new synthesis.

2. Robert Nisbet, *The Sociological Tradition* (New York, 1965), 47. On the importance of rural models see Raymond Plath, *Community and Ideology: An Essay in Applied Social Philosophy* (London, 1974), 24–25. Plath and Nisbet discuss the German, English, and American ideals of community. Raymond Williams discusses the appeal of the countryside as a retreat from capitalism in *The Country and the City* (New York, 1973). On Adams see Howard W. Odum, ed., *American Masters of Social Science* (New York, 1927), 99–127.

3. Lockridge, *A New England Town*, 16–22, 170, 168–69.

4. Ruth Sutter, *The Next Place You Come To: The Town in North America* (New York, 1973), 33; Lockridge, *A New England Town*, 172; Russo, *Families and Communities*, 156.

5. Frederick Jackson Turner, *The Frontier in American History* (New York, 1920), 30. Merle Curti et al., *The Making of an American Community: A Case Study of Democracy in a Frontier County* (Stanford, Calif., 1959), 65–77, quote on 67; James C. Malin, "The Turnover of Farm Population in Kansas," *Kansas Historical Quarterly* 4 (1935):339–72; Mildred Thorn, "Population Study of an Iowa County in 1850," *Iowa Journal of History* 57 (1959):305–30; Peter Coleman, "Restless Grant County: Americans on the Move," in Harry Scheiber, ed., *The Old Northwest* (Lincoln, Neb., 1969), 260–86.

6. Charles J. Galpin, *Rural Life* (New York, 1923), 86–87, reprints the earlier 1915 study. A few years earlier Warren H. Wilson similarly argued that "the country community is defined by the team haul"—the maximum distance for hauling farm produce to market; see *The Evolution of the Country Community* (Boston, 1912). For the neighborhood studies see especially John H. Kolb, *Rural Primary Groups: A Study of Agricultural Neighborhoods* (Madison, Wisc., 1921). For other references and

discussion see Lowry Nelson, *Rural Sociology: Its Origins and Growth in the United States* (Minneapolis, 1969). David B. Danhom, *The Resisted Revolution: Urban America and the Industrialization of Agriculture, 1900–1930* (Ames, Ia., 1979), sets the development of rural sociology within its historical context.

7. A. J. Reiss, "The Sociological Study of Communities," *Rural Sociology* 24 (1959):118.

8. A series of "rural life studies," prepared under the auspices of the Bureau of Agricultural Economics in the early 1940s, represented a high point in the early methodological work of rural sociology; these studies included examinations of not only economic life but of visitation, kinship, ritual, and institutional development, and as such approached a much fuller notion of community than the earlier work of Galpin and his associates. At the same time, these studies represented a turning away from the dynamic connection of open country and village to the more easily conceptualized and traditionally fashionable "little community." See Bureau of Agricultural Economics, *Rural Life Studies* nos. 1–6 (Washington, D.C., 1941–43). For complete citations of these important works see Nelson, *Rural Sociology*, 204 n. 17.

9. W. Stein, quoted in G. J. Lewis, *Rural Communities* (London, 1979), 135.

10. Galpin, *Rural Life*, 70.

11. Although he does not make much of these relationships, they are all implicit in Lockridge's analysis; see *A New England Town*, passim, but especially 65, 69–70, 80, 140.

12. This essay is a condensation of research to be published as *Sugar Creek: Life, Love, and Land in the Illinois Country, 1760–1860* (New Haven, Conn., in press).

13. From the earliest mention of Sugar Creek settlements in county records, observers noted a distinction between the upper and lower sections of the creek, suggesting that they thought there was a certain maximum boundary to the size of a single settlement. With population expansion the geographic boundaries contracted to include a manageable number, but rarely exceeded about 10 miles at their greatest length. Within such a settlement it was possible to visit nearly any location and return home, within one day. See County Commissioners Court (hereafter cited as CCC), Minute Books, 5 June 1821; 2 May 1825; 6 March 1826; 6 March 1827, typescript, Illinois State Historical Library, Springfield, Ill. (hereafter cited as ISHL). For purposes of this study I will confine myself to the 100 sections of upper Sugar Creek in the townships of Auburn, Divernon, Chatham, and Ball, Sangamon County. (See Figures 8.2–8.4.)

14. Persistence measured as the number of heads of household recurring on the manuscript schedules of the federal population census as a percentage of all households: see Table 8.1. All population figures in this article are taken from the Federal Census of Population, manuscript schedules, for Sangamon County, Illinois, available for the years 1830 to 1850 on microfilm from the National Archives, but more conveniently available in a set of publications issued by the Sangamon County Genealogical Society of Springfield, Illinois (hereafter cited as SCGS): *Federal Census, 1830, Sangamon County, Illinois*, trans. Ruth Z. Marko (Springfield, Ill., n.d.), *Federal Census, 1840, Sangamon County, Illinois*, trans. Ruth Z. Marko (Springfield, Ill., 1980), and *Sangamon County, Illinois, 1850 Census and Mortality Schedule* (Springfield, Ill., n.d.).

15. The technique of mapping the census returns was accomplished by linking

the names of householders with taxation, land title, and plat map data, a tedious process made much easier through use of the published transcriptions of census manuscript schedules by the SCGS. In addition to SCGS census volumes see SCGS, *Early Federal Land Sales Within the Present Boundaries of Sangamon County, Illinois* (Springfield, 1978). For tax records see Marilyn Wright Thomas and Hazelmae Taylor Temple, comp., *1835 Tax List, Sangamon County, Illinois* (n.p., n.d.), and "Taxable Lists for Sangamon County, 1832–1838," manuscripts, Illinois State Archives, Springfield, Ill. (hereafter cited as ISA). The earliest available county plat map, showing landowners, home sites, and roads, was compiled by Joseph Ledlie, county surveyor, and published by H. C. Whitley and S. B. Wheelock of St. Louis in 1858; a copy is available at ISHL. The Proceedings Files of the CCC also contain much valuable information on roads and bridges, including many beautifully composed maps by Ledlie and other county surveyors; see manuscripts, Illinois Regional Archive Depository, Sangamon State Archives, Sangamon State University, Springfield (hereafter cited as IRAD/SSU). See also SCGS, *Combined Atlases of Sangamon County, Illinois, 1874, 1894, 1914* (Evansville, Ind., [1981]). For a discussion of the mapping techniques employed here see William A. Bowen, *The Willamette Valley: Migration and Settlement on the Oregon Frontier* (Seattle, 1978), 97–103.

16. In 1835 some local boosters attempted to create a village in the area. "Auburn" was platted and lots sold, but for lack of a need for such a center the "town" never contained more than five or six structures. In 1853 a new town was platted on the rail line about a mile southeast, and eventually claimed the older name; the former site reverted to cornfield. *History of Sangamon County, Illinois* (Chicago, 1881), 750–52.

17. Eddin Lewis's accounts for 1847–50, included in Job Fletcher, Jr., Account Book, 1848–63, manuscript, ISHL. I checked the names against all available sources of residential information (see n. 21, below) at the county level. For 1849 I was able to geographically locate twenty-six of Lewis's thirty-one visitors; for 1861, twenty-six of Fletcher's forty-eight visitors. The chances are that some of the unidentified names were men from out of the county, but the lack of dispersion of the identified names outside the upper Sugar Creek area suggests that these individuals might have been local residents who moved on, or otherwise missed being counted in the record.

18. Moses Wadsworth, "Sugar Creek Country in 1840," typescript, 20, ISHL. On mills see *History of Sangamon County*, 749, 791; Mrs. Anthony W. Sale, "The Old Mills of Sangamon County," *Journal of the Illinois State Historical Society* 18 (1926):1056–58; Elizabeth Wier and Edward Hawes, "Mills and Mining in the Clayville Area," typescript, SSU; CCC, Minute Books, 5 September 1825, 2 July 1827, 1 March 1830, ISHL; CCC, Proceedings Files, box 1, September term, 1825, IRAD/SSU.

19. D. W. Meinig, "The Beholding Eye: Ten Versions of the Same Scene," in D. W. Meinig, ed., *The Interpretation of Ordinary Landscapes* (New York, 1979), 46. Robert V. Hine, *Community on the American Frontier: Separate But Not Alone* (Norman, Okla., 1980), 21–26.

20. J. B. Jackson, *The Necessity of Ruins* (Amherst, Mass., 1980), 122. For the public record on road construction see CCC, Proceedings Files, IRAD/ SSU.

21. For the location of the polling place see CCC, Minute Books, 3 July 1827; it

was relocated slightly west in 1847; Minute Books, 1 March 1847, ISHL. Successful candidates for office were generally no more wealthy than the average, but were invariably property owners. Calculated from election returns in Office of County Clerk, Election Papers, manuscripts, IRAD/ SSU. Richard S. Alcorn, "Leadership and Stability in Mid-Nineteenth-Century America: A Case Study of an Illinois Town," *Journal of American History* 61 (1974–75):685–702, finds a high degree of control of local leadership by the most persistent families in a town some 100 miles east of Sugar Creek. For a discussion of elections in another Sangamon community see Benjamin Thomas, *Lincoln's New Salem*, rev. ed. (New York, 1954). I have discussed frontier male culture at some length in John Mack Faragher, *Women and Men on the Overland Trail* (New Haven, Conn., 1979), 112–21, 134–36.

22. William J. Butler, "Indian and Mexican Wars," in Newton Bateman and Paul Selby, eds., *Historical Encyclopedia of Illinois and History of Sangamon County*, 2 vols. (Chicago, 1912), 2:905.

23. William Riley McLaren, "Reminiscences of Pioneer Life in Illinois," typescript, 1916, ISHL. On education see Bateman and Selby, eds., *Historical Encyclopedia*, 2:792–96. On the relationship of neighborhood and community to the organization of rural schools see Harold W. Foght, *The American Rural School* (New York, 1910), and Mable Carney, *Country Life and the Rural School* (Chicago, 1912).

24. See G. G. Hudson, "Sugar Creek Cumberland Presbyterian Church. Eightieth Anniversary of its Organization," in Edith Drennan Sprinkell, comp., "Records of Some Early Churches in Sangamon County, Illinois. Sugar Creek Congregation of the Cumberland Presbyterian Church, 1825–1870," typescript, 1928, 5, in Daughters of the American Revolution, Illinois Chapter, Genealogical Collections, ISHL; and SCGS, *Cumberland Church of Auburn, Illinois* (Williamsville, Ill., 1971). SCGS, *Marriage Records, Sangamon County, Illinois, 1821–1840* (Springfield, [1977]), 2:13. Edgar Lee Masters, *The Sangamon* (New York, 1942), 125; *History of Sangamon County*, 752, 792.

25. SCGS, *Methodist Church, Auburn* (Williamsville, Ill., n.d.); Sangamon Association of Regular Predestinarian Baptists, Minutes, 1823–82, manuscripts, ISHL; Joseph J. Thompson, *Diocese of Springfield in Illinois: Diamond Jubilee History* (Springfield, [1927]), 231–32; *History of Sangamon County*, 748, 752, 755–56, 793. T. Scott Miyakawa, *Protestants and Pioneers: Individualism and Conformity on the American Frontier* (Chicago, 1964), 214. See also Stuart Blumin, "Church and Community: A Case Study of Lay Leadership in Nineteenth-Century America," *New York History* 56 (1975):393–408; and William Warren Sweet, *Religion on the American Frontier*, 4 vols. (New York, 1964).

26. Charles Watts to Edward Watts, Greenfield, Ill., 20 June 1841, "Watts Letters, 1836–1852," ISHL. Greenfield is about 20 miles southwest of Sugar Creek. The literature on self-sufficing farming is enormous; among the more interesting works with direct relevance for Sugar Creek farming see Arthur F. Raper, "The General and Self-Sufficing Areas," in Carl C. Taylor et al., eds., *Rural Life in the United States* (New York, 1949), 446–63; Harriet Arnow, *Seedtime on the Cumberland* (New York, 1960); James A. Davis, *Frontier America, 1800–1840* (Glendale, Calif., 1977), 20, 138, and ch. 7; Michael Merrill, "Cash Is Good to Eat: Self-Sufficiency and Exchange in the Rural Economy of the United States," *Radical History Review* 3 (1977):42–71, as well as Christopher Clark, "The Household Mode of Production:

A Comment," *Radical History Review* 18 (1978):166–71, James W. Wessman, "A Household Mode of Production—Another Comment," and Michael Merrill, "So What's Wrong with the 'Household Mode of Production?'" *Radical History Review* 22 (1979–80):129–46; James A. Henretta, "Families and Farms: *Mentalité* in Pre-Industrial America," *William and Mary Quarterly* 3d ser. 35 (1978):3–32.

27. Willis Berry, Memoranda Book, 1837–58, manuscript, ISHL. Lucy Maynard, La Harpe, Ill., to Libbit and Able Pipper, 3 December 1839 and 15 July 1840, "Lucy Maynard Letters," ISHL.

28. John Smith, Account Book, manuscript, ISHL. Lemira Gillett, "Reminiscences of Pioneer Life in Springfield and Logan County, Illinois," typescript, 1901, 2, ISHL. "On the halves" refers to the millers' common practice of taking a share of the milled grain as their fee. By state law a miller could charge a maximum of one-eighth of the total sacks of wheat flour, one-seventh of corn, oats, or buckwheat. See Wier and Hawes, "Mills and Mining," 5.

29. Paul Angle, *"Here I Have Lived": A History of Lincoln's Springfield* (Springfield, 1935), 54–55, 144–48, 159–64; Arthur C. Boggess, *The Settlement of Illinois, 1778–1830* (Chicago, 1908), 141–42, 158, 163; Judson Fiske Lee, *Transportation as a Factor in the Development of Northern Illinois Previous to 1860* (Chicago, n.d.), 24–27, 35, 71, 76, 83; John Henry Krenkel, *Internal Improvements in Illinois, 1818–1848* (Cedar Rapids, Ia., 1958), 2–3; Bateman and Selby, eds., *Historical Encyclopedia,* 2:617, 640–42, 773. Wadsworth, in *History of Sangamon County,* 176; Angle, *"Here I Have Lived,"* 22, 36, confirms Wadsworth's statement.

30. R. G. Bergen, quoted in Bateman and Selby, eds., *Historical Encyclopedia,* 2:984. Solon Robinson, "Notes of Travel in the West," quoted in Angle, *"Here I Have Lived,"* 154; Timothy Flint, *A Condensed Geography and History of the Western States* (Boston, 1833), 398.

31. I have discussed the division of labor and the implications for women's history at greater length in *Women and Men on the Overland Trail,* and in John Mack Faragher, "History from the Inside-Out: On Writing the Social History of Women in Rural America," *American Quarterly* 33 (1981):537–57.

32. Distribution of property calculated from 1838 tax list and 1850 federal agricultural census, manuscripts, ISA. For comparison see Jackson Turner Main, *The Social Structure of Revolutionary America* (Princeton, N.J., 1965); Edward Pessen, *Riches, Class and Power Before the Civil War* (Lexington, Ky., 1973); David Klingman, "Individual Wealth in Ohio in 1860," in David Klingman and Richard Veeder, eds., *Essays in Nineteenth Century Economic History: The Old Northwest* (Athens, Ohio, 1975); Lee Soltow, *Men and Wealth in the United States, 1850–1870* (New Haven, Conn., 1975).

33. Wadsworth, in *History of Sangamon County,* 78. See *Early Federal Land Sales,* passim; Paul W. Gates, *Landlords and Tenants on the Prairie Frontier* (Ithaca, N.Y., 1973), 77–78, 149, 245–47, discusses Grigg, Ware, and the Berrys.

34. Allan Bogue, *From Prairie to Corn Belt: Farming on the Illinois and Iowa Prairies in the Nineteenth Century* (Chicago, 1963), 66. On tenancy and hired labor in general see Bogue, as well as Gates, *Landlords and Tenants,* and David Schrob, *Hired Hands and Plowboys: Farm Labor in the Midwest, 1815–1860* (Urbana, Ill., 1975).

35. Wadsworth, "Sugar Creek." I have traced kin connections with the use of the manuscript censuses in combination with the family histories and genealogical ma-

terial in *History of Sangamon County*; Bateman and Selby, eds., *Historical Encyclopedia*; John Carrol Power, *History of the Early Settlers of Sangamon County, Illinois* (Springfield, 1876); and miscellaneous genealogical materials at ISHL. F. Carlene Bryant, *We're All Kin: A Cultural Study of a Mountain Neighborhood* (Knoxville, Tenn., 1981), discusses a similar pattern of endogamy and community in an east Tennessee village.

36. Allan Bogue, "Social Theory and the Pioneer," *Agricultural History* 34 (1960): 21–34.

37. Stanley Elkins and Eric McKitrick, "A Meaning for Turner's Frontier," *Political Science Quarterly* 69 (1954):321–53, 565–602.

KATHLEEN NEILS CONZEN

# 9. Peasant Pioneers

## GENERATIONAL SUCCESSION AMONG GERMAN

## FARMERS IN FRONTIER MINNESOTA

Over the course of the nineteenth century, hundreds of thousands of European peasants transplanted themselves, their families, and their farming operations to the fields and plains of America.* By the end of the century, they and their children made up more than one-quarter of all those who earned a living from agriculture in the United States.[1] The peasant world that so many of the immigrant farmers had left behind revolved around the central relationship between the family and its land. The land nourished the peasant family, determined its status in the community, indeed shaped its very structure. Recent scholarship has illuminated the ways in which family strategies to insure sufficient labor to work the land and to pass it on to the next generation influenced every aspect of the peasant family, from its size, composition, residential patterns, and life cycle to its internal relationships and its external links to the wider world.[2] For many peasants, it was the final realization that this traditional symbiosis was no longer viable in the changing homeland that led to emigration.[3]

What then was the fate of traditional patterns of peasant family life as the family reestablished itself amid the very different conditions of America? Historians of rural America, obsessed with questions of farming technology and the income and status of farmers, have paid little attention to the "family" component in nineteenth-century "family farming." Conventional wisdom postulated loose family ties among American farmers, early dispersal of family members, and lack of sentiment surrounding family land and its inheritance.[4] Until recently, Turnerian notions of frontier individual-

*I wish gratefully to acknowledge the support of the American Council of Learned Societies and the Charles Warren Center for Studies in American History of Harvard University for the larger project of which this is a part. I am also grateful to Carolyn Walker and Andrew Yox for their research assistance; to the Zapp Abstract Co. of St. Cloud, Minnesota, for making available to me its abstracts of land transactions within St. Martin township; and to William L. Cofell of St. John's University, Collegeville, Minn., for sharing with me his special insight into twentieth-century St. Martin.

ism, combined with later perceptions that older American rural family strategies were simply incompatible with market agriculture, served to discourage reexamination of how families functioned in the context of husbandry. Impressed by the readiness with which immigrant farmers adopted American settlement forms, crops, and methods of cultivation, historians tended to find peasant cultural baggage of little relevance to nineteenth-century American farming.[5]

But the question remains open, if only because work in other contexts has repeatedly demonstrated that the family was a fundamental carrier of traditional values. Immigration historians, for example, have demonstrated the extent to which traditional family strategies and goals influenced the accommodation of European peasants to American cities.[6] A study of the adaptability of traditional peasant family patterns to the American farming frontier provides an opportunity both to assess the utility of customary family strategies in mediating adjustment to American life and to delineate one possible relationship between family and farm under conditions of nineteenth-century frontier agriculture. The detail necessary to illuminate that relationship can be achieved only at the local level. Accordingly, this essay investigates the strategies toward land and family adopted by German immigrant farmers in a central Minnesota community, from the establishment of the community in the late 1850s through the second generation's coming of age in the early twentieth century.

I

The area examined here is the 36-square-mile federal survey township of St. Martin, Minnesota, located in the heart of Stearns County some 70 miles northwest of Minneapolis on the Sauk River, an unnavigable tributary of the Mississippi (see Map 9.1). The township functioned as the basic unit of local government and was, for most of the period, virtually coterminous with the Catholic parish from which it took its name. Except for several sections of excellent prairie, most of the land was rolling to hilly, of moderately good soil quality and initially covered by a mixture of hardwood forest and scrub. At the time of initial settlement in the late 1850s, St. Martin lay on a branch of the territory's major route, the legendary ox-cart trail linking the fur-rich Red River Valley with St. Paul and the Mississippi River system. Its first railroad shipping point was established in 1872 about 6 miles beyond the township's boundaries. In the southeastern corner lay St. Martin's only nucleated settlement, a small village of the same name that grew up around the church, the general store, and several other small businesses serving the surrounding rural area. St. Martin's pioneer farmers participated in the wheat boom of the Minnesota frontier, but were beginning a

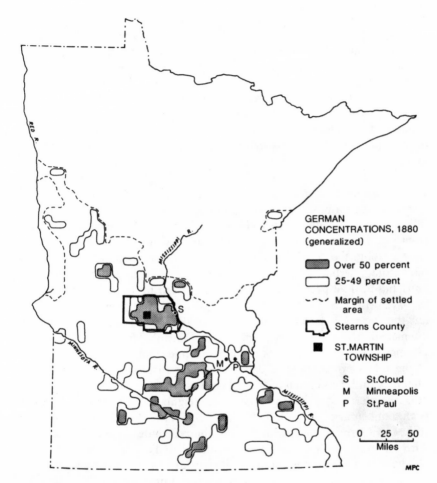

GERMAN
CONCENTRATIONS, 1880
(generalized)

▨ Over 50 percent

▢ 25-49 percent

⌁ Margin of settled
area

▢ Stearns County

■ ST.MARTIN
TOWNSHIP

S   St.Cloud
M   Minneapolis
P   St.Paul

0   25   50
Miles

MPC

*9.1. Location of St. Martin Township and Stearns County, in the context of German settlement concentrations in Minnesota, 1880 (derived from Map 8.3, "Germans in Minnesota Rural Areas, 1880," in* They Chose Minnesota: A Survey of the State's Ethnic Groups, *ed. June Drenning Holmquist, St. Paul: Minnesota Historical Society Press, 1981, p. 156.)*

transition to dairying as the pioneer generation ended its farming career. It was in 1897 that the first local cooperative creamery was established.[7]

By 1851, when the area of Stearns County was opened for settlement, Germans were becoming the nation's single largest immigrant group and were moving rapidly into agriculture. German farmers had already staked out large settlement areas in Missouri, Texas, Wisconsin, and elsewhere in the Midwest; they now turned their attention to the new Minnesota frontier.[8] The enthusiastic letters of a missionary priest published in German Catholic newspapers in the United States and Europe attracted the first German Catholic settlers to Stearns County. When a German Benedictine monastery was founded within the county in 1856, its German and Catholic future was assured. By 1870 twenty of the county's thirty-seven townships were at least 60 percent German and largely Catholic; nine of them were over 80 percent German. The county's 3,053 German-born residents constituted 21.5 percent of its total population and 58.5 percent of its foreign-born population; the native-born population included many children of German parents.[9]

The first German pioneers arrived in St. Martin township in 1856 or 1857. They included four families that had migrated westward from a German Catholic farming settlement in Fond du Lac County, Wisconsin, and a fifth that had initially located elsewhere in Stearns County after arriving from Germany the previous year. Several New Yorkers settled across the river at about the same time. By 1860, the pioneer community of 116 was multiethnic, harboring 12 German, 9 Yankee, 4 Irish, and 2 Scandinavian households. The pace of settlement slowed during the Civil War and the Sioux Uprising of 1862, so that the population in 1870 was still only 267, but the flow of new settlement soon quickened, and German domination intensified. By 1880, 76 percent of St. Martin's 86 households were of German stock; by 1905, 86 percent of 118 households were German. Most of the non-Germans were German-speaking Alsatians, Luxemburgers, or Dutch, with the exception of a small core of Irish families, who were beginning to intermarry with their German neighbors.[10] As late as the mid-twentieth century, almost nine-tenths of St. Martin household heads would still be of German stock, with most of the remainder at least half German. The community still remained exclusively Catholic.[11]

The cultural traditions and familial values of St. Martin's immigrant generation of German farmers were nurtured primarily in Prussia's Rhine Province, in the isolated, backward villages of the rugged Eifel uplands and in the bordering Rhine and Moselle valleys (see Map 9.2). Because St. Martin was not the product of group colonization and subsequent chain migration from a circumscribed German locality, the precise origins of its settlers are difficult to trace. Local tradition insists that St. Martin's immigrant farmers were "Germans from the banks of the Rhine and the Mosel," and indeed they named their church and their community for one of that region's most venerated saints.[12] But specific information on place of origin is available for only fourteen St. Martin families, eleven of which came from the Eifel or neighboring areas. Migration chains certainly continued to link the township with the Eifelers who had originally settled the Fond du Lac County, Wisconsin, community from which St. Martin's pioneers had set out, and undoubtedly also with the Rhine Province itself. Federal and state

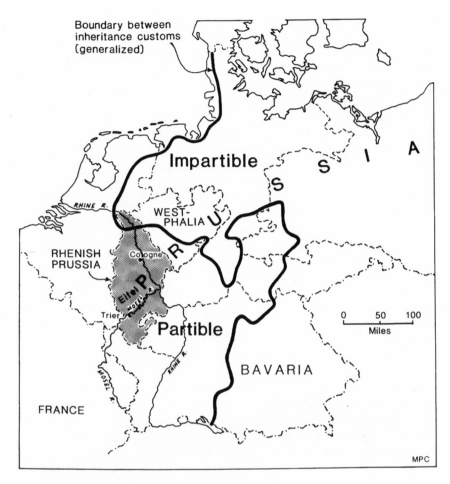

*9.2. Location of the German States of Origin of St. Martin Settlers, in relation to traditional areas of partible and impartible inheritance customs in Germany (derived from map in Lutz K. Berkner, "Inheritance, Land Tenure and Peasant Family Structure: A German Regional Comparison," in* Family and Inheritance: Rural Society in Western Europe, 1200–1800, *eds. Jack Goody, Joan Thirsk, and E. P. Thompson, Cambridge, Eng.: Cambridge University Press, 1976, p. 75.)*

censuses, however, tell us only that the great majority of St. Martin's Germans were Prussians, with Bavarians temporarily forming a small secondary group in the 1880s.[13]

In the mid-nineteenth century, the Rhine Province south of the Cologne–Aachen line was still an area of traditional village agriculture, where marginal soil and poor accessibility everywhere except in the wine-growing regions along the major rivers confined most peasants to little more than subsistence agriculture. The three-field system remained dominant, with each farmer owning widely scattered parcels in the open fields that lay around the village, as well as rights in the village's meadow, pasture, wasteland, and forest commons. The small size of individual parcels meant that communal decisions necessarily regulated farming operations, but the years of French occupation during the Napoleonic era had left most of the Rhineland an area of small peasant freeholders.[14]

The imposition of the Code Napoléon during those same years confirmed the partible inheritance customs traditional throughout most of this part of the Rhine Province. Sons and daughters inherited equally. Estates were frequently distributed during the lifetimes of the parents, whose support in retirement by one or more of the heirs constituted part of the settlement agreement. Each individual parcel of land might be divided, or the parcels could be distributed among the various heirs. Although it was unusual for sibling groups to hold and work their land cooperatively, it was not uncommon for one heir to sell or rent his or her land to another, thereby creating larger, more viable economic units. Marriage meant the pooling of two inheritances as well as creating the basis of the workforce. The system encouraged neolocal residence and nuclear families; it tied succeeding generations to the village, though it clearly could not link family identity over time with any particular piece of land. The residence, however, the visible symbol of the family in the community, could pass only to a single heir, in return for extra compensation to the parents or the other heirs.[15]

By the mid-nineteenth century these inheritance customs had created a "dwarf economy" of tiny marginal holdings in much of this part of the Rhine Province. Only widespread opportunities for supplementary earnings in small-scale mining, metal working, textile production, and similar activities permitted the system to function. In the 1840s, when poor harvests coincided with the collapse of the region's traditional cottage industries in the face of outside industrial competition, many peasants were forced to consider emigration. Between 1840 and 1871, the nine administrative districts of the Eifel alone registered 24,333 emigrants. Two-thirds to four-fifths of the emigrants were peasants, the remainder mainly artisans sharing the values of the peasants among whom they lived. Probably an equal number emigrated illegally. America was the goal for the majority.[16]

Even those St. Martinites who came from areas of Germany where impartible inheritance prevailed—Bavaria, for instance, or Westphalia—would have shared many of the familial expectations of the Rhinelanders. Partible inheritance was associated with open-field agriculture; impartible inheritance prevailed in areas of larger, unified holdings where peasants lived on their own farms. Impartible inheritance encouraged the creation of stem families in which the parental couple and the single heir and his family shared a common residence, either before or after the heir took over legal possession of the estate. It encouraged large farming units and considerable geographic mobility among nonheirs or those not marrying heirs.[17] But, at least in principle, nonheirs received compensation from the estate in forms other than land. The heir's wife's dowry provided needed cash for the settlements, and premortem division followed by support during retirement was common. Moreover, inheritance that was effectively partible could still occur in times of economic prosperity, when additional land might be purchased for other children.[18]

Both systems thus rested upon essentially similar conceptions of what has been termed the "perennial family." Under this general pattern, joint inheritances of the parental couple and the joint labor of parents and youngsters provided a stake in life for the children in the earlier phases of the family cycle. In the later phases, it facilitated the retirement of parents, which in turn provided the means and incentive for children to remain on the land, insuring that the bond of land, family, and village would endure for another generation.[19]

Emigrants from the Rhineland undoubtedly took it for granted that such traditional family strategies would continue to guide their actions in the New World. A government official in Trier reported in 1847 that one of the main reasons for the unprecedented emigration from this part of the Rhine Province the previous year was the uncertain future that peasants perceived for their children in their home villages. "By contrast," he went on to note, "America opens up to them the seductive prospect of being able to acquire with a small capital a considerable property and to leave to their children and their children's children a farm capable of providing them with an abundant livelihood."[20]

Many achieved the security they dreamed of, but it is less clear whether the immigrant farmers were equally successful in transplanting the familial patterns which that security was meant to support. Research, much of it designed to test Frederick Jackson Turner's hypothesis of rapid Americanization in frontier settings, has tended to stress the extent to which immigrant farming operations paralleled those of nonimmigrant neighbors. In place of communal villages and open fields, immigrants settled on dispersed farmsteads set in the midst of their own acres; production of staple crops for market replaced mixed subsistence farming and cottage industry; traditional house and barn types yielded to American-style farmsteads. The physical and economic context of farming was so different, the impact of American example so strong, that historians examining numerous groups in a variety of different settings have found few major differences attributable to ethnicity in farming practices, tenure, or persistence and success rates, except in isolated instances in which homogeneous groups of religiously motivated emigrants established their own colonies. "The old ways proved ineffective under new conditions and the new life quite different from the old," Oscar Handlin has argued. The differences "were not only in the surface appearance of things; they penetrated his whole life as a farmer."[21]

Yet, where such studies *have* found distinctive ethnic patterns, particularly among German immigrant farmers, they are precisely in those areas where one could expect traditional familial strategies to reveal themselves. Nineteenth-century German-Americans cherished what they saw as a stereotypical contrast between Yankee and German farmers. The Yankee farmer, according to this image, lacked any kind of sentimental attachment to his land. Ever ready to sell out for a profit and move further west, he planted the same crop year after year, paying little attention to the fertility of his soil, the well-being of his livestock, or the condition of his tools and machinery, and he plowed too much of his profit back into an elegant dwelling and a genteel life for his womenfolk. By contrast, the German farmer was stereotyped as deeply rooted in an intimate, permanent relationship with his land. His farm was an object of care and piety rather than of speculation. His deepest desire was to leave it debtfree to succeeding generations. He placed the comfort of his stock over that of his family. He carefully manured his land, chose his crops rationally to suit the soil, and let "painful order" rule in field and farmyard. His wife and children worked alongside him in the fields as the family slowly built up the capital to expand operations and to support a more comfortable existence.[22]

Central to this imagery is the German's view of the land as a family trust in traditional terms; this conception has been supported by scholarly findings of greater geographical stability, emphasis on ownership, soil conservation practices, and both intensity and productivity of farming practices. All of these characteristics can be traced to a perception of the farm as a long-term "home place" and vocation for the family over generations, rather than as a short-term investment.[23]

It seems clear, for example, that family strategies devised with that end in view would have placed little obstacle in the way of new farming practices or farmstead layouts if such innovations helped to achieve the economic security the immigrant family sought. The economic deficiencies of open-field village agriculture were likewise sufficiently evident that even newcomers accustomed to that pattern must have greeted the prospect of owning and residing on their own farms with relief and enthusiasm. So too, American customs of equal inheritance for all offspring were compatible with the assumptions underlying either German inheritance system.

It is equally clear, however, that the strategies adopted to achieve traditional familial goals must have undergone sometimes significant modification. Could those who made the transition from open-field to farm-based agriculture, for example, expect to continue traditional practices of land parcelization, or would they have to find new incentives to insure their children's continued presence on the farm and in the community? Families were, of course, more likely to replant old values when supported by their new communities. Where a settlement was sufficiently large and ethnically homogeneous, it could presumably achieve the degree of cultural autonomy necessary to insulate its children from values at odds with those of the peasant family. And where the community also possessed a strong religious focus, both the autonomy and the commitment to traditional familial values would be further reinforced. To the extent that such values insured the continuing presence of the founding families in the community, they were fundamental to the survival of the ethnically distinctive character of the community itself.

St. Martin, with its ethnic homogeneity, religious solidarity, and institutional self-sufficiency, offered a relatively favorable environment for old values to put down new roots. Did St. Martin's German farmers attempt to maintain an approximation of the peasant bond linking families, land, and community? If so, what strategies did they adopt to achieve that bond under the conditions of the Midwestern frontier and postfrontier farming? Answers to these questions can be sought in the ways in which they resolved the basic problems of first retaining their children as a family labor force, and then of guaranteeing the transmission of the farm to the next generation.

II

A letter to the editor published in Stearns County's German newspaper, some twenty years after St. Martin was first settled, suggests some of the obstacles immigrant farmers faced in transplanting customary family patterns. A young farmer's son pointed out that if local farmers wished to keep their sons working on their farms, they would have to realize that young men desire amusement as well as work, that sons had to be given interesting tasks, responsibility, praise, some money of their own ("don't say it will all come to him in ten or fifteen years anyway, most would rather have a dollar now than ten dollars in ten or fifteen years"), and some land to manage for themselves.[24]

Another article printed in the same paper that year makes clear that many families were successfully adapting traditional patterns of behavior to combat the lure of life away from the farm. This second article, entitled "A Stearns County Wooing," embedded a local genre piece within a vignette advertising Stearns County businesses. The story begins one morning just after Christmas, as Heinrich, a young man of twenty-three, was addressed by his father:

"I'm getting old. I don't want to and can't really work the way I used to, and God be thanked, I've set enough aside so that I can spend the rest of my days with the old one there"—and here he grinned at his wife who was sitting behind the stove—"without such tiring work. And so I thought," he continued, glancing at his wife as if he expected her agreement, "that you should take over the farm, which you've been running anyway for several years now." "Yes," interjected the old woman, "as far as taking over goes, it's like this: I don't want to spend the whole day, and the evening too, on my feet any more. I'd have absolutely no rest. No, no, it doesn't matter, if he'll take over the farm—I have no objections, I'll be happy—but he should get married first."

Heinrich blushed, and it soon became clear that he was favorably inclined toward a certain Katie, the daughter of another Stearns County German farmer, though he had said nothing to her. Heinrich's father assured him that if he could get married within the month, he could take over the farm in the spring, and that once Heinrich had won Katie's hand, the two fathers could get together to make the necessary arrangements. Heinrich immediately hitched the horses to the buggy and set out with a friend to visit Katie, stopping, it seemed, at nearly every tavern along the route for courage. Katie, his friend had told him on hearing of the impending courtship, "is really a fine young lady, and I think she'll make a good housewife too." The two young men finally arrived at Katie's father's farm, bearing presents for Katie and her family. "As the two arrivals came into the house, the girls put aside their work and shook hands with the young men. Heinrich, who was inching his chair ever closer to Katie, made his offer in a few words, and Katie answered happily, yes. Then he went into the next room, where her parents were sitting, and soon walked out beaming with joy." The following Monday found the engaged couple on a shopping spree in the county seat buying clothing, furniture, a stove, and other iron and tinware for their new home.[25]

Laid out in this vignette are many of the elements of traditional family strategy seemingly intact on the Minnesota frontier—the retirement of the parents, the transfer of the farm to the son who had been working it, the dependence of the transfer on his marriage, his reluctance to go wooing until he was assured of farm ownership, the importance given to the housewifely attainments of his intended, the hint of dowry arrangements, the businesslike nature of the whole romance. It is necessary to turn to the complex record of intrafamilial land transactions, however, to document the prevalence of such strategies in St. Martin, the means by which they were realized, and some of their consequences for farm, family, and community.[26]

The relative cultural homogeneity necessary to support a communitywide set of norms regarding farm and family was achieved as non-German families moved away or died, new German families replaced them, and earlier German families expanded their holdings and persisted (Table 9.1). Such dominance came only gradually. Through 1880 the German community grew absolutely, owing to the arrival of newcomers and the expansion of the number of farms under cultivation; it grew relatively owing to the failure of groups other than the Germans and Irish to maintain themselves. After 1880 the number of farms in the township stabilized and the proportion of newcomers declined in the face of cumulative persistence and the increasing pace of takeover of farms by the second generation.

Nearly all farmers after the initial period were landowners. From 1880 onward, the proportion of persons listed as farmers in the census whose local land holdings could be documented in deeds records remained at 94–95 percent. Such high levels of landownership by farm operators are one indication that retired St. Martin farmers preferred to alienate the land they were no longer farming rather than rent it out. The figures also help account for the high levels of farm family persistence, particularly among those who arrived early in St. Martin. Some 73 percent of the 1860 initial census cohort of German farm families were still farming in the township after twenty years, and 54 percent of the second cohort after twenty-five years, though only 38 percent of the third cohort persisted for a similar interval. In 1880, 55 percent of all landowners had been in the township less than a decade. By 1895, 37 percent of the landowners had arrived sometime during the previous fifteen years. Ten years later, only 15 percent of the landowners had arrived during the previous decade.[27]

Such figures begin to suggest that St. Martin farmers were indeed able to convert homesteads into enduring "home places." By 1895, 24 percent of all German-stock farm owners in St. Martin were members of the second generation to farm in the township; a decade later, the offspring of local farmers made up 38 percent of the German-stock farm owners. Comparable figures for the much smaller Irish community were even higher: 33 percent and 46 percent, respectively. Among the new farm owners of the 1895–1905 decade, there were 2.5 members of the second generation for every outsider who had purchased township land. By 1905, almost half of the pioneer German families of the late 1850s and 1860s had successfully established one or more children on local farms, while another sixth were still farming themselves (Table 9.2). Two-thirds of the Irish families had similar success in setting up their children on local farms. None of the original Yankee settlers was succeeded by his children, however, including the four who continued to hold their township land until retirement or death.

As in the old country, direct family aid played a crucial role in guarantee-

9.1. *Arrival and Survival Cohorts of St. Martin Farmer-Owners by Generation*

| Census Year | Total Farmers (Census) | Farmer-Owners (Deeds) | Farmer-Owners Wh | | | |
| | | | 1860 | | 1870 | |
| | | | 1st Gen. | 2d Gen. | 1st Gen. | 2d Gen |
|---|---|---|---|---|---|---|
| **1860** | | | | | | |
| Germans | 23 | 15 | 14 | 1 | | |
| Irish | 6 | 6 | 6 | — | | |
| Yankees | 11 | 8 | 8 | — | | |
| Other | 2 | 2 | 2 | — | | |
| **1870** | | | | | | |
| Germans | 31 | 26 | 10 | 1 | 15 | — |
| Irish | 7 | 6 | 3 | — | 3 | — |
| Yankees | 4 | 4 | 2 | — | 2 | — |
| Other | 5 | 5 | — | — | 5 | — |
| **1880** | | | | | | |
| Germans | 57 | 53 | 10 | 1 | 11 | 2 |
| Irish | 15 | 15 | 3 | — | 4 | — |
| Yankees | 2 | 2 | 1 | — | — | — |
| Other | 5 | 5 | — | — | 2 | — |
| **1895** | | | | | | |
| Germans | 81 | 76 | 6 | 7 | 8 | 6 |
| Irish | 13 | 12 | 2 | 1 | 1 | — |
| Yankees | 1 | 1 | — | — | — | — |
| Other | — | — | — | — | — | — |
| **1905** | | | | | | |
| Germans | 83 | 78 | 1 | 8 | 2 | 12 |
| Irish | 13 | 13 | 1 | 3 | 1 | 1 |
| Yankees | — | — | — | — | — | — |
| Other | — | — | — | — | — | — |

Source: Manuscript population schedules of the federal census (microfilm, National Archive Washington, D.C.) and the Minnesota state census (microfilm, Minnesota Historical Society St. Paul, Minn.); Deed Record, Register of Deeds, Stearns County Courthouse, St. Cloud, Minn.; abstracts, Zapp Abstract Co., St. Cloud, Minn.; manuscript agricultural schedules of the federal census (Minnesota State Archives, St. Paul, Minn.).

| | | | | |
|---|---|---|---|---|
| **ily First Appeared in Census in:** | | | | |
| *1880* | *1895* | | *1905* | |
| *2d* *Gen.* | *1st* *Gen.* | *2d* *Gen.* | *1st* *Gen.* | *2d* *Gen.* |
| — | | | | |
| — | | | | |
| — | | | | |
| — | | | | |
| 3 | 26 | 2 | | |
| 2 | 2 | 1 | | |
| — | — | — | | |
| — | — | — | | |
| 8 | 21 | 2 | 12 | — |
| 2 | 1 | — | 1 | — |
| — | — | — | — | — |
| — | — | — | — | — |

ing that the next generation would continue to farm in the township. It is possible to trace some of the means by which farms were obtained for twenty-six of the thirty second-generation farm owners in 1905.[28] Deeds records indicate that twenty-one of these twenty-six young farmers had acquired at least some of their land directly from other family members. Only one of those twenty-one had acquired all of his land from his family through inheritance alone. Fifteen acquired their land solely from family members, five from both family and nonfamily members, and two by that combination plus inheritance. The average age at which the first parcel of land was acquired was 28.5. Birth order played little clear role in determining which sons remained as farm owners in the community.

### III

The minimal role played by inheritance in land acquisition among the second generation and the relatively early age at which sons became landowners indicate the extent to which St. Martin's immigrant farmers succeeded in maintaining traditional customs of lifetime transmission of land to their children. At the same time, however, American conditions apparently made it unnecessary to tie such land transmission to a single distribution among all heirs at the time of the farmer's retirement. It remained possible, of course, to deed over the land at the time of retirement in return for a support agreement of the kind familiar in Germany. Such agreements were common in other areas of German settlement in the Midwest and appear with some frequency in Stearns County deeds records, but were used only twice in family transactions in St. Martin. In a third instance, a childless couple deeded their land to a neighbor in return for an essentially similar support agreement.[29] Far more common was a gradual process of land transfer to one or more sons (and occasionally sons-in-law) as they matured, culminating in the father's retirement and the final distribution of the remaining land. This process of land distribution was generally preceded or accompanied by a period of additional land acquisition by the father. The terms of transfer were not recorded with any consistency, but it seems clear that in most instances sons were not simply given land, but purchased it from the father, who frequently financed the purchase.

Several examples illustrate the strategies used. One extreme instance is represented by a thirty-eight-year-old farmer who settled on 160 acres of mortgaged land in 1869. His wife would bear him ten children, five of them sons. When his eldest boy was twenty and his second fifteen, the farmer took out another mortgage to acquire an additional 160 acres, and four years later added a third quarter-section, also mortgaged. The following year, he sold one of the quarter-sections to his eldest son (then twenty-five

9.2. *Patterns of Land Transfer among Arrival Cohorts in St. Martin*

| | Germans | | Irish | | Yankees | | Other | |
|---|---|---|---|---|---|---|---|---|
| | No. | % | No. | % | No. | % | No. | % |
| **Farmer-Owners in 1860 Who:** | | | | | | | | |
| a) completed the sale of all holdings to nonfamily members during the interval ending: | | | | | | | | |
| 1870 | 2 | 13 | 1 | 17 | 3 | 43 | 2 | 100 |
| 1880 | — | — | — | — | — | — | — | — |
| 1890 | 1 | 7 | — | — | 3 | 43 | — | — |
| 1905 | 3 | 20 | — | — | 1 | 14 | — | — |
| b) still held land in 1905 and had transferred none to the second generation | 2 | 13 | — | — | — | — | — | — |
| c) were in the process of or had completed transferring land to the second generation by 1905 | 7 | 47 | 5 | 83 | — | — | — | — |
| **New Farmer-Owners in 1870 Who:**[a] | | | | | | | | |
| a) 1880 | 3 | 19 | — | — | 1 | 50 | 3 | 60 |
| 1890 | 1 | 6 | — | — | — | — | 2 | 40 |
| 1905 | 2 | 13 | 1 | 33 | 1 | 50 | — | — |
| b) | 3 | 19 | 1 | 33 | — | — | — | — |
| c) | 7 | 44 | 1 | 33 | — | — | — | — |
| **New Farmer-Owners in 1880 Who:**[a] | | | | | | | | |
| a) 1890 | 8 | 27 | 3 | 38 | — | — | 2 | 66 |
| 1905 | 6 | 20 | 1 | 12 | — | — | 1 | 33 |
| b) | 11 | 37 | 2 | 25 | — | — | — | — |
| c) | 5 | 17 | 2 | 25 | — | — | — | — |
| **New Farmer-Owners in 1895 Who:**[a] | | | | | | | | |
| a) 1905 | 4 | 16 | — | — | — | — | — | — |
| b) | 15 | 60 | — | — | — | — | — | — |
| c) | 6 | 24 | 1 | 100 | — | — | — | — |

[a]Headings are the same as those for 1860.

Source: Manuscript population schedules of the federal census (microfilm, National Archives, Washington, D.C.) and the Minnesota state census (microfilm, Minnesota Historical Society, St. Paul, Minn.); Deed Record, Register of Deeds, Stearns County Courthouse, St. Cloud, Minn.; abstracts, Zapp Abstract Co., St. Cloud, Minn.; manuscript agricultural schedules of the federal census (Minnesota State Archives, St. Paul, Minn.).

years of age and either recently married or about to marry). Three years later his second son, now twenty-four, was also ready for marriage and purchased one of the two remaining quarter-sections from his father.

The next two sons were at that point eighteen and sixteen, respectively. The father, reduced to his original homestead, again entered the rapidly constricting local land market. The 40 acres he was able to purchase outright in 1892 were insufficient when his third son reached twenty-five and was ready for marriage, so the father sold him the original homestead. The farmer was now sixty-five years old, with one daughter and two sons, aged twenty-two and eighteen, still at home. As the depression years of the 1890s began to wane, and as his fourth son's twenty-fifth birthday approached, the farmer returned once more to the land market, laboriously putting together a farm from small lots as they became available, picking up 20 acres here, 48 acres there, 30 acres from another seller. By 1898 he had 138 acres to transfer. By 1903 the widowed father, now seventy-two, could finally settle down to well-earned retirement with the family of one of his daughters. Only the youngest son's fate was still unclear.

The financial arrangements between this father and his sons are as interesting as the pace of land acquisition and transfer. Clearly, the father was pooling his labor and that of his growing sons, along with his established credit, to finance the initial purchases of land. Then, as each son withdrew from the family "pool," the money with which the son purchased land from the father helped finance further land acquisition and, ultimately, the father's retirement. The first son paid his father using a mortgage obtained from a Massachusetts bank. The second son (who would later sell out and leave the township in 1905) evidently paid with cash or with an unsecured note. The father accepted his third son's mortgage note himself. The arrangement apparently encountered problems, however, as this son was forced to resell the land to his father in 1898, using a bond for deed to gain final title by 1903. Perhaps for this reason, when the fourth son purchased his land in 1898, he too signed a deed contract, whereby he would receive title only when the $3,700 purchase price had been repaid at 7 percent annual interest. He was able to pay his father and gain title in 1903, using a $2,700 mortgage from an outside lender. It was only then, when the third and fourth sons finally paid their father, that the farmer's retirement became possible.

This saga represents one father's heroic attempts to provide equally for all of his sons as they came of age. More typical in its mixed success was the case of another farmer, who purchased 280 acres in the township in 1884. He was already fifty-two years old at the time, with five children, including three sons over age twenty. The eldest son seems to have quickly struck out on his own, and the second son purchased a local quarter-section without recorded involvement of his father. Four years later, however, the father sold 160 acres to his youngest son, retaining 120 acres for himself and his wife, which he still held at the time of his death. His widow then sold these in equal shares to the two sons still in the township, undoubtedly to provide for her own old age.

Other German farmers attempted to follow essentially similar strategies in establishing their sons locally, but without success. Take, for example, the case of a Civil War veteran, thirty years old when he first took up a quarter-section homestead in 1869. His family would include five sons and seven daughters. In 1890, as his children were growing up, he used a mortgage to purchase an additional 120 acres, but sold the new farm outside the family two years later. His oldest son had married and left town in 1889 at the age of twenty-four; the second and fourth sons would follow, one to join a religious order. The third married in 1898 and evidently continued to farm the home place with his father and youngest brother. Then the youngest left home, and when the sixty-five-year-old father was ready to retire in 1904, he gave the third son a deed contract for the homestead. This son, however, was either unwilling or unable to make a go of farming on his own to fulfill the contract. After trying and failing to assist at least one and possibly more of his children to farm ownership and community permanence, the farmer was forced to finance his retirement in 1906 by sale of the homestead to a nonfamily member.

As these examples suggest, St. Martin's German pioneers developed a complex set of strategies, all based upon the expanding resources of the family as maturing sons joined their father in working family land, and all aimed at assisting the sons to establish themselves as independent farmers at an early age, retaining the home place within the family, and making possible the parents' retirement. Fathers could not simply give the land to their sons, because they had to consider the claims of other children and the desirability of maintaining parental independence in old age. One alternative, of course, would have been to rent out the family land (either to children or outsiders), use the rental income to support retirement, and distribute the land to the children as an inheritance after death. Data from ownership records and the census, however, suggest that extended rental was relatively uncommon in St. Martin's German families. Without the security of ownership, a son would have little incentive to invest heavily in the farm; indeed, without ownership, evidently few married sons were willing to remain in town.

With parental help, a son could acquire a farm much sooner than would otherwise be possible, and would be more likely to remain in the township. With children safely settled in the area, parents, in turn, could rest assured that what they had created in America would remain an enduring "home place" for the family, and that children would be available to comfort (and if necessary, support) their old age. As a farmer of German descent in a neighboring township would later recall, "Dad said, 'I am getting old and I cannot work the farm anymore.' That's how I was hooked with it; I couldn't say no and leave them sit there. I could have gotten a job somewhere, gone away. But I couldn't do that to my parents."[30] German parents could not preserve their children from knowledge of opportunities elsewhere, but they did create a local culture that offered both positive inducements and internalized norms to keep some at least of the next generation on the farm and in the community.

## I V

As in the last example cited, many in the first two pioneer cohorts who farmed for at least a decade in the township—long enough to be regarded as permanent settlers—but who failed to establish their children, probably also shared the familial values of those who were more successful. Another example of a family with fourteen children, none of whom continued to farm in the township, indicates the possibility of alternative values. In this household, the only offspring to remain in St. Martin was a storekeeper who had received a normal school education. Two other "unsuccessful" farmers in these two pioneer cohorts were childless, a third lost his land through foreclosure in 1894, and a fourth lost two sons to out-migration but could at least rejoice that his eldest son was well-established on a prosperous father-in-law's property in a neighboring township. In the latter case, the farmer—an Alsatian, not a Prussian, as it happens—retained his land until his death after his eightieth birthday. By that time all of his thirteen children had departed. None was apparently willing to return and take up farming on the family land; the children gradually sold their inheritance to neighbors.

Closer examination of those cases in St. Martin in which land transfer was delayed until after a father's death suggests that the transfer frequently involved similar risks for farm and family. Sixty-one conveyances of real estate at death occurred in St. Martin between 1859 and 1915, forty-four of which involved the estates of persons of German birth or stock. Of those forty-four persons, 43 percent died intestate. The wills of an additional 9 percent effectively used standard intestacy provisions, whereas in two instances wills were set aside in favor of the more liberal widow's rights under Minnesota's intestacy statutes.[31] Ten of the remaining twenty-one testators used their wills to make more favorable provision for their spouses; one left his property to a woman in Fond du Lac County, Wisconsin; the remaining ten made more complex arrangements for the division of their property within the family.

In general, intestacy characterized farmers who either died very young, had few or no children or had little land to dispose of, or who died at a ripe old age having already made some provision for their children. In cases in which the estate was complex, the children numerous, and the farmer not caught by early death, there was usually a will. In one case in which the husband died intestate at age seventy-five, after having transferred land to his elder but not to his younger son, we can see some of the complications that wills were often designed to avert: His widow, oldest son, and two daughters had to enter into a complicated series of arrangements to insure that the youngest son could purchase from the other heirs the land clearly meant for him after a three-year rental period intended to permit him time to accumulate the needed funds.

Often the continuity of intrafamily land transfer already under way was secured by leaving the land to the widow. In other instances, however, the will spelled out more detailed procedures. One father who died as his son was approaching twenty-one, for example, left everything to his wife, with the proviso that should she choose to sell, she was to give $1,000 to each of their two daughters and $1,200 to the son, assuming that he had reached twenty-one; she in fact soon sold the land to the son. In another example, a mother's will made explicit the relationship between previous help given by parents to children, aid from children to parents, and inheritance, by leaving an extra $400 to the daughter who had remained at home to care for her widowed mother, and by making no provision for two sons who "have received their full share during my lifetime." The same connection was made evident in another instance in the terms of a sale of land from father to son: The son purchased his father's land for $1,100 down, $100 a year for the next four years, and $3,000 at 5 percent interest to be paid to the estate one year after the death of the last parent—obviously to provide for the other children. The proviso was added that if the son sold the land in the meantime (i.e., alienated it from family ownership), "then the balance will be at six per cent interest."

Where intestacy provisions applied, by law daughters received shares in the estate equal to those of their brothers. Most wills likewise treated daughters simply as "children" who participated equally in the division of the estate. Their shares, however, were generally converted to cash rather than taken as land. Two instances in which wills attempted to provide monetary settlements for daughters and land for sons make such norms explicit, but such expectations are equally evident in the complex intrafamily arrangements that frequently followed upon the "undivided" transmission of estates to all heirs in cases of intestacy. Here the usual pattern was for female heirs to sell their interests to one or more brothers, unless the estate was sold out of the family altogether. Undoubtedly, daughters also received premortem assistance as did their brothers, but in the form of dowry or other kinds of payments rather than in land.

V

The effective functioning of such a system among the pioneer generation was a product of the relatively slow pace of settlement within the township and of generous federal land laws that encouraged rapid accumulations of acreage far larger than the family was initially able to farm. About half of the township land was alienated from the federal government by the early 1860s, most of the remainder by 1870, leaving only a few scattered pockets (as well as the two state sections of school land) for later sale.[32] About half of the land in the township was acquired under the provisions of the Homestead Act, mainly by Germans. The fifteen German landowners present in 1860 were able to acquire an average of 264 acres each before 1880 or their first sale of land, with no accumulations smaller than a quarter-section and one as large as 400 acres. Such large initial claims could be divided into farms and brought into production as family needs and labor supply dictated; as late as 1880, St. Martin's ratio of improved to unimproved land was only one to two.

Early speculator activity within the township provided a further land bank upon which German farmers could draw as more acreage was needed. Of the ten quarter-sections still held by three Yankee speculators in 1880, for example, four were sold to German newcomers by 1900 and the other six provided additional land for already established German families. The state land of sections 16 and 36 performed a similar function as it was sold on credit during the 1880s and 1890s, approximately half to established families and half to German newcomers. Another section or so of land had been broken up early into numerous parcels, some as small as 10 acres, and sold as woodlots to settlers on the treeless prairie of the neighboring town. This land, too, found its way into the hands of members of three established and one new St. Martin German family once it had been stripped of its timber. Finally, as Yankees and other early settlers moved on or died, Germans took their places. One German pioneer of 1860 was able to add two Yankee farms to his holdings, two other Yankee farmsteads passed into the hands of two second-generation German brothers, and German newcomers moved onto other parcels. The only land still in Yankee ownership by 1905 was held in litigation by the heirs of its original patentee.

St. Martin's land, of course, was ultimately as finite as that of any European village. By the late 1880s further stocks of available land for German expansion within the township were becoming increasingly rare, and St. Martin itself was surrounded by other German-settled townships with similarly expanding populations. In this situation, however, St. Martin farmers did not resort to the parcelization of land characteristic of much of the Eifel and neighboring areas in Germany. Mean size of individual holdings remained relatively constant. Indeed, the proportion of farmers with holdings over 200 acres increased from 4 percent in 1860 to 16 percent in 1880 and 32 percent by 1905, as the number of farms first rose from thirty-seven in 1870 to ninety by 1895, and then ten years later dropped to eighty-two. One early will of 1870 attempted to break up a farm into three 40-acre parcels for distribution to each of three sons, but such a strategy found few imitators. During the pioneer decades farmers were able to expand their holdings to provide land for their sons; when that possibility receded, they proved reluctant to revert to a practice of subdivision below local norms of viable farm size. By the turn of the century, no more than 20 percent of the farms were smaller than a quarter-section.

Nor did St. Martin farmers effectively reduce the size of their families as they began to exhaust the abundance of the frontier period. There was a slight decline in the fertility ratio from the extreme peaks of the early frontier period, but traditional values continued to encourage exceptionally large families.[33] The mean number of children residing in homes of mothers in their forties—a rough estimate of completed family size—remained stable at 4.7 between 1880 and 1905. As late as 1940 St. Martin would have a fertility ratio higher than that exhibited in 1875 by a comparable Yankee-dominated Minnesota township.[34]

Moreover, the nuclear family remained the dominant context of both residence and farm labor. Despite the frequency with which a son took over the family farm upon his father's retirement, there is little evidence of a tendency toward the stem family form often associated with farm-based agriculture in Germany. In 1880, 70 percent of all households contained only a nuclear family, extended neither by other relatives nor by hired hands. By 1905, when the variety of kin relationships within the community was much greater than twenty-five years earlier, 69 percent of all households still contained only a nuclear family. Only about 5 percent of all households in either census year contained a second-generation married couple, and fewer than 8 percent had one or more grandparents sharing the dwelling. Parental households could expand temporarily to take in a married child and family, as occurred at one point during the family cycle in four of the pioneer 1860 cohort of German families. A second-generation household might expand to harbor a widowed parent (two of the pioneers found themselves in such a situation) or to house a single sibling of the head (as occurred twice for this pioneer cohort). But the norm was for married children to establish separate households quickly, even if on the same farmstead, and for aging parents likewise to maintain their own households, either on the farm or in the village, until the death of one spouse brought the likelihood of residence with a married child for the surviving partner. The nuclear family was flexible in its willingness to take in other relatives at various phases in the family cycle, but extended coresidence of an heir and his family with his parents, or of a retired parental couple with the family of the child who had taken over the farm, was never the norm.[35]

The combination of large families, separate and usually nuclear households, stable size of holdings, and limited availability of land inevitably meant that over time increasing numbers of children would have to leave the community at maturity (Table 9.3). By 1885, 37 percent of the males who had resided in the township in 1875 were no longer present, a proportion that increased to 50 percent for the 1895–1905 period. Future out-migrants were 57 percent of males between the ages of ten and nineteen in 1875, 70 percent by 1895. By the late 1890s more than two-thirds of the maturing generation of young men were leaving their community in their teens and early twenties. About one-sixth of these could be traced to other Stearns County townships in 1900 and 1905; the remainder sought their fortunes further afield.[36]

For those who remained in St. Martin, however, the result was a familial system strong enough to endure long after the pioneer period—indeed, well into the twentieth century, as William Cofell documented in a 1950 study of St. Martin families. Only 7 percent of the farm owners at that time had inherited their farms, whereas 88 percent had acquired them by purchase (no information was available on the remaining 5 percent). Of the purchasers, however, 85 percent had acquired their farms from relatives, usually parents. Then as during the pioneer period, fathers aimed at purchasing additional land as sons began to reach maturity. Father and sons worked the farm together, all income accruing to the father to help repay his initial investment. When a son decided to marry, the father rented him the land for a year or two and, if he proved successful, the father sold him the farm for significantly less than the initial purchase price. Sons were also often furnished with machinery and livestock; daughters who married farmers received gifts of money, household articles, and perhaps livestock. The advantages of such strategies, as Cofell pointed out, were that the father could expand his operation while his family laborforce was growing, decrease it as his sons left home, avoid a cash outlay as each son married, yet still provide as much aid as possible. As one interviewee put it, "while we're waiting for the son to get married his farm is paying for itself." At an appropriate time, the home farm itself would then be sold to one of the children, and the parents would retire.[37]

VI

Frontier Minnesota conditions permitted German immigrant farmers and their children to maintain and revitalize traditional familial values through adaptations of old-country strategies. They continued to place central em-

9.3. *Out-Migration and Persistence of St. Martin Males by Age, 1875–1905*

*Out-Migration*

| Age Group | 1875 Males No Longer Present in 1885, by Age in 1875 | | 1895 Males No Longer Present in 1905, by Age in 1895 | |
| --- | --- | --- | --- | --- |
| | No. | % of Age Group | No. | % of Age Group |
| 0–9 | 77 | 21 | 127 | 45 |
| 10–19 | 51 | 57 | 74 | 70 |
| 20–29 | 21 | 52 | 103 | 41 |
| 30–39 | 18 | 33 | 41 | 51 |
| 40–49 | 20 | 35 | 23 | 39 |
| 50–59 | 17 | 41 | 17 | 47 |
| 60–69 | 7 | 29 | 20 | 50 |
| 70–79 | — | — | 14 | 86 |
| 80 + | — | — | — | — |
| Total | 211 | 37 | 419 | 50 |

*Persistence*

| Age Group | 1885 Males Present Since 1875, by Age in 1885 | | 1905 Males Present Since 1895, by Age in 1905 | |
| --- | --- | --- | --- | --- |
| | No. | % of Age Group | No. | % of Age Group |
| 10–19 | 85 | 72 | 102 | 75 |
| 20–29 | 52 | 42 | 59 | 53 |
| 30–39 | 23 | 43 | 41 | 51 |
| 40–49 | 20 | 60 | 33 | 70 |
| 50–59 | 24 | 54 | 25 | 76 |
| 60–69 | 24 | 63 | 12 | 75 |
| 70–79 | 4 | 100 | 8 | 100 |
| 80 + | 2 | 100 | 5 | 80 |
| Total | 235 | 59 | 285 | 67 |

Source: Manuscript population schedules of the Minnesota state census, 1875–1905 (microfilm, Minnesota Historical Society, St. Paul, Minn.).

phasis upon the assistance of their children toward an early start in farming. They retained the principle of treating all children equally. They continued to stress early retirement from both farming and landownership in order to provide incentives for children to remain as farmers on the family land and to preserve the family name in the community.

The means by which these traditional goals were achieved underwent modifications, of course. The early commercialization of local agriculture made it far easier to convert joint interests in the family enterprise into cash or credit than it had been in the old country, and the expanding national economy offered ample opportunities elsewhere, both agricultural and nonagricultural. One result was that the inefficient subdivision of land that had characterized the Rhineland system of partible inheritance could be abandoned even while maintaining the *principle* of partible division. The home place was frequently transmitted to only one child, as under the German system of impartible inheritance, but this did not create disadvantages for other children, who could be assisted toward other land purchases or careers, initially within the township itself. The practice of joint households, sometimes characteristic of German areas in which a single son took over the family land, was never necessary in St. Martin. The perennial cycle of the family farm maintained itself, from intergenerational cooperation to retirement, generational succession, and renewed father–son cooperation. But it could proceed more gradually, without the single climactic act of a succession agreement, and it could be embodied now in commercial conveyances that replaced old in-kind payments with cash installment or interest payments.

The successful transplantation of elements of peasant family goals rested in large part on the "window of opportunity" that frontier conditions offered the immigrant generation. This is not to dismiss the back-breaking toil and adversity faced by these pioneers, or the significant number who failed. Nevertheless, their traditional familial orientation served St. Martinites well in the task of frontier farm making. The labor of the entire family, more willingly invested when all perceived an equal stake in the outcome, replaced the capital the family lacked; large families meant that the increasing needs of the family were matched by the growing productivity of both the maturing workforce and the virgin acreage that it gradually brought into production. The initial abundance of land held out the promise of the traditional manner of provision for all children, which American law with its emphasis upon equal inheritance only confirmed.

Community support, however, was equally fundamental to the maintenance of traditional family values. The willingness of parents to forgo the psychological dividends of landlord status and parental power in their later years, the willingness of at least some children to resist the siren call of other ways of life, the ability to close the local land market to outside purchasers—all this required a value consensus that the ethnic and religious homogeneity and relative isolation of St. Martin were able to provide. In turn, the continuity of families on the land and expansion onto neighboring territory insured the survival and extension of the ethnic culture.[38]

In this respect at least, St. Martin farmers fit the old stereotype of the German farmer in America. Their counterparts in other areas of rural German-American concentration may have been equally successful in transplanting the basic bond of farm and family. The tendency for many initial clusters of German immigrants to expand through the acquisition of land previously owned by non-Germans is well documented, and rural sociologists earlier in the twentieth century often found farmers in such areas generally more successful in keeping the farm in the family than were most other Midwestern farmers. Family strategies similar to those of the St. Martinites were often the reasons.[39]

But German peasants from other parts of Germany brought different customs with them to America, and encountered varying circumstances where they chose to settle. American farming communities, even when solidly German, frequently included persons of German origins sufficiently different to necessitate a kind of cultural syncretism even in the absence of much contact with American customs.[40] Variations among areas of rural German settlement were probably as significant as the commonalities. By the late nineteenth century, for example, some Wisconsin German settlers had reportedly begun to honor old-country customs of family land subdivision. Similar subdivision characterized a central Illinois community of low German-speaking Lutheran East Frisians, where it combined with reduced levels of fertility to allow the survival of the ethnic community but not its expansion.[41] Further research is needed to document the differences and similarities in family strategies and their consequences for farm and family in rural German settlement clusters.

Such research is also necessary, of course, to clarify the strategies of other Midwestern farmers, and of Germans living outside their ethnic clusters. There is evidence to suggest, for example, that a different pattern developed in some Midwestern areas settled by native-stock farmers in the mid-nineteenth century, a pattern that accords more closely with the notorious restlessness of the American farmer and the speculative nature of the frontier. Although familial behavior fairly close to German patterns seems to have characterized many Yankee farmers in older settled areas, studies by rural sociologists and land economists in the early decades of the twentieth century found that many native-stock Midwestern farmers preferred to retain their land until death before bequeathing it equally to all children. Retirement for them usually involved a gradual withdrawal from farming and the leasing rather than the sale of the land. Sons often worked their fathers' land, but usually as tenants. If a tenant son desired to take over the farm after his father's death, he would reach an accord with his coheirs to buy out their interests or he would take a chance at the inevitable public auction, even though he would have had little chance to build up equity or credit. By the 1930s, scholars were coming to realize the extent to which increasing levels of tenancy resulted from the normal life cycle when combined with a set of values that encouraged transmission primarily through inheritance and multigeniture. Rather than the establishment of generations of stable families of owner-operators as in St. Martin, the results were more often high levels of tenancy and turnover, difficult prospects of ultimate ownership for the next generation, and low community cohesiveness.[42]

How widespread this latter pattern was and what factors were associated with its emergence require historical documentation. Ethnicity is clearly only one of many factors influencing processes of generational succession among farm families, and both the nature and the success of specific strategies could vary, not only from group to group and area to area but even from family to family, as St. Martin patterns suggest. Nevertheless, it is clear that the few Yankees who settled in St. Martin failed to follow the German course. There were six native-stock families (four farming families and two speculators) who held land within the township for a significant length of time. One farmer sold out and left town when he was seventy-six. The heirs of the other three husbandmen, as well as those of one of the speculators, first leased and then sold their inheritances after a period of joint ownership, while the legacy of the other speculator was still being contested at the end of the period. Although the German character of St. Martin obviously gave Yankee heirs little incentive to remain, it may be significant that most Yankee farmers waited until death to deal with the disposal of their land.[43]

St. Martin's Irish, unlike the Yankees, succeeded in establishing very stable intergenerational farms, but did not expand their holdings in the manner of the Germans. Although their numbers are too small to permit much generalization, there are indications of a tendency among Irish farmers to retain their land until extreme old age or death, to assist only one son directly (or at least to differentiate treatment among sons), and to reside in old age with the child who would ultimately inherit the land. In the case of one extensive Irish clan, the pattern more closely approached a process traditional in Ireland and also evident among the central Illinois Irish studied by Sonya Salamon, than it did either the practices of their Yankee neighbors or the American adaptation worked out by their German fellow Catholics.[44]

Other groups may have exhibited still other variations. Robert Ostergren, in a significant study of several mostly Swedish communities in Isanti County, Minnesota, found patterns resembling those of St. Martin among communities settled by farmers drawn from a relatively isolated area of Sweden. Farmers from more commercialized areas of Sweden, and those who settled outside the Swedish communities, exhibited the same Yankee tendency to prefer post- to predeath settlements and similarly low rates of interfamily farm transmission. Emphasis on educating children for nonfarm occupations rather than preserving the family farm may have had similar consequences, as other studies of Scandinavian-American farming communities suggest.[45]

Stearns County's Germans were able to develop and preserve a distinctive ethnic culture firmly based on the triad of farm, family, and community, which has to a significant degree endured to the present. Neither the content of that culture nor its survival can be understood without taking into account the extent to which pioneers were able to transplant traditional values supporting family continuity on the land. To look only at farming practices in the strictest sense is to miss, as Ostergren has pointed out, the critical familial nexus that linked the economic sphere, where the immigrant readily assimilated, to the cultural and social sphere, where traditional values usually retained their force.[46] To overlook the family is, in fact, to overlook the medium in which those values were nurtured. Agricultural commercialization in America proved consonant with a variety of different family strategies and goals, whose contours remain to be explored by historians. Attention to patterns of inter vivos land transmission as well as to inheritance, as demonstrated in this essay, should be combined with examination of the widely varying ethnic heritages of those who settled the Midwestern heartland and the differing ideals by which they defined "success" on the farming frontier. For many a Yankee, such accomplishment may well have meant expansive acreage and money at interest. But for most St. Martinites, at least, and for others like them, it was the successful transplanting of the perennial bond between family, land, and community.

NOTES

1. U.S. Senate, *Abstracts of Reports of the Immigration Commission*, document no. 747, 61st Cong., 3d sess., 1911, 799. There were 2,105,766 first- and second-generation German farmers and farm laborers in the country in 1900.

2. Michael Mitterauer and Reinhard Sieder, *The European Family: Patriarchy to Partnership from the Middle Ages to the Present* (Chicago, 1982); Heidi Rosenbaum, *Formen der Familie: Untersuchungen zum Zusammenhang von Familienverhältnissen, Sozialstruktur und sozialem Wandel in der deutschen Gesellschaft des 19. Jahrhunderts* (Frankfurt am Main, 1982), 47–120; Tamara K. Hareven, "The Family as Process: The Historical Study of the Family Cycle," *Journal of Social History* 7 (1974):322–29; H. J. Habakkuk, "Family Structure and Economic Change in Nineteenth-Century Europe," *Journal of Economic History* 15 (1955):1–12; Lutz K. Berkner, "Rural Family Organization in Europe: A Problem in Comparative History," *Peasant Studies Newsletter* 1 (1972):145–56; Lutz K. Berkner, "Inheritance, Land Tenure and Peasant Family Structure: A German Regional Comparison," in Jack Goody, Joan Thirsk, and E. P. Thompson, eds., *Family and Inheritance: Rural Society in Western Europe, 1200–1800* (Cambridge, Eng., 1976), 71–95; David Sabean, "Aspects of Kinship Behavior and Property in Rural Western Europe before 1800," in Goody,

Thirsk, and Thompson, eds., *Family and Inheritance*, 96–111. The extensive debate on the exact definition of peasant society is not critical for present purposes: "Peasant" here refers to primarily, although not exclusively, subsistence farmers with vested rights in their land who exist within a larger political and social system. See Walter Goldschmidt and Evalyn Jacobson Kunkel, "The Structure of the Peasant Family," *American Anthropologist* 73 (1971):1058–76; Teodor Shanin, "Peasantry: Delineation of a Sociological Concept and a Field of Study," *Peasant Studies Newsletter* 2 (1973):1–11. For present purposes, immigrants of "sub-peasant" status without full rights in land can be presumed to have shared the familial norms of their peasant neighbors.

3. For a classic statement of this theme, see Marcus Lee Hansen, *The Atlantic Migration, 1607–1860* (Cambridge, Mass., 1940).

4. Arthur W. Calhoun, *A Social History of the American Family*, repr. (New York, 1973), 9–77, 131–48. Richard Easterlin and his associates have suggested that declining rural fertility rates were related to the desire of American farmers to provide their children with land in their vicinity, but cite little evidence on land transmission patterns to support their suggestion; see Richard A. Easterlin, "Factors in the Decline of Farm Family Fertility in the United States: Some Preliminary Research Results," *Journal of American History* 63 (1976):600–614; Richard A. Easterlin, George Alter, and Gretchen A. Condran, "Farms and Farm Families in Old and New Areas: The Northern States in 1860," in Tamara K. Hareven and Maris A. Vinovskis, eds., *Family and Population in Nineteenth-Century America* (Princeton, N.J., 1978), 22–84.

5. For a discussion of this literature, see Kathleen Neils Conzen, "Historical Approaches to the Study of Rural Ethnic Communities," in Frederick C. Luebke, ed., *Ethnicity on the Great Plains* (Lincoln, Neb., 1980), 1–18.

6. For example, see Josef J. Barton, *Peasants and Strangers: Italians, Rumanians, and Slovaks in an American City, 1890–1950* (Cambridge, Mass., 1975); Virginia Yans-McLaughlin, *Family and Community: Italian Immigrants in Buffalo, 1830–1930* (Ithaca, N.Y., 1977); Tamara K. Hareven, "Family Time and Industrial Time," *Journal of Urban History* 1 (1975):365–89; John Bodnar, "Immigration and Modernization: The Case of Slavic Peasants in Industrial America," *Journal of Social History* 10 (1976):44–71.

7. Minnesota Historical Records Survey Project, Works Projects Administration, *Inventory of the County Archives of Minnesota: No. 73, Stearns County* (St. Paul, 1940), 4–23; Cyril Ortmann, *Saint Martin: A Century of Catholic Parish and Community Life* (St. Martin, Minn., 1958), 19–20, 62–64; Surveyor's Field Notes, Township 124 N, Range 32 W (1856), Minnesota State Archives, St. Paul; Merrill E. Jarchow, *The Earth Brought Forth: A History of Minnesota Agriculture to 1885* (St. Paul, 1949), 165–222. Stearns County's reported wheat output expanded from about 56,000 bushels in 1860 and 370,000 in 1870 to about 1.1 million in 1880, 2 million in 1890, and 3 million in 1900, while its fluid milk production climbed from 108 gallons in 1870 to about 43,000 gallons by 1880, over 3.9 million gallons in 1890, and 7.7 million gallons in 1900; *Eighth Census* (Washington, D.C., 1860), Agriculture, 80–81; *Ninth Census* (Washington, D.C., 1870), Wealth and Industry, 180–83; *Tenth Census* (Washington, D.C., 1880), Agriculture, 194, 159; *Eleventh Census* (Washington,

D.C., 1890), Agriculture, 372, 293; *Twelfth Census* (Washington, D.C., 1900), Agriculture, Part I, 170, 607.

8. Max Hannemann, "Das Deutschtum in den Vereinigten Staaten: seine Verbreitung und Entwicklung seit der Mitte des 19. Jahrhunderts," Ergänzungsheft Nr. 225, *Petermann's Mitteilungen* (1936); Hildegard Binder Johnson, "The Location of German Immigrants in the Middle West," *Annals of the Association of American Geographers* 41 (1951):1–41.

9. Ingolf Vogeler, "The Roman Catholic Culture Region of Central Minnesota," *Pioneer America* 8 (1976): 71–83; U.S. Census, *Population* (Washington, D.C., 1880), 515. By 1890, 68.1 percent of the native-born population of the county was of foreign parentage.

10. St. Martin's population was 516 in 1880, 692 in 1890, 623 in 1900, 601 in 1910, and 752 in 1920. The community included thirteen Irish households in both 1880 and 1905, as well as three Yankee and five other nationality households in 1880, which declined to one and two, respectively, by 1905, according to manuscript federal (microfilm, National Archives, Washington, D.C.) and state (microfilm, Minnesota Historical Society, St. Paul, Minn.) census schedules.

11. William L. Cofell, "An Analysis of the Formation of Community Attitudes Toward Secondary Education in St. Martin," M.S. Thesis, University of Minnesota, 1958.

12. Ortmann, *Saint Martin*, 21; Adam Wrede, *Eifeler Volkskunde* (Bonn, 1960), 175, 329. In attempting to link St. Martin families to their German villages of origin and to places of earlier settlement in the United States, I have drawn upon materials in the collections of the Stearns County Historical Society, St. Cloud, Minn., including oral histories; obituary files and other newspaper clippings; and interviews conducted by the Works Progress Administration. I have also consulted Civil War veterans pension records in the National Archives, Washington, D.C.; biographical compilations in William Bell Mitchell, *History of Stearns County, Minnesota*, 2 vols. (Chicago, 1915), in Western Historical Company, *The History of Fond du Lac County, Wisconsin* (Chicago, 1880), and in Maurice McKenna, ed., *Fond du Lac County, Wisconsin: Past and Present* (Chicago, 1912); and two Wisconsin parish histories: P. Corbinian Vieracker, *Geschichte von Mount Calvary, Fond du Lac County, Wis.: Ein Festgabe zum Goldenen Jubilaeum der ersten Ordensniederlassung der Kapuzinerväter in Nordamerika, 25 Juni 1907* (Milwaukee, n.d.) and B. J. Blied, *St. John the Baptist Congregation, Johnsburg, Wisconsin* (Johnsburg, Wis., 1957). Minnesota naturalization papers for this period (deposited in the Minnesota State Archives, St. Paul, Minn.) do not record village or province of origin.

13. In 1870, 86 percent of St. Martin's German household heads were born in Prussia, 72 percent in 1880, and 91 percent in 1895. Bavarians comprised 5 percent, 26 percent, and 3 percent of the St. Martin population, respectively, in each of the census years; manuscript population schedules of the federal census, 1870 and 1880 (microfilm, National Archives, Washington, D.C.); manuscript population schedules of the Minnesota state census, 1895 (microfilm, Minnesota Historical Society, St. Paul, Minn.).

14. Richard Graafen, *Die Aus- und Abwanderung aus der Eifel in den Jahren 1815 bis 1955. Forschungen zur deutschen Landeskunde*, 127 (Bad Godesberg, 1961); Josef

Mergen, *Die Amerika-Auswanderung aus dem Stadtkreis Trier im 19. Jahrhundert* (Trier, 1962); Max Sering, "Das Moselland in der Vergangenheit und Gegenwart," in Max Sering, ed., *Das Moselland* (Leipzig, 1910), 1–34; Franz Brümmer, "Der Notstand in der Eifel, seine Ursachen und die Massnahmen der Staatsregierung zu seiner Behabung," in Sering, ed., *Das Moselland*, 157–74.

15. Karl Rogge, "Gegenwartsfragen der Freiteilung des ländlichen Grundbesitzes in Westdeutschland," in Max Sering and Constantin von Dietze, eds., *Die Vererbung des ländlichen Grundbesitzes in der Nachkriegszeit* (München and Leipzig, 1930), 331–84; Brümmer, "Notstand in der Eifel"; Max Sering, ed., *Die Vererbung des ländlichen Grundbesitzes im Königreich Preussen*, 3 vols. (Berlin, 1899), 1:1–154.

16. Graafen, *Aus- und Abwanderung*, 43–52; figures cited on 50–51.

17. Berkner, "Inheritance, Land Tenure and Peasant Family Structure," and Lutz K. Berkner, "The Stem Family and the Developmental Cycle of the Peasant Household: An Eighteenth-Century Austrian Example," *American Historical Review* 77 (1972):398–418; Michael Mitterauer and Reinhard Sieder, "The Developmental Process of Domestic Groups: Problems of Reconstruction and Possibilities of Interpretation," *Journal of Family History* 4 (1979): 257–84; Michel Verdon, "The Stem Family: Toward a General Theory," *Journal of Interdisciplinary History* 10 (1979):87–105. The technical terms for the two inheritance systems are *Realteilung* (partible) and *Anerbenrecht* (impartible); there is a considerable literature relating to the relationship between the two systems and the incidence of emigration; see Walter D. Kamphoefner, "Transplanted Westfalians: Persistence and Transformation of Socioeconomic and Cultural Patterns in the Northwest German Migration to Missouri," Diss., University of Missouri, Columbia, 1978, 28–72.

18. Helmut Röhm, *Die Vererbung des landwirtschaftlichen Grundeigentums in Baden-Württemberg* (Remagen/Rh., 1957); Peter Brugger, *Das Anerbe und das Schicksal seiner Geschwister in mehreren Oberämter des Württ. Oberlandes. Berichte über Landwirtschaft* 21 (1936), Sonderheft; Ulrich Planck, "Hofstellenchronik von Bölgental 1650–1966: Strukturwandlungen in einem fränkischen Weiler," in Heinz Haushofer and Willi A. Boelcke, eds., *Wege und Forschungen der Agrargeschichte* (Frankfurt am Main, 1967):242–66; Joseph Baumgartner, "Die Vererbung des landwirtschaftlichen Grundbesitzes in Bayern rechts des Rheins," in Sering and von Dietze, eds., *Vererbung*, 397–405.

19. Mitterauer and Sieder, *European Family*, 152; see also Ulrich Planck, *Der Bauerliche Familienbetrieb: Zwischen Patriarchat und Partnerschaft* (Stuttgart, 1964).

20. Quoted in Mergen, *Amerika-Auswanderung*, 45.

21. Oscar Handlin, *The Uprooted* (New York, 1951), 83, 86. See Joseph Schafer, *The Social History of American Agriculture* (New York, 1936), 209–16; Merle Curti et al., *The Making of an American Community: A Case Study of Democracy in a Frontier County* (Stanford, Calif., 1959); Allan G. Bogue, *From Prairie to Corn Belt: Farming on the Illinois and Iowa Prairies in the Nineteenth Century* (Chicago, 1963); Michael P. Conzen, *Frontier Farming in an Urban Shadow* (Madison, Wisc., 1971); Seddie Cogswell, Jr., *Tenure, Nativity, and Age as Factors in Iowa Agriculture, 1850–1880* (Ames, Ia., 1975); D. Aidan McQuillan, "Adaptation of Three Immigrant Groups to Farming in Central Kansas, 1875–1925," Diss., University of Wisconsin, Madison, 1975; Donald L. Winters, *Farmers Without Farms: Agricultural Tenancy in Nineteenth-*

*Century Iowa* (Westport, Conn., 1978); see also Robert P. Swierenga, "Ethnicity and American Agriculture," *Ohio History* 89 (1980):323–44, for a summary of this work.

22. For a representative rendering of the stereotype, see Wilhelm Hense-Jensen, *Wisconsins Deutsch-Amerikaner*, 2 vols. (Milwaukee, 1900), 1:282–85.

23. Terry G. Jordan, *German Seed in Texas Soil: Immigrant Farmers in Nineteenth-Century Texas* (Austin, 1966); Russel L. Gerlach, *Immigrants in the Ozarks: A Study in Ethnic Geography* (Columbia, Mo., 1976); Arthur B. Cozzens, "Conservation in German Settlements of the Missouri Ozarks," *Geographical Review* 33 (1943):286–98.

24. *Der Nordstern* (St. Cloud, Minn.), 12 July 1876.

25. Ibid., 28 December 1876.

26. The following discussion rests upon linked analyses of the manuscript population schedules of the federal censuses of 1860 through 1880 and 1900 (microfilm, National Archives, Washington, D.C.); manuscript population schedules of the State of Minnesota decennial censuses of 1865 through 1905 (microfilm, Minnesota Historical Society, St. Paul, Minn.); the manuscript agricultural schedules of the federal censuses of 1860 through 1880 (Minnesota State Archives, St. Paul, Minn.); the St. Martin parish marriage register (St. Martin rectory, St. Martin, Minn.); the Assessment Books for St. Martin township (Stearns County, Auditor, Stearns County Courthouse, St. Cloud, Minn.), sampled at five-year intervals 1860–1905; and a complete reconstruction of all land transactions within the township from its founding through 1915. (Because of the necessity of linking ownership to residence within the township, the present discussion is confined largely to ownership patterns through 1905 only.) The files of the Zapp Abstract Co., St. Cloud, Minn., which are arranged by section within the township and by parcels within each section, made it a relatively straightforward process to compile basic data on individual land transactions by parcel for the entire township; it was then possible, where necessary, to compile further information on individual transactions from the Deed Record, the Mortgage Record, the Mortgage Satisfaction Record, and the other miscellaneous records of the Register of Deeds, Stearns County Courthouse, St. Cloud, Minn. The chaotic alphabetizing within the grantor-grantee indexes of the Register of Deeds made it far more difficult to trace purchases by St. Martinites of land outside the township. Because this discussion cannot take into account land held outside the township, its estimates of landownership and intrafamily assistance must be regarded as *minimums* only.

27. Scholars generally have found a positive correlation between landownership and persistence in farming communities; see the summary discussion in Conzen, *Frontier Farming*. Because retired landless farmers are not classified by the census as farm operators, they do not affect the percentages relating to landownership among farmers. "Cohort" as used here refers to all farmers who were listed in the same census for the first time, that is, who had arrived during the preceding decade.

28. A variety of possible types of assistance went unrecorded, and cannot be included in this discussion; they could range from monetary gifts, unsecured loans, and advantageous rental agreements to dowries, gifts of livestock and machinery, and labor assistance. Thus the *minimal* nature of these estimates of intrafamily arrangements must be emphasized again.

29. H. W. Spiegel, "The Altenteil: German Farmers' Old Age Security," *Rural*

*Sociology* 4 (1939):203–17; Carl F. Wehrwein, "Bonds of Maintenance as Aids in Acquiring Farm Ownership," *Journal of Land and Public Utility Economics* 8 (1932): 396–403. The provisions of one such St. Martin agreement (Book H, p. 614, Deed Record, Register of Deeds, Stearns County Courthouse, St. Cloud, Minn.) specify that "in consideration of the sale by the first parties unto the second party of the lands described. . . . The said party of the second part hereby contracts and agrees to furnish unto first parties, or either of them, during their remaining years of life . . . the sum of $100 in cash annually any day within the year due, 100 lbs. pork and 25 lbs. beef each year in the customary season, 200 lbs. best wheat flour, delivered as needed 1 lb. butter weekly, also 1 doz. eggs each week, potatoes as much as needed from time to time, besides ready made fuel necessary for comfortable use, also free lodging, either with family in the same house, or, if preferred, erect necessary comfortable abode separate from family home, same preferred by said first parties to be located upon the lands above described."

30. Quoted in *Stones and Hills: Reflections—St. John the Baptist Parish: 1875–1975* (Collegeville, Minn., 1975), 67.

31. Minnesota law in 1878 abolished the traditional right of dower, giving the surviving spouse a life interest in the homestead (not to exceed 80 acres) and an undivided one-third of all other land in fee simple in cases of intestacy; children were also to receive equal and undivided shares of the remaining land, as well as of the homestead after the death of the surviving spouse; *Minnesota Statutes Annotated* (1975), sect. 525.16, 510.02, 525.145. This discussion is based on analyses of the wills of St. Martin landowners recorded in the Wills Book, Register of Deeds, Stearns County Courthouse, St. Cloud, Minn.; the recording of probate judgments in the Deed Record, and the subsequent ownership histories of the estates involved as reconstructed for this project from the Deed Record and the abstract files of the Zapp Abstract Co.

32. The following statements are based upon data extracted from federal and state land entry records, Minnesota Historical Society, St. Paul.

33. The fertility ratio (defined as the ratio of children under the age of five to women aged twenty to forty-four multiplied by 1,000) was 1,490 in 1875, 1,380 in 1884, 1,280 in 1895, and 1,100 in 1905.

34. Douglas C. Marshall, "The Decline in Farm Family Fertility and its Relationship to Nationality and Religious Background," *Rural Sociology* 15 (1950):42–49.

35. Cross-sectional analysis of life cycle stages for 1860, 1880, and 1905 suggests that at no point in the middle years of the life cycle did more than one-quarter of the households have parents residing with them. One-third and one-half of the households headed by parents in their sixties had married children resident in 1880 and 1905, respectively, but this involved only six households in the first census year, four in the second. In 1880, twelve of the seventy-four married women in St. Martin between the ages of eighteen and twenty-nine were living with their husbands' parents, and one married man in the same age group was living with his wife's family; this was characteristic of no other age group. There were no sons-in-law and only four daughters-in-law resident in parental households in 1905. Cf. Goldschmidt and Kunkel, "Structure of the Peasant Family": "It is our impression that when a rural community becomes highly monetized, the heirs tend to translate their

rights into cash rather than to entangle themselves in joint family economic enterprises" (1069).

36. It is impossible to determine at this stage in the research the extent to which they also benefited from parental assistance; they certainly shared equally in the distribution of estates after the deaths of their parents.

37. Cofell, "Community Attitudes," 19–20.

38. For the character and continuity of St. Martin's distinctive culture well into the twentieth century, see Cofell, "Community Attitudes"; Ronald G. Kleitsch, "The Religious Social System of the German-Catholics of the Sauk," M.A. Thesis, University of Minnesota, 1958; Marian MacNeil Deininger, "Some Differential Characteristics of Minnesota's Major Ethnic Groups in Selected Rural Townships," Diss., University of Minnesota, 1958; Douglas G. Marshall and Milo Peterson, "Factors Associated with Variations in School Attendance of Minnesota Farm Boys," *Minnesota Agricultural Experiment Station Paper* no. 635, Miscellaneous Journal Series (July 1948); Marshall, "Decline in Farm Fertility"; Samuel Lubell, *The Future of American Politics* (New York, 1952); Paul Folsum, "Rural Ministry: A Response to Change," Doctorate of Ministry Pastoral Project, Aquinas Institute of Theology (Dubuque, Ia., 1976); Roberta Walburn, "Stearns Syndrome Only Hurts If You Don't Laugh," *Minneapolis Tribune*, 2 January 1979.

39. For an area with customs very similar to those of St. Martin, see Oscar F. Hoffman, "Culture of the Centerville-Mosel Germans in Manitowoc and Sheboygan Counties, Wisconsin," Diss., University of North Carolina, 1942; see also Joseph Schafer, *The Winnebago-Horicon Basin: A Type Study in Western History* (Madison, Wisc., 1937), 162–66, 239–40; Walter L. Slocum, "Ethnic Stocks as Cultural Types in Rural Wisconsin," Diss., University of Wisconsin, 1940; Kenneth H. Parsons and Eliot O. Waples, "Keeping the Farm in the Family: A Study of Ownership Processes in a Low Tenancy Area of Eastern Wisconsin," *Wisconsin Agricultural Experiment Station Research Bulletin* no. 157 (1945); George S. Wehrwein, "The Problem of Inheritance in American Land Tenure," *Journal of Farm Economics* 9 (1927): 163–75; A. B. Hollingshead, "Changes in Land Ownership as an Index of Succession in Rural Communities," *American Journal of Sociology* 43 (1937):764–77; Marian Deininger and Douglas Marshall, "A Study of Land Ownership by Ethnic Groups from Frontier Times to the Present in a Marginal Farming Area of Minnesota," *Land Economics* (1955): 351–60; Cozzens, "Conservation in German Settlements"; Jordan, *German Seed in Texas Soil*; Gerlach, *Immigrants in the Ozarks*.

40. Cf. Ns. Gonner, *Die Luxemburger in der neuen Welt* (Dubuque, Ia., 1889), 184–88, for an excellent contemporary discussion of such syncretism in German regional dialects in American settlements.

41. Ibid., 164; Sonya Salamon, "Ethnic Differences in Farm Family Land Transfer," *Rural Sociology* 45 (1980): 290–308.

42. The literature from which this model is derived includes Don Kanel, "The Land Tenure Process in American Agriculture: The Competitive Status of Family Farms and their Adjustment to the Life Cycle of Farm Families," Diss., University of Wisconsin, 1953; Robert Diller, *Farm Ownership, Tenancy, and Land Use in a Nebraska Community* (Chicago, 1941); Richard Ely and Charles J. Galpin, "Tenancy in an Ideal System of Landownership," *American Economic Review* 9 (1919 suppl.):

196–211; Kenneth H. Parsons, "Research in the Succession of Farms: A Comment on Methodology," *Land Economics* 24 (1948):293–302; Sidney Henderson, "A Plan for Transfering the Farm from Father to Son," *Land Economics* 34 (1948):82–85; Harold A. Pederson, "A Cultural Evaluation of the Family Farm Concept," *Land Economics* 26 (1950):52–64; James D. Tarver, "Intra-Family Farm Succession Practices," *Rural Sociology* 17 (1952): 266–71; W. A. Anderson, "The Transmission of Farming as an Occupation," *Rural Sociology* 4 (1939):433–48; W. J. Spillman, "The Agricultural Ladder," *American Economic Review* 9 (1919 suppl.):170–79; Erven J. Long, "The Agricultural Ladder: Its Adequacy as a Model for Farm Tenure Research," *Land Economics* 26 (1950):268–73. For earlier American patterns, see, for example, Philip J. Greven, *Four Generations: Population, Land, and Family in Colonial Andover, Massachusetts* (Ithaca, N.Y., 1970); James A. Henretta, "Families and Farms: *Mentalité* in Pre-Industrial America," *William and Mary Quarterly* 3d ser. 35 (1978):3–32; Mary P. Ryan, *Cradle of the Middle Class: The Family in Oneida County, New York, 1790–1865* (New York, 1981), 18–59.

43. Mark Friedberger's recent study of inheritance practices in several Iowa and Illinois townships, though not directly addressing the question of ethnic differences, does provide data that support an argument for the general dominance of transfer through inheritance rather than inter vivos transmission, and for distinctive differences among German Catholics; see his "The Farm Family and the Inheritance Process: Evidence from the Corn Belt, 1870–1950," *Agricultural History* 57 (1983): 1–13.

44. Conrad Arensberg and Solon T. Kimball, *Family and Community in Ireland* (New York, 1940); Salamon, "Ethnic Differences." The only St. Martin farmer to partially disinherit one son for "dissolute" behavior was a member of the pioneer generation of Irish farmers.

45. Robert C. Ostergren, "Land and Family in Rural Immigrant Communities," *Annals of the Association of American Geographers* 71 (1981):400–411; Peter A. Munch, "Social Adjustment among Wisconsin Norwegians," *American Sociological Review* 14 (1949):780–87; Deininger, "Differential Characteristics of Minnesota's Major Ethnic Groups"; Robert Harold Brown, "The Upsala, Minnesota Community: A Study in Rural Dynamics," *Annals of the Association of American Geographers* 57 (1967):267–300.

46. Ostergren, "Land and Family."

HOWARD LAMAR

# 10. From Bondage to Contract

ETHNIC LABOR IN THE AMERICAN WEST,

1600–1890

The old dream of coming west to claim the promised land and with it a secure position in American society continued to exert a powerful attraction. As late as 1915 a member of the Industrial Workers of the World complained that for years "the Golden West has been the Mecca in the dream of the misguided worker in all parts of the country. If I can only get West, has been his only thought."[1]

One of the most arresting images in American historiography has been that of America as a virgin land. Frederick Jackson Turner's famous essay "The Significance of the Frontier in American History" suggests that white pioneers penetrated an empty—and therefore innocent—preindustrial continent in which the absence of laws and organized society reduced Europeans to a more simple, open, free, and democratic status.[2] The Edenic qualities of the American wilderness have also been the subject of countless historical studies, works of fiction, and critical essays.[3] The latest of these, Ray Allen Billington's *Land of Savagery/Land of Promise: The European Image of the American Frontier*, chronicles the powerful impact of both the wilderness and the virginal image on Europeans from 1600 to the present.[4] This ideal of preindustrial innocence was projected into the settlement period by Thomas Jefferson when he pictured the yeoman farmer as a self-sufficient person beholden to none and therefore truly free and independent.

These various images—as arresting and as useful as they sometimes are —create more problems than they solve. The frontier, for example, is associated with freedom and democracy, and the American West with rugged individualism. The mountain men of the fur-trade era are associated with freedom amounting to anarchy. Even the obviously fraudulent concept of "manifest destiny" has been accepted as an ex post facto rationalization for extending the area of political freedom.[5] Such approaches do not allow for the fact that precontact Indian societies not only flourished in North America, they had a large variety of labor systems that persisted into the contact period and were frequently adjusted to fit the economic demands of the European intruders. Indians working for or in alliance with whites constituted the first ethnic laborforce in colonial America.[6] Very early on the Europeans developed trading and mercantile systems, one of which was the fur-trading company, which reached far beyond the frontiers of settlement to affect all native societies in North America.

It is also incontrovertible that many persons in the colonial economies of both North and South America were not free when it came to a definition of their status as laborers. Instead, they were slaves in slave societies (as was the case of Indian societies in the Pacific Northwest) or slaves in slave-owning societies (as was the case in Mexico and the American South), or they had the status of indentured servants (as in the British colonies) or were the victims of debt-peonage or harsh labor contracts (as was the case in Mexican New Mexico, Mexican California, and Russian Alaska). These conditions were so common in regions west of the Mississippi River that the question must be asked: Was the American West and the Western frontier more properly a symbol of bondage than of freedom when it comes to labor systems? A second related question has emerged from this study: How much so-called frontier or western violence has stemmed from economic conditions in which labor was abused, rather than from race hatred between Indians and whites, or between ethnic groups, or from the excesses of rugged individualism—although all three of these factors were very much in evidence?

It is clear that romantic perceptions of the frontier have dominated nearly all Western historiography until very recently, as can be seen in rousing narrative histories of the fur trade, the cattle industry, and the mining rushes.[7] On the other hand, a much more realistic perception of life and labor in the American South has characterized the writings of historians of black slavery in the United States. Indeed, the history of black slavery has been such a major preoccupation of outstanding historians from Ulrich B. Phillips to Eugene Genovese that there has been a relative lack of emphasis on other forms of slave, bonded, or contract labor in this country.[8] Put more specifically for the purposes of this essay, the labor history of the American West has yet to be meshed with the history of American slavery or with the history of labor generally. Those who do discuss Western labor tend to write about it regionally or in terms of craft or race; they treat, for example, the Chinese laborer, the Mexican worker, the Basque sheepherder, the cowboy, the hardrock miner, and the Anglo and Chicano migratory worker.[9] There is nothing wrong with these specific approaches, and they do stress ethnicity, but they lack a national or comparative perspective.

In various ways the Trans-Mississippi West presented the same problem that had occurred at Jamestown after 1607: where to find an adequate labor supply. In Virginia, the first answer was indentured servants who, because of the availability of free lands, could not be fully controlled. The second solution was to import African bondsmen. Edmund S. Morgan has brilliantly analyzed how the presence of slaves paradoxically helped enhance the sense of freedom in whites that we see as the cornerstone of American democracy.[10]

Morgan's argument is fully persuasive, but one should also keep in mind the further observation of H. J. Nieboer, a Dutch scholar who wrote in 1900 that "Slavery will generally occur where there is still some free land available," for "where there are still open resources, no one is dependent on another for his earning, and it is necessary to use force if others are to be made to work for an individual." On the other hand, Nieboer concluded that in a closed resource system free people will work in order to make a living.[11]

Evsey D. Domar enlarges on Nieboer's thesis in his article "The Causes of Slavery or Serfdom: A Hypothesis," in which he argues that the opening of new lands in Russia caused such a shortage of labor that the landowners enserfed their already indebted workers.[12] Domar maintains that the land to labor ratio has an intimate relation to serfdom and slavery in a way that seems to deny the argument used by Walter Prescott Webb in *The Great Frontier*. There Webb states that the surplus of land that became available after the European discovery of America stimulated the rise of capitalism while providing the necessary space and surplus production of foodstuffs and goods to allow freedom and democracy to develop.[13] Nieboer's and Domar's observations turn both Turner's and Webb's theses on their heads by asserting that the frontier will always be an area of bondage where labor is concerned.

Such generalizations are attractive and intriguing, but one must remain somewhat skeptical because frontier situations, although they have certain elements in common, represent unique combinations of circumstances based on hundreds of factors. The peculiarities of the frontiers of southern Africa and colonial North America are cases in point. In the first, the labor of the native populations, which always greatly outnumbered that of the whites, was coopted by the Dutch and English settlers.[14] In the British Atlantic colonies, the Indians voluntarily supplied food to the Europeans during the very early stages of settlement, but eventually were forced to do so in such a way that the tribute was a cause of early Indian–white conflicts.[15]

In the long run, Indian labor, though a mainstay of the Atlantic colonial fur trade, was not used as generally as it was in the early Spanish, Russian, and British systems in the Trans-Mississippi West. Moreover, the hunting of furs was an occupation that fitted the life-style of the Indians while drawing on the seemingly boundless animal resources of their forested environment.[16] No sooner had they adjusted to this new economy, however, than Europeans began to come in such numbers that they were able to supply their own labor and could, indeed, reproduce a European economy based on agriculture and commerce rather than on hunting and trading. It was also the case that disease had so decimated the Indian populations of eastern America by the eighteenth century that they could not be counted on as a realistic source of labor.[17]

In southern Africa the resistance of the native populations to smallpox, the limited resources of the environment, and the reverse ratio of white and black created a very different situation. Unlike the European experience in Mexico or southern Africa or elsewhere, by the nineteenth century native labor had no practical meaning for Americans, and so Indian-Americans were placed on small reservations and their few remaining lands were taken from them.[18] In an ironic way Frederick Jackson Turner was right when he argued that it was a virgin land into which the white settler could move, but it was a virginity achieved by the cauterizing surgery of epidemic, abuse, and removal.

I

The first European observer of the American Southwest was Alvar Nuñez Cabeza de Vaca, who was a member of a Spanish exploring party ship-wrecked on the coast of Texas in 1528 after the group had experienced a disastrous sojourn in Florida.[19] During the eight years that Cabeza, a few companions, and a Moorish slave Estevanito worked their way westward in the hope of reaching the northern borders of New Spain, they were captured and enslaved by local Indian tribes. Later they worked as indentured servants for other Indians, and finally secured a freedom of sorts by becoming successful medicine men with a large following. Thus Cabeza ran a gamut of native labor systems in his memorable but miserable trek across the American Southwest. He described it as a world of cruelty in which his few surviving companions had become so fearful that some refused to flee with him when the opportunity arose. They preferred bondage to danger and possible death. Ironically, Cabeza learned that he had reached civilization when, near Culiacán in Sinaloa, he encountered terrified and wounded Indians fleeing from Spanish slave-hunting parties from central Mexico. He recalled that "we gave many thanks to God our Lord. Having almost despaired of finding Christians again, we could hardly restrain our excitement."[20] It is instructive to learn that after Cabeza returned to his job as a crown official he worked for the remainder of his life as an opponent of slavery.

When Francisco Vasquez de Coronado came to New Mexico in 1540–41 in search of the golden cities of Cibola, he found slaves from the Caddoan villages of Kansas living in the Pueblo towns along the Rio Grande.[21] Soon after the Spanish settled in New Mexico in 1598, the governor of that province began trafficking in Indian slaves taken from the Navaho tribes, and sent them south to work in the mines of New Spain.[22] In essence the Spanish allied themselves to an already existing trade and raid system that had been carried on between the Pueblos and the Plains Indians for generations.[23]

Although Spain tried to prevent the exploitation of Indians by detailed legislation dealing with tribute and labor, France V. Scholes has found that "almost without exception the governors of New Mexico were interested in using the Indians for their own profit, and instead of curbing abuses, were often the worst offenders."[24] The efforts to supply mining labor to New Spain occurred in the seventeenth century, but they bore some resemblance to the sale of Indian captives from the Yamasee War (1715) by South Carolina officials. In the latter case captured Indians were sent to the Caribbean Islands as a labor supply.[25]

After the Spanish brought the sedentary Pueblo Indians of the Rio Grande Valley under tribute, they forced them to manufacture *mantas* (cloth), deliver salt, travel to the Plains to bargain with Apaches for hides and slaves, collect piñon nuts for the Mexico City market, and serve as carpenters and artisans for the Spanish settlers. Indians were also shanghaied to serve as muleteers and cartmen for the supply trains that periodically went from Santa Fe to Chihuahua. At the end of the trip many did not receive pay and, indeed, were often abandoned in Chihuahua. When Governor Mendizabal of New Mexico had his accounts reviewed by the Crown in 1661, he was found to "owe 2,400 pesos to Indians for various services, or an equivalent of 19,000 days of labor at the rate of one real a day."[26]

The actual enslavement of adult Pueblo Indians in Spanish New Mexico was rare; if it occurred it was as a punishment for certain crimes. On the other hand, soldiers could seize Pueblo orphans as house servants. It was more common for Spanish settlers to use captive Apache boys and girls as house servants, however, and, as Scholes has noted, "the governors received their share of these spoils of frontier warfare."[27] Apache children were estimated to be worth 30–40 pesos, or the value of a good mule. An adult Apache slave was worth four oxen.[28] In 1662 Governor Mendizabal owned or had an interest in ninety Apache slaves. Later Governor Diego de Penaloso "sent several Apache boys and girls to Mexico City as gifts for friends."[29] The Lipan Apaches of Texas were under double jeopardy because the Spanish raided them from the west while the Pawnees to the east sold captured Apache slaves to the French in the Mississippi Valley.[30] Apaches for their part often captured Spanish children as well as the offspring of other Indian tribes to use as their own laborforce or to sell.

With the Pueblos paying multiple tribute in the form of corn to mission fathers, blankets and labor to the governor, and work days to Spanish settlers, it is no wonder that the Revolt of 1680 took place. In that upheaval the Pueblos and their allies killed 400 Spaniards and drove out some 1,900 more.[31] The point I would like to argue here is that this revolt was not an Indian–white frontier war or a race war in the usual sense of such terms, but a revolt of slave or bonded labor.

It took the Spanish fourteen years to reestablish their authority in the Rio Grande Valley, but this time they gave the Pueblos better treatment. Even so, trafficking in captives continued in the border towns of Pecos and Taos where annual trade fairs were held. There Plains Indians sold captives for horses. By 1720, Ute Indians were selling Jicarilla Apache women and children at Taos and some Pawnee captives were still coming in from Kansas. By this time, however, the captives went to local citizens rather than to the mining towns of New Spain.[32]

In his study of the American Southwest during the Mexican period (1821–46), David J. Weber has noted that

> from California to Texas, *gente de razón* [people of reason] continued the practice of taking captives in Indian campaigns, or purchasing or ransoming them from other Indians. These captives became involuntary members of Mexican households, received baptism, and "performed domestic chores in exchange for their board and education." . . . Mexicans referred to these servants as *criados* (literally "those being raised"), and rarely as *escalvos* or slaves, since theoretically they were free.[33]

Eventually the eastern Apaches suffered such a decline in strength and numbers that between the 1780s and the Mexican War it was the Comanches who carried on the trade in captives.[34] In April 1849, a party of gold seekers crossing Texas on the southern trail to California caught a glimpse of this situation when they ran into fifteen Comanche Indians accompanied by five or six Mexican boys herding about 500 Mexican horses and mules to Torrey's Station, a trading post near present-day Waco, Texas. The post was owned by two Connecticut Yankees who, it is said, had Sam Houston as a silent partner. At first the Indians and the whites were sociable and actually participated in a joint dancing contest in the evening. But the gold seekers soon learned that the boy herders and the horses had both been captured in a devastating raid on a Mexican village a few days before. Infuriated by this news, the overlanders wanted to ambush the Comanches, but one of the Torrey brothers argued against this plan, saying that such an act would start a war. Instead the Torreys appear to have purchased the boys from the Indians and probably some of the horses as well.[35]

By concentrating on black slavery in the United States, historians have tended to ignore the practice in the Southwest of older, more classic forms of bondage that had existed in Greece and Rome, and in parts of Africa and

Asia. And, as had been the case in the Old World, it was a system in which captives were often incorporated into households and even became citizens of the tribes or province that had captured them.[36]

II

While Spanish-Mexicans were busy capturing Indians and Indians were capturing Spanish-Mexican children, another form of bondage appeared in New Mexico during the eighteenth and nineteenth centuries, especially before 1848. In this system of debt-peonage, a *patron* or head of a family with a flock of sheep lent cash and some of the herd to a young man, often a relative. The recipient had to pay an annual rent of so many ewes for the sheep and for supplies. In most cases the recipient never quite paid off his debt. By this so-called *partidaro* system the *patron* became the head of an enormous extended family.[37] Some observers have noted that by 1800 this system had concentrated the economic and political power of New Mexico into the hands of some twenty prominent families. In 1821 William Becknell, father of the Santa Fe trade, said that New Mexico society was characterized by "the rich keeping the poor in dependency and subjugation." As late as 1900 one such *patron*, Pedro Perea, controlled 27,000 sheep through a variation of the *partidaro* system.[38] Of course one sees parallels to this system everywhere. John M. Gullick has noted that in the Malayan Peninsula, those in debt-bondage followed their creditors about, lived in their households, were part of the same society as their masters, and rarely exercised the right of debt redemption.[39] Both the New Mexican *patrons* and the *partidaros* would have understood their Malayan counterparts.

In some ways this system was not unlike sharecropping in the American South after the Civil War. It also bore some resemblance to the clientage system in southern Africa whereby native tribesmen became laborers for white farmers and ranchers in return for support and protection. Even that system built on an older one, for before white settlers penetrated southern Africa, San hunters supplied settled Bantu farmers with skins and meat in return for grain, an exchange that Pueblos and Apaches would have recognized as similar to their own exchange system before the arrival of the Spanish.[40]

Tribute systems between whites and Indians in the late eighteenth and early nineteenth centuries could also be found in Spanish California, where intruding Europeans—in this instance Franciscan missionaries—resorted to coercion in order to maintain both a congregation and a labor supply. For purposes of efficient Christianization, Indians were congregated around the California coastal missions and, along with religious instruction, were taught to ranch and farm. The records reveal that they were whipped if they neglected their duties, and soldiers were stationed nearby to insure obedience.[41] Such treatment seems all the more tragic because recent studies of the Indians of California assert that they were so peaceful they could be called "Red Quakers." Not only were they pacifists by and large, they also possessed such a strong sense of territoriality that they were able to prevent conflict by a careful avoidance of trespass on the land of another tribelet.[42]

Yet, if the Spanish mission system seemed coercive, what followed during the period of secularization after 1833, when the mission laborforce—as well as its lands—were taken over by private individuals, was worse. As David J. Weber has observed:

> Without the protections of the Franciscans, many former mission Indians fell easily into a system whereby Californios advanced them goods, money, or liquor, then required them to repay their debts. Father Narciso Durán described the condition of two or three hundred Indians living in debt peonage on the edge of Los Angeles in 1833: "All in reality are slaves, or servants of white men who know well the manner of securing their services by binding them for a whole year for an advanced trifle. An Indian who tried to flee," Durán said, "experiences the full rigor of the law."[43]

Despite the consequences, Indians did begin to flee to the foothills of the Sierras to escape forced labor. They also began to form fighting bands to resist local authorities sent out to recapture them or to recruit fresh labor from inland *rancherias*.[44] At the same time the crowded conditions of the native quarters of the missions had increased the frequency of endemic diseases which, when combined with white epidemic diseases and the atmosphere of abuse and despair, reduced the native population from 275,000 during the Spanish-Mexican years to less than 150,000 by the time the Americans arrived on the scene in the 1840s.[45]

After 1848 California Indians were quick to see that gold could be used to purchase white luxuries and joined in the gold rush as miners. American miners regarded them as a nuisance and quickly reduced their numbers still further by shootings, small wars, and arbitrary removals—this despite the perceptive comment of John Marsh, the California rancher, who wrote in 1846, "The Indians are the principal laborers: without them the business of the country could hardly be carried on."[46] Indeed, Albert L. Hurtado has found that between 1846 and 1860 Hispanic and Anglo farmers, ranchers and townspeople in California—as opposed to miners—continued to use Indian labor, particularly in the southern and central coast areas. As Major John Bidwell noted, there was "hardly a farm house—a kitchen without them."[47] Bidwell himself depended on Indians for his grain farming. Although many California Indians seemed willing to work for whites voluntarily, they were also forced to do so by state laws which provided for the "arrest and indenture of loitering and intoxicated Indians."[48]

Hurtado has also found that Anglo ranchers and farmers in certain areas, whether they employed the more numerous male Indians as workers or the less numerous females, tended to segregate the sexes in living arrangements so that Indians could not reproduce at a normal rate. This situation, combined with the continued toll of white diseases on the California tribes had, by 1860, reduced the native population to 35,000.[49]

## III

The labor system in Russian Alaska for the period 1780 to 1867 furnishes still other examples of bondage that ranged from the extremes of forced labor to the more moderate forms of written contracts and even symbiotic trade relations between Indians and whites.

In the Russian expansion across Siberia in the sixteenth and seventeenth centuries, Cossack parties and semimilitary fur-hunting groups brought the natives under a system of fur tribute known as the *yasak*, which lasted until 1788 when it was replaced by a compulsory labor tribute.[50] By the time the Russians had penetrated Alaska, the possibility of a mobile labor supply from Russia itself had been reduced by the institution of serfdom: Russian serf owners understandably objected to an exodus of their labor. The landed nobility also argued on the grounds of social class that they could not let mere merchants have serfs.[51] Faced with this situation, the Russian American Company sought labor from at least six alternative sources.

First, they recruited workers from an idle population that could be found in Siberian villages from Irkutsk to Okhotsk. Arthur Okun noted in his study of the Russian American Company that they were "runaway peasants, small merchants and artisans who had lost everything," and who had gone "east" to escape the authorities. Mixed in with them was a floating population of ex-soldiers and sailors.

A few days before the ships sailed for American Alaska, all the drinking establishments in Okhotsk would be crowded with promyshlenosty [fur hunters], whom the company entertained lavishly, without sparing expense. Here in the saloons the recruiting agents would slip the contracts into the hands of the promyshlenosty for their signature, contracts which would bind them for many years to come, and in which, in the guise of advance pay, was included the cost to the last penny of the entertainment at the time of enlistment.[52]

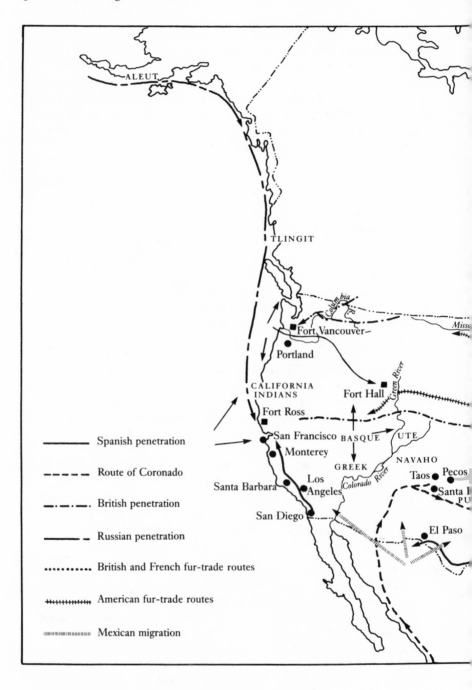

10.1. *Encounters between Europeans, Americans, and Native Peoples*

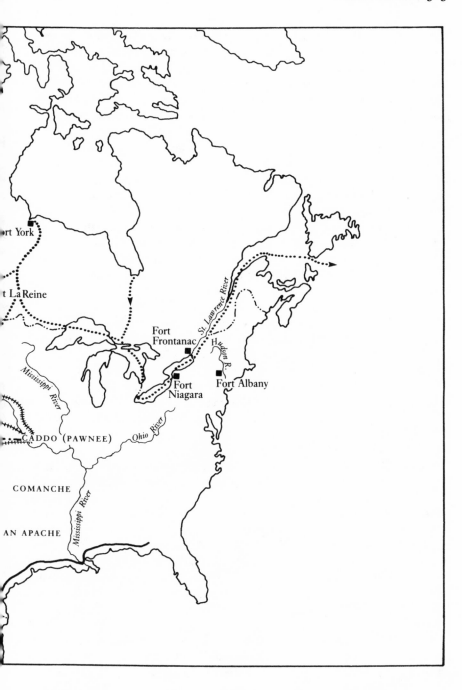

They were in effect shanghaied; once on board, if the ship was not at sea, their clothes were taken away and the newly contracted workers wrapped in sacks.[53] In somewhat similar fashion agents in London and Bristol enticed men, women, and children to the English colonies as indentured servants. Meanwhile, in Europe, "Newlanders" sought out Rhinelanders who would be willing to accept indentured status in return for their passage to America.[54]

Okun has concluded that although most of the Russians thus hired to hunt made a "considerable sum of money in the course of their stay in the colonies," the deductions for purchases at the company store, for His Majesty's taxes, and for the sums sent to families back on the mainland, combined with deceit and cheating, often left the hunters in debt and thus unable to return home. In the early period hunters were not paid in cash but in peltry. Each catch was divided equally between the workers and the company, the worker receiving a so-called half-share. It was, observed Okun, "a system based on a piece wage, with the pay not in money but in kind."[55]

The ways in which these workers were defrauded almost compels admiration. Prices at the company store were twice those at Okhotsk. Workers recruited from the Siberian mainland were often told not to lay in food because the company would feed them; in fact the company charged them for the food they got from the company store. They were also forbidden to manufacture homebrew vodka, but if they bought vodka at the store, they could be fined for drunkenness. In a revealing letter from Alexander Baranov, the local company director, to Baroness Shelikov, the widow of the head of the firm, he reassured her that the labor supply would be forthcoming for "liquor will always get them into debt."[56]

In the half-share division one finds again a form of sharecropping or a variation of the *partidaro* system. In Alaska, however, the working conditions and abuses proved to be so brutal that labor shortages occurred, and in 1815 the Russian American Company was forced to pay the men with wages, although the currency of such wages appears to have been stamps, good only at the company store. Moreover, the wages were so low that the workers continued to fall into debt, which meant that they could not leave the colony. "The longer a man worked," Okun writes, "the more debts he accumulated," as a laborer made only 350 rubles a year while it took 728 to live. "To all intents and purposes," concludes Okun, "it was a condition of slavery."[57]

The second source of labor for the company was the native population of the Aleutian Islands. Some 20,000 persons lived on this attenuated chain when the Russians first appeared in Alaska during the 1740s. The use of Aleut labor was necessitated by the fact that although the Russians were excellent hunters on land, they had neither the skills nor the patience to hunt the sea otter, the most valuable fur-bearing animal in the northern Pacific. The Aleuts, on the other hand, could sit for hours in their small bobbing kayaks or *bidarkas* waiting with their harpoons for the sea otter to surface. To persuade the Aleuts to do the hunting, the Russians used brute force or held women and children hostage until the Aleut males brought in a catch. Once the system was stabilized Aleut men were expected to serve the company from age eighteen to fifty. In season the Russians went to a village and drafted one-half of the men for service. When the furs had been taken, the Aleuts had to sell theirs to the firm at the company price and accept company stamps in payment.[58] The company also acted to control the use among the Aleuts of such luxury items as bread, tea, and other European foodstuffs.[59]

As the more northern sea otter herds declined, the Aleut hunters were moved to the Alaskan Panhandle and eventually down to California to exploit the herds found there. Meanwhile, the company had learned to secure its labor supply by manipulating the chiefs or *toyons*. "Do not forget," wrote one official, "to send over for the toyons twenty of the best suits of clothes with flashy trimmings; . . . we must attach them to us."[60] Writing in 1800, Alexander Baranov instructed a subordinate in the handling of Aleuts. Treat them kindly, he said, and help them with food in bad weather. "The more eminent are to be singled out whenever possible and should sometimes be seated with the Russians at table during the holidays, for instance the Kalmai toion Gavril, [and] toion . . . Charnov."[61]

At the same time Baranov observed that the Aleuts were naturally lazy, rough, and ignorant.

> We must hope that time will improve their opinion of us and order will tame them because these people being used to natural freedom since the creation of the world have never thought of nor know how to submit to the will of others and can bear no slight without retaliating. . . . It is important that you bear this in mind as well as their uncontrollable greed, covetousness and ingratitude. Therefore, do not accept a single item from them without bargaining, and forbid anyone else to take anything without payment or by force.[62]

Baranov's letter bears comparison with that of a Southern slave owner writing directions to his overseer. The *toyons* or elders gave orders to the Aleut workers and became, in effect, drivers. In searching for a comparable system Okun points to the "mita" or *repartimiento* system in the gold and silver mines of Peru and Mexico. In Mexican mining communities, for example, one-fourth of the village males had to work for the Spaniards, and there, too, the chiefs were the labor factors.[63]

The Aleut population declined during the period of Russian control from an estimated 20,000 at the beginning of white contact to 4,000 or less in

1859. Here as elsewhere in North America epidemics took a fearful toll of the population, but forced labor also helps account for the shrinking numbers. The tragedy was the greater because the Aleuts appear to have enjoyed the work of hunting and went at their task with zeal. On the eve of the transfer of Alaska to the United States, a member of the governing board of the Russian American Company concluded that "neither the Negro of Guinea, nor the Chinese Coolie, nor the European worker can take the place of the Aleut in the art and practice of hunting."[64]

As a third source of labor the Russians sought to subdue the Tlingit Indians of the Alaska Panhandle. The latter, however, not only resisted becoming workers, but sometimes attacked the Russians at their posts and occasionally drove them out. Nevertheless, after years of open hostility, the Tlingits began to supply the Russians with food. By the 1820s these Indians annually filled from 160 to 250 boats with potatoes, wild mutton, and berries to sell to the Russians at New Archangel. As the Tlingits had slaves of their own, perhaps they understood all too well the disadvantages of working for the Russians.[65]

The fourth source of labor was provided by the offspring of Russian men and native women. They became the mainstay of the clerical bureaucracy or entered the workforce as sailors and artisans. But as Okun has noted, "they, too, were in a state of servile dependency upon the Company."[66]

When the Russians established Fort Ross in California in 1812 in the hope of raising grain and cattle to supply Alaskan workers, they imported Aleut hunters to farm and herd cattle. The Aleuts were unsuccessful at the first task and hated dealing with cattle. The Russians then tried to persuade the local Pomo Indians to farm and milk cows, but as James R. Gibson has reported in his *Imperial Russia in Frontier America*, this experiment also failed: "Indians hired to do harvest became bored and left. If the harvest failed the Indian laborers were held responsible and made to remain to redeem the lost crop with other work. So they became understandably reluctant to toil for the company. At first they worked voluntarily for the Russians, but eventually they had to be recruited by force."[67] By 1835 the California Indians living near the Russians had become so hostile they began to steal wheat from company fields and in 1838 tried to rustle Russian cattle at Fort Ross.

Faced with perennial labor shortages, the handful of Russians in Alaska and California grew so desperate for help that in the 1830s they sent agents to Hawaii to recruit Kanakas, the sixth source of labor. Perhaps as many as 1,000 came to serve as sailors or workers, an arrangement that allowed half of the Aleuts in California to return to their home islands to carry on sea otter hunts there.[68] Certainly the Russian American Company is a classic example of a mercantile monopoly manipulating the factors of isolation, distance, debt, and force for their own advantage. Although the ways in which they recruited and held a laborforce together were not unusual, there were marked excesses in terms of exploitation and cruelty.

## I V

Some 2,000 miles east of the Russian American Company, the Hudson's Bay Company, founded in 1670 to exploit the fur-bearing lands of the northern reaches of the present Canadian provinces of Ontario, Quebec, and Manitoba, brought a vast territory into dependence on British goods and firearms. They achieved this by turning Canadian Indians with whom they came into contact into professional hunters.[69] In the short run, the Indians may not have viewed the change as particularly great; but as Arthur Ray has observed, the shift for many was not only significant culturally but eventually catastrophic, for the tribesmen now hunted animals for furs to sell rather than food or clothing. And when they traded these furs for guns, sugar, coffee, rum, or other luxuries, the benefits often went to the male hunter rather than to his tribe or his family, who were then obliged to seek food as best they could.[70] In this way the Hudson's Bay Company succeeded in achieving a voluntary form of labor tribute to the company.

In the years between 1670 and the end of the French and Indian War in 1763, when Great Britain acquired French Canada, the custom had been for Indians to bring furs to the factories (outposts) established by the British.[71] By the late eighteenth century such factories could be found from Hudson's Bay all the way south to the northern edge of the Great Lakes. After the British acquired French Canada, however, the company found itself competing with Montreal traders, the XYZ Company, and other firms. One consequence was that all groups began to seek furs by sending trappers and traders into the wilderness to hunt and trade. This highly mobile system, spurred by ruthless competition between the North West Company and the Hudson's Bay Company until 1821 (when the latter won out by absorbing its rival) pushed the trading area all the way to the present-day states of Washington and Oregon and the Canadian province of British Columbia.[72]

In the mobile fur brigades could be found Englishmen, Scots, French Canadians, Iroquois Indians from the St. Lawrence Valley, local tribesmen, and even Hawaiian Kanakas. Despite killings and ambushes of one party of trappers by another, and many abuses, the trappers and traders appear to have signed contracts for a given wage for a set number of years of service. They also appear to have had far more freedom than did laborers for the Russian American Company, if we can believe the comments of an old voyageur to Alexander Ross in 1825. "There is no life as happy as a voyageur's life; none so independent; no place where a man enjoys so much variety and freedom as in the Indian country."[73] The point to be stressed, however, is that whether the Indian hunted for furs on his own to trade at the factories, or became a member of a fur brigade, he was crucial to the success of a vast European mercantile operation that stretched over a large part of North America for more than two centuries.[74]

Considering the whole range of labor systems employed in the Trans-Mississippi Rocky Mountain fur trade between 1822 to 1850, however, some curious contrasts and contradictions become evident. In 1822 the federal government ended its efforts to control the fur trade through designated official trading posts and licensed traders—although it was still necessary to get a license to enter Indian country. This government withdrawal allowed fur companies to create their own posts and to downplay the role of Indians in the trade by sending brigades of American white trappers into the wilderness. It was a period of intense rivalry between firms and equally intense exploitation of the animal resources of the Great Plains and Rockies. Thus workers could choose between outfits. Moreover, the use of decentralized brigades consisting largely of white trappers stressed efficiency through freedom rather than by control.[75]

In short, no American fur firm, whether it was William Ashley's Rocky Mountain outfit or John Jacob Astor's more centrally controlled and hierarchical American Fur Company, had the authority of the Russian American Company or the Hudson's Bay Company over its laborforce or over the territory and its peoples. And although blacks and Indians were occasionally to be found in a brigade, the sense of ethnic difference usually centered on the fact that perhaps a third of the trappers were of French or French-Canadian origin, although outfits operating out of Taos, New Mexico, or Bent's Fort in present-day Colorado, may have been largely Spanish-Mexican.[76] In any case it did not mean that one ethnic group dominated or exploited another. Although French-Canadians often occupied the more menial positions as keelboatmen or camp tenders and were referred to as the "cheerful slaves of the fur trade," the fact was that many of the most successful fur-trade entrepreneurs in St. Louis were of French descent.

American trappers voluntarily signed contracts to hunt and/or trade for one or more years. They were charged high prices at the trading posts or at the annual rendezvous on the Green River. It is true they frequently drank or gambled away their earnings, and were forced to return to the mountains in order to pay off the new debts. But it should be understood that the contractual arrangements and the degree of control were far less coercive than they were in Russian Alaska.

Finally, it should be noted that American fur trappers exhibited two characteristics that protected them from exploitation. First, they were exceptionally mobile. Not only did they move over much of the inland West, they also moved from company to company or became independent trappers.

Many returned to Missouri after years in the mountains, while others migrated to California and Oregon or New Mexico. Still others allied themselves with an Indian tribe or opened a trading post at some spot on the overland trails. Second, and equally significant, they often moved into new occupations. Jim Bridger, for example, began as a trapper, then became a post trader on the California–Oregon Trail during the 1840s, and later served as a guide for the U.S. army and for railroad survey parties.[77] Rather than ordinary laborers, they were small entrepreneurs or incipient capitalists prepared to work at whatever job or trade promised a good living.[78] For these reasons it appears that the 3,000 or more persons engaged in the Rocky Mountain fur trade did enjoy some of the freedom and excitement that has so often been associated with that trade.

V

In the early 1820s Dr. O. Hotchkiss, a kindly Yale professor, found a Hawaiian youth named Obookiah weeping on the steps of the Yale College Library. Obookiah was what seafaring men called a Kanaka sailor. He had been brought to Connecticut by one Captain Brintnall.[79] Natives from Hawaii and other Pacific islands often shipped as sailors on the vessels of all nations from the eighteenth century onward, but they were usually found on Yankee whaling vessels or British, Russian, and American ships engaged in the seal and sea otter fur trade of the Pacific. Obookiah was taken in, educated, and cared for in New Haven until he died at an early age.

Kanakas laboring under three-year contracts first appeared on the Pacific coast of North America in 1788, long before they were recruited by Russians for work in Alaska. As was the case with the Aleuts, native governors served as the labor factors who supplied sailors for ships and workers for the fur trade, for which they received a percentage of the wages paid. John Meares, one of the earliest British traders in the Pacific Northwest, established a colony of Chinese laborers on Nootka Sound and gave them Hawaiian wives, possibly, writes George V. Blue, with the idea that the less conversation between married folk, the more the harmony.[80] Captain Robert Gray had a Kanaka on board when he named the Columbia River, and Captain George Vancouver had two Hawaiian women on his vessel when he charted the waters of the Pacific Northwest coast. Twenty-four Kanakas were on board John Jacob Astor's ill-fated boat, the *Tonquin*, when it was attacked by Indians and then destroyed by a gunpowder explosion.[81]

By the 1830s some 300 to 400 Kanakas could be found working at the British port of Fort Vancouver under a three-year contract paying $10 a month. In addition to collecting furs, the Kanakas served as herders for the sheep and cattle of the Hudson's Bay Agricultural Company located in

Puget Sound.[82] When the North West Company established Fort Walla Walla in 1818, the operation included 25 Canadians, 32 Kanakas, and 38 Iroquois workers. Nathaniel Wyeth, the Boston ice merchant who went into the Western fur trade in 1834, sent 20 Kanakas to work at Fort Hall, his outpost in Idaho. Narcissa Whitman, wife of Dr. Marcus Whitman of the Walla Walla Mission, employed a Kanaka servant.[83]

Kanakas were also to be found at Sutter's Fort in California, and we know from Richard Henry Dana's *Two Years Before the Mast* that carefree Kanakas lived in huts on the southern California beaches until the exhaustion of their resources forced them to return to their jobs as sailors. Dana befriended them and after daring briefly to enjoy their easy life-style, returned to Boston to pursue a distinguished career as a lawyer.[84] After the California gold rush, Kanakas there who had been converted to Christianity were sent as missionaries to the Digger Indians in Nevada.

But as with other nonwhite ethnic groups, the impact of white diseases and labor demands devastated the aboriginal population of Hawaii. At the time of first contact Hawaii's population appears to have been about 300,000. By 1823 smallpox had reduced the number to 134,750. At this time probably as many as 1,000 males a year were leaving the islands, and by 1848 the number of departing Kanakas had risen to 3,500 from a population base that was now only 82,000. By 1860, as Janice Duncan has found, 12 percent of the population over the age of eighteen had left the islands.[85] The crucial role Kanakas played in the first laborforces assembled in the Pacific Northwest cannot be exaggerated; yet when white American settlers came to Oregon, they declared that the Kanakas should be viewed as Indians—that is, as noncitizens—and should be fired from their jobs or deported. After they had petitioned unsuccessfully for citizenship in Oregon, many Kanakas moved to California.[86]

The Kanaka experience once again demonstrates that white Americans, having become accustomed to a plentiful labor supply by virtue of immigration, saw other ethnic groups either as competitors or as having no useful function in their economy or their society. In gold-rush California, this took the form of relegating local Indians to a nonproductive role in mining, and of seeing Californios, Sonorans, Chileans, and indeed all foreigners as competitors.[87]

VI

Undoubtedly the supremely ironic twist to the convoluted history of ethnic labor in the West can be found in the story of the first black migration to California. When the news of gold discoveries reached the East in 1848–

49, Frederick Douglass and other leading abolitionists urged free blacks to go West for a new start. Nearly 3,000 black Americans had reached California by 1850 in what was one of the most intriguing invisible migrations in American history. Not all of them were free, for some came with Southern masters, but the fact is that for most it was a voluntary trip—the first large voluntary migration of blacks to take place in the United States.[88]

According to Rudolph Lapp, many of the blacks were articulate and able leaders who tried to found schools, secure the vote, and serve on juries once they had arrived in California. But antiblack legislation in the 1850s persuaded some 800 to migrate to Vancouver Island in Canada, while those remaining in California had to accept the status of second-class citizens and were confined to working as unskilled laborers, farm hands, domestics, or barbers.[89] A second wave of voluntary migrants came during World War I, and a third in World War II, but it was not until the 1960s that blacks achieved their civil rights.[90] Paradoxically, it was the black westward migrant who reflected the desire for a new start and freedom that Turner says characterized the American westward movement.

At first, Americans in California also resisted the presence of Chinese immigrants whom they saw as competitors. But the Chinese arrived at a crucial moment in the industrialization of the American Far West. First, the prospect of making millions by large-scale investments in quartz mining, and especially the deep shaft mines of Nevada's Comstock Lode, left placer mining and even the tailings of quartz mines available to Chinese workers who moved into this less attractive side of the mining business. They were so patient and so thorough at the task of recycling that they not only managed to make a living, they constituted the majority of the population in some mining areas.[91] Second, when the urgent need for labor to build the Central Pacific Railroad developed in the 1860s, Chinese labor proved essential. The result was a blending of the older mercantile system of contract labor—in this instance the Chinese workers were supplied by labor factors from the Pearl River delta in China—for a new industrial system that sought cheap labor wherever it might secure it.[92]

It is not the purpose of this essay to recount the well-known history of Chinese workers in America, but simply to observe that they, like the Kanakas, came as temporary laborers. In this instance it was on a "credit ticket" system requiring them to work in order to pay their fare over and back. That arrangement, writes Gunther Barth, left them the slaves of their own countrymen. Understandably, they obeyed the "invisible control" of the labor agents as they were not only in debt to these men, but also dependent on them for the pay needed by families back home. Of the 200,000 Chinese who came to America in the nineteenth century some 100,000 returned to China. Despite the fact that only 50 percent remained, American labor's fear of competition led to the Chinese Exclusion Act of 1882, to the violent anti-Chinese outbursts in the Pacific Northwest in 1884, and to the killing of twenty-eight Chinese at Rock Springs, Wyoming, a year later.[93]

Chinese laborers working as railway laborers, small-scale shopkeepers, domestics, or in the canneries of the Pacific Northwest, have received ample coverage by historians. Less well documented are the 80,523 Chinese who served in American merchant shipping between 1876 and 1896. Indeed, by 1900 some 80 percent of this nation's seamen were foreign-born, and of these many were Chinese.[94] The LaFollette Seamen's Act of 1915, sometimes hailed as the first piece of progressive legislation under Woodrow Wilson, was also a device to get rid of Asians in the merchant marine.[95]

In the case of California, it is interesting to see the oldest and newest labor systems existing side by side. On 2 October 1854, the *Alta California* reported that people were stealing Indian children in the north and selling them to *rancheros* in the southern part of the state. Later it was estimated that between 3,000 and 4,000 children had been stolen in the fifteen-year period from 1852 to 1867.[96] Meanwhile, in the gold camps, individual Anglo-Americans feared that Sonoran peons or Southern capitalists with gangs of slaves would exploit the gold fields in such an efficient way that free labor would be driven out. When Thomas Jefferson Green of Texas appeared at Rose Bar on the Yuba River with his slaves to work the placers, the miners unceremoniously tossed him out and put into effect a local code prohibiting all master–servant teams in mining operations no matter what their relationship. The ordinance was originally directed at Mexican and Chilean mining *patrons* and their workers, but it was also applied to Mr. Green of Texas.[97]

## VII

Another variation of an imported labor supply system in the West can be seen in the history of the Basques who came to California in the gold rush period but soon turned to cattle and sheep-herding enterprises that stretched eastward into Nevada, Utah, and other interior states or territories. Because of a rise in world wool prices in the 1870s, Basque *patrons* in the West, such as Pedro Altube, successfully engaged in sheep ranching in California and Nevada by persuading kinsmen and fellow villagers to come to America as herders. They had to agree to a three- or four-year contract and to take part of their wages in ewes. "Once his flock was large enough to support him," writes William A. Douglass, "the migrant would break away and move to marginal lands."[98] By 1910 there were probably 10,000 Basques in the West. Americans derisively called them tramps or "Black Bascoes," levied special taxes on them, and sometimes drove them off the range; yet when the restrictive immigration laws of the 1920s removed the source of Old World Basque herders, there was such a shortage of workers that "it produced a labor crisis in the sheep industry." When a similar shortage occurred in the 1940s and the 1950s, 383 Basques jumped ship to join relatives in sheep-raising states. The outcome was that private bills were introduced into Congress to legitimize their presence. During the 1950s Congress finally passed a law allowing a given number of Basques to immigrate each year if they would sign a three-yar sheepherders contract. "By June, 1970," according to Douglass, "some 5,495 herders had entered the West under this plan."[99]

Examples of ethnic contract labor in the American West since 1860 are seemingly endless. Italian laborers operating under a contract system came to California in large numbers after 1865 to work either in construction or in vineyards or agriculture.[100] By 1900 a large part of the laborforce for the maintenance of Western railroads consisted of Mexican-Americans living away from home. During the 1920s, as Julian Nava has observed, "American recruiters actually ranged over Mexico hiring people to fill labor ranks in the United States," and "immigration officials looked the other way as thousands crossed the border."[101] In the depressed 1930s, however, there was a reversal of policy and Mexican immigrants were urged to return or were deported. Even today Mexican nationals continue to operate under conditions that are far from ideal, as the career of Cesar Chavez has so eloquently reminded us.[102]

On the surface the early labor history of Mormon Utah seems at odds with all the foregoing accounts, for the Latter-Day Saints initially came to the Great Basin in such numbers that there was no labor shortage. Moreover, the converts they recruited from Europe came largely from Great Britain and Scandinavia, so that ethnic distinctions in the laborforce were absent. Nor did the Mormons coopt the labor of local Indian groups although they did befriend them. The Mormon church also used a system of labor tithes, but the evidence does not suggest that specific groups, ethnic or otherwise, were exploited.[103]

On the other hand, the historian of labor in twentieth-century Utah can point to disturbing parallels to Aleut *toyons* or Hawaiian contract governors in the chronicle of Leonidas Skliris, a powerful and demanding labor *padrone*, who pushed the number of his Greek countrymen in the state from 3 in 1900 to 4,000 in 1910.[104] Although the Greek immigrants worked as regular laborers, some were used as strike breakers in the Bingham Canyon area, said by observers to have been one of the most miserable mining camps in the United States. Here again one finds the blending of the old and the new: a traditional form of labor recruitment to supply a modern industrial operation.

This confrontation between a traditional labor system and the new industrial order brings us back to the questions posed at the outset of this essay. First, was the American West and the Western frontier more properly a symbol of bondage than freedom when it came to labor systems? And second, how much so-called frontier or Western violence has stemmed from the economic conditions in which labor has been abused rather than from race hatred or other factors?

To the first, the answer must be that it was indeed an area of bondage exemplified by captive Indians in New Mexico, cowed mission neophytes in California, and Aleutian forced labor in Alaska; but it was also a place where capitalist competition in the fur trade and flood migration of white labor into the mining industry either used traditional systems of native labor without unduly abusing the workers, or, in the case of mining, ignored the presence of a potential native laborforce. In short, varying conditions of bondage and freedom existed side by side.

Thus it is nearly impossible to say when these earlier conditions of slavery and/or debt-peonage were replaced by a system of job contracts and cash wages. Certainly the ratification of the Thirteenth Amendment in 1865 outlawing slavery and involuntary servitude was a symbolic turning point, for although it was directed at the South, the amendment applied to the entire nation. And Congress, not unmindful of the fact that debt and Indian peonage had long existed in New Mexico, passed *An Act to Abolish . . . The System of Peonage* on 2 March 1867 and had it proclaimed in New Mexico a month later. The law was not really enforced, however, until 1868, and even then master and servant relations did not change significantly.[105] As every student of Reconstruction knows, Southern black workers continued to live in conditions of debt-peonage after 1865 in the South and elsewhere. The persistence of debt-peonage led the Supreme Court to declare in 1911 that all forms of peonage were unconstitutional. Perhaps the best evidence that we have passed from a tolerance of involuntary labor is the public's reaction of shock when it hears, for example, that an entire village in India is burdened by debt-peonage or that Mexican laborers in Arizona have been held in chains by an employer on an isolated Arizona ranch.

A search for the causes of labor violence in the West must also bring forth a mixed response. Spanish abuses of native labor in New Mexico and California, and the Russian attempts to control the Aleuts and Tlingits in Alaska naturally provoked resistance. Here again no clear-cut evolution from early bad conditions to later better conditions can be assumed. American conflicts with Chinese laborers did not occur in early frontier situations but in cities and in mining towns in the 1880s. The real cause of conflict was economic competition for jobs, yet it must be admitted that the hatred provoking the conflict was also racially inspired.

In this and other instances ethnic conflict in the West derived not so much from frontier conditions as from two basic economic characteristics, one Western in origin, the other projected from Eastern states. The Western economy in the nineteenth century tended to focus on a single commercial product in a given region. That vast region could be said to have a series of monotheme economies: furs and the Indian trade in the early years, metal mining in other areas, cattle ranching in the Great Plains, lumber and canning industries in the Pacific Northwest, and large-scale agriculture in California. When depression hit one or more of these economies the result was disaster for the local workers, and tension and conflict inevitably occurred.

The Eastern factor is best described in Richard Lingenfelter's fine study, *The Hardrock Miners*, in which he correctly asserts that violence in the Western mines was not due to the "lawlessness of the frontier."

In the early disputes, when law enforcement was least effective, the miners acted with the greatest restraint. Only as the law grew stronger and the owners began to manipulate it as a tool of repression, and only as the freedom of the frontier faded, did the miners in their frustration turn to violence. Both the labor repression and violence in the western mines were, in fact, but an imitation of that already rampant in the more settled and civilized eastern states. Troops and hired gunmen were called in to break strikes in the coal pits of the East well before they were used in the Amador war and in Leadville; the same may be said of blacklisting, Pinkerton spies, lockouts, and injunctions; even the Haymarket dynamiting preceded the dynamiting at Grass Valley where it had been peacefully used for nearly two decades; and it was the violent eruption at Homestead that helped trigger that in the Coeur d'Alene. Thus it was the "taming of the frontier," not frontier lawlessness, that spurred the violence—that heritage of conflict—that left so lasting a scar on labor relations in the western mines.[106]

At the same time there also seems to be evidence that labor violence in the American West in the late nineteenth and early twentieth centuries arose from the fact that older, preindustrial ethnic labor systems were joined with a modern industrial system, subject to boom and bust markets in an environment that could be called frontier. Further, ethnic laborers found themselves working side-by-side with white Americans or Europeans who were jealous of their rights both as wage earners with contracts and as free citizens. Certainly the condition in the mining communities of Bingham Canyon, Coeur d'Alene, Leadville, and Ludlow suggest this.[107] And finally, as Carlos A. Schwantes has indicated, workers going West in the late nineteenth century embraced an "ideology of disinheritance" after they failed to realize dreams of success and wealth. Accordingly, they joined political and labor protest movements such as the Alliance, the Populist party, the Western Federation of Miners, and the Industrial Workers of the World. Certainly the juxtaposition of all the incompatible elements described in the foregoing pages combined with this "ideology of disinheritance" made labor violence virtually inevitable after 1880.[108]

## VIII

As a way of placing the discussion of bonded and contract labor in the American West in some larger perspective, the observations of M. I. Finley are instructive.

> Throughout most of human history labor for others has been performed in large part under conditions of dependence or bondage; that is to say the relations between the man who works and his master or employer rested neither on ties of kinship nor on a voluntary revocable contract of employment, but rather on a birth into a class of dependents or debtors or some other precondition, which by custom and law automatically removed from the dependent, usually for a long term, some measure of choice or action.[109]

From Finley's point of view labor in the early American West seems more traditional than unique. Thus it appears even more remarkable that there have been so few comparisons of the age-old ethnic labor systems of the West with those of the South, or with African, Asian, or European systems. By neglecting the story of labor, Western historians have missed an opportunity to explain Western race relations more fully, the nature of the Western economy, Western violence, and the remarkable continuity between the bonded labor system of the past and the contract labor systems of the nineteenth and twentieth centuries.

It is also the case that the history of many groups—such as that of the Mexican-Americans—is sometimes better explained by focusing on labor history than on political or racial history. As David J. Weber has noted:

> Race ... did not constitute an insurmountable barrier to upward social mobility on the Mexican frontier. A rigid, hierarchical social structure, with status determined in large part by race, had been a feature of Mexican life since the sixteenth century, but had broken down in the late colonial period and had never been firmly planted on the northern frontier. In the Far North the shortage of an easily exploitable native labor pool and the need to work with one's own hands made it impossible to maintain firm racial distinctions. In the colonial

era, some persons classified as "Spaniards" had worked as servants on the frontier, while Indians, blacks and mixed bloods had moved up the social ladder.[110]

This brief and selective survey should suggest that economic expectations rather than racism sometimes account for slavery or bondage in an abundant land, although racism can easily become a rationalization for slavery or abuse. At the same time, this essay may also suggest why bondage did not flourish on other American frontiers. A comparative approach to the history of bonded and contract labor within the whole of the United States cannot help but place slavery in the antebellum South in a new perspective. And finally it may be hoped that such a study also helps to explain the possibly ironic and yet profound meaning of Turner's belief that free land meant free people and a democratic society. For Turner, like Jefferson, insisted on talking about an ideal West rather than a real West. We may celebrate the names of both men one day, not for their presentation of the grim facts, but for their vision of what the West and America itself could mean.

NOTES

1. Carlos A. Schwantes, "Protest in a Promised Land: Unemployment, Disinheritance, and the Origin of Labor Militancy in the Pacific Northwest, 1885–1886," *Western Historical Quarterly* 13 (1982):390.

2. Frederick Jackson Turner, "The Significance of the Frontier in American History," *American Historical Association Annual Report, 1893* (Washington, D.C., 1894).

3. Frederick Jackson Turner, *The Frontier in American History* (New York, 1920); Ray Allen Billington, *Westward Expansion: A History of the American Frontier* (New York, 1949, rev. ed. 1982); Henry Nash Smith, *Virgin Land: The American West as Symbol and Myth* (Cambridge, Mass., 1950); Robert Penn Warren, *Brother to Dragons: A Tale in Verse and Voice* (New York, 1953); R. W. B. Lewis, *The American Adam: Innocence, Tragedy, and Tradition in the Nineteenth Century* (Chicago, 1955); Edwin Fussell, *Frontier: American Literature and the American West* (Princeton, N.J., 1965), vii–ix; G. Edward White, *The Eastern Establishment and the Western Experience: The West of Frederick Remington, Theodore Roosevelt, and Owen Wister* (New Haven, Conn., 1968); Roderick Nash, *Wilderness and the American Mind* (New Haven, Conn., 1973); John Logan Allen, *Passage Through the Garden* (Urbana, Ill., 1975); Frederick Merk, *History of the Westward Movement* (New York, 1978); Lee Clark Mitchell, *Witness to a Vanishing America: The Nineteenth-Century Response* (Princeton, N.J., 1981); William K. Wyant, *Westward in Eden: The Public Lands and the Conservation Movement* (Berkeley, Calif., 1982).

4. Ray Allen Billington, *Land of Savagery/Land of Promise: The European Image of the American Frontier* (New York, 1981).

5. Frederick Merk, *Manifest Destiny and Mission in American History* (New York, 1963).

6. George T. Hunt, *The Wars of the Iroquois* (Madison, Wisc., 1940); Allen W. Trelease, *Indian Affairs in Colonial New York* (Ithaca, N.Y., 1960); Verner W. Crane, *The Southern Frontier, 1670–1732* (Durham, N.C., 1961); Francis Jennings, *The Invasion of America: Indians, Colonialism, and the Cant of Conquest* (New York, 1976), 63–64, 89–90; J. Leitch Wright, *The Only Land They Knew: The Tragic Story of the Indians in the Old South* (New York, 1981), esp. ch. 6–7.

7. See, for example, Edward E. Dale, *The Range Cattle Industry* (Norman, Okla., 1930); Ernest S. Osgood, *The Day of the Cattlemen* (Minneapolis, 1929); Louis Pelzer, *The Cattlemen's Frontier* (Glendale, Calif., 1936); Philip Durham and Everett L. Jones, *The Negro Cowboy* (New York, 1965); Jimmy M. Skaggs, *The Cattle Trailing Industry: Between Supply and Demand* (Lawrence, Kans., 1973).

8. See, for example, Ulrich B. Phillips, *American Negro Slavery* (New York, 1918); Kenneth M. Stampp, *The Peculiar Institution* (New York, 1956); Eugene D. Genovese, *Roll, Jordan, Roll: The World the Slaves Made* (New York, 1974); Edmund S. Morgan, *American Slavery, American Freedom: The Ordeal of Colonial Virginia* (New York, 1975). Recent studies of indentured labor suggest a changing perspective. See, for example, David Galenson, *White Servitude in Colonial America* (Cambridge, Eng., 1982).

9. Excellent accounts of these groups may be found in the following studies: Gunther Barth, *Bitter Strength: A History of the Chinese in the United States, 1850–1870* (Cambridge, Mass., 1964); Carey McWilliams, *North From Mexico: Spanish Speaking People of the United States* (Westport, Conn., 1968); Carey McWilliams, *Factories in the Fields* (Hamden, Conn., 1969); William A. Douglass and Jon Bilbao, *Amerikanuak: Basques in the New World* (Reno, Nev., 1975); I. Emerson Hough, *The Story of the Cowboy* (New York, 1897, repr. 1924); Joe B. Frantz and Julian E. Choate, Jr., *The American Cowboy: The Myth and the Reality* (Norman, Okla., 1955); Rodman W. Paul, *Mining Frontiers of the Far West, 1848–1880* (New York, 1963); Vernon H. Jensen, *Heritage of Conflict: Labor Relations in the Nonferrous Metals Industry up to 1930* (Ithaca, N.Y., 1950); Richard E. Lingenfelter, *The Hardrock Miners: A History of the Mining Labor Movement in the American West, 1863–1893* (Berkeley, Calif., 1974); Robert Coles, *Migrants, Sharecroppers, and Mountaineers* (Boston, 1971); Carol Norquest, *Rio Grande Wetbacks: Mexican Migrant Workers* (Albuquerque, N.M., 1972); Lloyd S. Fisher, *The Harvest Labor Market in California* (Cambridge, Mass., 1953); Vernon M. Briggs, Jr., Walter Fogel, and Fred H. Schmidt, *The Chicano Worker* (Austin, 1977).

10. Edmund S. Morgan, "Slavery and Freedom: The American Paradox," *Journal of American History* 59 (1973):5–29.

11. Nieboer is quoted in translation in Robin W. Winks, ed., *Slavery: A Comparative Perspective* (New York, 1972), 195–96.

12. Evsey D. Domar, "The Causes of Slavery or Serfdom: A Hypothesis," *Journal of Economic History* 30 (1970):18–32.

13. Walter Prescott Webb, *The Great Frontier* (Boston, 1952).

14. Howard R. Lamar and Leonard M. Thompson, eds., *The Frontier in History: North America and Southern Africa Compared* (New Haven, Conn., 1981), 16, 309.

15. Bernard Sheehan, *Savagism and Civility: Indians and Englishmen in Colonial Virginia* (New York, 1980).

16. See Ramsay Cook, "The Social and Economic Frontier in North America," in

Lamar and Thompson, eds., *The Frontier in History*, 176–77, 179–80, 186–88, 195–97. Also see William Cronon, *Changes in the Land: Indians, Colonists, and the Ecology of New England* (New York, 1983).

17. Cook, "The Social and Economic Frontier," 192–93.

18. Lamar and Thompson, eds., *The Frontier in History*, 34–35, 206–7.

19. Alvar Nuñez Cabeza de Vaca, *Adventures in the Unknown Interior of America*, trans. and annotated by Cyclone Covey (New York, 1972).

20. Ibid., 122–25.

21. George P. Hammond and Agapito Rey, eds., *Narratives of the Coronado Expedition*, Coronado Historical Series vol. 2 (Albuquerque, N.M., 1940), 188, 219, 234–37.

22. See Jane E. Scott, "New Aspects of the Indian Slave Trade: Indian Contributions to Commerce in New Mexico, 1540–1775," paper presented at Yale University, December 1975, 8. Also see Charles W. Hackett, ed., *Historical Documents Relating to New Mexico, Nueva Viscaya, and Approaches Thereto to 1773* . . ., 3 vols. (Washington, D.C., 1923), 1:140, 156, 161–62.

23. Elizabeth Ann Harper, "The Taovayas Indians in Frontier Trade and Diplomacy, 1765–1779," *Southwestern Historical Quarterly* 57 (1953):181–201; Jack D. Forbes, *Apaches, Navaho, and Spaniard* (Norman, Okla., 1960), 120–21, 148–49, 151. Jane E. Scott writes: "there were institutions in Southern Plains societies—the taking of captives, the enslaving of captives, and the buying and selling of captive slaves—which provided the framework out of which a slave trade with the Spaniards developed." See Scott, "New Aspects of the Indian Slave Trade," 19.

24. France V. Scholes, "Civil Government in New Mexico in the Seventeenth Century," *New Mexico Historical Review* 10 (1935):81.

25. "Yamasee Indians," in Howard R. Lamar, ed., *Reader's Encyclopedia of the American West* (New York, 1977).

26. Scholes, "Civil Government," 81–82; France V. Scholes, "The Supply Service of the New Mexico Missions in the Seventeenth Century," *New Mexico Historical Review* 5 (1930):93–115, 186–210, 386–404.

27. Scholes, "Civil Government," 83.

28. Ibid., 83–84, 109.

29. Ibid., 85.

30. Alfred Barnaby Thomas, *The Plains Indians and New Mexico, 1751–1778*, Coronado Cuarto Centennial Publications vol. 2, 1540–1940, ed. by George P. Hammond (Albuquerque, N.M., 1940), 6.

31. Oakah L. Jones, Jr., *Pueblo Warriors and Spanish Conquest* (Norman, Okla., 1966); E. H. Spicer, *Cycles of Conquest: The Impact of Spain, Mexico, and the United States on the Indians of the Southwest, 1533–1960* (Tucson, Ariz., 1962).

32. Scott, "New Aspects of the Indian Slave Trade," 14–15; Spicer, *Cycles of Conquest*, 213.

33. David J. Weber, *The Mexican Frontier, 1821–1846: The American Southwest Under Mexico* (Albuquerque, N.M., 1982), 212.

34. See Charles L. Kenner, *A History of New Mexican–Plains Indian Relations* (Norman, Okla., 1964), ch. 4. See also J. Evetts Haley, "The Comanchero Trade," *Southwestern Historical Quarterly* 38 (1935):157–76; Carl Coke Rister, *Border Captives: The Traffic in Prisoners by Southern Plains Indians, 1835–1857* (Norman, Okla.,

1940); Frank McNitt, *Navajo Wars: Military Campaigns, Slave Raids, and Reprisals* (Albuquerque, N.M., 1972).

35. Benjamin Butler Harris, *The Gila Trail: The Texas Argonauts and the California Gold Rush*, ed. and annotated by Richard H. Dillon (Norman, Okla., 1960), 35–37.

36. The characteristica of Old World slavery are briefly summarized in C. Duncan Rice, *The Rise and Fall of Black Slavery* (New York, 1975), 1–23. See also M. I. Finley, ed., *Slavery in Classical Antiquity: Views and Controversies* (Cambridge, Eng., 1960); G. Macmunn, *Slavery Through the Ages* (London, 1938, repr. Westport, Conn., 1970).

37. William J. Parish, *The Charles Ilfeld Company: A Study of the Rise and Decline of Merchant Capitalism in New Mexico* (Cambridge, Mass., 1961), 150–53; Weber, *Mexican Frontier*, 211. John M. Coatsworth in "Obstacles to Economic Growth in Nineteenth-Century Mexico," *American Historical Review* 83 (1978):80–100, argues that in Mexico itself "debt peonage ... was effectively practiced only in part of the sparsely populated geographical extremities of the country." Although no real feudal power existed, he concludes that "coercion, however, was widespread and pervasive" (96). The larger question of whether peonage was an "oppressive" system of labor or simply "the stark reality of rural structure" has been explored in Arnold J. Bauer, "Rural Workers in Spanish America: Problems of Peonage and Oppression," *Hispanic American Historical Review* 59 (1979): 34–63, and in a response by Brian Loveman, "Critique of Arnold J. Bauer's 'Rural Workers in Spanish America,'" *Hispanic American Historical Review* 59 (1979):478–85. The question has also been brilliantly explored by Magnus Mörner in "The Spanish-American Hacienda: A Survey of Recent Research and Debate," *Hispanic American Historical Review* 53 (1973): 183–216.

38. Larry M. Beachum, *William Becknell: The Father of the Santa Fe Trade*, Southwestern Studies no. 68 (El Paso, Tex., 1982), 30; Weber, *Mexican Frontier*, 210; Howard R. Lamar, *The Far Southwest, 1846–1912: A Territorial History* (New Haven, Conn., 1966), 187.

39. John M. Gullick, "Debt Bondage in Malaya," in Winks, ed., *Slavery*, 57.

40. Lamar and Thompson, eds., *The Frontier in History*, 18–19, 83.

41. R. F. Heizer and M. A. Whipple, comps. and eds., *The California Indians: A Source Book* (Berkeley and Los Angeles, 1971), 566–71.

42. This is a theme of George H. Phillips, *Chiefs and Challengers: Indian Resistance and Cooperation in Southern California* (Berkeley, Calif., 1975), and A. L. Kroeber, "The Tribe in California," in Heizer and Whipple, eds., *California Indians*, 367–84.

43. Weber, *Mexican Frontier*, 211.

44. Heizer and Whipple, eds., *California Indians*, 567; George H. Phillips, *The Enduring Struggle: Indians in California History* (San Francisco, 1981), 24.

45. Heizer and Whipple, eds., *California Indians*, 66–68, 566.

46. Marsh is quoted in Weber, *Mexican Frontier*, 211.

47. Albert A. Hurtado, "'Hardly a Farm House—A Kitchen Without Them': Indian and White Households on the California Borderlands Frontier in 1860," *Western Historical Quarterly* 13 (1982):245 n. 44, 260, 249–50, 256–58.

48. Ibid., 252.

49. Ibid., 269; Phillips, *Enduring Struggle*, 343–45; Carvel Collins, ed., *Sam Ward in the Gold Rush* (Stanford, Calif., 1949), 23–24; Sherburne F. Cook, *The Population*

*of California Indians, 1769–1970* (Berkeley, Calif., 1976), 42–44, 59, 60, 70, 199–202.

50. James R. Gibson, *Imperial Russia in Frontier America: The Changing Geography of Supply of Russian America, 1784–1867* (New York, 1976), 32.

51. Arthur Okun, *The Russian American Company*, (Cambridge, Mass., 1951), 171–73.

52. Ibid., 175.

53. Ibid.

54. Galenson, *White Servitude in Colonial America*, suggests that over half of the white colonists arriving in British North America sold themselves into bondage to pay for passage.

55. Okun, *Russian American Company*, 177.

56. Ibid., 178–79. It is intriguing to see the parallels between the excessive charges of the Russian American Company store and the company stores (*tienda de raya*) supplying the late colonial haciendas in Mexico, as well as comparable attempts to create debt-peonage. See especially Friedrich Katz, "Labor Conditions on Haciendas in Porfirian Mexico: Some Trends and Tendencies," *Hispanic American Historical Review* 54 (1974):9 n. 29.

57. Okun, *Russian American Company*, 180–81, 185–86.

58. Gibson, *Imperial Russia*, 8–10.

59. Okun, *Russian American Company*, 193–98.

60. Ibid., 198–99.

61. Richard A. Pierce, ed., *Documents on the History of the Russian American Company* (Kingston, Ont., 1976), 121.

62. Ibid., 115.

63. Okun, *Russian American Company*, 200. Also see David A. Brading, *Miners and Merchants in Bourbon Mexico, 1763–1810* (Cambridge, Eng., 1977), 5, 23. The fate of Indian slaves in Mexico is treated in the early portion of Colin A. Palmer, *Slaves of the White God: Blacks in Mexico, 1570–1650* (Cambridge, Mass., 1976), 3–35. Useful materials may also be found in E. C. Frost, M. C. Meyer, J. F. Vasquez, and L. Diaz, eds., *Labor and Laborers Through Mexican History* (Tucson, Ariz., 1979).

64. Okun, *Russian American Company*, 193–94. Dorothy M. Jones, *Aleuts in Transition: A Comparison of Two Villages* (Seattle, 1976), 18, argues that the Aleuts had declined to less than 2,000 by 1825.

65. Okun, *Russian American Company*, 203–5; Gibson, *Imperial Russia*, 13.

66. Okun, *Russian American Company*, 215; Gibson, *Imperial Russia*, 10–13.

67. Gibson, *Imperial Russia*, 130–31.

68. Janice Duncan, "Minority Without a Champion: Kanakas on the Pacific Coast, 1788–1850," *Oregon Historical Society* brochure (Portland, Ore., 1972), 13. Also see Raymond H. Fisher, *Records of the Russian-American Company, 1802, 1817–67* (Washington, D.C., 1971).

69. The standard history of the firm is E. E. Rich, *The History of the Hudson's Bay Company, 1670–1870* (London, 1958–59), vols. 1–3. See also Joseph Burr Tyrrell, *Documents Relating to the Early History of Hudson's Bay* (Toronto, The Champlain Society, 1931).

70. Arthur J. Ray, *Indians in the Fur Trade: Their Role as Trappers, Hunters, and Middlemen in the Lands Southwest of Hudson Bay, 1660–1870* (Toronto, 1974).

71. See Arthur J. Ray and Donald Freeman, *"Give Us Good Measure": An Economic Analysis of Relations Between Indians and the Hudson's Bay Company Before 1763* (Toronto, 1978).

72. Some confusion exists as to when the practice of sending companies of men into the wilderness to hunt and trade evolved into a brigade system. Billington suggests that the brigade system was used by Dr. John McLoughlin, factor at Fort Vancouver, in the 1820s. At that time he "began concentrating his brigades on the Pacific Slope." But McLoughlin also sent his brigades east to create a "fur desert" in present-day eastern Oregon and Washington as well as Idaho and Utah to discourage penetration by American trappers. Meanwhile, the Rocky Mountain Fur Company inaugurated its own version of the brigade with mountain men in 1822 and thereafter. See Ray Allen Billington, *The Far Western Frontier, 1830–1860* (New York, 1962), 41–42; LeRoy R. Hafen, ed., *The Mountain Men and the Fur Trade of the Far West*, 10 vols. (Glendale, Calif., 1965), 1: introduction.

73. Examples of the ways the XYZ and Northwest companies used contracts and indebtedness to control workers can be found in Bruce M. White, comp., *The Fur Trade in Minnesota: An Introductory Guide to Manuscript Sources* (St. Paul, 1977), 30–31, 32–39. Contracts signed by free hunters in the Amerian trade may be found in Hiram M. Chittenden, *The American Fur Trade of the Far West*, 2 vols. (Stanford, Calif., 1954), 2:941–45. There are numerous records of contracts and settlements between fur-trade companies and trappers or engages. See, for example, John C. Luttig, *Journal of a Fur Trading Expedition on the Upper Missouri, 1812–1813* (New York, 1964), xvi, 113–14. The democratic nature of the articles of association by the Missouri Fur Company described here stand in stark contrast to those of the Russian American Company as reported in Okun, *Russian American Company*, 192–213, and Alexander Ross, *The Fur Hunters of the Far West*, 2 vols. (London, 1855), 2:236–37.

74. Howard R. Lamar, *The Trader on the American Fronter: Myth's Victim* (College Station, Tex., 1977), 16–17.

75. The major characteristics of the Rocky Mountain fur trade are summarized succinctly in Billington, *Far Western Frontier* 57–68. The classic older account is Hiram M. Chittenden, *A History of the American Fur Trade of the Far West*, 2 vols. (New York, 1902). Two more recent accounts are Paul C. Phillips, *The Fur Trade*, 2 vols. (Norman, Okla., 1961); and David J. Wishart, *The Fur Trade of the American West, 1807–1840* (Lincoln, Neb., 1979).

76. David J. Weber, *The Taos Trappers, 1540–1846* (Norman, Okla., 1971); Elinor Wilson, *Jim Beckwourth: Black Mountain Man and War Chief of the Crows* (Norman, Okla., 1972).

77. J. Cecil Alter, *James Bridger* (Salt Lake City, Utah, 1925); Stanley Vestal, *Jim Bridger, Mountain Man* (New York, 1946).

78. This idea is brilliantly developed in William H. Goetzmann, "The Mountain Man as Jacksonian Man," *American Quarterly* 15 (1963):402–15.

79. "Memoirs of Thomas Hopoo," *Hawaiian Journal of History* 2 (1968): 42–54.

80. Duncan, "Minority Without a Champion," 1–4; George V. Blue, "Early Relations Between Hawaii and the Northwest Coast," *Thirty-third Annual Report of the Hawaiian Historical Society* (Honolulu, 1925):17.

81. Duncan, "Minority Without a Champion," 3.

82. Ibid., 5–7; Blue, "Early Relations," 17.

83. Duncan, "Minority Without a Champion," 12.

84. Richard Henry Dana, *Two Years Before the Mast* (London and New York, 1840, repr. 1972). Dana's classic has been through many editions. It should be remembered that Dana himself crusaded for a reform of sailors' rights and particularly for the abolition of the custom of flogging. In 1841 he published *The Seaman's Friend*, which became the standard manual of naval law regarding sailors. The many kinds of ethnic labor on board whalers is discussed in Elmo Paul Hohman, *The American Whaleman: A Study of Life and Labor in the Whaling Industry* (New York, 1928). The abuses of sailors' rights aboard whalers is explored in Gaddis Smith, "Whaling History and the Courts," *The Log of Mystic Seaport* 30 (1978):67–80.

85. Janice Duncan, "Kanaka World Travellers and Fur Company Employees, 1785–1860," *Hawaiian Journal of History* 7 (1973):111.

86. Duncan, "Minority Without a Champion," 16–17. Oregon settlers were anti-black while being antislavery. It was not uncommon for Oregon overland companies to express this feeling in their articles of incorporation. An 1843 constitution stated, for example, "No Black or Mulatto person shall, in any case or any circumstances whatever, be admitted to the Society, or permitted to emigrate with it." Sandra L. Myres, *Westering Women and the Frontier Experience, 1800–1915* (Albuquerque, N.M., 1982), 85.

87. See especially Leonard Pitt, *The Decline of the Californios* (Berkeley, Calif., 1966), 50–52, 55–56, 58–59, 63–64.

88. Rudolph M. Lapp, *Blacks in Gold Rush California* (New Haven, Conn., 1977), 12–48.

89. Ibid., 158–254.

90. Rudolph M. Lapp, "Negroes in the Far West," in Lamar, ed., *Reader's Encyclopedia of the American West*, 813–16.

91. Paul, *Mining Frontiers*, 143–44, 149.

92. See Barth, *Bitter Strength*; Rose Hum Lee, *Chinese in the United States of America* (Hong Kong, 1960).

93. Gunther Barth, "Chinese Immigration," in Lamar, ed., *Reader's Encyclopedia of the American West*, 208; Schwantes, "Protest in a Promised Land," 373–90; Alexander P. Saxton, *The Indispensable Enemy: Labor and the Anti-Chinese Movement in California* (Berkeley, Calif., 1971); Willard B. Farwell, *The Report of the Special Committee of the Board of Supervisors of San Francisco on the Condition of the Chinese Quarter of the City* (San Francisco, 1885).

94. Robert J. Schwendinger, "Chinese Sailors, America's Invisible Merchant Marine, 1876–1905," *California Historical Society Quarterly* 57 (1978):62.

95. Interviews with Patricia Nelson Limerick and John Morton Blum (September 1982, New Haven, Ct.) regarding their joint research on the LaFollette Seamen's Act of 1915.

96. John W. Bingaman, *The Ahwahneechees* (Lodi, Calif., 1966), 45, quotes *Alta California*, 2 October 1854; the Butte County *Record*, 23 October 1857; and the *Petaluma Journal*, 6 December 1861.

97. Pitt, *Decline of Californios*, 58.

98. William A. Douglass, "Basques," in Lamar, ed., *Reader's Encyclopedia of the American West*, 79. Also see Douglass and Bilbao, *Amerikanuak*, 224–30, for early examples of contracts.

99. Douglass, "Basques," 79.

100. See Andrew Rolle, *The Immigrant Upraised: Italian Adventurers and Colonists in an Expanding America* (Norman, Okla., 1968).

101. Julian Nava, "Mexican-Americans," in Lamar, ed., *Reader's Encyclopedia of the American West*, 727.

102. Ibid.; Peter Matthieson, *Sal si puedes: Cesar Chavez and the New American Revolution* (New York, 1969). See also Cletus E. Daniel, *Bitter Harvest: A History of California Farm Workers, 1870–1941* (Ithaca, N.Y., 1981); James C. Foster, *American Labor in the Southwest: The First Hundred Years* (Tucson, Az., 1982).

103. Leonard J. Arrington, *Great Basin Kingdom: An Economic History of the Latter-Day Saints, 1830–1900* (Cambridge, Mass., 1958); Michael Scott Raber, "Religious Polity and Local Production: The Origins of a Mormon Town," Diss., Yale University, 1978, 413–24.

104. I am indebted to Peter M. Blodgett's research paper, "Mormon Economic Policy and the Mining Industry, 1847–1912," Yale University, 1977, 30–31, for much of the preceding information. See also Allen K. Powell, "The Foreign Element and the 1903–04 Carbon County Coal Miners' Strike," *Utah Historical Quarterly* 43 (1975):125–54; Helen Z. Papanikolas, "Life and Labor Among the Immigrants of Bingham Canyon," *Utah Historical Quarterly* 33 (1969):290–91; Helen Z. Papanikolas, "Toil and Rage in a New Land: The Greek Immigrants in Utah," *Utah Historical Quarterly* 38 (1970):100–203.

105. Lamar, *Far Southwest*, 131.

106. Lingenfelter, *Hardrock Miners*, 227–28.

107. See Jensen, *Heritage of Conflict*.

108. Schwantes, "Protest in a Promised Land," 374–75, 379.

109. M. I. Finley, "The Extent of Slavery," in Winks, ed., *Slavery*, 4.

110. Weber, *Mexican Frontier*, 214. See also Frost, Meyer, Vasquez, and Diaz, eds., *Labor and Laborers Through Mexican History*, 463–505, which summarizes the origins and development of the Mexican working class in the United Sttes between 1600 and 1800.

# PART IV

# The Countryside after the Great Transformation

HAL S. BARRON

# 11. Staying Down on the Farm

## SOCIAL PROCESSES OF SETTLED RURAL LIFE

## IN THE NINETEENTH-CENTURY NORTH

I

Although the rapid development of a modern industrial society was the most dramatic aspect of American social history during the second half of the nineteenth century, many Northerners continued to live in settled rural communities where they were also affected by the new social and economic order.* Yet historians have paid scant attention to Northern rural society during this period, assuming instead that social change in the countryside followed and paralleled urban trends. A careful study of one older rural community suggests, however, that the urban and rural North experienced the great social and economic transformations of the nineteenth century in markedly different ways.

Certain aspects of rural development during the second half of the nineteenth century do resemble the changes occurring in urban society. Agricultural historians have detailed the rise after the Civil War of large-scale farming operations utilizing increasing amounts of capital and relying on wage labor or tenants from outside the owner's family. As rural wealth became concentrated in fewer hands, class divisions rigidified and the social structure of rural communities came to approximate that of cities. Various scholars have also noted the increasing prevalence of "modern" attitudes and urban cultural patterns in the countryside. Clarence Danhof and Allan Bogue discuss the new entrepreneurial attitudes of farmers who took a more calculating, businesslike view of their farming operations; and Lewis Atherton narrates the transition of "Main Street" in the Middle West from a dynamic social force and cultural arbiter into a shrill mimic of the big city.[1]

*An earlier version of this essay was presented at the 1981 annual meeting of the Social Science History Association in Nashville, Tennessee. I thank Martin Ridge and Katherine Kobayashi for their helpful comments and acknowledge the assistance provided by a Faculty Summer Research Award from Harvey Mudd College.

327

The case for parallel development, however, is by no means clear cut. Commercial farm operations in the late nineteenth-century North were not, for the most part, factories in the field. The overwhelming majority of farmers relied primarily on family members for labor and management. Although the incidence of wage labor and tenancy increased after 1865, the social positions of these laborers and tenant farmers remained more ambiguous than those of industrial workers. Evidence also indicates that the rise of "modern" attitudes and the ascendance of urban values met heightened resistance in the countryside. Instead of assuming that commercial farmers acted as fully rational economic individuals, Anne Mayhew argues for a distinct set of agrarian values when she interprets farm protest between 1870 and 1900 as a reaction to the growing market orientation of Plains agriculture. Don S. Kirschner's study of state legislation in Illinois and Iowa indicates persisting, if not increasing, rural animosity toward city ways well into the twentieth century.[2]

Unfortunately, there are few studies of older rural communities in the North that provide a clear understanding of late nineteenth-century agrarian society. Because of the pervasive influence of Frederick Jackson Turner's theories about the frontier, depictions of rural life during this period typically focus on the development of new farm areas and give little consideration to settled rural conditions. Although several American social historians have devised a different theoretical framework to explore the *mentalité* of the colonial and antebellum countryside and the social bases for the emergence of the market economy, there has been little effort to examine farm society after the transition to a commercialized economy. And those who have studied established rural conditions have concentrated on the economic aspects of agricultural development rather than on the social context or consequences of that development.[3]

As a result, our perception of rural society in the North during this period is confused and contradictory. The characteristics of urban industrial society are not wholly satisfactory models for understanding the changes in farm communities after the commercialization of agriculture, and Turner's mythic portrayal of frontier society or other notions of premodern village life are also inappropriate. Instead, settled rural life during the late 1800s appears simultaneously to exhibit characteristics associated with both traditional communities and modern society.

Any attempt to resolve this contradiction must consider the fact that older agrarian communities experienced patterns of development fundamentally different from either late nineteenth-century cities or earlier frontiers. In contrast to the rapid and continuous expansion typical of frontier development and urban industry, economic growth in established farm communities slowed and then leveled off. Moreover, while the population in both newly settled rural areas and cities typically increased rapidly between 1850 and 1900, older rural communities commonly lost population. The key to understanding the social history of older farm areas, it would seem, lies in a detailed consideration of the ramifications of this diminished growth.[4]

Slowed economic development and demographic growth were not necessarily new features of rural life in America during the late nineteenth century. As studies of colonial New England communities demonstrate, Puritan villages often became saturated by the third generation of settlement and only migration to newer areas served to alleviate population pressure. Unlike early New England towns, which contended primarily with local problems of subsistence and land distribution, nineteenth-century rural communities were buffeted by much larger forces than those present during the colonial period—urbanization, industrialization, the imperatives of a national market, and competition from newer agricultural areas. Economic development and migration decisions became more than simply a function of local conditions.[5]

The first rural communities to achieve maturity and grow old after the great transformations of the nineteenth century were townships of northern New England and eastern New York that had been settled during the last decades of the eighteenth century. This essay will attempt to delineate the social processes characterizing settled rural life by focusing on one such community: Chelsea, Vermont. This township is not necessarily representative of the rural North in any absolute or statistical sense. Based on a consideration of appropriate theoretical issues and available comparative data, however, the patterns of change in Chelsea are indicative of trends in other rural areas as they, too, became old.

## II

The traditional social and economic history of northern New England during the nineteenth century has been a tale of woe. Harold Fisher Wilson refers to the periods between 1830 and 1870 and between 1870 and 1900 as the "autumn" and "winter" of that region's history, and cites contemporary observers alarmed by the sight of deserted farms and the specter of closed and dilapidated schools and churches. These observers were convinced that the region suffered from an incurable blight brought on by the rise of the West and the lure of the city. Thus, the predominant image of rural New England during the 1800s is an abandoned and decaying township where only the graveyard flourished.[6]

Chelsea, Vermont, was just the sort of community anxious contemporaries had in mind when they chronicled the decline of northern New England. Nestled in the hills of eastern Vermont, Chelsea grew rapidly from its settlement in the late 1790s through the 1830s, reaching its peak of almost 2,000 people in 1840. Commercial agriculture developed extensively during these years as Chelsea farmers produced wool for sale to regional manufacturers, and the principal village in the township contained a modest array of stores and workshops. From 1840 on, Chelsea's population declined at a fairly steady rate until it stabilized at 1,070 in 1900, about half of its maximum size. Both the timing and the pattern of this population decline were typical of the other adjacent townships in Orange County as well as many other rural areas throughout New England and New York.[7]

In contrast to the traditional view of decline and decay, however, an analysis of Chelsea reveals a pattern of stability marked by little real deterioration, but also by little growth. Rather than being subjected to a fatal plethora of social and economic evils, Chelsea and northern New England were simply growing old.

In Chelsea, almost no farms were abandoned in spite of an overall loss of almost half of the population. Throughout the "autumn" and "winter" of northern New England's history, the township always contained about 200 farms whose size, location, and value changed very little. Agricultural production also stayed constant, and from 1850 until the end of the century, wool, butter, and maple sugar remained the principal farm products in more or less fixed proportions.[8]

There was, however, little potential for local agricultural expansion. By 1850, all of the township's available acreage was already in farms; because there was no new land and because local opportunities outside of farming were limited, Chelsea failed to attract or retain younger men starting out in life. Consequently, after the Civil War, Chelsea farmers faced a shortage of farm labor that caused them to continue raising sheep even though the market for wool was weakening. They could not effect a successful transition to dairying because, although it was more profitable, it was too labor-intensive. Instead, local farmers utilized higher-yielding breeds of sheep to offset the high price of labor and adverse market conditions. Moreover, even if there had been a shift to dairying, the number of farms would have been the same because both sheep raising and dairying required equivalent amounts of land. Chelsea's farm economy was stable, but the number of opportunities to farm available to the younger generation remained more or less fixed.[9]

The changing structure of Chelsea's nonagricultural economy also reflects a leveling of economic growth. Most villagers did not farm but served the needs of the larger agricultural population. Again, however, there was little potential for expansion. The rise of mass-production industries in southern New England during the 1840s and 1850s displaced a number of Chelsea artisans who had produced for local consumption, and wiped out the few small factories in Chelsea that had manufactured goods for external markets. Village merchants filled much of the economic gap created by these changes as they retailed the new centrally manufactured goods. And in several cases local craftsmen actually became merchants, relying less on the production of their own stock in trade and more on the sale of factory-made shoes, furniture, and clothing. The trends in Chelsea's nonagricultural economy thus belie traditional notions of wholesale economic collapse; yet they also indicate a situation of limited economic opportunity rather than growth.[10]

In varying degrees, this constriction of economic opportunity occurred throughout the northern countryside and spread into the Midwest. As the processing of agricultural produce and the manufacturing of consumer goods became centralized in the nation's cities, smaller factories closed and artisans were displaced in many rural areas. In his 1895 essay "The Doom of the Small Town," Henry U. Fletcher lamented the precipitous decline of village industry, not in New England, but in Iowa. "One by one," he wrote, "these little centers of industrial activity succumbed to the inevitable: every one of them tells a sad story of heroic struggles with conditions which they but dimly understood and were powerless to resist. Yet this region is a portion of the State of Iowa where crops never fail and where nature has done everything to encourage a prosperous population."[11]

Although Fletcher did not raise the issue, there were limits to Iowa's agricultural prosperity as well. Farming in Iowa and other Northern states was more profitable than in Chelsea, but development in both areas was limited by the supply of the least mobile and least flexible factor of production—land. Once a given location was settled and put into farming, the number of family farm sites neared its maximum. To the extent that later adjustments to new market conditions and new technologies altered the configuration of local farm sites, they usually resulted in fewer opportunities for local farm families.

A comparison with the process of urban economic development will clarify this point. Throughout the 1800s American cities expanded dramatically by creating new jobs and economic opportunities. Jane Jacobs defines this process as adding new work to old work; and Allan Pred, in his more formal model of American metropolitan growth, delineates a multiplier effect in which a city's manufacturing activities led to still other endeavors. Such increased economic activity simultaneously enhanced the probability of new inventions or innovations, which further accelerated the multiplier effect to new levels. The expansive spiral of economic growth continued almost unabated until it ran into problems such as high land costs due to overcrowding.[12]

There was no local multiplier effect in rural areas. During the second half of the nineteenth century, mechanization decreased rather than increased the number of jobs in older farm communities. The adoption of new farm machinery and improved farming practices were mostly one-time changes that shifted farm production to a new plateau, but not into an upward spiral. Farmers reinvested increased returns in their farms, bought additional land from less successful neighbors, invested outside of the community, or gave profits to their children. In any event, although individual farmers may have prospered, the structure of the local economy did not expand appreciably, and few new local agricultural opportunities were created. In writing about a farming area so far removed from Chelsea as the bonanza wheat fields of the Red River Valley of North Dakota and Minnesota, one historian described the achievement of "maturity" after the settlement period:

> The term mature is applicable because, for all practical purposes, the present-day pattern of land use came into existence in the valley during the twenty-five years after 1895. During this period the rural population reached its highest point, declined somewhat, and then remained at approximately the same figure until World War II. Farmers purchased most of the unused land, they put an increasing percentage of their holdings into crop, and they established long-lasting trends in the ownership, number, and size of farms.[13]

The maturation of a local economy does not mean that settled agriculture failed to contribute to the general process of economic growth. On the contrary, the connections between farming and the other sectors of the economy remained essential and were probably much more pronounced in prosperous regions such as Iowa and the Red River Valley than in the hill country of Vermont. Changes in eastern Iowa in 1900 or in western Minnesota in 1920 did not replicate the experiences of rural Vermont in 1850. In all of these areas, however, the number of available opportunities stabilized after the settlement period had passed, and this local economic stabilization distinguished older rural communities from both the earlier frontier and the contemporary city.

## III

As a consequence of economic stabilization, rural population growth also slowed and even declined after the period of settlement. Depopulation began in the Northeast and spread westward over the course of the nineteenth and twentieth centuries as former frontier regions matured. Although not all rural areas lost as large a proportion of their population as Chelsea, most eventually declined in size. Even areas that continued to grow often grew more slowly than the natural population increase.[14]

The most commonly accepted explanation for this population decline is out-migration. The pulls of the city and the frontier were certainly the focuses of contemporary anxieties about rural decline and have received the greatest amount of scholarly attention. But persistence rates in Chelsea were higher than any measured in nineteenth-century rural communities that were growing, suggesting less out-migration rather than more. Taking into account the effect of mortality, these persistence rates reveal that almost half of all males, two-thirds of the household heads, and over three-fourths of the farm operators in Chelsea simply did not leave the township during the second half of the nineteenth century.[15]

Population loss was not caused primarily by excessive out-migration, but by the community's inability to produce or attract new inhabitants to replace those who died or left. The limited number of local economic opportunities failed to lure newcomers: Between 1860 and 1880, the township replaced only 46 percent of those whose names disappeared from local enumerations; and between 1880 and 1900, it replaced only 34 percent. The population of Chelsea became progressively older because both out-migration and the lack of in-migration were selective according to age. This also contributed to population loss as larger proportions of local inhabitants were more likely to die while fewer Chelseans were in their family-forming years.

Those who did leave Chelsea moved out because they had fewer economic or social ties to the community than those who stayed. Displaced artisans, for example, were much more likely to leave town than were farmers or merchants. Similarly, property owners usually stayed while the propertyless were apt to move on. Natives of Vermont persisted more often than those born out of the state; and young men under thirty, especially those who were single, were much more footloose than were older men with families. Virtually the same kind of selective migration is found in other studies of nineteenth-century mobility in newer rural communities with much higher rates of population turnover; and in Chelsea, these patterns remained more or less constant over the second half of the century.

Gradually, after decades of repeated selective out-migration coupled with declining in-migration, an increasing percentage of the local inhabitants were bound to the community by firm social and economic ties. Consequently, persistence rates in Chelsea were higher than those in more recently settled farm areas in the Midwest because the people least likely to leave formed a larger proportion of the township's total population. These higher rates do not reflect any absolute difference in the behavior of individuals so much as the changed structure of the community's overall population. The result, however, was that Chelsea became more stable and homogeneous as its population declined, and it was much less subject to the constant turnover and flux that characterized newer rural communities.

None of the processes contributing to this demographic stability was peculiar to Chelsea or northern New England. What distinguished Chelsea from newer rural communities was primarily the duration of those processes, and, in some cases, their degree. The gradual aging of settled rural communities is well documented, and demographic evidence suggests that absolute fertility as well as the number of women in their child-bearing years also declined in Northern farm families after the frontier era had passed. Migration throughout the Northern countryside was selective according to the same social and economic ties to the community that existed in Chelsea. For example, James C. Malin's work indicates that persistence rates in rural Kansas also increased steadily after the settlement period, and the number of in-migrants declined. Moreover, high levels of persistence are not uncommon in present-day rural communities that lose population.[16]

Slowed population growth, then, was both a cause and a consequence of increasing demographic stability rather than a symptom of instability. As a whole, those who lived in older rural communities were more persistent and homogeneous than those who lived in the cities or on the frontier. They were influenced by numerous ties to their communities, and, in the words of the proverbial hymn and sampler, these are the ties that bind.

## I V

Family ties were the most important, and in Chelsea families helped ease the adjustments of their members to limited local opportunities. The farm family's strategies for transferring its land to the next generation, its provisions for those children who did not take over the home farm, and the continuous assistance that relatives gave each other throughout their lives all served to establish and maintain the well-being of family members. This nexus of aid and obligation linked kinfolk closer to each other and kept them close to home.

The family farm usually passed to the youngest son. Thus, most of the farmers between the ages of thirty and thirty-nine listed in the 1880 census, who spent their entire lives in Chelsea, were either the youngest or one of the younger children of local husbandmen. When a youngest son was in his mid-twenties, he typically entered into a partnership with his father and was deeded title to one-half of the farm with the expectation of receiving the other half after his father's death. Chelsea farmers favored their youngest sons because they came of age when the father turned sixty-five or seventy and was ready to retire or reduce the scope of his activity. This meshing of life cycles was necessary because the average farm was simply not large enough to support the father's full household and the oldest son's growing family at the same time.[17]

As the price of his guaranteed legacy, the youngest son incurred considerable responsibilities that bound him to his family and his community. Various sources indicate a common array of obligations: He promised to continue farming the land with his father, assumed his father's debts and liabilities, and avoided selling his part of the farm while his parents were alive. He also had to house and care for his father, mother, and any unmarried sisters, and, if his father died, he was obliged to provide dowries for his sisters at their weddings. Thus, the timing of the partnership between father and youngest son insured not only a continuous level of farm production, but also security for the elderly farm couple in their remaining years, while keeping at least one member of the next generation at home.

The older sons from farm families had to find other means of livelihood. A few managed to buy another farm in Chelsea and others tried their hand at local nonagricultural occupations. According to church records, Civil War militia rolls, and other genealogical information, sons who left Chelsea to farm after 1850 often moved nearby, usually to a neighboring township where they continued to benefit from family aid. It was not unusual for several brothers to make such a move together, providing a ready-made network of support.

Whether in town or nearby, family assistance was essential for continued security and stability. Farmers tried to give all their sons enough money for a down payment on a farm, and to provide their daughters with dowries which might be put toward purchasing a homestead if they married a farmer. Later in their lives, children who had left the family farm might inherit shares of their father's half of the operation which they usually sold back to their younger brother. Parents or some other relative also typically supplied mortgages and underwrote loans for children or kinfolk who were nearby, providing much lower rates of interest and easier terms than were available from local merchants or the bank. Mortgaging with the family had other advantages as well. One local farmer, Eugene Thorne, held a mortgage for his farm with his father. When the father died, Eugene as administrator of the estate simply dismissed the remainder of his obligation, along with another mortage that his father held from Eugene's sister and her husband.

As the foregoing example indicates, relatives by marriage were also important resources. Of nineteen permanent farmers who were between thirty and thirty-nine in the 1880 census and who married, fourteen wed local women—six literally married the girl next door. In the same vein, several farmers lived near their brothers-in-law by their sisters' marriages. In all cases, kinfolk swapped labor and financial assistance. Those who stayed in Chelsea were bound by ties within the generations as well as between them.

By contrast, the sons of Chelsea merchants and professionals were less likely to stay at home or move nearby. Local opportunities were either too few or too confining. Unlike the continuity experienced by local husbandmen, none of Chelsea's doctors, lawyers, or larger merchants had their practices or businesses taken over by their sons. Instead, the sons of local farmers and craftsmen often filled these roles. As a result, the village and countryside became increasingly intertwined by the bonds of kinship, and the tensions between farmers and nonfarmers, which had been troublesome earlier in the century, eased significantly.

Again, Chelsea was not unique in this regard; several studies suggest the increasing prevalence and continued importance of family ties after the first generation of settlers. James M. Williams's 1906 sociological study of "Blanktown" (actually the rural township of Waterbury, New York) shows that in 1845, a few families in the community were related to perhaps one or two other households in their immediate neighborhood, but to no one elsewhere in the township. By 1900, however, well over half had family connections in other neighborhoods, and over one-third had kin living in the larger village center of "Blankville." A recent study by an anthropologist of kinship patterns in nineteenth-century Londonderry, Vermont, provides a more direct comparison. As in Chelsea, Londonderry farmers sold land to kinfolk, lived near relatives, and married women from families who also lived in the area; and these ties became most widespread after the settlement period. "The extent to which patterns of family and social stability were established principally through premortem land transfers . . . and sustained by continued residence," this scholar noted, "cannot be emphasized enough."[18]

Numerous social surveys taken during the early twentieth century also provide evidence for the stability and importance of family ties in older rural areas. Throughout the North, older farming communities consisted chiefly of people who were born in the vicinity as farm children stayed near their home townships and benefited from the proximity of kinship networks. A 1917 survey of three separate Iowa townships shows that 84 percent of the local residents were born in their township or an adjoining one. Three-fourths of the farmers in a later survey of different Ohio communities were born within 25 miles of their farms. A similar study of rural families in Genessee County, New York found that two-thirds of the men who remained in their home townships married women from that township or one that was adjacent. Moreover, in both Ohio and New York, the sons and daughters who had left their parents' homes were usually close by. Over one-half of the New York children were on farms or in villages in Genessee County, and around 70 percent of their counterparts in Ohio lived within 20 miles of the parental homestead.[19]

The importance of the kinship network in rural life has often been noted. Recently, James Henretta and others have argued that concern for the family line was the basis of the *mentalité* of the preindustrial countryside. These authors assume that this emphasis on the family was ultimately incompatible with a market economy, but the evidence from Chelsea and elsewhere demonstrates the centrality of family ties in commercialized farming communities. In Chelsea inheritance patterns during the second half of the nineteenth century represented a continuation of older strategies to provide for the family line in spite of an increasing involvement in a capitalist economy; and throughout the North the family farm remained the dominant unit of production, facilitating the continued prevalence of family ties in older rural communities. Indeed, the conflicts between familial concerns and economic realities may have been much less pronounced in older rural areas than in urban and industrial society. One could argue that rural family bonds grew stronger over time rather than weaker as the ties that bind developed after the settlement period and as kinship networks responded to challenges created by stabilizing local opportunities.[20]

V

The increasing interconnections and homogeneity of settled rural inhabitants were also apparent at the community level. Like many rural communities, Chelsea's early history was fraught with social divisions and turmoil. During the course of the 1800s, however, a local consensus gradually developed that paralleled and reinforced the economic and demographic trends towards homogeneity; and in place of earlier social conflicts, a single, though not singular, point of view emerged.

Chelsea's early settlers did not come as a covenanted group, but as individuals and families from a variety of New England backgrounds. As a result, the religious and political tempests that eddied about New England and New York before the Civil War created numerous local factions that mirrored similar splits in other northeastern communities. Baptists and other Arminian sects opposed the more established Congregationalists. In the political arena, Jeffersonian Republicans, later Jacksonian Democrats, fought with Federalists and Whigs. The local anti-Masonic movement in Chelsea was an attack on the well-to-do that pitted the countryside against the village, and the temperance crusade also sharply divided the community.[21]

By the end of the century, few of these divisions still existed in Chelsea, and little social conflict was evident. Chelsea was a one-party town with Republicans regularly capturing over three-fourths of the local vote. Instead of fighting, local churches cooperated with each other and members of their congregations intermarried. Numerous voluntary associations now dominated town society, and these groups drew leaders as well as members from a wide cross-section of Chelsea's population. Unlike their fraternal forebears, for example, Masons in late nineteenth-century Chelsea were no longer an elite group, and included members from local farms as well as the village. The series of events sponsored by these organizations involved people throughout the community, and the less public socializing recorded in private diaries and local newspapers also cut across denominational, occupational, and neighborhood lines.

Temperance, the source of some of the most dramatic conflicts in Chelsea's history, had also disappeared as a divisive issue by 1900. In 1852, when Vermont narrowly passed statewide prohibition, Chelseans voted against the measure by 250 to 142. In the face of this substantial opposition, local enforcement of the law proved extremely difficult, but temperance advocates gradually gained the upper hand, and active drinkers became an increasingly insignificant and ostracized element of town life. One local physician, for example, was reported to be a drinker in the R. G. Dun and Company credit ratings. Although he was respected during the 1860s, he saw both his practice and his credit rating erode during the 1870s because of liquor. Given such active sanctions, Chelsea soon became a dry town, and when the issue of prohibition came up for a statewide referendum in 1903, Chelsea voters rejected its repeal by almost 4 to 1.

Perhaps the best way to describe the emergence of shared attitudes in Chelsea is with a story. The scene is the second meeting of the local debating club on 8 November 1897; the topic for consideration was "Resolved that New England farms can be made to pay." The debate must have been a contentious one, because the three judges turned in a split decision with two in favor of the affirmative and one for the negative. When the question was turned over to the audience for a vote, however, they voted unanimously, 21 to 0, that New England farms could be made to pay. Quickly, the debaters who argued the opposite position motioned for adjournment, but the motion did not carry and the other club members all stood up and sang "Hurrah for Old New England." There is a postscript: Neither Edward Bicknell nor Richard Emanuel who argued against the viability of local farming was still in town three years later. Their opponents, however, continued to live in Chelsea and to farm their fathers' land.[22]

No doubt the change from social conflict to social consensus occurred in other older rural communities as well. Initial turmoil was endemic to the settlement process throughout the North as disparate groups of people found themselves cast together in new communities. For example, two sociological studies from the early 1900s see factions and quarrels as the most pervasive aspects of the initial years of "Aton," Indiana, and "Blanktown," New York. Similarly, Allan Bogue, Don H. Doyle, and others have delineated numerous social fault lines in their more recent studies of Midwestern community formation.[23]

According to scattered evidence from various studies, however, these differences often abated as time passed. In contrast to its early contentiousness, disagreements in "Blanktown" were much less acrimonious by the turn of the century, a change attributed to the broadening association of local inhabitants to the detriment of partisanship and personal cliques. Social differences also faded in the multiethnic village of Germantown, Ohio, which was "spared the dynamic tension of change and diversity," and "became a community of no little homogeneity and congruity."[24]

In many settled rural communities, clubs and associations institutionalized this emerging social consensus. These voluntary associations filled the social gap created by the declining influence of the church after the Civil War, and served, in Doyle's phrase, as bridges across the troubled waters that had previously divided the community into numerous factions. In the large number of communities that were predominantly pietistic and Protestant, temperance reform and prohibitionism were also important devices for establishing a local consensus and defining the social boundaries of the community. This commitment to temperance often served as a substitute for the social covenant that was lacking in communities settled randomly by diverse groups of people.[25]

It is, of course, wrong to overstate the universality of social consensus of older rural communities. Voluntary associations can institutionalize social differences as well as transcend them. In more diverse communities, ethnic divisions were pronounced, especially over the temperance issue. Relatively little is known, however, about the scope and dimensions of ethnicity in older rural areas, or about how interethnic relations changed over time. Settlements that began as communal or covenanted colonies often experienced their own versions of declension as new social and economic realities altered and eroded initial religious and ideological unity. Moreover, images of vicious gossip and enduring quarrels permeate literary depictions of settled rural life, although the authors were usually those who chose to leave town rather than those who stayed.[26]

Nevertheless, diminished economic and demographic growth created a degree of inertia in settled rural life that distinguished it from the volatility of the frontier or the city. More than elsewhere, society in Chelsea and other older rural communities was characterized by a pervasive equilibrium among economic opportunities, the size and composition of the local population, familial and individual expectations, and local institutions and social life. To the extent that social divisions persisted in some older rural communities, they were probably static rather than dynamic aspects of local society. Potentially disrupting forces from the larger society were mitigated to a large degree by the stability and constancy of family and social ties and by the localism that continued to dominate the world view of settled rural inhabitants.

VI

Those who lived in older rural communities in the North, then, experienced the great transformations of the nineteenth century in ways profoundly different from their contemporaries in newer rural areas or in the nation's cities. In contrast to rapidly expanding cities and frontier communities—typified by population turnover, social diversity, and social flux—older rural communities like Chelsea became increasingly staid, uniform, and uneventful. An understanding of those differences can shed new light on the bitter urban and rural splits that permeated American political and cultural debates during the period. In this vein, rural advocacy of prohibition may have been more than simply a reaction to the cultural threat posed by the cities. In Chelsea, it was also an affirmation of the experiences of a settled rural society in which lessened growth culminated in a social consensus dependent upon sobriety as a social boundary of community life. Further consideration of the differences between older rural communities and those settled more recently can also help to explain why Populism was not a significant movement in areas where established social patterns provided additional buffers against the vicissitudes of the market economy.

The history of Chelsea and older rural societies is also very suggestive from a theoretical point of view. The social consequences of diminished economic and demographic growth in settled rural communities underscore the inadequacy of the categories used in developmental theories as well as the fallacious assumption that those categories are mutually exclusive. Although the transitions from feudal to bourgeois, from traditional to modern, or from gemeinschaft to gesellschaft may characterize the broad path traveled by nation-states, they do not reflect accurately changes in smaller rural communities. Rather, Chelsea and other older rural towns were, to play on Robert Wiebe's famous phrase, island communities against the stream where local farmers were at once tied to larger national markets and also entwined in a face-to-face local life.

NOTES

1. Clarence Danhof, *Change in Agriculture: The Northern United States, 1820–1870* (Cambridge, Mass., 1969); Allan Bogue, *From Prairie to Corn Belt: Farming on the Illinois and Iowa Prairies in the Nineteenth Century* (Chicago, 1963); Lewis Atherton, *Main Street on the Middle Border* (Bloomington, Ind., 1953).

2. William Parker discusses the persistence of the family farm in Northern agriculture; see his "Agriculture," in Lance Davis, Richard A. Easterlin, and William N. Parker, eds., *American Economic Growth: An Economist's History of the United States* (New York, 1972), 369–417. Donald L. Winters, *Farmers Without Farms: Agricultural Tenancy in Nineteenth-Century Iowa* (Westport, Conn., 1978), 3–11, 78–91; Anne

Mayhew, "A Reappraisal of the Causes of Farm Protest in the United States, 1870–1900," *Journal of Economic History* 32 (1972):464–75; Don S. Kirschner, *City and Country: Rural Responses to Urbanization in the 1920s* (Westport, Conn., 1970).

3. James A. Henretta, "Families and Farms: *Mentalité* in Pre-Industrial America," *William and Mary Quarterly* 3d ser. 35 (1978):3–32; Michael Merrill, "Cash Is Good to Eat: Self-Sufficiency and Exchange in the Rural Economy of the United States," *Radical History Review* 3 (1977):42–71; Christopher Clark, "The Household Economy, Market Exchange and the Rise of Capitalism in the Connecticut Valley, 1800–1860," *Journal of Social History* 13 (1979):169–89; Winifred B. Rothenberg, "The Market and Massachusetts Farmers, 1750–1855," *Journal of Economic History* 41 (1981):283–314. For a recent but preliminary attempt to integrate Turnerian theory with the different approaches of the new social history, see Robert P. Swierenga, "Theoretical Perspectives on the New Rural History: From Environmentalism to Modernism," *Agricultural History* 56 (1982):495–502.

4. Certain cities also slowed down or even lost population during the second half of the nineteenth century, but these were exceptional cases. In any event, studies of two such cities, Newburyport, Massachusetts, and Poughkeepsie, New York, demonstrate patterns of population turnover and mobility akin to those found in urban areas that were growing rapidly. See Stephan Thernstrom, *Poverty and Progress: Social Mobility in a Nineteenth Century City* (Cambridge, Mass., 1964); and Clyde Griffen and Sally Griffen, *Natives and Newcomers: The Ordering of Opportunity in Mid-Nineteenth-Century Poughkeepsie* (Cambridge, Mass., 1978).

5. Darrett B. Rutman, "People in Process: The New Hampshire Towns of the Eighteenth Century," *Journal of Urban History* 1 (1975):268–92; Charles Wetherell, "A Note on Hierarchical Clustering," *Historical Methods Newsletter* 10 (1977):109–16; Daniel Scott Smith, "A Malthusian-Frontier Interpretation of United States Demographic History Before c. 1815," in Woodrow Borah et al., eds., *Urbanization in the Americas: The Background in Comparative Perspective* (Ottawa, 1980), 15–23.

6. Harold Fisher Wilson, *The Hill Country of Northern New England: Its Social and Economic History, 1790–1930* (New York, 1936), is the most important formulation of the traditional view. Many towns in New England experienced industrialization and urbanization during this period, but this essay is concerned with areas that continued to rely primarily on agriculture.

7. For a more extensive description of Chelsea, see Hal S. Barron, *Those Who Stayed Behind: Rural Society in Nineteenth-Century New England* (New York, 1984).

8. The local economy is discussed more thoroughly in Hal S. Barron, "The Impact of Rural Depopulation on the Local Economy: Chelsea, Vermont, 1840–1900," *Agricultural History* 54 (1980):318–35.

9. Barron, "The Impact of Rural Depopulation."

10. Barron, *Those Who Stayed Behind*, 68–77.

11. Henry U. Fletcher, "The Doom of the Small Town," *The Forum* 13 (1895): 214–23.

12. Jane Jacobs, *The Economy of Cities* (New York, 1969); Allan Pred, "American Metropolitan Growth: 1860–1914, Industrialization, Initial Advantage," in Allan Pred, *The Spatial Dynamics of U.S. Urban-Industrial Growth, 1800–1914* (Cambridge, Mass., 1966), 12–85.

13. Stanley N. Murray, *The Valley Comes of Age: A History of Agriculture in the Valley*

*of the Red River of the North, 1812–1920* (Fargo, N.D., 1967).

14. Wilbur Zelinsky, "Changes in the Geographic Patterns of Rural Population in the United States, 1790–1960," *Geographical Review* 52 (1962):492–524.

15. The following discussion of migration and persistence in Chelsea is based on an extended analysis of manuscript census schedules and other quantitative sources. For a more complete description of methods and conclusions, see Barron, *Those Who Stayed Behind,* 78–92.

16. Richard A. Easterlin, "Population Change and Farm Settlement in the Northern United States," *Journal of Economic History* 36 (1976):45–83; Richard A. Easterlin, "Factors in the Decline of Farm Fertility in the United States: Some Preliminary Research Results," *Journal of American History* 63 (1976):600–614; Michael B. Katz, Michael J. Doucet, and Mark Stern, "Migration and the Social Order in Erie County, New York: 1855," *Journal of Interdisciplinary History* 8 (1978):669–701; Michael Conzen, *Frontier Farming in an Urban Shadow* (Madison, Wisc., 1971), 44–51; James C. Malin, "The Turnover of Farm Population in Kansas," *Kansas Historical Quarterly* 4 (1935):339–72; Calvin L. Beale, "Rural Depopulation in the United States: Some Demographic Consequences of Agricultural Adjustments," *Demography* 1 (1964): 264–72.

17. Although census persistence rates are useful for delineating the static characteristics of the ties that bind, they provide little sense of how such ties developed and how they influenced individual behavior. An analysis of the careers of the men in Chelsea between ages thirty and thirty-nine who were listed in the 1880 census sheds additional light on these questions. These career patterns were reconstructed using a variety of additional sources including Hamilton Child, *Child's Orange County Gazette, 1762–1888* (Syracuse, N.Y., 1888); Grand Lists of Taxes for 1880 and 1895, manuscripts, Office of the Town Clerk, Chelsea, Vt.; Land Records and Vital Records for Chelsea, Vt., manuscripts, microfilm, Vermont State Division of Public Records, Montpelier, Vt.; H. F. Wallings, *Map of Orange County Vermont* (New York, 1858); F. W. Beers, *Atlas of Orange County Vermont* (New York, 1877). The age group thirty to thirty-nine was selected because these men lived in the township throughout the entire period of this study. See Barron, *Those Who Stayed Behind,* 92–111.

18. James M. Williams, *An American Town* (New York, 1906); Robert A. Riley, "Kinship Patterns in Londonderry, Vermont, 1772–1900: An Intergenerational Perspective of Changing Family Relationships," Diss., University of Massachusetts, Amherst, 1980, 168.

19. Paul S. Peirce, "Social Surveys of Three Rural Townships in Iowa," *University of Iowa Monographs, Studies in the Social Sciences* 5 (1917); C. E. Liveley and P. G. Beck, "Movement of the Open Country Population in Ohio, I. The Family Aspect," *Ohio Agricultural Experiment Station Bulletin* no. 467 (1930); C. E. Lively and P. G. Beck, "Movement of the Open Country Population in Ohio, II. The Individual Aspect," *Ohio Agricultural Experiment Station Bulletin* no. 489 (1931); W. A. Anderson, "Mobility of Rural Families, I.," *Cornell University Agricultural Experiment Station Bulletin* no. 607 (1934); W. A. Anderson, "Mobility of Rural Families, II.," *Cornell University Agricultural Experiment Station Bulletin* no. 623 (1935).

20. Henretta, "Families and Farms"; Clark, "The Household Economy"; Merrill,

"Cash Is Good to Eat." See also Mary P. Ryan, *Cradle of the Middle Class: The Family in Oneida County, New York, 1790–1865* (New York, 1981), 27–31.

21. Barron, *Those Who Stayed Behind*, 112–31, discusses this change from social conflict to social consensus in greater detail. For more general analyses of early social conflict in Vermont, see David Ludlum, *Social Ferment in Vermont, 1791–1850* (New York, 1939); and Randolph A. Roth, "Whence This Strange Fire? Religious and Reform Movements in the Connecticut River Valley of Vermont, 1791–1843," Diss., Yale University, 1981.

22. Manuscript records of the Chelsea Debating Club, 1897–98, Chelsea Historical Society, Chelsea, Vt.

23. Newell Sims, *A Hoosier Village* (New York, 1912); Williams, *An American Town*; Don H. Doyle, *The Social Order of a Frontier Community: Jacksonville, Illinois, 1825–1870* (Urbana, Ill., 1978); Allan Bogue, "Social Theory and the Pioneer," *Agricultural History* 34 (1960):21–34.

24. Williams, *An American Town*; Carl Becker, *The Village: A History of Germantown, Ohio, 1804–1976* (Germantown, Ohio, 1981).

25. Doyle, *The Social Order*; Page Smith, *As a City upon a Hill: The Town in American History* (New York, 1966).

26. The work of Kathleen Neils Conzen and Robert Swierenga will help overcome this shortcoming. See Conzen's essay in this volume; her earlier "Historical Approaches to the Study of Rural Ethnic Communities," in Frederick C. Luebke, ed., *Ethnicity on the Great Plains* (Lincoln, Neb., 1980); and Swierenga, "Ethnicity and American Agriculture," *Ohio History* 89 (1980): 323–44.

# Contributors

STEVEN HAHN holds a Ph.D. from Yale University and is associate professor of history at the University of California, San Diego. His book, *The Roots of Southern Populism: Yeoman Farmers and the Transformation of the Georgia Upcountry, 1850–1890* (1983) received the Allen Nevins Prize and the Frederick Jackson Turner Award. He is an associate of the Freedmen and Southern Society Project and is now at work on a study of the black political experience in the South from 1860 to 1900.

JONATHAN PRUDE earned his Ph.D. from Harvard University and is currently associate professor of history at Emory University. He is author of *The Coming of Industrial Order: Town and Factory Life in Rural Massachusetts, 1810–1860* (1983) and is presently engaged in studying the changing appearance of working people in nineteenth-century America.

HAL S. BARRON received his Ph.D. from the University of Pennsylvania and is associate professor of history at Harvey Mudd College. He won the Vernon Carstenen Award for the best article in *Agricultural History* in 1981 and is author of *Those Who Stayed Behind: Rural Society in Nineteenth-Century New England* (1984). He is currently pursuing the study of localism and cosmopolitanism in small-town America from 1880 to 1930.

KATHLEEN NEILS CONZEN, a Ph.D. recipient of the University of Wisconsin, is associate professor of history at the University of Chicago. She has written *Immigrant Milwaukee, 1830–1860: Accommodation and Community in a Frontier City* (1976), along with numerous scholarly articles, and is now studying German immigrants in rural settings.

THOMAS DUBLIN received his Ph.D. from Columbia University and is associate professor of history at the University of California, San Diego. He has written *Women at Work: The Transformation of Work and Community in Lowell, Massachusetts* (1979), for which he won both the Bancroft Prize and the Merle Curti Award, and has edited *Farm to Factory: Women's Letters, 1830–1860* (1981). He is now completing a study of women's careers in nineteenth-century New England.

JOHN MACK FARAGHER holds a doctorate from Yale University and is associate professor of history at Mount Holyoke College. His book, *Women and Men on the Overland Trail* (1979), received the Francis Parkman Prize. He is presently finishing a study of Sugar Creek, Illinois, in the nineteenth century.

DAVID JAFFEE received his Ph.D. from Harvard University. He teaches history at Georgetown University, works as a historian at the National Museum of American History, and is currently writing a book on the commercialization of crafts in rural America during the nineteenth century.

GARY KULIK holds a doctorate from Brown University and is chairman of the department of social and cultural history at the Smithsonian Institution's National Museum of American History. He has edited *The New England Mill Village, 1790–1860* (1982) and *Rhode Island: An Inventory of Historical and Engineering Sites* (1978), and he is now writing a book on the invention of the American factory.

HOWARD LAMAR is Coe Professor of History at Yale University and Dean of Yale College. His books include *The Dakota Territory, 1861–1889* (1956), *The Far Southwest, 1846–1912* (1966), *The Reader's Encyclopedia of the American West* (1977), and, with Leonard Thompson, *The Frontier in History: North America and Southern Africa Compared* (1981). He is currently at work on a study of labor systems in the West.

ROBERT C. MC MATH, JR. received his Ph.D. from the University of North Carolina and is professor of history at the Georgia Institute of Technology. He is author of *Populist Vanguard: A History of the Southern Farmers' Alliance* (1975) and co-author of *The American People: A History* (1981) and *Engineering in the New South: Georgia Tech, 1885–1985* (1985). At present, he is studying the technological transformation of Southern agriculture since the 1930s.

JOHN SCOTT STRICKLAND received his Ph.D. from the University of North Carolina at Chapel Hill and is assistant professor of history at Syracuse University. He is currently revising his doctoral dissertation, "Across Space and Time: Conversion, Community, and Cultural Change among South Carolina Slaves," for publication.

# Index